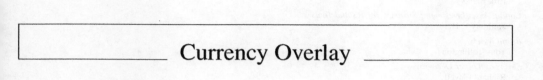

Currency Overlay

Wiley Finance Series

Currency Overlay

Neil Record

WILEY

Other Wiley Editorial Offices

John Wiley & Sons Inc., 111 River Street, Hoboken, NJ 07030, USA

Jossey-Bass, 989 Market Street, San Francisco, CA 94103-1741, USA

Wiley-VCH Verlag GmbH, Boschstr. 12, D-69469 Weinheim, Germany

John Wiley & Sons Australia Ltd, 33 Park Road, Milton, Queensland 4064, Australia

John Wiley & Sons (Asia) Pte Ltd, 2 Clementi Loop #02-01, Jin Xing Distripark, Singapore 129809

John Wiley & Sons Canada Ltd, 22 Worcester Road, Etobicoke, Ontario, Canada M9W 1L1

Wiley also publishes its books in a variety of electronic formats. Some content that appears
in print may not be available in electronic books.

Library of Congress Cataloging-in-Publication Data

Record, Neil.
   Currency overlay / Neil Record.
      p.   cm.
   Includes bibliographical references and index.
   ISBN 0-470-85027-2 (Cloth: alk. paper)
1. Currency overlay.   I. Title.
HG4529.5 .R43   2003
332.4′5—dc22   2003014721

British Library Cataloguing in Publication Data

A catalogue record for this book is available from the British Library

ISBN 0-470-85027-2

Typeset in 10/12pt Times by TechBooks, New Delhi, India

This book is printed on acid-free paper responsibly manufactured from sustainable forestry
in which at least two trees are planted for each one used for paper production.

To Julie, Chris, Rob, Helen, Katy and Guy – a cure for insomnia!

Contents

List of Boxes

Biography

Neil Record was educated at Balliol College, Oxford, where he studied Philosophy & Psychology; Essex University and University College, London, from where he gained an MSc in Economics with Distinction. His first job, in 1977, was as an Economist in the Economic Intelligence Department of the Bank of England. While there he had his first taste of large-scale economic modelling, and his first exposure to an exchange rate forecasting model. It was notable then that the exchange-rate forecasting model was one of the weaker elements of the Bank's model of the UK economy.

In 1979, Neil moved to work as a commodity price forecaster at the chocolate maker Mars in Slough, UK. He quickly moved into line responsibility for buying commodities, and then to buying forward currency for the company's commodity and import needs. While at Mars he developed an innovative process for controlling currency risk and exploiting currency market inefficiency.

In 1983, aged 29, Neil left Mars to establish his own specialist currency management business, Record Treasury Management (renamed Record Currency Management in 2001). Record Currency Management was a pioneer of currency overlay for pension and investment funds, and in April 1985 it was awarded the worldwide first-ever institutional currency overlay mandate – from the UK Water Authorities' Superannuation Fund.

Today, 20 years after founding Record Currency Management, Neil remains Chairman and CEO. He divides his time between client liaison, currency overlay design work, and speaking and writing about currency overlay. His other interests include a non-Executive Directorship of RDF Media – a leading UK independent TV production company – opera, baroque music, tennis, skiing, travel, art, architecture and watching his childrens' sporting activities. He is divorced and lives with his partner, Julie, and his three children and her two children.

Acknowledgements

I am indebted to my colleagues at Record Currency Management, particularly Peter Wakefield, Leslie Hill, Bob Noyen, Mike Timmins, Ian Harrison, Joel Sleigh, Dave Murphy, Simon Williamson, James Dyas, Sebastian Jans and Dmitri Tikhonov for their technical input, advice and debate. I am also grateful to Chris Jackson, Jane Deane and Julia Edbrooke for their administrative support. I am also indebted to Brian St.J. Hall of Hewitt Bacon & Woodrow for advice and comments on earlier drafts. Finally, I must thank Julie for putting a glass of wine in my hand after particularly heavy days!

1

Introduction

Currency overlay is a new branch of investment management. Not surprisingly, the literature is equally new; in particular, there does not exist at the time of writing (2003) any comparable comprehensive book on currency overlay.

Because currency overlay is new, I have chosen to write this book in such a way that it fulfils two functions: the first as a primer; the second as a reference book. Writing for a heterogeneous audience is difficult at the best of times; writing for a heterogeneous audience and to fulfil two functions is doubly challenging. I have chosen to enlist a number of techniques to help in this effort.

- **Argument from first principles**
  Where possible, I try to limit the reference to external theories or academic literature. In theory, I would like the able and mathematically literate reader to be able to grasp the arguments in this book without having prior knowledge of the currency world or any of the literature that surrounds it.
- **Use of mathematics**
  I will use only sufficient mathematics to explain my point or make my case. I have avoided advanced maths where at all possible. Generally, the only references to 'given' mathematical theories are in statistical formulae, where there is simply not enough space to derive them from first principles.
- **Boxes**
  I will use a technique used by Norman Davies in *Europe – a History*,[1] in which he creates 'boxes' with self-contained 'stories'. While a full description of currency overlay is clearly nowhere near as multi-stranded as the history of Europe, nevertheless I believe the reader will find it helpful to have text which is not fully 'linear'. I also use boxes to explain or describe vocabulary which may be unfamiliar.

This book is aimed at a wide audience. I anticipate that it will include readers from currency overlay managers, from the wider investment management industry, from investment consultants and actuaries, from the more investment-literate pension fund managers, from the investment management desks of insurance companies, from foreign exchange dealing banks and from custodian banks. It will inevitably also appear on the desks of students in finance and related disciplines, although it is not written as a textbook.

What distinguishes this book from a similar one written as a textbook? Firstly, it is not designed to fit in with any class, course, degree or qualification. Secondly, it is not designed to be fully rigorous. This is deliberate – full rigour would significantly expand the size of the book without adding to the core content. Thirdly, a textbook would not typically aim at a heterogeneous audience. A readership of, say, graduates following an AIMR[2] qualification or a

---

[1] Davies, N., *Europe – a History*, Oxford University Press, December 1996; ISBN 0-195-20912-5.
[2] Association for Investment Management & Research – the highly respected American asset management trade association and the awarder of the CFA qualification.

postgraduate degree course would expect a great deal less introductory finance and economics, and a great deal more mathematical rigour.

Currency overlay is not, to my knowledge, part of the syllabus of any investment management or other finance course at the moment. When, and if, it becomes part of standard graduate or professional courses, a textbook will undoubtedly emerge.

1.1   INVESTMENT BACKGROUND

Readers completely unfamiliar with investment may like a brief primer as to the key investment instruments and the key investor categories. I do this because I will be referring to these instruments throughout the book. The reader familiar with basic investment principles might like to skip this short section, and turn to p. 14.

1.1.1   Investor instruments

There are two main investment classes: equities and bonds, and both of these are also instruments. There is a larger range of smaller asset classes (cash, property, private equity, hedge funds, commodities), although some of these (e.g. hedge funds) are not instruments.

Box 1.1   What is currency overlay?

An investor – say a US investor – decides to invest in the UK stock market. The decision to invest in the UK is not determined by the investor's view on the prospects for the UK pound, but by the good prospects for the UK stock market and a desire for diversification. However, to buy the UK stocks, the US investor has to buy pounds with dollars on the foreign exchange market. He then buys the UK stocks with the pounds. Each month, the investor will get a valuation of this investment, and two markets (not one) will affect this valuation – (i) the general level of UK stocks in pounds and (ii) the level of the pound against the dollar.

The investor may decide that the uncertainty brought about by the variation in the dollar/pound exchange rate is undesirable, and choose to get rid of (or 'hedge') it. He hires a currency overlay manager, whose remit is to maintain a portfolio of forward currency contracts to offset any movements in the dollar/pound exchange rate. Broadly speaking, these contracts commit the investor to sell fixed amounts of pounds against the dollar at fixed dates in the future. This 'overlay' does not require any investment on the part of the investor; only a credit line with foreign exchange banks to enable the overlay manager to have the ability to deal in forward contracts with the banks on behalf of the investor.

The 'returns' of currency overlay come in two ways: forward currency contract valuations and cash settlements on maturing forward contracts. These two combine to become the contribution to return of currency overlay. The overlay manager who maintains the currency hedge over a constant proportion of the portfolio is conducting 'passive overlay'; the manager who varies it according to his view on the prospects for the pound is running 'active overlay'.

The expression 'currency overlay' has been extended recently to cover active mandates which are purely return-seeking, rather than risk-reducing. These mandates are not restricted purely to forward contracts to sell currencies already owned in the portfolio against the base currency – they can utilise any currency pair in either direction.

Equities (or shares) are a share in a limited liability company, and entitle the holder to the residual value on winding up of a company, and to regular payments in the form of dividends of surplus profits after other claims on the business have been discharged. Quoted equities (those that trade on recognised exchanges) are generally sufficiently liquid to maintain a 'second-hand' price in the market. This market price is the key for much of the later discussion in this book about international equities and currency risk. For the time being it is worth noting that the currency in which equities are quoted (which is generally, but not exclusively, the same as the currency in which the company reports its accounts) is important for the initial categorisation of equities' currency risk.

Bonds are on the face of it much simpler instruments than equities. They are a loan from the investor to a company or other economic entity. Bond-issuing entities include companies, asset-holding special purpose vehicles, governments, international organisations and mixed public/private sector groups. The bond (and I find it easiest even in this electronic world to think of it as a piece of paper) represents a promise of a series of payments by the issuer to the holder. These payments are a fixed amount of cash (the coupon), say $6 per year, until a particular date, and then a payment of principal, which is almost always by convention $100 (or £100 or Eur100 depending on the currency of the bond). Bond coupon payments are usually made either annually (mainly governments) or semi-annually. For annual payments, the last payment date (when the principal is repaid) is also usually the payment date of the coupon. There are a huge range of variations on this simple theme – most importantly that there are bonds where both the coupon and the principal are linked to an index of consumer or retail prices ('index-linked' bonds), and where the amount of the coupon varies according to prevailing short-term rates, rather than being fixed ('floating rate' bonds).

Bonds can be and are issued in a variety of currencies, although they are for practical purposes traded (in the second-hand market) in the same currency as their issue currency.

1.1.2   Key investor categories

Who are the main investors in equities and bonds? The ultimate answer is 'individuals', but most of this ownership is diffused through one or more intermediary layers, so that the majority of the influential decision-making is made by the managers of large pools of assets. These are commonly called 'institutional investors', although this is something of a misnomer, since they are mainly professional commercially-orientated managers, rather than representatives of 'institutions'.

Investment is about deferring consumption. There are many different reasons for deferring consumption, but by far the most important now is the deferral of income from the period while an individual is working to their retirement. This used not to be the case, at least in public securities' markets. In the heyday of nineteenth century capitalism, the majority of investors were rich men intent on getting richer – not thinking about their retirement, and insurance and provident companies investing small contributions from policyholders to provide for life's disasters – death, injury, fire – but not generally retirement. Few women in this period were economically active (in the sense of having paid jobs), and men were expected to work until 60 or 65.

The fundamental changes in the economic and social structure of western societies in the late twentieth century have changed that – families no longer expect to look after their elderly relatives, life expectancy in the developed countries has been extended markedly and average retirement age has, if anything, gone down. See Box 1.2. It is not untypical for a worker to retire in their mid to late fifties and live to their early eighties. This requires 25 years of income – income that governments are either unwilling, or now increasingly unable, to provide. Providing this income is the principal concern of the investment management industry.

Box 1.2   Life expectancy

Life expectancy in developed countries has been increasing almost continuously for two centuries. However, the pattern of mortality has also changed, and this has a significant impact on the need and scale of retirement provision. Taking the UK as an example, the striking thing about the change in mortality patterns is the collapse in *early* death rates. In the nineteenth and early twentieth centuries, people died at every age group – mainly through infectious diseases and what would be regarded now as avoidable causes – accidents, childbirth, etc.

In the late twentieth and early twenty-first centuries, death is almost exclusively the preserve of the elderly. This means that the population is becoming increasingly elderly, and the ratio of working years to retirement years has collapsed. In 1841, only 30% of males born reached 65; in 2000, 83% reached 65. Life expectancy for those lucky enough to reach 65 has changed less markedly. In 1841, the life expectancy of a 65-year-old man was 76 years; in 2000, 81 years.

This effect can be seen graphically in male life expectancy at ages 0, 45 and 65:

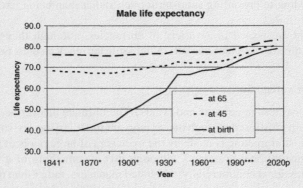

Source: UK Government Actuary's Department.

The female experience is very similar: just a few years longer at every age. So both the continuous rise in the solid line, and the recent rise in the dotted and dashed lines, are making the provision of retirement income so much more difficult and material.

These changing social and economic trends mean that the majority of investment is by pension funds. While there is a large sector which is explicitly labelled 'pension funds', there are also mutual funds and insurance company investments which, even if not labelled so, are also largely for the purpose of securing individual income in retirement.

Pensions are divisible into two key types – defined benefit and defined contribution.

1.1.3   Defined benefit pensions

Defined benefit (DB) pensions are just that. They are a promise by an employer, or a government, to pay a defined amount of annual pension between a retirement date and death. The

---

Box 1.3   Defined benefit pensions

The key characteristic of defined benefit (DB) pensions is that the pension they deliver is
not affected by any factors except the number of years of pensionable employment and the
employees' final (or, more rarely, average) salary. DB pensions are typically expressed in
the form '1/60 of final salary for each year of pensionable employment'. In the UK, but not
the US, they are now required to be index-linked (0–5% p.a. limits) after retirement. They
are typically offered to men and women on the same terms, although the expected cost to the
employer is higher for women than for men because of the higher life expectancy for women.

    The cost of DB pensions is highly sensitive to real investment returns, salary increases and
longevity. If the cost of providing a DB pension were outsourced to a third-party provider
like an insurance company, then it would be possible to calculate from financial economics
the annual cost to the employer that the insurance company would have to charge. I assume
here that the insurance company is prepared to take mortality (annuity) risk (which is
diversified), but not investment risk (which is systematic), and that the contract is priced
at cost. The graph below shows the annual pension cost compared to employee age on the
following assumptions: UK pension; investment only in I/L gilts; 2.5% real returns for I/L;
I/L pension (no cap or floor); UK average mortality; annual salary increase 3% p.a. higher
than inflation; continuous employment with one employer for 40 years; retirement at 60;
1/60th accrual. Later years are so much more expensive to the employer because of the
uprating of accrued rights with salary increases. And just to be clear, this graph means that
the *annual* cost to the employer of a male aged 59 is 60% of his salary!

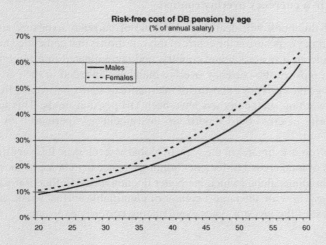

On these assumptions, the average cost per year to the employer is 26% p.a. for males, and
30% p.a. for females.

defined amount may go up (in the UK it routinely increases with inflation for example), but it will never go down. The level of pension is not dependent on the performance of any underlying assets guaranteeing the pension – only on the rules of the pension. This is the distinguishing feature from defined contribution pension schemes.

1.1.4   Defined contribution pensions

Defined contribution (DC) pension schemes are not really pension schemes. They are basically mutual funds or unit trusts with a beneficial tax-wrapper. The 'tax-wrapper' is usually that governments will allow income tax relief on investment into a DC scheme, and allow the income and capital gains to roll up inside the fund tax-free.[3] By way of compensation, governments usually tax all of the subsequent capital value as income when it is received by the pensioner, which will usually be by way of annuity receipts.

DC pension schemes allow individuals to build their own 'pot' of assets, often with contributions also coming from their employer. Most jurisdictions require retiring DC members to buy an annuity with much or all of this 'pot'. An annuity is a promise from a provider (usually an insurance company) to pay a fixed annual amount from the date of purchase until the annuitant's death. Payments from an annuity are, in effect, a pension. Annuities are priced by the market, which is run by insurance companies. They pool the mortality risk they are taking, and then replicate the payments required by holding bonds. If bonds are expensive (i.e. bond yields are low), then annuities will be expensive (i.e. a fixed outlay will buy less annual pension).

The DC investor therefore runs two very significant financial risks: (1) the risk of poor performance of his investments up to the point at which he retires, and (2) the risk that annuities will be expensive, thereby reducing his pension.

1.1.5   Investors in a currency overlay context

The remainder of this book will deal with the issue of currency exposure and institutional investors. The currency exposure at the centre of this question is that embedded in the ownership of securities outside an investor's home country, and denominated in a foreign currency. As a practical matter, most of the currency overlay mandates awarded in the period 1985–2002 have been to manage the currency exposure of international *equity* portfolios. In addition, most of the investors awarding such contracts have been DB pension funds. This has come about because the majority of cross-border portfolio investment is experienced by DB schemes' equity portfolios.

Table 1.1 shows rough estimates of the scale of global asset classes. It is very difficult to make sensible estimates of total cross-border asset holdings, hence my choice to show estimates for DB cross-border holdings alone (which are better documented). Suffice it to say at this stage that *international equities* are the largest creator of identifiable currency risk, and *DB pension funds* are the largest of the investor types experiencing currency exposure.

---

[3] In the UK, the notorious 1997 withdrawal of ACT relief for pension fund holders of UK equities was a partial withdrawal of this tax-free status. The position with regard to bonds is now anomalous – bond interest cost is fully tax-relievable for UK corporates, and not taxable in the hands of pension funds.

Table 1.1   Estimates of global asset ownership ($ bn)

	Total world market cap	Of which owned by DB funds	Of which DB cross-border	DB% total	Cross-border% DB
Equities	23 800	5200	1126	22%	22%
Bonds	18 000	3466	125	19%	4%
Total	41 800	8666	1251		

Sources: Lehman Bros; MSCI; Record Currency Management, December 2002.

2

The Problem

2.1 ASSET AND LIABILITY VALUATIONS, VOLATILITY AND SOLVENCY

2.1.1 Funded pension schemes

Pension funds as distinct financial entities are a post-war phenomenon. They emerged in scale in the 1950s in the US and UK, and they largely invested in domestic, mainly government, bonds. Domestic bonds were regarded as a safe investment, and trustees, in many jurisdictions hedged around with legal limitations, had neither the expertise nor the incentive to invest in any other instruments.

The idea of establishing trustees in a statutory framework to oversee the investment of a separate fund was gradually enshrined in legislation in the US,[1] UK, Australia, Canada, Netherlands and Switzerland, as well as several smaller economies. Notably, the major economies of continental Europe, Germany, France and Italy, did not adopt this model, and to a great extent have not done so to this day. Japan is a special case, with substantial funded schemes, but not in the standard employer-sponsored model.

Pension funds were only established because the sponsoring employer had made a pensions promise to its staff. Generally speaking, these promises consisted of the employee 'earning' a proportion of his final salary for each year of employment. A typical pension scheme might offer 1/60 or 1/80 of the final salary as pension for each year's service. In the US this remains a promise which is not linked to inflation after retirement; in the UK defined benefit pensions are now required to be given limited price indexation – in effect linked to retail prices with a 5% p.a. cap and 0% p.a. floor. Governments and regulatory authorities were rightly wary of allowing companies to take on long-tail financial obligations to employees (who are also voters!) without putting in place some mechanism to ensure that these promises were fulfilled. Hence the pension fund, legally distinct from the company, and able to survive the insolvency of the company without danger of attack by the liquidator.

Clearly, the desirable aim for the security of pensioners and future pensioners is to ensure that in the event of the insolvency of the sponsoring company, the assets in the pension fund are sufficient to pay all the outstanding promises in full. This opens the door to an area of significant controversy. I feel that in order to fully explore the concept of investment risk in a pension fund, I need to lay out some elements of that controversy.

2.1.2 Asset valuations

In the modern world of electronic communication, real-time market price screens and large and liquid securities' markets, it might seem that the question of establishing how much the assets of the pension fund are worth was a relatively trivial one. Why not look up the price of all the

---

[1] Michael Clowes, editor for many years of the premier pension trade journal (*Pensions & Investments*) in the US, has written a detailed post-war history of US pension funds. Clowes, M. J., *The Money Flood*, John Wiley & Sons; ISBN 0-471-38483-6.

constituent stocks, and sum the consequent value of each holding over the whole portfolio? While there might remain some question over the pricing of unquoted securities and of property, nevertheless the realisable value would be established with a narrow margin. This procedure has now been adopted in many, but not all, of the major funded pension jurisdictions. Even in those where market valuation is now the standard, this change has in many cases happened within the last 10 years.

What can possibly have been the alternative basis? The answer to this is dependent on the jurisdiction, and the practices of the profession responsible for pension fund valuation – actuaries.

In the UK and the US, until fairly recently, many pension fund asset valuations were made on the basis of 'discounted cash flow'. Discounted cash flow valuation ignores market values of otherwise perfectly marketable securities, and instead values them on the basis of a valuation model. As this applies to equities, the model runs something like this:

- **Step 1**   Establish the current dividend yield of the security or index
- **Step 2**   Project the dividend out into the future using a dividend growth assumption
- **Step 3**   Calculate the stream of dividend cash flows arising from these assumptions
- **Step 4**   Discount the stream of cash flows to a present value (PV) at an arbitrary discount rate
- **Step 5**   Call this PV the valuation of the assets

There are numerous objections to this valuation methodology, not least that the valuation so devised will not be the asset sale value. Other objections include the arbitrary nature of the dividend growth assumptions and the discount rate, neither of which can be readily determined by reference to a market. Indeed, it could be argued that the only possible reference to the market would be to derive an implied dividend growth rate and equity dividend discount rate from the market's valuation of the security – which then makes the whole exercise plainly circular.

Discounted cash flow valuations have all but been replaced by market valuations in pension fund valuations (see Table 2.1), so the discussion may seem a little academic. However, the culture that created actuarial valuations for assets lives on in the valuation of liabilities. Table 2.1 shows that the market value valuation methodology, while the largest category of asset valuation, is by no means the only methodology. 'Smoothed value' (taking only a proportion

Table 2.1   Asset valuation method relative frequency in North America

	US		Canada	
	Small plans	Large plans	Small plans	Large plans
Number of responses	5799	3168	274	311
Asset valuation group				
Fair market value	65.3%	48.6%	90.5%	47.3%
Discounted cash flow	0.0%	0.1%	0.0%	0.3%
Book value	27.8%	13.9%	1.1%	4.5%
Smoothed value	6.9%	36.4%	8.0%	42.1%
Other (including combination of methods)	0.1%	1.0%	0.4%	5.8%

Source: Survey of Asset Valuation Methods for Defined Benefit Pension Plans, Society of Actuaries, 1999.

of the asset value changes each year) and 'book value' (essentially cost) are also remarkably widespread.

It is worth noting that 'During the period from 1988 through 1996, plan assets were "marked to market" sparingly in the U.S. (a low of 0.3% of all plans in 1989 to a high of 2.6% of all plans in 1996) and very rarely in Canada' (SOA 1999 Survey). So the change to market valuation has come very recently and very rapidly. The reader will notice 'book value' as a valuation alternative, which is essentially asset purchase cost (or possibly market valuation if less). Since most assets will have been long-held, book value will not acknowledge any volatility in valuation brought about either by equity market fluctuations, or by currency fluctuations.

2.1.3 Liability valuations

Liabilities do not on the face of it fall as neatly as assets into market-based valuations. DB pension funds' liabilities to future cash outflows are not certain. They are subject to a number of uncertainties, including:

- Mortality (currently on an unfavourable trend)
- Pensions-in-payment inflation (depending on the pensions promise)
- Salary inflation prior to retirement
- Early leavers (a favourable risk to the fund)
- Early retirement (variable effect)

These factors combine to make the calculation of future cash flows an educated guess, or a range of values with probabilities assigned, rather than an exact value. However, all of these uncertainties can be estimated with more or less precision, and the estimates are unlikely to change rapidly (mortality), or can be hedged (inflation). One key uncertain variable is left to bring these future cash flows back to today's values – a discount rate.

2.1.4 Liabilities' discount rate

The value, and the underlying calculative principles, of the discount rate are by no means a settled question, and indeed at the time of writing have been raised right to the top of the political agenda in the UK, and to a lesser extent in the US and elsewhere. What is so contentious?

There has been a considerable history around the subject of liabilities' valuation. The position in most of the developed economies with funded pension sectors is that liabilities are valued in two or three different ways depending on context. In the US, funds are required by ERISA[2] to undergo a regular solvency examination to determine whether they meet minimum solvency requirements. This was the context of the asset valuation results shown in Table 2.1. The valuation of liabilities is similarly varied, with no pension funds reporting their liabilities discounted at the risk-free discount rate. In addition, companies are required to report their net liabilities and pension expense under the US accounting standard FAS87. However, this allows for smoothing of asset valuations, as well as a choice of three key variables for the liability valuation – salary inflation, 'expected rate of return' and the discount rate.

In FAS87 parlance, the discount rate is commonly applied to pensions in payment, and to a lesser extent future pensions at the shorter end of the maturity spectrum. The 'expected rate of return' is the discount rate applied to longer maturity liabilities. The nomenclature is revealing:

---

[2] The US Employee Retirement Income Security Act 1974.

liabilities do not have an expected rate of return; assets do. Why should the returns of a fund's assets affect the calculation of the PV of the liabilities?

Box 2.1   Discounting

A pension fund has obligations to pay its pensioners out into the distant future. How does the fund value this liability in today's money? This is important if only because it gives a guide as to how much it needs in assets valued today to cover the liabilities. Assume for the moment that a pension fund owes a level £10m per year from today to 2050, after which it has no further obligation. (Pension liabilities do not have this level payment characteristic – it is for illustration only.)

We can calculate a PV of this liability using a risk-free rate (say 4% p.a.) – the rate of return from investing in government bonds of the appropriate maturity. We can also value it at higher discount rates, representing a 'hope' that the assets in the fund (on the other side of the balance sheet) will yield a return yield than or equal to the higher assumed rate. We can show the huge impact of changing the discount rate in the following table:

Discount rate	PV (£m)	% risk-free PV
4% (risk-free)	222	100%
5%	191	86%
6%	167	75%
7%	147	66%
8%	132	59%
9%	119	54%
10%	109	49%

The answer, I believe, lies in the *realpolitik* of the actuaries' profession. Profit-maximising companies wish to minimise their payments to their pension funds, commensurate with the funds remaining solvent. As they increased their holdings of equities in the 1950s and 1960s, the superior returns of equities meant that each year the discount rate used for the valuation of their funds' liabilities looked over-conservative. If their assets went up, on average, faster than their liabilities, then was there not a case for adjusting the discount rate of the liabilities to more closely match the returns achieved in the investment portfolio?

The pressure from companies on their actuaries, and then from actuaries to government regulators (via their position on working groups, etc.) began to enshrine in law the idea that a risk-free rate for the liabilities' discount rate was a luxury they neither needed nor could afford. In its place was put a series of discount rates, each applying to different types of liability (pensions in payment, active staff members, deferred pensioners (ex staff), roughly reflecting the maturity of the liability and its 'certainty'. 'Uncertain' liabilities, particularly those of young active staff members, could be discounted at 'assumed equity' returns (in 2000, these were about 9% p.a. in the UK, versus a risk-free rate of about 5.5%).

What has escaped most governments (despite a regular trickle of underfunded pension schemes in bankrupt companies) is that enshrining 'long-term' rates of return in the liability discount rates ensures that there is a strong likelihood that the primary purpose of pension funds – to secure promise payments to pensioners – will fail. The turn of the twentieth to the twenty-first century has seen interest rates (and inflation) across major industrialised countries fall to 40-year lows. This has not only created well-publicised problems for insurers like

Equitable Life in the UK (who promised (high) Guaranteed Annuity Rates to some of its savers), but has also made the equity return assumption for the liability discount rate increasingly untenable.

2.1.5   FRS17

A new accounting standard, introduced in the UK in 2001 and originally coming fully into force in 2003 (but now delayed until 2005 to mesh with the move to international accounting standards), requires UK companies to put the assets of their pension fund less pension liabilities on the parent balance sheet (in the interim, in the notes). Not only is this the first time that UK companies have had to do this, but they are required to value assets at realisable market value on the balance sheet date, and liabilities at a discount rate equal to the AA corporate bond rate prevailing on the balance sheet date. There is no 'smoothing' and no 'assumed rate of return'. This standard has almost always shown that pension funds reporting in 2001 and 2002 are in deficit, and sometimes by very large absolute and relative amounts. Bizarrely, the new standard, which goes some way in allowing the owners of companies to know what their net pension obligations are, is under attack from an unholy alliance of unions, business leaders and politicians. The unions want the standard postponed or abolished because they fear the bad news it brings will prompt the company to abandon final salary pension schemes; businessmen want it postponed or abolished because it introduces an 'uncontrollable' element of volatility onto their balance sheets, and they can't afford to eliminate the volatility by investing in bonds; and politicians of all hues want it postponed or abolished because they fear it will lead to the closure of final salary pension schemes, which will not only be unpopular amongst a significant proportion of the electorate, but will also put more pressure on the state and the taxpayers to fund retirement.

Those in favour are a small group of informed accountants and actuaries, who are attempting to provide financial transparency and objectivity to the users of company accounts – the equity holders. Ironically, pension funds form a significant proportion of equity holders, and they have remained mute in this role. This group will most likely win the battle – the Equitable Life debacle in the UK, and Enron in the US, very different in both cause and result, will ensure that the call for transparency is going to be politically irresistible.

2.1.6   IAS19

The UK and other EU members are committed to adopting international accounting standards by 2005, and the US will wish to move to closer harmony with these if at all possible. US and international standards currently allow smoothing and non-market liability discount rates – the outcome of the next few years' debate will determine whether the new UK principles will prevail at international level.

2.1.7   Summary on assets and liabilities

The result of the changing valuation culture is to make pension funds more sensitive to the risks they are running with their investments. Generally speaking, for DB pension funds, this risk is principally in holding assets other than bonds. Bonds are a low-risk investment because they are increasingly forming the basis of the liability calculation (and are the only instrument capable of securing future pension liabilities with a high degree of certainty).

By far the largest category of non-bond assets is equities. For several investing countries, the next largest is currencies, since several (smaller) countries have large allocations to international equities. This is followed (in decreasing importance) by property, private equity, hedge funds and other, ad hoc, assets. The latter are less important sources of risk simply because they are smaller average allocations.

I will devote the remainder of this chapter to examining the role of currencies and the consequent investment risk that they create. At the end of the chapter I will also look briefly at cross-border investment by entities other than pension funds.

2.2   HISTORY OF PENSION FUND CROSS-BORDER PORTFOLIO INVESTING

The countries with the two largest funded pension sectors are the US and the UK. Both have different histories of international investing

2.2.1   US

Until 1980, the entire US pension sector had less than \$1bn invested outside the US (or about $\frac{1}{4}$% of the roughly \$390bn 1980 total in pension assets). In that year, several pension funds adopted new asset allocations, driven by the desire to diversify and the ascendancy of the new quantitative modelling of risk, and the amount invested abroad quintupled to \$5bn, or more than 1% of total assets. This heralded a trend which continued throughout the 1980s and much of the 1990s. By 2000, the US defined benefit pension sector had about \$7000bn in total assets, of which about \$800bn, or about 11%, was invested outside the US. US pension funds, with 11% in total of international assets, are low in the international league table of international diversification by percentage, but by far the largest in absolute value. By far the majority of the international assets that the US holds are equities, and it is equity portfolios, as we shall see, that form the basis for the growth of the currency overlay sector.

2.2.2   UK

The growth of the UK funded pension sector paralleled that of the US. But the UK's experience in international investing is very different, and can be divided firmly into two halves – pre-1979 and post-1979. Why 1979?

Before October 1979, the UK maintained exchange controls. These had been introduced at the beginning of the Second World War as part of the panoply of measures put in place then to create, in effect, a command or 'planned' economy. Even though most of the legacy of regulation and control was scrapped by the middle of the 1950s, one overarching regulation remained – exchange controls.

Exchange controls required that UK residents apply to the Bank of England for permission to acquire foreign currency. Permission would be given for specified purposes, including the importation of necessary foreign commodities and goods, and £50 per year (raised to £200 in the 1970s) for each individual for the purposes of foreign travel. However, permission would not be given for the purchase of overseas assets. Here the Bank of England was faced with a difficulty – at the imposition of exchange controls, there was a considerable pool of British capital invested abroad. The government decided that this could stay, but that when a UK investor wished to repatriate his investment, he could sell his foreign currency to another UK investor who wished to invest abroad.

This created an arbitrary, but largely fixed, pool of overseas capital which had to be competed for by UK investors. It was called the 'dollar' pool, and it traded at a premium to the normal exchange rate. The premium varied according to supply and demand, and was called, unsurprisingly, the 'dollar pool premium'. This strange corner of the financial world had one major effect on UK pension funds – they could not as a group increase their holdings of international assets, every individual increase was matched with a compensating decrease in international holdings elsewhere. Then, in 1979, in the first months of the new Conservative administration under Mrs Thatcher, exchange controls were summarily and totally abolished. The dollar pool (and premium) disappeared (incidentally causing a one-off loss for those funds already invested abroad), and from that point UK funds could invest abroad unhindered.

Figure 2.1 shows the proportion of assets invested overseas by UK funds in the 20 years to end-2001. It includes equities and bonds, but overseas equities are the dominant asset class. At the end of 2001, UK pension assets were about £800bn; this puts international assets held by UK funds at about £220bn.

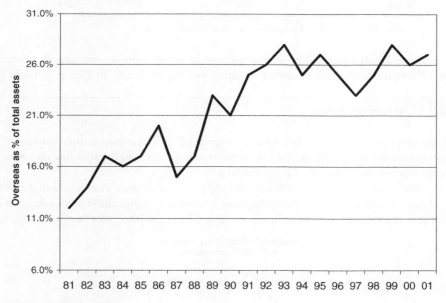

Source: WM Company.

Figure 2.1   Overseas asset allocation 1981–2001 (UK pension universe weighted average)

Table 2.2 is a very rough 'guesstimate' based on asset values at the end of 2002, for the extent of international asset allocation. It has been compiled by the author from a range of diverse and sometimes incomplete sources, so it should be relied upon only as a general guide, not a source of definitive values. It should be noted that for the three years ending December 2002, there has been a significant decline in the size of international portfolios arising from the general decline in equity values.

2.3   CURRENCY VOLATILITY

Against the background of these increasingly internationalised investment portfolios, what role does currency play?

Table 2.2   Geographical market analysis, end-2002 estimates

Country	Approx. size of funded DB pension funds (US$bn)	International assets %	International assets US$bn
US	5688	10%	569
UK	1120	26%	291
Switzerland	298	40%	119
Netherlands	400	25%	100
Japan	643	10%	64
Canada	222	15%	33
Sweden	71	40%	29
Australia	75	30%	23
Hong Kong	15	50%	8
Germany	60	15%	9
Belgium/France	76	10%	8
Total	**8666**	**14%**	**1251**

Source: Record Currency Management Estimates, December 2002.

The measure I will adopt to record the movement in the currency markets is 'currency surprise'. Currency surprise is described in detail in Chapter 3, and in Box 2.2. There is a

Box 2.2   Currency surprise

Currency surprise is the difference (usually expressed in percentage terms) between the forward rate at the start of the period (say month) in question, and the spot rate one month later (or whatever the frequency being measured).

It is called 'surprise' because whereas the appreciation or depreciation implicit in the forward rates is anticipated, any deviation from this implicit depreciation or appreciation is a 'surprise', and is equally likely to be up as down. The graph illustrates currency surprise:

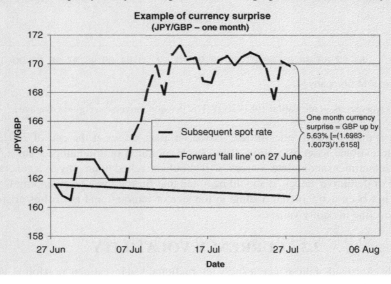

The reason that currency surprise is attractive is because it represents the only exploitable measure of currency movements. Since an investor can buy or sell a currency forward (at the forward price), the profit or loss he will experience when that contract reaches maturity will be equal to the currency surprise.

Note that to allow currency surprise to be added to or deducted from asset returns, the algebra of the calculation has the spot rate at the start as the denominator. This is a unique feature of currency surprise – all other assets have their start value as the denominator. See text for a more detailed discussion of this point.

large quantity of high-quality historical currency data available. Currency surprise can be readily calculated from this data, and so we have a lot of information about currency surprise.

If we take the past 20 years (1981–2001), we can illustrate the scale of currency surprise movements for major currencies in a matrix (Table 2.3). I have chosen six currencies [US dollar (USD), Japanese yen (JPY), Deutschmark/euro (DEM), pound sterling (GBP), French franc/euro (FRF)]. Note that the three-letter abbreviations in brackets are the 'Swift' codes (see Box 2.3) for the currencies in question – Swift codes are the currency codes internationally recognised by the banking system. I will generally use them for labels and captions, and only with introduction elsewhere. Note also that for the two largest member states of the Eurozone, I have combined the euro rates post-1999 with the individual currency rates pre-1999.

Table 2.3 illustrates a number of important characteristics of long-term currency surprise:

(a) Currency surprise is zero sum if taken from all base currencies – this is logically true, not just empirically true.

Table 2.3 Currency surprise matrix 1981–2001

	Numerator						
Denominator	USD	JPY	DEM/EUR	GBP	FRF/EUR	CHF	Average
USD		1.39% (13.15%)	2.03% (12.00%)	0.36% (11.67%)	0.90% (11.91%)	2.65% (13.05%)	**1.47%**
JPY	−1.42% (13.25%)		0.62% (11.64%)	−1.04% (13.06%)	−0.50% (11.75%)	1.24% (11.64%)	**−0.22%**
DEM/EUR	−2.02% (12.04%)	−0.63% (11.59%)		−1.64% (9.27%)	−1.11% (2.58%)	0.62% (4.76%)	**−0.96%**
GBP	−0.40% (11.61%)	1.01% (12.93%)	1.65% (9.21%)		0.51% (9.41%)	2.28% (10.12%)	**1.01%**
FRF/EUR	−0.92% (11.86%)	0.49% (11.64%)	1.12% (2.54%)	−0.55% (9.39%)		1.74% (5.26%)	**0.37%**
CHF	−2.65% (13.12%)	−1.26% (11.62%)	−0.63% (4.77%)	−2.26% (10.21%)	−1.73% (5.34%)		**−1.71%**
Average	**−1.48%**	**0.20%**	**0.96%**	**−1.03%**	**−0.39%**	**1.71%**	**0.0%**

Box 2.3   Swift codes

In 1973 the international banking community formed a co-operative ('Society for World-wide Interbank Financial Telecommunication' (SWIFT) to allow efficient international electronic cash transfer using common standards. SWIFT has devised unique three-letter codes for all the world's currencies. These are becoming increasingly used not just across the market-making community, but also across the user community. They are superseding a variety of less formal abbreviations for currencies, although in common usage informal abbreviations will undoubtedly continue to have an existence.

As an example, the Swift code, and the informal abbreviations, for the Swiss franc are as follows:

Swift code:	CHF
Informal abbreviations:	SFr, SwFr, SF

Swift codes for a selection of the more common traded currencies are shown below in alphabetical order:

Country/currency	Swift codes	Country/currency	Swift codes	Country/currency	Swift codes
Argentine peso	ARS	Indian rupee	INR	Russian ruble (new)	RUB
Australian dollar	AUD	Indonesian rupiah	IDR	Saudi Arabian riyal	SAR
Brazilian real	BRL	Israeli shekel	ILS	Singapore dollar	SGD
British pound	GBP	Japanese yen	JPY	South African rand	ZAR
Canadian dollar	CAD	Kenyan shilling	KES	Swedish krona	SEK
Chilean peso	CLP	Korean won	KRW	Swiss franc	CHF
Chinese yuan	CNY	Malaysian ringgit	MYR	Taiwan dollar	TWD
Czech koruna	CZK	Mexican peso	MXN	Thai baht	THB
Danish krone	DKK	New Zealand dollar	NZD	Turkish lira	TRL
European euro	EUR	Norwegian krone	NOK	US dollar	USD
Hong Kong dollar	HKD	Philippine peso	PHP	Venezuelan bolivar	VEB
Hungarian forint	HUF	Polish zloty	PLN	Zimbabwe dollar	ZWD

(b) It is empirically the case that many individual currency pairs have low or zero currency surprise returns. We will come back to 'expected return' from currency later.
(c) Annual volatilities in currencies are mostly in the 4–12% range – higher than bond volatilities (average $c.$ 6% p.a.) but lower than equities (average $c.$ 17% p.a.).

It is also worth noting that despite the fact that the calculations are all done via logs, the returns of the same relationship turned upside down (i.e. JPY/USD and USD/JPY) are not identical. This is because we have defined currency surprise as:

$$\text{Currency surprise \%} = (\text{Spot rate}_t - \text{Forward rate}_{t-1})/\text{Spot rate}_{t-1}$$

not

$$\text{Currency surprise \%} = (\text{Spot rate}_t - \text{Forward rate}_{t-1})/\text{Forward rate}_{t-1}$$

In the latter case, all the inverse currency surprises would be identical as long as we converted the currency surprise % to logs.

The 20-year volatility averages mask very significant variations in the volatility of currencies. Popular economic history will remind most readers that there are occasional currency 'crises', in which one or more currencies suffer a sharp movement versus others. These cannot be called 'crashes', because unlike the equity market, when one currency 'crashes', another currency has to do the opposite of crash – it soars. We will return to this relative nature of exchange rates (one man's gain is another man's loss) later.

We can show the variability of currency volatility by charting 20 years' worth of 3-month moving averages of annual volatility calculated from daily prices. Figure 2.2 shows two currency pairs that illustrate this well – USD/GBP and JPY/USD. Each of the spikes are particular events which are well documented. For example, Sep 1985 in USD/GBP is the 'Plaza Accord' – the G5 meeting that agreed to 'manage the dollar down'. The spike in Oct 1998 for the JPY/USD is the rapid appreciation of the yen as hedge funds unwind their 'yen carry'[3] positions.

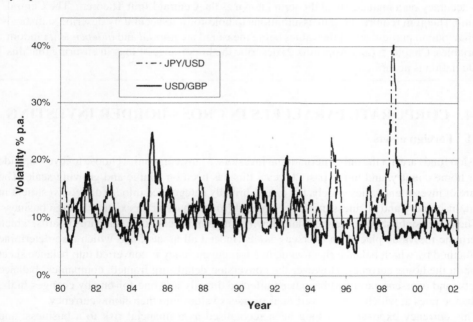

Figure 2.2   JPY/USD and USD/GBP volatility (3-month moving average annualised volatility calculated from daily prices 1980–2002)

So to summarise, international investors have chosen to invest in international assets (mainly equities) for their diversification properties. In doing so, they wittingly or unwittingly have also invested in the currency surprise between their base currency and the currency of denomination of their equities. For the remainder of the book, whenever I refer to currency returns, I will be referring to currency surprise.

---

[3] 'Yen carry' positions were those that took advantage of lower interest rates in the yen compared to the dollar to 'borrow' yen and invest the proceeds in dollars, and be 'paid' for the privilege. (The 'borrowing' and 'lending' can be replicated cheaper using forward currency contracts.) This tactic only works if the yen appreciates by less than the interest rate differential over the horizon of the trde.

Box 2.4   Volatility

The measure *volatility* as used in the financial world is a measure (normally annualised) of the *standard deviation* of the periodic returns of an investment, asset class or portfolio. This is the most commonly used measure of the risk of investments, and the formula for its calculation is:

$$ SD = \sqrt{\dfrac{\sum\limits_{i=1}^{n} (r_i - \bar{r})^2}{n - 1}} $$

where r_i = ith period return, $\bar{r}$ = average value of r in the sample, and n = number of observations in the sample.

   If the periodic returns that are recorded are, say, monthly, then the convention is to annualise by multiplying the calculated monthly volatility by $\sqrt{12}$. This conversion relies for its accuracy on a mathematical theorem known as the Central Limit Theorem. The Central Limit Theorem requires certain assumptions to hold for it to accurately describe statistical behaviour, in particular that the values being measured are *normal* and *independent* random variables. Chapter 5 (and Appendix 2) describe the importance of logs in ensuring that this calculation is accurate.

2.4   CORPORATE PARALLELS IN CROSS-BORDER INVESTING

2.4.1   Foreign assets

Pension funds are not the only international investors. Many companies choose to invest outside their home country, and in the past 20 years this has been on a large and growing scale. The nature of investment varies widely, but can be broadly categorised into (a) direct investment in plant, machinery and business infrastructure and (b) purchase of an existing foreign business.

   There are established guidelines[4] laid down by national accounting standards boards, which determine the value placed on overseas assets (indeed all assets), and which also determine the method by which balance sheet value in a foreign currency is converted into balance sheet value in the home currency. However the conversion details are framed, companies' balance sheets (and overseas earnings) have been affected directly and one-for-one by changes in the exchange rates at which they convert their overseas values into their home currency.

   This currency exposure has long been recognised as a financial risk to a business, and companies have employed financial and other strategies to reduce or eliminate the risk. Before we look at the economic impact of those strategies, we should look very briefly at the other side of the balance sheet – foreign debt.

2.4.2   Foreign debt

As we will see below, companies with foreign assets routinely take on foreign debt. But large and/or international companies also routinely tap the international bond markets for long-term

---

[4] These are called Generally Accepted Accounting Principles in the US, similar in the other major standard setters (UK). There is also an International Accounting Standards Board which has a remit to standardise all major standards under its auspices by 2005.

Box 2.5   The euro

At the time of writing (2002), the euro is the single currency for 12 EU member states (Germany, France, Italy, Spain, Netherlands, Austria, Belgium, Finland, Portugal, Ireland, Greece, Luxembourg). The euro was launched in January 1999 with 11 members – Greece not joining initially because it failed the economic assessment. Greece subsequently joined in January 2001.

Three EU member states are not members of the Eurozone – UK, Denmark and Sweden. Denmark held a referendum (in September 2000) in which the Danes voted 53% to 47% not to join the European Single Currency. The UK government has said that it will not enter the Eurozone without a referendum, and that may be held before 2005. Sweden has not held a referendum yet, but will be doing so, according to the Prime Minister, 'before 2005'.

The euro is governed by the European Central Bank, set up under EU Treaties. The ECB has the sole responsibility for monetary policy in respect of the euro. There is a common interest rate across the Eurozone, and rules limiting the fiscal flexibility of member states. The principal rule is that fiscal deficits must not exceed 3% p.a.; failure by individual states to meet this target will be met, in theory, by fines, although these have not yet been required or imposed. Portugal's 2001 public accounts show that it has become the first state to break the 3% limit; Germany has admitted it will break the limit in 2002.

---

debt financing at the most competitive rates. They may borrow in currencies in which they have no natural exposure. However, is it extremely unusual for companies to choose to borrow in a foreign currency on price or investor-demand grounds, and to leave such currency exposure unhedged.

The instrument of choice for hedging foreign debt (or foreign bond issues) is the currency swap.

2.4.3   Economic impact of corporate currency exposure

Balance sheet currency exposure is not welcomed by CFOs. They intuitively understand that it brings unrewarded volatility, even if they have not thought in detail about the rewards or the risks, nor examined the historical evidence. As a result, they expend a considerable amount of time and effort in minimising their net currency exposure.

In modern reports and accounts, companies spend a significant effort in disclosing their currency exposure, the instruments they have used to reduce or eliminate that exposure, and analyses of the sensitivities of the profit and loss and balance sheet to exchange rate movements. This highlights the mismatch between the sensitivity with which companies treat their 'own' balance sheets, and the lack of perceived investor interest in the financial exposures of the company's pension fund.

If we make the assumption that the company is the 'owner' of their pension fund assets net of pension fund liabilities, and that this is symmetrical (i.e. surpluses can ultimately be recovered by the company – deficits certainly will!), then we can make an assessment on a stylised company of the relative importance of direct balance sheet foreign assets versus pension fund foreign assets. Let us take a UK company, with foreign subsidiaries accounting for 30% of gross assets, and 15% of net assets (i.e. funded with foreign currency debt). It has a pension fund equal to 100% of its net assets, and it has 30% in international assets. The

---

Box 2.6 Swaps

Swaps are a class of 'derivative' contract. They were developed and became popular in the 1980s and 1990s to allow companies to tap bond finance in countries where there was investor demand, or to alter the maturity of the interest rate fix, again to match the different needs of both the company and investor.

In a currency swap, the contract provides for one party to pay to the other a stream of interest payments, plus principal at maturity in one currency, while the other party agrees to pay a stream of interest payments plus principal at maturity in another currency. The interest rates applying to the two currencies will be different, and will reflect the domestic monetary conditions in the two countries.

In an interest rate swap, the contract provides for one party to pay to the other a stream of floating interest payments (e.g. linked to LIBOR) in one currency, while the other party agrees to pay a stream of fixed interest payments in the same currency. The interest rates applying to the fixed payments, and the LIBOR-based floating payments, will reflect the monetary conditions in the currency concerned.

There are many other swaps now available to convert one type of financial payment into another – the scope is almost limitless. The 'financial engineers' who develop and market swaps are investment banks, who will trade and hedge them on their own account.

---

currency exposure in the pension fund of such a company (and these figures are typical for the UK) will be double that of the exposure in the company. It is safe to assume from the reporting conventions that companies currently adopt, that such a company would spend at least a page, and probably more, describing the profit and loss and balance sheet sensitivity to currency, and a similar length explaining treasury policy, instruments and risk control in relation to currency risk. It is quite likely that an effectively identical risk (currency risk in the pension fund) will not even be published, let alone analysed. This 'immunity' that CFOs believe they have in the pension fund may be one of the reasons that the standard remains unhedged currency exposure for pension foreign assets, but hedged in the balance sheet 'proper' exposures.

3
Currency Hedging

3.1 INSTRUMENTS AVAILABLE

The purpose of currency hedging is to reduce or eliminate currency exposure. Currency exposure as it relates to investment assets means that the market valuation of foreign assets varies (positively) with movements of the foreign currency. It follows that an instrument whose market valuation varies negatively with that foreign currency will reduce or eliminate (if held in the right quantity) the currency variations of the asset. What instruments are there that can perform such a task?

Listed here is a full (but not necessarily comprehensive) selection of the principal ones:

- Foreign debt
- Forward currency contracts
- Currency swaps
- Currency futures contracts
- Currency options

Let us take these five instruments in turn, looking at three issues for each: the *nature* of the instrument; the *costs* of using the instrument; and the shape of the instrument's *sensitivity* in market valuation to currency movements.

3.1.1 Foreign debt

3.1.1.1 Nature

Foreign debt is fairly self-explanatory (and was briefly discussed in the previous chapter), but to recap: foreign debt will act as a hedge to a foreign asset if the proceeds from the debt are converted into the home currency (and these proceeds put on term deposit or used to buy a monetary investment that matches the term of the loan). If the proceeds of the loan are used to buy the foreign asset in the first place, then the proceeds do not need to be repatriated, since there will not need to be a purchase of foreign currency to buy the assets. The one attractive feature of using debt to hedge foreign assets is the lack of 'interim cash flow'. That is, during the life of the debt, there will be no call on the investor for extra cash.

The use of foreign debt by pension funds to hedge is extremely rare, in fact almost unheard of, because the majority of pension trust deeds do not allow borrowing. The use of foreign debt is also rare in life funds, but is much more common in investment trusts or other less heavily regulated vehicles.

3.1.1.2 Costs

Using debt as a hedging instrument (without the need for the debt for gearing in the fund) is expensive. If the debt is short- to medium-term (say 1–5 years), a typical spread over LIBOR for an otherwise ungeared investment fund, acting clearing within its powers, would be in the

50–100 bp[5] range. The equivalent deposit rate for the same entity would be at LIBID, which is 8–12 bp below LIBOR, depending on the currency. In addition, a lending institution would require documentation a couple of inches thick. This will all have a cost associated with it. It might be possible for a fund to borrow money much more cheaply (say <10 bp p.a. credit spread) if the debt was fully collateralised. But this would severely limit the flexibility of the fund as to the nature of acceptable capital and its active management.

In summary, an annual cost estimate for the use of foreign debt to hedge foreign currency debt is 60–110 bp, say average 75 bp.

3.1.1.3 Sensitivity

Foreign currency debt is a 'straight line' hedge – that is, if the debt value equals the asset value, then it will fully eliminate foreign currency risks. As a simple example: suppose a fund, denominated in dollars, invests $100 in the UK markets, with an initial exchange rate of $/£ = 1.50. The cost of the asset in sterling terms will be £66.66. Assuming for the moment that the underlying asset does not move in sterling terms, how does the value of the asset move in dollar terms in relation to $/£ movement? Figure 3.1 shows the shape of the value.

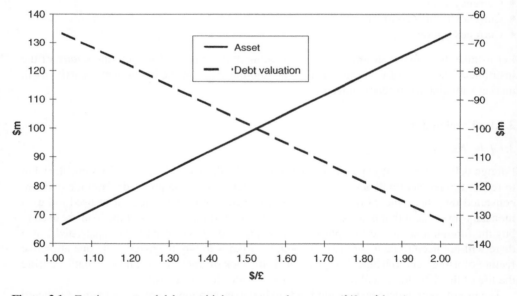

Figure 3.1   Foreign asset and debt sensitivity versus exchange rate ($/£ to $ base)

However, this simple picture is complicated by a number of factors. The first is that the asset value will not be constant. If the asset value rises, then the level of debt will need to be increased to equal the new asset value. If the debt is not increased, then the asset will be less than 100% hedged, and exchange rates will begin to affect the net asset value (i.e. asset and debt together). Conversely, if the asset value falls, the debt will need to be reduced to avoid over-hedging.

---

[5] 1 bp = 1 basis point = 0.01%.

Secondly, the proceeds of the debt will need to be invested. This deposit needs to match as closely as possible the characteristics of the debt, otherwise there will be relative valuation mismatches.

Which brings us to the third point. If the investor has a marked-to-market valuation regime, then the debt should be valued at market, rather than its face value (i.e. the amount owed). This may drive an additional wedge between the asset and debt values, which will need to be adjusted for if a full hedge is genuinely desired.

In summary, foreign debt is an unwieldy and expensive means to achieving the desired end.

3.1.2 Forward contracts

3.1.2.1 Nature

Forward currency contracts are contracts between two parties for the exchange of an agreed amount of currencies at a fixed exchange rate on a fixed date in the future (see Box 3.1). They rely on the mutual creditworthiness of each party for the other to fulfil its obligations, irrespective of the profitability of the deal by the time it reaches maturity. They are generally, although not exclusively, for maturities up to one year.

Box 3.1   Forward currency contracts

Forward currency contracts are very simple instruments – they are contracts between two parties for the exchange of currencies at a fixed exchange rate on a fixed date in the future. The amounts of currency, the direction of flow, the exchange rate and the date are all agreed on a voluntary basis between the parties at the start of the contracts. The only fulfilment required of each party is to deliver a specified amount of a currency to the other on a given date.

Forward currency contracts are easy to understand, and they were for many years the natural instrument for hedging foreign exchange. Why do I use the past tense?

Until the advent, in the 1980s and 1990s, of large and sophisticated corporate treasuries, and the development of cross-border investing, the vast bulk of the needs of banks' customers worldwide were for contracts to ensure the delivery of foreign currency they owed or were owed at a fixed exchange rate. As a result, forward contracts became a very widely-used and liquid instrument. Fierce competition between market makers led to a continuous lowering of the cost of transactions (the bid/offer spread). This, together with a lack of regulatory intervention, meant that forward contracts became the contract of choice for all the users of the currency market, not just those who needed to make or take physical delivery of currencies. Forward contracts are now most commonly used to hedge the market impact of foreign currency movements, not to secure future currency flows.

Forward contracts rely on the mutual credit status of the parties to each bilateral deal. Each of the parties has to be prepared to wait until the contract maturity date for their money, with no 'top-ups' or margins during the life of the contract.

A forward contract is initiated with a maturity date agreed between the parties. This will be a business day, and is the date on which two currencies have to be mutually delivered, for 'value' that day (i.e. no further time for 'clearing' required). There is an established process within the currency market for establishing which days are business days – i.e. avoiding Bank Holidays and weekends.

The contract's 'expiry date' is two working days prior to the maturity date. This is the date on which the reversing deal would be a spot deal, and so is the last convenient date on which avoiding action can be taken if delivery of the principal is not contemplated. Spot deals in the currency market are, by convention, for delivery of the principal in two business days' time.

Forward contracts are not, strictly speaking, derivatives. They are not contractually dependent on any other market for their fulfilment or their final settlement. However, when marked to market, their value varies with exchange rates linearly (but note comments in Box 5.1 later).

3.1.2.2 Costs

Forward contracts do not have any costs 'built in' to them. The process of delivery may have small transmission costs associated with it, but the convention is for currency to be delivered to the recipient free of all charges. The way in which the foreign exchange market-makers make their living is by quoting higher prices to sell, lower to buy (see Boxes 3.2 and 3.3).

The market provides customers with a great deal of information about pricing via FX screen networks. Prices are fed into the networks by bank market-makers, and these are instantly disseminated to users worldwide. The scale and activity of the market is such that new quotes are entered every few seconds at the busiest times of day.

Box 3.2 FX swaps

FX swaps (not to be confused with interest rate or currency swaps) are a pair of currency transactions wrapped up into one price. They allow a customer to simultaneously, say, sell a currency spot and buy it forward for delivery at a fixed date in the future.

If a spot currency rate for currencies A and B is expressed as A/B (i.e. the number of units of A to buy B), A is the numerator and B is the denominator. Suppose A is $ and B is £; the bid and offer quotes might be 1.4363/65. This means that the bank will buy (the bid) sterling (the denominator) from the customer at 1.4363, and sell (the offer) sterling to the customer at 1.4365. The first quoted number is always the lower one, and it is called the 'left-hand side' (LHS) of the quote. The other side is the RHS.

Swaps are quoted as the difference, in FX points (in this case 1/10 000th dollar) between the spot rate and the forward rate. The quote for the same exchange rate as above, but this time for delivery in one year, might be 1.3998/1.4004. If we subtract the spot rate from each side of the quote, we get values (called 'FX swap points') – in this case −365 points (1.3998 − 1.4363) for the LHS, and −361 points (1.4004 − 1.4365) for the RHS.

These swap points are generally quoted stand-alone (−365/−361) – and it is possible for the customer to undertake the swap without the associated spot deal. Suppose the customer is on the LHS (wishing to sell sterling forward). This would entail the customer contracting to sell sterling (vs. dollars) at 365 FX points lower than the rate at which he buys sterling spot.

In such a deal, a notional spot rate (the market rate at the time) is agreed to allow fixed prices to be assigned to each leg of the contract. The bank will want to use the RHS of the spot, to disadvantage the spot deal from the perspective of the client (and simultaneously advantage the distant deal), and the customer will want the LHS of the spot rate for the same reason. This is because of differences in the timing of the cash flow, although the overall effect is very slight. See also Box 3.3.

Table 3.1 WM/Reuters London close exchange rates 6 Jan 2003

Currency pair	Spot		1m Fwd		2m Fwd		3m Fwd		6m Fwd		12m Fwd	
	LHS	RHS	LHS	RHS	LHS	RHS	LHS	RHS	LHS	RHS	LHS	RHS
USD/EUR	1.0478	1.0483	−0.00148	−0.00146	−0.00269	−0.00265	−0.00386	−0.00381	−0.00722	−0.00712	−0.01210	−0.01180
GBP/EUR	0.6504	0.6508	0.00059	0.00062	0.00111	0.00115	0.00169	0.00175	0.00356	0.00367	0.00760	0.00793
JPY/EUR	124.4263	124.5380	−0.33294	−0.32802	−0.61067	−0.60261	−0.88523	−0.87448	−1.71204	−1.69061	−3.30114	−3.25718
CHF/EUR	1.4563	1.4570	−0.00303	−0.00295	−0.00561	−0.00547	−0.00818	−0.00801	−0.01597	−0.01563	−0.02976	−0.02822
USD/GBP	1.6109	1.6111	−0.00377	−0.00374	−0.00692	−0.00688	−0.01017	−0.01009	−0.01991	−0.01981	−0.03730	−0.03700
JPY/GBP	191.2944	191.3987	−0.68876	−0.68220	−1.26926	−1.25850	−1.86239	−1.84550	−3.67052	−3.64396	−7.26185	−7.21324
CHF/GBP	2.2379	2.2403	−0.00673	−0.00661	−0.01250	−0.01229	−0.01845	−0.01819	−0.03673	−0.03630	−0.07149	−0.06939
JPY/USD	118.7500	118.8000	−0.15000	−0.14800	−0.27900	−0.27500	−0.40900	−0.40400	−0.82100	−0.81100	−1.80000	−1.79000
CHF/USD	1.3892	1.3905	−0.00093	−0.00088	−0.00180	−0.00170	−0.00270	−0.00260	−0.00570	−0.00550	−0.01250	−0.01140

The market in forward contracts is so well developed, and so liquid, that the bid/offer spreads that market-makers are able to charge are extremely small.

Table 3.1 is an example of quotes given on a day in January 2003 (6/1/03) for nine major exchange rates. I have used WM/Reuters rates, as these are representative of the average of quotes of several major market-makers. The quotes are expressed as LHS/RHS, where LHS is the offer price of the first named currency. As an example, for the first named currency pair, USD/EUR, the spot price of 1.0478 USD per EUR is the price at which the quoting bank will sell the customer USD for EUR (i.e. the customer buying USD with EUR). The swap prices are similarly quoted (see Box 3.2). So as an example, the 1-month LHS quote of −0.00148 (or −14.8 FX points – an FX point being 1/10 000th of the exchange rate integer) is the difference from the spot rate, expressed in exchange rate terms, at which the bank will sell the customer USD vs. EUR for 1-month maturity, and simultaneously buy EUR vs. USD spot. The spot will be agreed between the bank and the customer, and will be the currency market rate, but the exact rate agreed is not material since if it benefits one party for one 'leg' of the transaction, it will equally disadvantage them on the other leg.

In this example, the following cash flows would be committed to if a customer rolled a long position in USD (vs. EUR) one month forward. It assumes the customer took the bank's LHS 1-month swap price, and agreed the spot at the LHS quote, for $10m. The cash flows are for the customer; for the bank they would be the exact reverse:

Date	USD	Rate	EUR
Spot (= +2 working days)	−10 000 000.00	1.04780	9 543 806.07
One-month (=spot date + 1 month)	10 000 000.00	1.04632 (= 1.0478 − 0.00148)	−9 557 305.60

The USD is at a premium in the forward market because it costs more euros to buy dollars forward than it does spot. This reflects the fact that, on this date, USD interest rates at one month were lower than euro interest rates.

We can turn the Table 3.1 into a 'spreads' table, in which we record only the difference between the LHS and RHS quotes. Table 3.2 shows this in FX points (1/10 000th of the

Table 3.2 Table of WM/Reuters FX bid/offer spreads (in FX points = 1/10 000th of integer)

Currency pair	Spot spread	Forward spreads				
		1m	2m	3m	6m	12m
USD/EUR	5.0	0.2	0.4	0.5	1.0	3.0
GBP/EUR	4.0	0.3	0.4	0.6	1.1	3.3
JPY/EUR	1117.0*	49.2	80.6	107.5	214.3	439.6
CHF/EUR	7.0	0.8	1.4	1.7	3.4	15.4
USD/GBP	2.0	0.3	0.4	0.8	1.0	3.0
JPY/GBP	1043.0*	65.6	107.6	168.9	265.6	486.1
CHF/GBP	24.0	1.2	2.1	2.6	4.3	21.0
JPY/USD	500.0*	20.0	40.0	50.0	100.0	100.0
CHF/USD	13.0	0.5	1.0	1.0	2.0	11.0

Note: It is a convention in the FX market that JPY-based quotes' FX points are 1/100th of an FX integer, not 1/10 000th. However, I have expressed them here as 1/10 000th for consistency.

integer, which would be recognised by a currency dealer), and Table 3.3 shows this in basis points (bp), which express all spreads in 1/100th of percentage point terms (i.e. 100 bp = 1%). Note that I have added two additional rows at the bottom, the unweighted average of the

Table 3.3 Table of WM/Reuters FX bid/offer spreads (in basis points = 1/100th of 1%)

Currency pair	Spot spread	Forward spreads				
		1m	2m	3m	6m	12m
USD/EUR	4.77	0.19	0.38	0.48	0.95	2.86
GBP/EUR	6.15	0.46	0.61	0.92	1.69	5.07
JPY/EUR	8.97	0.40	0.65	0.86	1.72	3.53
CHF/EUR	4.81	0.55	0.96	1.17	2.33	10.57*
USD/GBP	1.24	0.19	0.25	0.50	0.62	1.86
JPY/GBP	5.45	0.34	0.56	0.88	1.39	2.54
CHF/GBP	10.72	0.54	0.94	1.16	1.92	9.38
JPY/USD	4.21	0.17	0.34	0.42	0.84	0.84
CHF/USD	9.35	0.36	0.72	0.72	1.44	7.91
Unweighted averages	**6.19**	**0.35**	**0.60**	**0.79**	**1.43**	**4.25**
Average outright spreads	**6.19**	**6.54**	**6.79**	**6.98**	**7.62**	**10.44**

* This value omitted in the averages, for consistency with Table 3.4.

spreads (in bp) and the unweighted average of the outrights. Outrights are the spot spread plus the relevant forward swap spread added together. The outright is the deal required to open or close a forward hedging contract.

It is notable that the spreads across all the currencies vary widely. WM/Reuters have a particular methodology for calculating some cross rates which may exaggerate the spreads (CHF/GBP being one example), but this would not apply to, for example, CHF/USD, which also apparently has wide spreads. For many currencies, there is a sharp widening of spreads between 6m and 12m. As we will see below, this is not reflected in the prices actually obtained in live dealing.

How do these quoted rates compare to rates actually dealt? These are, after all, just one day's snapshot rates. Spreads can vary according to market conditions, competitive pressure, and the nature of the customer. In trying to answer this question, I will call upon proprietary

Box 3.3 Bid/offer spreads

The currency market enjoys transparent pricing, no commissions, taxes or levies. Its pricing transparency has been one of its strengths, and the competitive pressure of other jurisdictions has prevented governments from successfully imposing taxes and levies. Where these have been imposed, trading has moved to other, more accommodating, jurisdictions.

The form that the pricing of transactions in the currency market takes is bid/offer spreads. These are expressed by market-makers as the simultaneous issue of two prices at which they will deal – a price to buy the currency (bid) and a price to sell the currency (offer). Of course with currency rates, there are two currencies involved, not one, so a convention has grown up as follows.

If a spot currency rate for currencies A and B is expressed as A/B (i.e. the number of units of A to buy B), A is the numerator and B is the denominator. Suppose A is $ and B is £; the bid and offer quotes might be 1.4363/65. This means that the bank will buy (the bid) sterling (the denominator) from the customer at 1.4363, and sell (the offer) sterling to the customer at 1.4365. The first quoted number is always the lower one, and it is called the 'left-hand side' (LHS) of the quote. The other side is the RHS.

In market slang, this quote would be expressed as 63/65 on 'big figure' 3, i.e. the 1.40 is assumed, the 3 cents is the 'big figure' and the quote is in 'FX points' (1/10 000th) of a dollar. All FX market quotes are in FX points, and the rules above (LHS always a lower number than RHS) always apply. Market convention quotes some low value currencies (e.g. yen) with FX points equal to 1/100th of a yen rather than 1/10 000th. See also Box 3.2.

data from the currency overlay firm that I chair – Record Currency Management. This firm has collected bid/offer spread data from four years' history of dealing (1999–2002), and the results are shown in Table 3.4. The table is calculated from 6230 actual deals with an average size of some $10m each (i.e. total volume in this survey c. $60 bn). The figures shown are the bid/offer spreads – i.e. the cost of two deals, buying and selling. The cost of one deal is half the spread cost. To ensure wide coverage, we have categorised into the relevant month deals where the actual maturity date falls within 15 days of the exact maturity date. The table is laid out in an identical fashion to the previous tables.

Table 3.4   Table of actual FX dealing spreads spot and forward (in basis points = 1/100th of 1%)

Currency pair	Spot spread	Forward spreads				
		1m	2m	3m	6m	12m
USD/EUR	2.73	0.23	0.42	0.52	0.87	1.63
GBP/EUR	3.19	0.56	0.78	0.83	1.64	4.06
JPY/EUR	3.10	0.62	0.94	1.09	2.31	3.57
CHF/EUR	1.43	0.60	0.80	1.01	1.89	*
USD/GBP	2.50	0.22	0.33	0.39	0.75	2.20
JPY/GBP	4.37	0.46	0.90	0.93	1.78	3.80
CHF/GBP	3.33	0.64	0.79	1.10	2.30	5.00
JPY/USD	2.87	0.42	0.53	0.62	1.05	2.47
CHF/USD	2.26	0.40	0.59	0.76	1.30	2.97
Unweighted averages	**2.87**	**0.46**	**0.68**	**0.81**	**1.54**	**2.86**
Average outright spreads	**2.87**	**3.33**	**3.54**	**3.67**	**4.41**	**5.72**

*Insufficient number of deals for reliable average.

Finally, we can record the proportion of the quoted FX spread actually paid in long-term daily experience. Table 3.5 shows, for each table cell, the percentage of actual spread to quoted spread. For example, for USD/EUR spot = 57% = 2.73/4.77. The averages and outrights are the ratio of the averages in the source tables, not the averages of the percentage table.

In summary, the quoted bid/offer spot spreads from this WM/Reuters London close snapshot are (with the exception of USD/GBP) significantly wider than the prices achievable in practice. The spot spreads are by far the largest component of the outright spread for an outright forward

Table 3.5   Table of proportion of quoted spread actually paid

Currency pair	Spot spread	Forward spreads				
		1m	2m	3m	6m	12m
USD/EUR	57%	123%	110%	108%	91%	57%
GBP/EUR	52%	120%	128%	90%	97%	80%
JPY/EUR	35%	156%	145%	126%	134%	101%
CHF/EUR	30%	109%	83%	86%	81%	
USD/GBP	201%	119%	135%	79%	121%	118%
JPY/GBP	80%	135%	160%	105%	128%	150%
CHF/GBP	31%	120%	84%	95%	120%	53%
JPY/USD	68%	251%	158%	148%	125%	294%
CHF/USD	24%	112%	81%	106%	90%	38%
Unweighted averages	**46%**	**130%**	**112%**	**102%**	**108%**	**67%**
Average outright spreads	**46%**	**51%**	**52%**	**53%**	**58%**	**55%**

contract, and so this effect dominates the outright spreads, which range from 46% to 58% of the quoted outright spreads.

The story for swap spreads is quite different. With the exception of 12m maturity, swap spreads achieved are slightly wider than the swap spreads quoted. However, the absolute size of the spreads is very small, so the impact on overall costs is very small.

3.1.2.3   Sensitivity

Forward contracts are a 'straight line' hedge – that is, if the principal value of the contracts equals the asset value, then it will fully eliminate foreign currency risks.

Both the example and some of the caveats from Section 3.1.1 apply to forward contracts. However, forward contracts are very cheap and easy to adjust in size, they are ideal for hedging a changing asset value. They are also easy to value (using the forward currency market to mark them to market), and their change in value is dominated by the movements in the spot market rather than changing interest rate differentials.

3.1.3   Currency swaps

3.1.3.1   Nature

Currency swaps (to be distinguished from FX swaps, which are the shifting of maturities in the FX market) are long-term contracts which have developed out of the needs of the international bond market, and the need of companies and their corporate treasuries to easily hedge bonds that they issue in foreign currencies.

A currency swap is a contract between two parties (say *customer* and *bank*), in which the parties agree to exchange regular (quarterly, twice-yearly or yearly) payments in different currencies, and then one final, much larger, exchange at maturity. The purpose of currency swap is to convert the payment (or receipt) stream from a bond from one currency into another. As an example, Table 3.6 shows the payments for a USD/GBP swap for a sterling-based issuer, who has issued a USD fixed rate bond, but wishes to have only sterling fixed rate liabilities. (10-Year $100m bond; annual interest payments; fixed rate; bullet repayment; dollar coupon = 5% p.a.; sterling 10-year fixed rate market (for this issuer) = 7% p.a. All payments and receipts are from the perspective of the customer.)

Table 3.6 Payments for a USD/GBP swap

A	B	C	D	E	F	G	H	I
Years from issue	Coupon payments under bond ($m)	Repayment of principal ($m)	Swap annual receipts ($m)	Swap annual payments (£m)	Swap final receipt ($m)	Swap final payment (£m)	USD/GBP spot exchange rate	Net swap receipts/ payments (£m)
0	-7.00		7.00	-5.00			1.4000	–
1	-7.00		7.00	-5.00			1.3600	0.15
2	-7.00		7.00	-5.00			1.6150	-0.67
3	-7.00		7.00	-5.00			1.5050	-0.35
4	-7.00		7.00	-5.00			1.5300	-0.42
5	-7.00		7.00	-5.00			1.7100	-0.91
6	-7.00		7.00	-5.00			1.8100	-1.13
7	-7.00		7.00	-5.00			1.7500	-1.00
8	-7.00		7.00	-5.00			1.7400	-0.98
9	-7.00		7.00	-5.00			1.5500	-0.48
10	-7.00	-100.00	7.00	-5.00	100.00	-71.43	1.6200	-10.38
				Total net swap payments (£m)				**-16.17**

The mechanics of the swap is generally that the swap counterparties will make the dollar leg of the payments direct to the bondholders, and the customer will then only 'see' sterling payments. They will look for all the world like a sterling 7% fixed rate bond. However, swap payments can be netted (at the then current exchange rate), and just the sterling amount paid to or from the customer (column I). This is uncommon in currency swaps, but almost universal in another branch of the swap world – interest rate swaps.

A currency swap is the economic equivalent of an issue of a bond in one currency, and the investment of the proceeds in another. The astute reader will have noticed that a currency swap is like a series of forward contracts at increasing maturities, and one large forward contract at final maturity. However, whereas individually traded forward contracts would be conducted at the forward rates relating to the maturity, the currency swap exchange rates are all conducted at the spot exchange rate at initiation. The mechanics of the interest rate differential is accounted for by means of outgoing annual swap payments being higher or lower than annual receipts by the interest rate differential.

Why is this very specialised type of currency hedge relevant in currency overlay? The answer is that a currency swap, or its equivalent, is the only instrument capable of hedging a fixed rate foreign currency bond into a domestic currency fixed rate bond. Short-term currency hedges will not allow a pension fund or insurance company to match the domestic long-bond yield curve with long-dated foreign bonds. Short-term hedges will eliminate the spot (and short-term forward) exchange rate risk, but leave the investor with an unwanted foreign currency yield curve and not give the investor the desired domestic yield curve. A currency swap can do this.

However, the use of swaps in this area is rare. All the hedged benchmarks for international fixed income use 1-month rolling currency hedges, and short-term currency hedges remain overwhelmingly the currency hedge of choice for fixed income.

3.1.3.2 Costs

Currency swaps are a relatively restricted market, although they will be offered by the investment banking market in volume to interested customers. Bid/offer spreads, expressed in basis points of yield, are around 5–10 bp for 'straight dates' (i.e. exactly 10 years), plain vanilla contracts, collateralised and liquid currencies. While 5–10 bp may look similar to the costs of outright forward contracts (see above), 10 basis points of yield is 81 bp of NPV at a 4% discount rate. That is, if a customer wished to reverse a currency swap the day after he had initiated it, it would cost him 0.81% of the principal in bid/offer spreads.

Closing currency swaps, particularly where the original counterparty to the swap is asked to quote, is often more expensive than nominal spread quotes would imply. The 'odd' maturity date is a much less liquid market, and the original counterparty has a credit advantage over a new counterparty – the former is eliminating a credit risk, while the latter is taking a new risk on.

Finally, swap contracts are 'credit-intensive'. Unless a swap is collateralised (i.e. assets are regularly posted to cover losses either way), the counterparty will demand a significant credit premium, which will emerge in a wider bid/offer spread.

3.1.3.3 Sensitivity

A currency swap is another 'straight line' instrument as far as currency exchange rates are concerned. However, it can give convexity in its interest rate sensitivity, to counter the same convexity in bond valuation. This means that the marginal change in value of the swap as the domestic interest rate falls, rises as the domestic interest rate tends towards zero.

3.1.4 Currency futures

3.1.4.1 Nature

A currency futures contract is an irrevocable contract to buy or sell one currency for another at a fixed price, on a fixed date in the future. Currency futures contracts are almost identical to forward contracts in their economic effect, but are traded in standardised amounts, for standardised and fixed maturity dates on a formal futures exchange (see Box 3.4). Currency futures are widely used by retail 'investors' (in reality 'traders' rather than 'investors').

Box 3.4   Futures

Futures markets exist in a very wide variety of commodity, financial and money markets, including the currency market. Futures contracts are always issued by an organised exchange, and have certain common characteristics that set them apart from forward contracts:

- A futures contract is an agreement to buy (long contract) or sell (short contract) a fixed amount of a commodity, financial index or other market at a fixed price on a fixed date in the future.
- Futures are priced in public (at the exchange) and are available to anybody able to pay an initial cash deposit.
- A futures contract can be a 'contract for difference' or contract for delivery. A contract for delivery means that the holder of the long contract will be tendered the commodity in question at expiry of the contract. A 'contract for difference' means that the holder of the long contract will be paid/have to pay an amount of money equal to the difference between the contract rate and the official 'settlement' rate on the closing day of the contract.
- Futures contracts do not require any assessment of credit by either buyer or seller. Each futures contract is contracted with the issuing exchange, and the exchange requires a cash 'margin' from each participant sufficient to cover their marked-to-market liability to the exchange. If the contract become worth less (or negative) because of market movements, the exchange will ask for more cash (variation margin), and failing that will force the closure of the contract.

Although the exchange is the counterparty to all futures contracts, the fundamental principle of futures markets is that the exchange 'holds the ring' for independent traders, who contract deals with each other in the open outcry 'floor' of the exchanges. The exchanges' trading systems ensure that there are always exactly the same amount of long contracts outstanding as short contracts.

Users of futures contracts, whether retail or wholesale, are obliged to use a broker to execute the transaction on their behalf. The broker will be a clearing member of the exchange, which means that they can deal directly with the futures exchange, and represent the counterparty which the exchange looks to for margining. Futures brokers will make their money in three ways: through commissions charged to the client, through differential interest rates paid and received on margin accounts, and through acting as proprietary market-makers in the futures market. The futures market needs proprietary market-makers, just as the interbank currency market needs price-givers. They act as the lubrication of the system, taking short-term currency risk for a fee (the bid/offer spread). Bid/offer spreads in the currency market are highly dependent on activity in the particular market, and on the direction of sentiment (i.e. desired trades) on the floor. Currency futures markets are the most 'anchored' of any of the futures markets, because the massive interbank market is an exact match for hedging. This means that prices on futures exchanges never stray far from interbank prices.

Futures markets' margining systems allow anyone, with or without a credit status, to access the currency market. Margining works as follows.

3.1.4.2   Margining

To establish an initial futures position, a customer must first appoint a futures broker with whom he will transact the futures contracts. The broker will either be a clearing member of the futures exchange, or a customer of a clearing member. The smaller, or very 'retail' brokers may not be clearing members, but this will mean that they will have a higher cost base in the transaction 'chain'. We will assume for the purpose of this description, however, that the broker is a clearing member.

The customer will be required by the broker to deposit an amount of cash (an 'initial margin') with the broker to be able to undertake the first trade. This margin is calculated as a percentage of the face value of the contracts – typically 10%, although this can vary widely depending on the market conditions at the time, the market in which the customer is going to transact, and the requirements of the exchange. This initial margin is paid over to the exchange by the broker.

The arrangements for interest on margins varies. The broker may be paid interest by the exchange at something below market interest rates; most brokers will not pay interest on margin balances, but it is common for brokers (and sometimes the exchange) to accept interest-bearing instruments (say Treasury bills) as margin.

For retail investors, all that is required is an initial cash payment, and further cash payments if the contract loses money. Failure to pay the further cash payments results in automatic closure of the contract by the exchange, preserving the credit integrity of the contract (i.e. ensuring that the commitment is fulfilled in full). Futures contracts are generally cheap to deal by normal retail standards, although for large sizes, the combination of brokerage charge, bid/offer spread and margin interest arrangements will make futures not cost-effective. To my knowledge, no currency overlay manager of institutional accounts uses currency futures markets to any great extent – the interbank alternative is just too attractive.

Table 3.7 shows the futures exchanges that offer currency futures contracts, and the broad specification of the contracts.

3.1.4.3   Costs

It is not easy to generalise on the transaction costs of futures contracts – it depends on the charging structure of the broker, and the contracts which are being dealt. In currency futures, total transaction costs are almost invariably higher than the underlying cash (i.e. interbank) market. Bid/offer 'spreads' in futures, while not formally necessary, will in practice exist, and will be wider than interbank spreads. 'Spreads' in futures are a particular concept on which it is worth elaborating.

When a futures contract trades, it does so at one price. If a customer – buyer of a contract, and a customer – seller of the same contract, happen to wish to execute their trades simultaneously,

Table 3.7 Futures exchanges offering currency futures contracts

Futures exchange name	Currency pairs traded (vs. USD unless stated)	No. maturities per year	Max. maturity	Approx. lot (contract) size (USD' 000)	Average daily volume (USD m)
CME – Chicago Mercantile Exchange	AUD/CAD, AUD/JPY, AUD/NZD, AUD, GBP/JPY, GBP/CHF, BRL, GBP, CAD, CAD/JPY, EUR/AUD, EUR/GBP, EUR/CAD, EUR/JPY, EUR/NOK, EUR/CHF, EUR/SEK, E-mini Euro FX (E7), E-mini Japanese Yen (J7), Euro FX (EUR), JPY, MXN, NZD, NOK, RUB, CHF/JPY, ZAR, SEK, CHF	4 – except MXN, ZAR and BRL which are monthly (BRL & RUB cash-settled)	18m	60–125 depending on contract	**8345**
BM&F – Brazilian & Mercantile Futures Exchange	BRL, BRL Mini, EUR/BRL	12	24m	5 & 50	**2711**
FINEX (NY Board of Trade – Financials)	AUD/CAD, AUD/JPY, AUD, AUD/NZD, GBP/JPY, GBP/CHF, GBP, CAD/JPY, EUR/AUD, EUR/GBP, EUR/CAD, EUR/JPY, EUR/NOK, EUR/SEK, EUR/CHF, EUR, EUR (LGE), NZD, CHF/JPY, CAD, JPY, NOK, ZAR, SEK, CHF	4 – except ZAR which is monthly	12m	100–200	**644**
MexDer – Mexican Derivatives Exchange	MXN	12	48m	10	**3**
Sydney Futures Exchange	AUD	4	12m	50	**3**
PBoT – Philadelphia Board of Trade	AUS, GBP, CAD, JPY, CHF	12 quarterly maturities & 2 near-month maturities at any time	12m	50–100	**<1**
Euronext	EUR	12	36m	20	**<1**
SAFE – South African Futures Exchange	ZAR	12	15m	100	**<1**
TIFFE – Tokyo International Financial Futures Exchange	JPY	4	15m	50	**<1**
				Average total daily volume (USD bn)	**11 706**

Note: Other exchanges exist, for example the Korean Futures Exchange, Budapest Futures Exchange.

then they will do so without a bid/offer spread. However, the price at which they deal may be nearer the bid price in the interbank market, nearer the offer price, or in the middle. Exactly where it trades will depend on the dynamics of the market (which way it is moving, the pressure of other buyers and sellers), the respective elasticity of the buyer and seller, and the urgency of their need to deal.

The 'simultaneous order' is, however, a special case of the general case of a mixed selection of varied customer orders. In most futures markets, brokers are appointed by the exchange as 'official' market-makers – i.e. they are allocated the task of creating liquidity continuously throughout the trading day. They will be prepared to accept positions (i.e. act as buyer or seller) at a price which reflects the risk to them of taking the position. This is exactly analogous to the market-maker role in the interbank market. This often means that they will actively quote a bid and offer price simultaneously which is, *de facto*, the bid/offer spread (in the absence of new customer bids or offers).

Currency futures market bid/offer spreads are narrow in relation to other futures markets, reflecting the depth and liquidity of the underlying cash market.

3.1.4.4 Sensitivity

Currency futures contracts are straight-line instruments with respect to the exchange rate. With the exception of the cash effect of margins, their economic effect is identical to that of forward contracts.

3.1.5 Currency options

3.1.5.1 Nature

Currency options are highly complex instruments, despite their seemingly simple design. I therefore make no apologies for devoting some considerable attention to this section, in particular, their pricing.

Currency options are contracts which give the option buyer the right, but not the obligation, to take delivery of one currency in exchange for another at a fixed exchange rate on an agreed date in the future. By corollary, option sellers (writers) have the obligation, but not the right, to deliver one currency in exchange for another at a fixed exchange rate on an agreed date in the future. The fixed exchange rate is called the 'strike rate', and there are four dates relevant in each option: the deal date; the date for premium payment (2 working days later); the expiry date (2 working days prior to the maturity date); and the maturity date, when the exchange of principal amounts takes place.

There are a huge variety of option types now on offer, but there are two key 'plain vanilla' option types – European-style options and American-style options. European options can only be exercised on the expiry date (and mature only on the maturity date), while American options can be exercised by the option buyer at any time between the deal date and the expiry date. An early-exercised American option will also accelerate the maturity date, which will occur two days after exercise. European options are dominant in the OTC market, and increasingly dominant in the traded options market (see below). The subsequent discussion will concentrate on European-style options.

Options are traded at a premium, payable by the option buyer to the option seller on the grant of the option. Currency options can be traded in the interbank market, when they are generally called over-the-counter (OTC), and on futures exchanges, when they are called 'traded options'. The principal distinguishing features of these two types of options are the same as the distinguishing features of interbank forward contracts versus futures contracts. The former are bilateral contracts, the latter are contracts with an exchange.

Box 3.5   Currency options

Currency options are contracts which give the option buyer the right, but not the obligation, to exchange two currencies at a fixed rate (strike rate) on an agreed date in the future. They trade at a premium which reflects three principal elements: the relationship between the strike rate and the current market level (in- or out-of-the-money); the implied volatility for the currency market; the length of time remaining until the option matures.

Currency options are very different instruments from forward contracts. Forward contracts represent only a transfer of economic currency ownership; options represent a more fundamental transfer of market risk. This is because the option buyer cannot lose any more money than the option premium he pays the option seller. However, he can make theoretically unlimited amounts of money if the underlying currency market moves in a particular direction. If he has bought a 'call' on a currency, then he will profit if that currency is strong against the other currency in the pair; if he has bought a 'put', then he will profit if that currency is weak against the other currency in the pair.

The pricing of options has been the subject of intense academic debate, and by 'pricing' I mean the premium at which market participants will willingly buy or sell options. Modern option pricing is based on a seminal work by Black and Scholes in 1973, although their work must be considered a framework rather than a solution to the problem.

The currency options market is so well developed that there is, in effect, a secondary market in which players can pit their expertise against each other – that of currency market volatility. Players wish (put crudely) to sell volatility high and buy low, and it is arguable that this expertise might be quite separate from an ability to correctly predict the direction of the foreign exchange market.

There is one distinguishing feature of OTC options that sets them apart from forward contracts – one party (the option buyer) does not need to be creditworthy. This is because option buyers pay the premium for the option up front, and once that premium has been paid, the option buyer has no further obligations, only rights. By contrast, an option writer (option granter, option seller) needs to have a solid credit rating. The option writer receives a cash premium at the start of the option contract, and thereafter has a potentially unlimited liability to the option buyer, and no upside beyond the premium already received.

In traded options, the credit arrangements are very similar to those with futures: both the option writer and the option buyer are required to post initial margins; the option buyer's initial margin is the option premium; the option writer's margin is, in effect, the option premium plus an amount to reflect the market risk the writer is running.

3.2   OPTION PRICING

The theory of option pricing is a huge topic, and a full review is beyond the scope of this book (and the author's expertise!). However, the key elements in pricing theory are within the book's scope, and I have set them out below.

3.2.1   First principles

The core principle in establishing a theory for pricing options is that the theoretical 'fair' premium should be equal to the present value of the expected payoff of the option at maturity. If options trade at fair prices, then there will be no net transfer of value long-term between option sellers and buyers.

A fair price is not necessarily the price at which options will trade – that depends on the availability of risk capital willing to take the risk of selling options, and the demand for buying options from customers. Since option writers tend to be professional traders, why would an option writer wish to write an option at a theoretically correct price when there is no expectation of profit, but a certainty of risk? A commercial insurer will not write insurance unless he has an expectation that the average losses will be less than the premium plus accumulated interest.

Other things being equal, professional option writers will not write options without the expectation of profit, and that means they will write options at higher than 'theoretical prices' (or their view of them). However, they do need to know what the theoretical price is, and also a framework for judging the expected profit and the risk. A good model can provide all of this – although it is debatable, as we shall see, whether such a model exists. There are a number of competing theories of option pricing, but all boil down to trying to establish the expected payoff of an option at maturity.

3.2.2   Option pricing theory

3.2.2.1   Coin tossing

Let's take a simple example: coin tossing. Suppose that we score 1 point for heads and -1 point for tails whenever we toss a coin. The coin is true, and it is tossed once a period. The 'market price' is the sum of the points scored. We can (I hope with only mental arithmetic) devise and calculate the fair value for a one-period call at zero strike price and at one dollar per point. For simplicity, assume interest rates are zero. The answer is 50c. Why? Because there is a 50% chance that the score is minus one (when the option payoff is zero), and a 50% chance that the score is plus one (when the option payoff is $1). (50% × $0) + (50% × $1) = 50c.

What about a two-period option? Again the fair value is 50c: a 25% chance of two heads (payoff = $2), a 50% chance of one head/one tail (payoff = nil), and a 25% chance of two tails (payoff = nil). What about three-period? The answer turns out to be 75c, which the reader might like to verify himself.

This simple model has a number of attractive features. Firstly, the model is intuitively plausible – that is we believe it accurately describes a known physical process. Secondly, the underlying distribution (i.e. heads/tails) is known with confidence. Thirdly, the model makes few assumptions, and those that it does make can be tested with some rigour and verified. This pricing model would be called a binomial model (because the underlying distribution is objectively known to be binomial). Interestingly, an n-period price (where n is a large number, say 1000) would approximate to the Black–Scholes model price, which is derived from the normal distribution, because the Central Limit Theorem tells us that the distribution of the mean of a large binomial sample tends to normality.

This forms the ideal backdrop to a reliable valuation model, a backdrop that is regrettably diminished or absent when we move from manufactured distributions to those actually observed in the financial markets. Of course, option theorists do not necessarily regret the difficulties of modelling the real financial world – if the models worked most of them would be out of a job!

3.3 THE BLACK–SCHOLES MODEL

For practical purposes modern option theory can be dated from a seminal paper by Black and Scholes in 1973. In that paper the authors demonstrated for the first time the theoretical possibility of risklessly hedging written options using only the underlying security, and that this process produced 'costs' exactly equal to the 'fair' premium of the option. The process they described (although see below) was one of continuous adjustment of the underlying holding of the security, a process we now call 'delta hedging'.

The importance of the paper was that it provided a theoretical argument for claiming that the fair price of an option should be the expected payoff value without any additional risk premium, because it is risklessly replicatable using the underlying securities. Prior to this, pricing models had always tried to include a pricing of the risk taken by option writers.

This underpinning was seen to establish the fair price, and the maths to calculate it, as a legitimate price, one which traders could have confidence in. Ironically, the 'fair price' maths has been almost universally accepted (although Black and Scholes did not invent this); their innovation, the riskless replication, was always an illusion, since it relied on assumptions about the underlying markets which are clearly violated in practice. Black and Scholes knew at the time that their riskless replication was never available to real traders – and yet this is the model which has endured.

Without going into too much maths, what is the Black–Scholes model?

3.3.1 Market assumptions

The first, and most important, aspect of the Black–Scholes model is their assumptions about the characteristics of the market. Note also that these were assumptions made about a single equity market, not the currency market. The following are the key assumptions (there are others, but they are not key, or are not seriously violated in practice):

(a) The market price is a lognormal random walk in continuous time;
(b) Volatility ($= \sqrt{\text{variance}}$) is constant;
(c) There are no transaction costs, and any (fractional) amount of the option and the instrument can be traded in continuous time.

All three of these are seriously violated in all markets, and the currency market is no exception. If (a) held, then there would be no possibility for any active management, forecasting or systematic outperformance in the currency (or any) markets – all markets would be coin-tossing. But the violation of (c) is the most serious, since if transactions costs are present (as they always are), and if the market is not priced in continuous time (which it cannot be in a market run by humans, even in the imagination), then the maths of the Black–Scholes model breaks down.

Box 3.6 Normal and lognormal

The normal distribution is a feature of many types of random processes. Its 'bell-shaped curve' represents the likelihood of outcomes ranging from people's height to the number of peas in a bag of frozen peas. The normal curve is defined by its formula, which is quite simple, but more importantly has taken a place at the centre of the statistical world. There is no 'natural law' which makes the normal distribution the right one for modelling the real world, and indeed it is possible that its mathematical elegance is one of its main qualifications. However, the Central Limit Theorem" does lead directly to the normal distribution. The Central Limit Theorem says that if the average value of a sample of observations is taken (say the number of heads from tossing a coin 1000 times), then the normal distribution describes the likelihood of the number of heads being 450–500, 500–550, 550–600, etc. As long as the samples are large enough, this effect applies to a wide range of underlying distributions. Coin-tossing is 'binomial', the number of fish caught by fisherman is Poisson, and the length of telephone calls is exponential, but all of these will have normal distributions of sample means for large samples.

Lognormal processes are those where the randomness is multiplicative, say in the period returns of an asset. They are called lognormal because if returns are recorded as percentages, then '1+ percentage' is the factor by which to multiply the asset to get the next period value. If we take the natural log of these '1 + percentages', the resulting series is normally distributed.

Appendix 2 takes a full look at the mathematical implications of this phenomenon. It is not self-evident, however, that lognormal (i.e. a normal generator in a multiplicative environment) is the 'natural' distribution for financial markets. Indeed, the occurrence of so-called '7-standard deviation' events in the markets (or 'melt-downs') on a regular, if infrequent, basis does require us to abandon the normal hypothesis. 7-SD events occur under a stable normal distribution once in every 2 billion years.

3.3.2 The model

Black and Scholes derived their fair price not by simple calculus from the lognormal distribution (which had already been done), but by a peculiarly 'back door' method. They hypothesised that if the underlying market on which the option was written indeed satisfied the above assumptions, then it would be possible for a writer of a call option on x shares of underlying to hold an amount of shares $y(0 \leq y \leq x)$ which (measured instantaneously) would provide a riskless hedge. Rather bizarrely given the subsequent development of delta hedging, the way this was actually shown in the paper was that the holder of a fixed amount of underlying shares could hedge that risk by varying the amount of options written. If the amount x was varied continuously (and they mean *continuously*, not every 1/100th of a second!), then using continuous time maths (which allows calculus), they found that the formula for pricing the option which satisfied the 'no-risk' requirement created by this continuous adjustment method would be, hey presto, the fair value (which equals the expected payoff value of the option).

The Black–Scholes model, in its simplest form, has only three variables: the time to expiration, the market volatility, and the strike price in relation to the current market level. For currency options, the interest rate is relevant only insofar as it discounts future cash flows. If the option premium were payable at maturity, the interest rate would fall away.

The academic world regarded Black and Scholes' proof that options could be risklessly hedged with the underlying market instrument, and vice versa, as their major innovation. This 'discovery' ended the speculation as to the appropriate risk premium for options, since they 'proved' there had to be none.

This innovation spawned huge interest in option pricing theory, and set Scholes (with Merton) on their way to the 1997 Nobel Prize. Unfortunately Black died in 1995, and so missed out on the prize. It is a little ironic that the acclaim for this paper is based on the creation of riskless portfolios of options with underlying instruments. The moment there is serious violation of Black and Scholes' assumptions, the riskless nature of the hedge breaks down. What may appear to work in theory does not survive any practical tests – and under most scientific regimes this would be regarded as refutation of the theory.

3.3.3 Understanding option pricing

The Black–Scholes formula is set out in the footnote below.[6] I recommend that, unless you have a strong grasp of calculus, you should leave it unread. I think the best way to understand the pricing model is to visualise what it is trying to do.

When an option matures, it will have a 'payoff' value equal to the curve in Figure 3.2. Ignoring the lognormal element (and forward differentials) for the moment for simplicity, the normal distribution curve for, say, 8% annual volatility, and with the current market level at

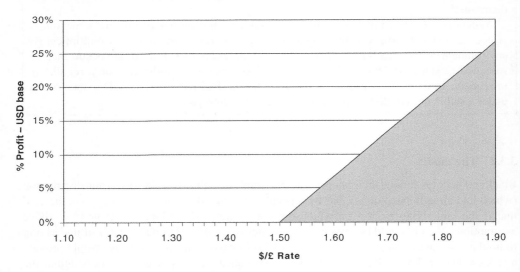

Figure 3.2 Payoff % at maturity of $/£ option – £ call; strike = 1.50

---

[6] $C = SN(d_1) - Ke^{(-rt)}N(d_2)$

where:

C = theoretical call premium	s = standard deviation of log returns
t = time until expiration	$\ln$ = natural log
r = risk-free interest rate	S = current stock price
e = 2.7183	K = option strike price
$d_1 = \dfrac{\ln(S/K) + (r + (s^2/2)t)}{s\sqrt{t}}$	N = cumulative standard normal distribution
$d_2 = d_1 - s\sqrt{t}$	

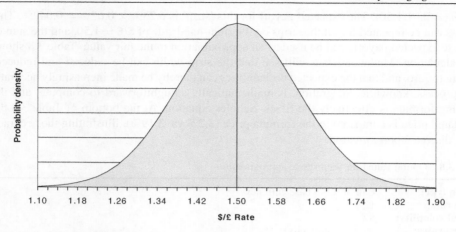

Figure 3.3 Normal distribution (SD = 8%)

1.50, would be as in Figure 3.3. This tells us the 'probability density' of the exchange rate one year from now. 'Probability density' allows us to determine the chance that the exchange rate lies between any two values. I have deliberately not put values on the left-hand axis, since without more information, the values of the curve do not mean a lot.

From the elements in these two graphs, we can visualise that the expected payoff value of a call option at 1.50 strike price is the sum of the likelihood of the end-year rate lying at each interval above 1.50, and the profit for the option holder at each of these intervals. To do this accurately is a job for calculus, but we can approximate it closely by using discrete ranges. Figure 3.4 shows the payoff curve superimposed on the normal distribution, and an area, between 1.50 and 1.52, marked out.

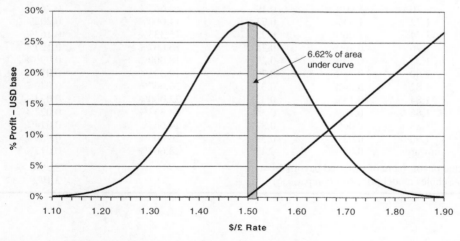

Figure 3.4 Payoff % at maturity of $/£ option – £ call; strike = 1.50

On the stated assumptions, the area under the normal curve between 1.50 and 1.52 (i.e. the likelihood that the exchange rate will end the year lying between these values) is 6.62%. The (approximate) average profit (i.e. the average of 1.50 and 1.52) to the option buyer is $0.01, or

0.67% (= 0.01/1.50). The expected payoff for this 'strip' is 6.23% × 0.67% = 0.042%. This process can be repeated for all the strips on the right-hand side of $/£ = 1.50, and the sum of all these expected payoffs can be used as an approximation to the fair value. Table 3.8 shows this calculation. Mathematicians will see that the strip width can be reduced and reduced, tending to zero, and that the expected probabilities can thereby be made increasingly accurate. This process, known as integration, is mathematically straightforward to compute, and the resulting formula is effectively the Black–Scholes equation. At the bottom of Table 3.8 the calculated price is compared to the formula price (3.2% vs. 3.19%), illustrating the accuracy of the discrete approximation.

Table 3.8   Option valuation – a discrete approximation

Option type:	Call on £ – $ base currency
Strike rate:	1.50
Annual volatility:	8%
Interest rates:	0% (for simplicity)

Exchange rate		Probability	Mean payoff ($)	Mean payoff (%)	Expected payoff (%)
(a)	(b)	(c)	(d)	(e) = d/((a + b)/2)	(f) = c × e
from	to				
0	1.50	50.00%	0	0.000%	0.000%
1.50	1.52	6.62%	0.01	0.667%	0.044%
1.52	1.54	6.44%	0.03	2.000%	0.129%
1.54	1.56	6.09%	0.05	3.333%	0.203%
1.56	1.58	5.60%	0.07	4.667%	0.262%
1.58	1.60	5.02%	0.09	6.000%	0.301%
1.60	1.62	4.37%	0.11	7.333%	0.320%
1.62	1.64	3.70%	0.13	8.667%	0.321%
1.64	1.66	3.05%	0.15	10.000%	0.305%
1.66	1.68	2.44%	0.17	11.333%	0.277%
1.68	1.70	1.90%	0.19	12.667%	0.241%
1.70	1.72	1.44%	0.21	14.000%	0.202%
1.72	1.74	1.06%	0.23	15.333%	0.163%
1.74	1.76	0.76%	0.25	16.667%	0.127%
1.76	1.78	0.53%	0.27	18.000%	0.096%
1.78	1.80	0.36%	0.29	19.333%	0.070%
1.80	1.82	0.24%	0.31	20.667%	0.049%
1.82	1.84	0.15%	0.33	22.000%	0.034%
1.84	1.86	0.10%	0.35	23.333%	0.022%
1.86	1.88	0.06%	0.37	24.667%	0.014%
1.88	1.90	0.03%	0.39	26.000%	0.009%
1.90	upwards	0.04%	0.43	28.667%	0.012%
Expected payoff (sum of expected payoffs by step)					3.20%
Black–Scholes model price (for comparison)					3.19%

3.3.3.1   The Greeks

Option theory has spawned a series of Greek letters to represent various rates of change (or elasticities) in an option's price. The main ones are:

- Delta (Δ, δ) – The change in the option value as a percentage of the change in the underlying instrument price. An option with a delta of 0.5 will change in value by 0.5% (of the principal) for every 1% move in the underlying market
- Gamma (Γ, γ) – The rate of change of the delta with respect to the price
- Theta (Θ, θ) – The rate of change of the option price with respect to time
- Vega (bizarrely, not a greek letter) – The rate of change of the option price with respect to changing (implied) volatility
- Rho (P, ρ) – The rate of change of the option price with respect to the interest rate

When option traders trade options, these 'Greek' values are the key ones for them in constructing hedges for their portfolios. By adding second- and third-derivatives (in the mathematical calculus sense), one could go on adding these letters for ever, so the ones above are just the most popular.

3.3.3.2   The portfolio insurance story

This surfeit of maths brings us to an interesting point about financial theory in general, and option pricing in particular. Financial theory starts by modelling an imaginary world where 'everything is perfect' (i.e. Black and Scholes' assumptions are not violated). As long as this world is maintained in the imagination, then a huge and complex set of theories can be created, all of which fit the world neatly. Actual markets, however, are not like physical laws. They not only do not conform at all closely to the assumptions of the imaginary world, but they are also reflexive. By reflexive, I mean that they change their nature depending on the theories about them that have common currency, and also by what other participants think yet other participants are doing.

While this is instinctively understood by market participants, there are numerous examples where this phenomenon has fundamentally undermined even the least heroic assumptions on which these mathematical models are based. Let's pick an example: the stock market crash of 1987. For several years prior to October 1987, US fund managers had sold programmes of 'portfolio insurance' to the major US institutional investors. These were based precisely on the Black–Scholes notion that by varying the underlying instrument, an investor could 'risklessly' create the payoff of an option – in this case a put option on the US equity market, the S&P 500. Generally, these programmes set the notional strike price somewhat out of the money, so that deltas were very low at the initiation of these schemes. (Remember that deltas represent the proportion of the underlying put that is held in a short futures position.) There had been a subsequent rising market, and so, despite some resetting upwards of strike prices, deltas were still very low. The providers of these programmes knew the processes they employed were not riskless because they could not trade costlessly in continuous time. However, they thought their proprietary ways of minimising the risks would work well enough. They could not have been more wrong.

In October 1987, an extraneous external factor caused a downturn in the S&P. This triggered some selling of the market, using S&P500 futures as the chosen instrument. In the absence of other buyers, and no new good news, this caused the equity market to fall (changes in stock futures market levels affect the underlying securities market by arbitrage). This fall in the equity market triggered more selling of the futures, as the deltas on the (notional) put options rose. This triggered yet more selling of the futures market, which increased deltas and also gammas (gamma is the rate of change of delta as the option goes towards the money).

These circular waves of selling and sell orders overwhelmed the market. There were inadequate buyers, the futures market continuously hit its 'limit' (when trading is suspended), and the underlying equity market was pulled down by arbitrageurs (probably the only futures buyers), who then realised that they could not sell the underlying securities because buyers had panicked and fled there too.

When the waves of selling finally subsided, the customers of portfolio insurance had not only failed to be effectively protected against these market falls, but where trades had been executed (many programmes were abandoned), they were at extremely disadvantageous prices – undermining the rationale of the programmes. The whole concept was consigned to the rubbish bin with little sophisticated reflection, and the world moved on.

3.3.4   The role of assumptions in option pricing

This example brings us to the key point on option pricing. The meat of option pricing is not the mathematics by which prices are arrived at, but the assumptions underpinning the application of each theory. The late Professor Fischer Black himself wrote 'I sometimes wonder why people still use the Black–Scholes formula, since it is based on such simple assumptions – unrealistically simple assumptions'.

This is not a trivial point. In many areas of scientific enquiry, simplifying assumptions are routinely made to limit the degrees of freedom or the complexity of the hypotheses. However in financial markets, such assumptions are not 'simplifying assumptions'. 'Assuming' that markets are lognormal is a very powerful statement. If it is true, then from this a large number of significant results flow, including the maths of option pricing. 'Assuming' that markets are costless to trade in continuous time is another very powerful statement, and it materially affects the construction of option pricing theory. It may be clever maths to use this assumption to 'prove' that there should be no risk premium in option prices, but if the assumptions are grossly violated, is this a useful proof?

Professor Black should probably not have been so surprised – or rather his surprise might have been redirected. The Black–Scholes model has become so popular – indeed the market standard – because it is elegant and logical, is easily calculable (particularly with modern computers), and because it validates and stands together with delta hedging and so is practically useable. Everyone who buys, trades or prices options knows (or should know) that many of the model assumptions are violated in real markets, but they feel more able to cope with these violations from the safe haven of the model. Abandon the model, they argue, and they are once again adrift with no reference points.

3.3.4.1   Implied volatilities

There is an interesting phenomenon which reflects this 'measured acceptance' of the basic Black–Scholes methodology, 'implied volatilities'. As I mentioned above, for a 'plain vanilla' option, the only market variables needed to fully price an option are (i) its maturity, (ii) its in- or out-of-the-moneyness, (iii) the interest rate, and (iv) the volatility. (i) to (iii) are known variables – they are fact. Only (iv) is not directly observable. What is observable, however, is the option price quoted in the market. This means that (iv) can be reverse-engineered, i.e. the terms of the option pricing equation can be rearranged to calculate the volatility that would have produced the option price quoted. The value so produced is called the 'implied volatility'.

Implied volatilities can be calculated for every specification of option. In the perfect world of the Black–Scholes assumptions, implied volatilities would not change (since Black and

Scholes assume that volatility is constant, and they would be independent of other variables, like in- and out-of-the-moneyness. In the world of real markets, however, implied volatilities are so volatile that many option traders, if asked, would claim that their principal job is to 'trade implied volatilities'. Not only do they move up and down in line with the short-term volatility expectations of the market, but there are 'bid' and 'offer' implied volatilities (depending on whether the option is bid or offered by the market), and changing implied volatilities dependent on the in- and out-of-the-moneyness of the option.

Figure 3.5 shows the history of implied volatilities for USD/EUR, 3m at-the-money options. It illustrates the distinct lack of stability in implied volatilities.

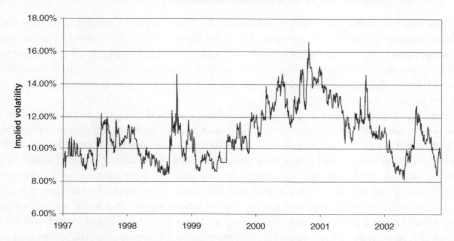

Figure 3.5   History of implied volatilities – USD/EUR (formerly DEM) options; 97–02; 3m maturity; offer price

Figure 3.6 shows a snapshot of the implied volatilities for one specification of option, but graphed against the extent to which it is in- or out-of-the-money. The fact that it shows a strong

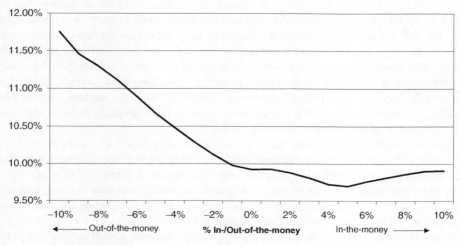

Figure 3.6   Implied volatilities for USD/EUR option versus in- or out-of-the-moneyness – euro call; 6m maturity; 18 Nov 02 quotes

skew represents in part the scepticism of the market about the lognormality assumption. The skew implies that either (a) extreme movements are more likely to happen than implied by the lognormal curve or (b) low time-value options (particularly very out-of-the-money) are more difficult, and more risky to hedge. Both of these possibilities are explicitly recognising failures in the Black–Scholes assumptions, and instead of adjusting or abandoning the model, they are adjusting one of the input variables. It is a bit like aiming a gun with skewed sights left of the target (rather than adjusting the sights) in an attempt to hit the target!

3.3.5   Practical implications of assumptions violations

One of the key issues that arises when discussing the Black–Scholes assumptions is 'what is the effect on expected return'? Remember that in the pure Black–Scholes world, the expected PV of all options is zero (and therefore it is irrelevant from a return perspective whether you are a buyer or a seller, or whether you buy or sell any particular currency against any other). In a world where these assumptions are routinely and grossly violated, what is the expected PV of an option?

For options on most underlying markets (equities, commodities), the consistent buyer of options would have lost money over time. One would have thought therefore that, by analogy, the option writer would have made money. This may, however, not have been true since most professional option writers will hedge their exposure using a dynamic (i.e. delta) hedge in the underlying market. If the average options premiums charged were lower than the frictional costs incurred by the option writer together with the calls on the writer by the option buyers, then it is possible that both could lose money. Those option writers that write options without matching them with a dynamic hedge will have a clearer run at profitability, but will suffer very high risk in periods of high volatility. For most financial houses, the risk/return trade-off of uncovered option writing is unattractive. Historical option pricing, and its effect on the profitability of options, is looked at in more detail in Chapter 10.

This brings me to a diversion which is briefly worth a mention. Although uncommon in the writing of currency options, it is common in the writing of equity options for an option-trading financial house to persuade an institutional investor to write what are termed 'covered calls'. These are call options on single equities or indices, but in the eyes of the institution they are 'covered' by their ownership of the underlying security. If the equity in question remains stable or falls, the call will not be exercised, and they will keep the option premium. If the equity price is strong, they will be called on the option they sold, and they will have to surrender the profits they would otherwise have made in that period from their ownership of the equity. Their compensation will again be the option premium. As a long-term strategy this will be profitable if the implied volatilities are higher than the actual volatilities, and the measurement of volatilities accurately reflects the market movements at the relevant horizon. I will come back to this point in a discussion of trends in Chapter 9.

As a formal risk-management exercise, 'covered call' writing leaves a lot to be desired. It is highly unlikely that the investing institution will be in a position to judge whether the implied volatilities are attractive (and higher than the long-term historical volatility); they are highly unlikely to be minimising the risk of option writing by matching the delta of the option with their holding, and they are unlikely to possess the analytical tools to determine whether writing options is diversifying or concentrating versus their liabilities.

In theory investing institutions with foreign currency exposure could, by analogy, write 'covered call' on foreign currencies. That they are more likely to do the opposite – hiring active currency overlay managers whose profits profile is option-like (from an option buyers' perspective) – is testament to the rather ill-thought-out nature of 'covered call' option writing.

3.4   CURRENCY OPTION PRICING HISTORY

Currency options have been available since November 1982. The first options were American-style options traded on the Philadelphia Stock Exchange. In the subsequent two or three years, a substantial over-the-counter market developed in the London interbank market and elsewhere.

A full and detailed analysis of historical option premium levels is beyond the scope of this book, but broadly speaking, option premiums in the period 1985–1992 were generally at levels at or below the actual average payoffs in the market, particularly for longer-maturity options. That is, over this period, passive buyers of currency options would have made average returns on their option premiums significantly higher than the risk-free rate of interest. Of course, the payoffs of options are highly variable, and can frequently be zero. So consistent buyers of options would ideally have had pre-existing currency exposure which option payoffs would be a hedge for. This is a highly unusual observation, and will not have been generally appreciated by the currency option community (although a number of banks entered the currency option market in this period as writers, and subsequently withdrew nursing losses).

In the period subsequent to 1992, it has been much less easy to make generalisations about average option premium levels. However, there remains in the currency market no obvious evidence that long-term writers of currency options are indulging in a profitable exercise.

3.4.1   Lognormality

In Appendix 2 we discuss lognormality in some detail, particularly in relation to the calculation of the volatility of a series of returns. Lognormality (i.e. the assumption that market prices from a lognormal random walk) represents one of the key assumptions in the construction of option pricing models. It is worth noting that lognormality is not entirely consistent with returns as we normally calculate them, unless we operate a very rigorous 'translation' process between the 'log world' and the world we actually observe.

The principle of lognormality is the assumption that the 'linking' variable, linking one period's security (or currency) value with the next, is multiplicative. This is best (and accurately) represented by converting the price into its natural log. The arithmetical differences between these sequential log prices are then normally distributed. Exactly the same result can be achieved by converting the percentage returns of sequential prices into logs by $R = \ln(1 + r)$, where r is the percentage return and R is the normally distributed variable.

The following are variables in the Black–Scholes model:

$$C = SN(d_1) - K \exp(-rt)N(d_2),$$

where:

C = theoretical call premium	s = standard deviation of log returns
t = time until expiration	S = current stock price
r = risk-free interest rate	K = option strike price
$\exp(-rt)$ = exponential function = e^{-rt}	N = cumulative standard normal distribution

$$d_1 = \frac{\ln(S/K) + (r + (s^2/2)t}{s\sqrt{t}}$$

$$d_2 = d_1 - s\sqrt{t}$$

When working in the 'log world', it has to be dealt with consistently. So, for instance, is the risk-free interest rate, r, the IRR annual return (the convention used in investment management), or is it a continuous rate of return $\ln(1 + r)$? Is the standard deviation expressed as a standard deviation of percentage returns, or of additive changes in the log price? Or $\exp(SD(\log \text{changes}))-1$? These questions have to be carefully considered when using the Black–Scholes or any other model.

3.4.2 Monte Carlo models

There is one other major class of models based on numerical analysis. The principal representatives of this class are Monte Carlo models. These take a very different approach to pricing, which can crudely be characterised as 'let's try it and see'. (Incidentally, they are called Monte Carlo because the Principality is a major gaming centre – the epitome of testing distributions by repeated sampling!) Generally used by banks and financial engineers to price more intractable or complex option instruments, Monte Carlo models take an externally determined price distribution (e.g. lognormal, lognormal+jump, binomial or whatever), and calculate one outcome of the option (i.e. whether it matures in- or out-of-the-money, and if in-the-money how big the payoff is) on the basis of a randomly generated price series. This process is then repeated (several thousands or tens of thousands of times) to generate a wide range of possible outcomes. The average of these outcomes (appropriately discounted if necessary) is then the 'fair value' of the premium.

Monte Carlo techniques are appealing where there are non-standard price distribution assumptions, where the option instrument is path-dependent or has other complexities, and where the model user wishes to 'stress test' the option instrument and examine the range and variety of outcomes. The disadvantage of Monte Carlo techniques is that they are a sampling process whose accuracy increases asymptotically with the number of simulations run. This can be a very heavy computing requirement for on-line pricing. Indeed some banks use Monte Carlo in regular batch runs, and then create 'look-up' tables with the results to get instant on-line quotes.

3.4.3 Costs

The premium of an option is not its 'cost'. In the Black–Scholes model world, the option premium equals the discounted average payoff value, and so neither buyer nor seller expect to gain on average over time. However, there has developed a particular approach to pricing the cost of an option which merits a brief discussion – that of implied volatility.

If we take an accepted model for the pricing of a currency option – say the Black–Scholes methodology with adjustments for the forward contract nature of the underlying – then with only four input values we can calculate the fair price. These inputs are:

(a) Maturity date
(b) % In- or out-of-the-money. This represents the difference between the current market price and the strike price. An in-the-money call option has a strike price lower than the current market price, and vice versa. In currency options, it is usual to measure the strike rate versus the forward market rate, rather than the spot
(c) Market volatility – we shall come back to this
(d) Interest rate for the option maturity period

With this information, we can price an option fully. Moreover, all but one of these values are definitive, known quantities. However one value, volatility, is not known. Its historical value can be estimated, there is a pool of information about the volatilities used to price other options, but it cannot be directly observed. What happens in practice is a little strange to the outside observer, and it is this. The market price at which options are offered or bid is recorded. Then the Black–Scholes calculations are 'put into reverse', and the level of volatility that would generate the observed premiums (all other factors remaining the same) is calculated. This can be done for both the offer bid and the bid price of the options, and these produce a value called the implied volatility – bid implied volatility and offered implied volatility.

Implied volatility is an excellent way of covering up the shortcomings of the market pricing mechanism, since it cheerfully reports different values for buying and selling options, different values for options that are heavily in- or out-of-the-money, and so on.

3.4.4   Sensitivity

Currency options are not straight-line instruments. Their sensitivity to exchange rates forms a curve, the slope of which is the 'delta' of an option. The typical curve looks as in Figure 3.7. This 'convex curve' characteristic of currency options gives them particular features in the hedging of currency exposure which we shall consider in later chapters. In particular, the 'delta' (the slope of the option valuation) will tend towards 50% over the long-term (assuming that options are bought at-the-money). This means that the risk-reducing properties of an overlay portfolio consisting of options are close to those of a passive overlay portfolio with a 50% hedge ratio.

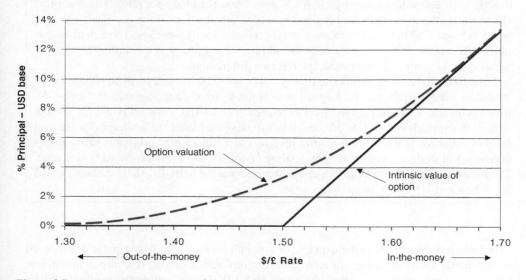

Figure 3.7   Option model prices % – $/£ option; £ call; strike = 1.50

3.5   INTEREST RATES AND FORWARD CURRENCY RATES

One of the distinguishing features of the currency market is its intimate relationship with the interest rate market. In particular, forward currency rates are not, except in very special circumstances, 'forecasts' of future exchange rates. Instead, they are a mathematical calculation based on the currency spot rates, and the respective interest rates of the two currencies in question. See Box 3.7 for descriptive details.

Box 3.7   Forward currency rates

Forward currency exchange rates are not guesswork by the market-makers, but the result of a two-way arbitrage with the respective interest rates of the two currencies in question. Let us take an example. Suppose the US dollar has interest rates at a 1-month horizon of $2^1/_8\%/2^1/_{16}\%$, and the UK has interest rates of $5\%/4^{15}/_{16}\%$, and the spot rate is 1.5345/47. In the interest rate quotes, the first number is the interest rate to borrow money (LIBOR) from the interbank market, the second the price to lend money (LIBID). In the exchange rate, the LHS (1.5345) is the rate to buy dollars, the RHS is the rate to sell dollars, and the rate is the amount of dollars per sterling.

   Assuming large amounts of money can be borrowed and lent by a creditworthy bank at these rates, then these rates determine the no-arbitrage boundary rates for the forward rates. The arbitrage works in two stages like this. Suppose a bank has £10m to deposit for one month. It can deposit in £ LIBID at $4^{15}/_{16}\%$, and have £10 041 146 in one month. Alternatively it can convert its cash into dollars, simultaneously sell the dollars 1-month forward, and deposit the dollars at $ LIBOR. The forward rate at which this exercise is exactly cash equivalent neutral is 36.6 FX points less than the spot rate. (The main text shows the maths workings.) An FX point is 1/10 000th of a $, so if the two deals are done at 1.5345 and 1.53104 then the £ cash at one month exactly matches. The calculation is ultimately one of interest rate ratios [forward rate = spot rate × ((1 + Int$)/(1 + Int£))] rather than, as commonly supposed, interest rate differentials.

   If the RHS dollar swap points rise (to say −37), then UK investors will be paid to invest in dollars via $ LIBID and the forward rate. If the forward swap rate falls (to say −36), then US investors will be paid to invest in pounds via £ LIBID. Forward points are subject to bid/offer spreads (say −37/−36), and this will raise the hurdles to arbitrage. The second level of arbitrage is where cash-neutral investors can 'round trip' profitably. This means borrowing in sterling, converting spot, lending in dollars, and selling forward (vice versa). The boundaries of this arbitrage (which has to overcome the LIBOR/LIBID spreads shown) are −37.4 and −35.8 FX swap points.

   The inset box takes a particular example of 1-month forward $/£. To recap, the $/£ forward rate is constrained by the ability of arbitrageurs to replicate a sterling one-month investment by means of conversion into dollars, investing in $ LIBID, and selling the resulting dollars forward to completely eliminate currency risk. We can examine the maths of this arbitrage in the 'perfect world', and also in the real world of LIBID/LIBOR, spot and forward spreads. Similarly, the constraint applies in the other direction: arbitrageurs can replicate a dollar one-month investment by means of conversion into sterling, investing in £ LIBID, and selling the resulting sterling forward. Finally, any market participant could borrow one currency and deposit the other, which sets the outer bounds of the arbitrage. The boundaries of the arbitrage are fully described in Appendix 1.

3.6 CURRENCY SURPRISE

3.6.1 What is currency surprise?

Currency surprise (see Box 2.2) is an expression first coined relatively recently, but now in common use in the currency overlay industry.[7] It represents a measure for the unanticipated deviation of the spot rate from the rates 'predicted' by past forward rates.

One of the difficulties that investors have faced as they internationalised their portfolios was to get adequate information about what their currency returns were. Custodians reporting on international portfolios quite naturally used their standard 'mark-to-market' technology for valuation. This was based on two valuation elements – the market valuation expressed in local (i.e. foreign) currency, and the spot rate to convert the local currency to GBP (or whatever the base currency was). This naturally threw up an attribution split – the local market returns and the currency returns (i.e. spot-to-spot). Unfortunately, this split has systematically biased the currency returns reported from those that are investable – because spot currency is not investable. The Association for Investment Management and Research (AIMR®) issued a paper on benchmarks[8] in 1998 which discusses this issue clearly and in some detail.

These investable elements are (a) currency return = currency surprise and (b) foreign asset returns = *hedged* asset returns expressed in the home currency (note *not* 'local' returns).

3.6.2 Currency surprise calculation

Currency surprise (C_t) for a foreign currency expressed as a percentage in period t is:

$$C_t = \left(\frac{(\text{Foreign currency spot rate}_t) - (\text{Foreign currency forward rate}_{t-1})}{\text{Foreign currency spot rate}_{t-1}} \right) \times 100\%$$

Assume for this example that the investor has a sterling base currency, so:

Foreign currency spot rate$_{t-1}$ = GBP/foreign currency at the end of period t
Foreign currency forward rate$_{t-1}$ = GBP/foreign currency forward rate at the end of period $t - 1$ for delivery at the end of period t

Most exchange rates are quoted foreign currency/GBP, so for currency surprise (expressed in this way) their reciprocals are used.

The denominator is the spot rate at the end of the prior period. While there is no fundamental necessity for this to be the case, there is a strong case that this is the best approach. This is because currency surprise has been created as a concept because it is an investible element in a portfolio. Investible means, as we have seen, also dis-investible. The mechanics of disinvesting in currency surprise for those investors with international assets requires currency hedging. It is computationally convenient if currency surprise and 'contribution from hedging' are exactly the same values, but with opposite signs. It also means that the 'contribution from hedging' can be combined with other asset returns within periods by addition. We have already discussed above the attraction of having currency hedging returns additive to unhedged returns of the underlying asset, and this requires the spot rate at the end of the prior period as the denominator. Hence it is adopted here for currency surprise.

---

[7] I first came across the expression coined by Grant W. Gardner in a 1994 Russell working paper. I immediately liked its descriptive power, so enthusiastically adopted it. Its extensive use in the AIMR paper cited below is largely as a result of my intervention.

[8] AIMR Benchmarks and Performance Attribution Subcommittee Report, John C. Stannard *et al.*, August 1998. This paper can be viewed on AIMR's website at www.aimr.com/standards/pps/benchmark.html., and is reproduced here as Appendix 3.

3.6.3   Why not spot returns?

Many investors measure their currency returns by reference to the movements in the spot exchange rates. If this is wrong, why is it wrong?

It is wrong because spot rates are 'uninvestible'. Let's take the example of a UK institutional investor buying $10m worth of US equities at the end of period 0. The values in Table 3.9 apply for the subsequent period (I ignore bid/offer spreads and commissions for simplicity).

Table 3.9   US equity returns for UK investor

End period	Equity value ($m)	Equity returns	Spot rate	Spot returns	Combined equity & spot returns
	(a)	$(b) = (a_t/a_{t-1}) - 1$	(c)	$(d) = (c_{t-1}/c_t) - 1$	$(e) = [(a_t/c_t)/(a_{t-1}/c_{t-1})] - 1$
0	10		1.5000		
1	10	0.00%	1.4000	7.14%	7.14%
2	11	10.00%	1.3000	7.69%	18.46%
3	10.5	−4.55%	1.3500	−3.70%	−8.08%
4	11.5	9.52%	1.4000	−3.57%	5.61%
5	11	−4.35%	1.4200	−1.41%	−5.70%
Cum.		**10.00%**		**5.63%**	**16.20%**

Note: The algebra for column (c) is inverted because the exchange rate is expressed as dollar/sterling, i.e. the price of sterling in dollar terms. In this context we need to calculate the price of the dollar in sterling terms, i.e. use the reciprocal.

It is very common for returns to be presented to investors in this way, and it is tempting for investors to argue, faced with this information, that their being exposed to the US dollar, which was strong over this period, yielded 5.63% cumulatively over the period, and therefore was profitable. But it is only possible to say whether an investment or exposure is profitable or not by reference to the alternative – in this case eliminating all exposure to the US dollar. Exposure to the dollar can only be eliminated by selling US dollars forward, let us say at a one-period horizon.

We have to examine the forward rates applying at each period (Table 3.10) to assess the impact of eliminating exposure using forward contracts.

Table 3.10   Example spot & forward rates

End period	Spot rate	Forward rate
0	1.5000	1.4700
1	1.4000	1.3700
2	1.3000	1.2700
3	1.3500	1.3200
4	1.4000	1.3700
5	1.4200	1.3900

We can calculate the profit or loss, both in cash and as a percentage of the initial amount hedged, from settling the one-period forward currency contracts necessary to fully hedge the equity exposure. Table 3.11 illustrates this.

If we add the % profit and loss each period to the combined equity and spot (or unhedged) returns, we get the hedged returns as given in Table 3.12 (we can add the percentage returns

Table 3.11   Currency hedge profit & loss

End period	Equity value ($m)	Spot rate	Forward rate	Currency hedge profit/loss (£m)	Currency hedge profit/loss (%)
	(a)	(b)	(c)	$(d) = (a_{t-1}/c_{t-1}) - (a_{t-1}/b_t)$	$(e) = d/(a_{t-1}/b_{t-1})$
0	10	1.5000	1.4700		
1	10	1.4000	1.3700	−0.34	−5.10%
2	11	1.3000	1.2700	−0.39	−5.50%
3	10.5	1.3500	1.3200	0.51	6.07%
4	11.5	1.4000	1.3700	0.45	5.84%
5	11	1.4200	1.3900	0.30	3.60%
Cum.				**0.53**	**4.30%***

* See Section 3.6.4.

Table 3.12   Hedged return calculation

End period	Equity value ($m)	Spot rate	Equity value (£m)	Unhedged equity return (%)	Currency hedge profit/loss (%)	Hedged equity return (%)
0	10	1.5000	6.67			
1	10	1.4000	7.14	7.14%	−5.10%	2.04%
2	11	1.3000	8.46	18.46%	−5.50%	12.96%
3	10.5	1.3500	7.78	−8.08%	6.07%	−2.01%
4	11.5	1.4000	8.21	5.61%	5.84%	11.46%
5	11	1.4200	7.75	−5.70%	3.60%	−2.10%
Cum.				**16.20%**	**4.30%**	**23.24%**

each period because they occur contemporaneously, and have the same denominator). The cumulative 23.24% is the return we get from taking US equity exposure only, and no currency risk. This mechanism, using forward contracts to sell currency forward (or the equivalent), is the only way to eliminate currency risk.

This allows us to complete the circle. Currency surprise is the difference between the hedged equity return and the unhedged equity return, and will therefore in this case be the negative of the currency hedge profit and loss %. This gives us Table 3.13, with the equity and currency

Table 3.13   Correct attribution of equity & currency returns

End period	Unhedged equity return (%) (a)	Currency surprise (b)	Hedged equity return (%) (c) = a − b
0			
1	7.14%	5.10%	2.04%
2	18.46%	5.50%	12.96%
3	−8.08%	−6.07%	−2.01%
4	5.61%	−5.84%	11.46%
5	−5.70%	−3.60%	−2.10%
Cum.	**16.20%**	**−5.46%**	**23.24%**

components correctly divided into their investible parts. So we discover that, far from being a strong currency, which contributed to investment returns, the dollar has in fact been a weak currency, which has detracted from investment returns.

Box 3.8   Local currency returns

It is universal in the casual reporting of international equity market behaviour to use the currency of the target country. This is always implicit, rather than explicit, because equity markets are expressed in index numbers, not currency prices. So when a commentator says that the 'Nikkei is down 0.6% to 10 100', the value and percentage change is always expressed in yen. However, for a non-Japanese investor, yen returns are unattainable. The only returns that are obtainable are (a) yen returns converted to the home currency at spot rates or (b) yen returns hedged to the home currency by forward contracts.

This may appear to be a little academic in the short run, but it is not academic at all in the long run. Under alternative (a), we are looking at a combination of currency spot exchange rate movements and equity returns. Under alternative (b), we are looking at only equity returns, with the effect of exchange rates eliminated.

If a US investor was to report the performance of the Nikkei for 20 years (say Dec 1981–Dec 2001), the index has gone from 7681.8 to 10 542.62, a rise of 37.2% or 3.2% p.a. But if a US investor had invested in the Nikkei in Dec 1981, and hedged the currency exposure to eliminate any effect of the yen spot rate, then the rise would have been 140.7% or 9.2% p.a. This is a very significant difference, and illustrates the importance of avoiding local-currency-denominated equity market analysis over anything but the shortest term.

This means that the realisable performance of any index is different depending on the base currency from which one views it. The 20-year Nikkei numbers shown above can be recalculated for a UK investor, and the effect is even more marked. A rise of 37.2% in local currency converts to a rise of 236.5% when expressed in sterling (and excluding exchange rate movements). This would mean the Nikkei, which stood at 7681.8 in Dec 1981 would be 25 852.3 for a sterling investor rather than the 10 542.6 that is reported in yen. The following graph illustrates this:

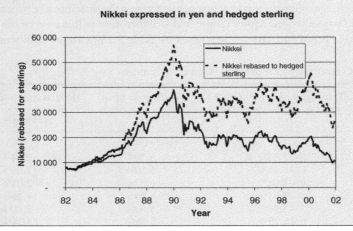

Nikkei expressed in yen and hedged sterling

Why is this methodology so compelling? Because an investor can only measure return series against alternative return series that are available. Since the alternative to investing in currencies (strictly speaking *currency exposure*) is *not* investing in currencies, the currency return series measured must be one that can be eliminated.

The importance of this methodology cannot be underestimated, nor the very substantial impact of interest rate differentials on long-term currency trends. Many investors have a distorted view of a particular currency's 'strength' or 'weakness' because they only look at the headline rate – the spot rate. Box 3.8 graphically illustrates the point.

3.6.4   Geometric linking and 'adding across'

All the cumulative figures are derived by geometrically linking the period returns. The reader will note that while period returns can be accurately 'added across' (since the percentages have the same base), multi-period returns appear not to be. This needs some analysis and explanation.

The way in which period returns can be cumulated, and how they can then be 'added across', depends crucially on the underlying nature of the combinations. There are three main types of 'asset combination types', and therefore three different ways of combining returns. Let us suppose we are talking about two return series; for simplicity, returns (a) and (b) in Table 3.13.

3.6.4.1   Assets in a portfolio

If a portfolio consists of two assets, (a) and (b), then their returns are combined by adding the underlying values, and then recalculating the returns from the combined values. In this example (Table 3.14), the assets are equally weighted at the beginning of the cumulating period, i.e. period 0.

Now if we just look at the three return series (Table 3.15), we can see that the period-by-period portfolio returns are 'arithmetically averaged across' as well as combined geometrically down. This is intuitively straightforward, and certainly convenient when dealing with returns at various levels in the portfolio.

Table 3.14   Returns in a two-asset portfolio

End period	Asset A $(a) = (c_t/c_{t-1}) - 1$	Asset B $(b) = (d_t/d_{t-1}) - 1$	Asset value A (c)	Asset value B (d)	Portfolio value $(e) = c + d$	Portfolio return (%) $(f) = (e_t/e_{t-1}) - 1$
0			50.00	50.00	100.00	
1	7.14%	5.10%	53.57	52.55	106.12	6.12%
2	18.46%	5.50%	63.46	55.44	118.90	12.04%
3	−8.08%	−6.07%	58.33	52.08	110.41	−7.14%
4	5.61%	−5.84%	61.61	49.04	110.64	0.21%
5	−5.70%	−3.60%	58.10	47.27	105.37	−4.77%
Cum.	**16.20%**	**−5.46%**				**5.37%**

Table 3.15 'Adding across' a two-asset portfolio

End period	Return asset A (%) (a)	Return asset B (%) (b)	Portfolio return (%) (c)	Weighted average (d) = weighted a + weighted b
0				
1	7.14%	5.10%	6.12%	6.12%
2	18.46%	5.50%	12.04%	12.04%
3	−8.08%	−6.07%	−7.14%	−7.14%
4	5.61%	−5.84%	0.21%	0.21%
5	−5.70%	−3.60%	−4.77%	−4.77%
Cum.	**16.20%**	**−5.46%**	**5.37%**	**5.37%**

3.6.4.2 International assets and the spot rate

The position gets more complicated when the two return series being evaluated are the local currency asset value and the spot rate. If we go back to Table 3.9, (reproduced as Table 3.16), we see not only that column (e) is the percentage change in the sterling value of the assets, but also that it can be calculated by geometrically linking (not arithmetically averaging) across the table the two returns, e.g. for period 2, 10% and 7.69% are combined as follows: $18.46\% = [(1 + 0.1) \times (1 + 0.769)] - 1$.

Table 3.16 Combining equity & spot currency returns

End period	Equity value ($m) (a)	Equity returns (b) = $(a_t/a_{t-1}) - 1$	Spot rate (c)	Spot returns (d) = $(c_{t-1}/c_t) - 1$	Combined equity & spot returns (e) = $[(a_t/c_t)/(a_{t-1}/c_{t-1})] - 1$
0	10		1.5000		
1	10	0.00%	1.4000	7.14%	7.14%
2	11	10.00%	1.3000	7.69%	18.46%
3	10.5	−4.55%	1.3500	−3.70%	−8.08%
4	11.5	9.52%	1.4000	−3.57%	5.61%
5	11	−4.35%	1.4200	−1.41%	−5.70%
Cum.		**10.00%**		**5.63%**	**16.20%**

The spot rate and the local currency are virtually the only variables in investment management that are combined in this way. This is because of the nature of these return series and their valuation – currency has a 'multiplicative' relationship with underlying investments, not additive. The cumulative returns are also geometrically linked both across and down, so the spot rate, despite being uninvestible, has a fully multiplicative relationship with the underlying international investment.

3.6.4.3 Assets and overlay/hedging

This tidy state of affairs is now to be contrasted with the maths associated with overlay (or hedging – in this context it is the same) (and also with attribution analysis).

Currency overlay is not multiplicative at the single period level – it is (as indicated by the maths of the hedged return above) additive. However, currency overlay is not an asset. You cannot put £100 into 'currency overlay' and receive returns each period which will compound up. Currency overlay is a source of a variable return which does not have a capital allocation. *This means that currency overlay/currency hedging returns cannot be geometrically linked alone.*

Geometric linking is the universal linking method for period-by-period returns, but it assumes that the full value of the asset at any period-end is available for reinvestment at the next period-start (which is simultaneous). Linking assumes that there is a 'carrier' investment with some starting value which can be increased or reduced by the amount of each period return. There is no such automatic 'carrier' investment in currency overlay or hedging. However, there are carrier investments which are commonly associated with overlay – in particular, and rather obviously, international assets. Once we have a 'carrier' asset, then we can geometrically link.

Let's take an example from the data above. Table 3.17 is a 'cut down' version of Table 3.12, which has the relevant information. The question that we would like to answer is: what is the contribution from currency hedging over time? There are at least three answers to this – none of which is indisputably right, and one of which is wrong. Let's start with the wrong one.

Table 3.17 Hedged equity return calculation

End period	Equity value (£m)	Unhedged equity return (%)	Currency hedge profit/loss (%)	Hedged equity return (%)
0	6.67			
1	7.14	7.14%	−5.10%	2.04%
2	8.46	18.46%	−5.50%	12.96%
3	7.78	−8.08%	6.07%	−2.01%
4	8.21	5.61%	5.84%	11.46%
5	7.75	−5.70%	3.60%	−2.10%
Cum.		**16.20%**	*4.30%*	**23.24%**

Geometric linking: The value reported (in italics) in the cumulative row under the 'currency hedge profit/loss' – *4.30%* – is the geometrically linked value of the period hedge return above. I have already described above that this is an incorrect way to calculate it, but I have not yet spelt out in full the problem.

At the end of period 1, the return from currency hedging is −5.10%. What does this mean? It means that in this context (1-month contracts), there is a cash outflow of 5.10% of the end-period value of the unhedged international asset – which is £6.67m. So 5.10% means an outflow of −5.10% × £6.67m = −£0.34m. But the key here is that −£0.34m is 5.10% of the *unhedged asset value*, not of 'itself' a period earlier. What would it mean, therefore, to say that the cumulative loss after two periods was $\{(1 - 0.0510) \times (1 - 0.0550)\} - 1 = -10.32\%$? It would imply that the principal had shrunk in the first period by 5.10%, and that therefore the impact of the second loss would be reduced. This will not be true, since the 5.50% loss is a percentage of the end-period 1 *unhedged asset value*, which has gone up by 7.14%. It may be that the cash outflow from hedging at the end of period 1 was funded by a sale of international equities (although in practice this is unlikely), but even if this was the case this would be accounted for in a performance measurement sense by the withdrawal of £0.34m from the amount invested in equities. No percentage returns would change. The nature of the calculation of currency hedging returns therefore rules out the geometric linking of stand-alone hedging.

Interestingly, if the relative weight of country equities in an international portfolio is determined by the market-cap, this is universally measured by the *unhedged* market-cap. This means that even if the rise in a country's relative weight is due to currency movements, this country will nevertheless keep that higher weight in the index, and therefore a fund would not rebalance the portfolio by selling that country's equity alone to fund the hedging loss.

Subtraction: A much more defensible way to report on the effect of hedging would be to subtract the cumulative (geometrically linked) return of the hedged equities from the unhedged equities. This gives the cumulative return of the hedging as $23.24\% - 16.20\% = 7.04\%$. This is a materially different figure from 4.30%, and more accurately reflects the way currency hedging has affected the return of the underlying securities. However, this value is also materially affected by the return behaviour of the underlying securities – meaning that the overlay manager is in part dependent on the performance of the hedging he controls on underlying returns that are entirely outside his control. For example, if the underlying security had exhibited zero returns over the period in question, the returns from hedging would have been 5.92% rather than 7.04%. There are no particular rules that govern this relationship – it depends on the detailed period-by-period returns to determine the 'interference' effects. On balance, however, subtraction is a mathematically and intuitively appealing approach, and is to be recommended. The one word of caution is that the subtraction approach does require an underlying carrier, and that the choice of carrier will influence the currency hedging returns.

Arithmetic: One final alternative is available. This is to arithmetically average returns, and then annualise using conventional geometric annualisation techniques. In this case we want the cumulative 5-period return, so let us suppose that the returns in Table 3.17 are monthly, then the cumulative return from hedging would be the arithmetic average of the monthly returns -0.98%, grossed up to 5 months by $[(1 + 0.0098)\char`\^5] - 1 = 5.00\%$. Normally, longer series would be annualised (i.e. raised to the power 12).

This is a fudge, but one with less stark faults than geometric linking. The fudge is that annualising using powers is, in effect, geometric linking, which we saw earlier was flawed. However, the practical effects of the flaw are minimised by arithmetic averaging, because by this method, the series is assumed to have constant return, which will avoid the large second-order-generated errors of highly volatile return series.

4
Foreign Exchange Market – History and Structure

4.1 BRIEF HISTORY OF THE FOREIGN EXCHANGE MARKET AND HOW INSTRUMENTS DEVELOPED

4.1.1 Bretton Woods

In the reconstruction that followed the Second World War, the Bretton Woods Agreement became for nearly 30 years the guiding principle for the management of exchange rates and intergovernmental financing. Bretton Woods was concluded in the belief that national governments were (or should be) overwhelmingly dominant in the conduct of national and international financial markets. It was also concluded in the belief that financial markets alone were not capable of lubricating the wheels of international trade and clearing the markets for currencies. This interventionist thinking found its source in the severe failure to clear of markets (particularly the labour market) in the 1930s, and developed to maturity with the seeming success of allied (particularly British) interventionist policies in the Second World War.

4.1.2 Central banks as buffer

In July 1944, despite the still raging war, an intergovernmental conference of 43 (allied) countries met in a small town in New Hampshire, US – Bretton Woods. Their agenda was to establish international arrangements to prevent the competitive devaluations, trade wars and protectionism of the 1930s. The feeling amongst the participants was that the economic conditions of the 1930s had bred fascism, and therefore ultimately war. The agreement that came out of Bretton Woods laid the foundations for two new institutions – the International Bank for Reconstruction and Development (IBRD), otherwise known as the World Bank, and the International Monetary Fund (IMF). The World Bank's brief was to provide long-term official loans to facilitate economic development, mainly in the less developed economies, the IMF's brief was to operate a system of controlled exchange rates and internationally co-ordinated monetary policies.

One of the guiding principles of the IMF was the implicit acceptance that national governments had responsibility for balancing external supply and demand of their domestic currency without exchange rates providing an automatic stabiliser. In short, making up any current account shortfall from reserves or mopping up any current account surplus by foreign currency purchases. In the world of the 1950s and 1960s, a world of credit controls, exchange controls and little private cross-border capital flows, this system worked tolerably well. Central banks did not generally have to bow to market pressures, and governments could conduct domestic monetary policy with virtually no external interference or linkage. There was broad exchange rate stability, punctuated by occasional realignments when persistent exchange deficits depleted reserves too far. There was very little international liquidity outside the central banks, so that relatively modest foreign currency reserves were adequate to iron out most supply and demand fluctuations.

4.1.3 Ad hoc foreign exchange market development

Most OECD countries emerged from the Second World War with stringent exchange controls, and these largely remained in place until well after the breakdown of fixed exchange rates in 1972/3. As a direct result of exchange controls, currency exchange arrangements were ossified in the structures dictated by central banks. Customers, usually commercial companies or individuals, were forced to buy and sell their foreign currency through retail banks, who effectively had a monopoly. For many years, the business of foreign exchange was seen as an (expensive) irritant by customers, and as a sleepy but lucrative backwater by the retail banks. In the fixed exchange rate environment of 1945–71, it was largely an administrative not a market activity.

Box 4.1   Capital flows

'Capital flows' are often cited as a relevant factor in the determination of exchange rates and exchange rate movements. But what are they? The expression is a loose one, and is used by observers of the currency market to describe or explain the movements of funds across the exchanges. Generally speaking, they have different meanings at different horizons. Let us take these in order.

Short-term: A market commentator, usually speaking from a bank market-maker's perspective, will talk about 'strong flows' in a particular direction – say to sell euros/buy dollars. What this generally means it that the bank's customers have been executing deals this way round in a trading day, and the bank has had to go to the interbank market to find buyers of euros. This is sometimes associated with a falling euro price ('it was all one way'), and so, in the desire to *ex post* rationalise market movements, the 'capital flows' out of the euro are described as having caused the price fall. Alternatively, it can be associated with stable or rising euro prices – in which case it is described as 'strong two-way volume'. In reality, of course, there will have been no net capital movements; every sell order of the euro being matched with a countervailing buy order. The perception of capital flows, therefore, is one of sectional interests and not about the whole market.

Long-term: Although all unrationed markets clear with equal volumes of buyers and sellers, it is still possible to categorise types of economic agents into homogeneous units (or at least sufficiently homogeneous to be useful). So, for example, the Japanese public and private sectors have a seemingly inexhaustible appetite for US paper assets – particularly US Treasury securities. This 'capital flow' has been extremely important in the evolution not only of the yen/dollar exchange rate, but also of all the related exchange rates (i.e. anything with a yen or dollar in it). Understanding the behaviour of this group (or maybe two groups – public and private) may provide valuable insights into the future behaviour of the exchange rate. This type of thinking is very widespread in the foreign exchange markets – and much research goes into analysing and understanding capital flows.

4.1.3.1 The 'Euro-market'

This settled state of affairs began to change in the late 1960s, and was given a massive spur at the beginning of the 1970s with successive oil price rises which created for the first time very large international liquidity. This sudden appearance of 'hot' money started the development of the huge, liquid and unregulated foreign exchange markets that we see today. For the first time large unofficial currency balances were held abroad. 'Unofficial balances' were the proceeds of oil sales to the west by OPEC countries, and these were not controlled by central banks, but by commercial and quasi-state entities with commercial aims. The balances were in the major OECD currencies (mainly dollars), and the scale of the net transfer of wealth to the OPEC countries was such that these balances were recycled back into the OECD economies. The balances were held in bank accounts (not even in securities) in offshore accounts (offshore to both the OPEC owners and the issuers of the currency), and these balances were free to move across the exchanges unfettered by domestic exchange controls. This heralded the growth (mainly in London) of what has rather euphemistically been called the 'Euro-market',[1] but which in reality was a black market. An abiding characteristic of 'black' or 'unofficial' markets, however, is that they clear at prices that express the genuine balance of desires to buy and sell the currency or commodity in question.

4.1.4 Free markets dominate

The scale of the new trading in the 1970s was sufficiently large that central banks no longer had the whip-hand. The visible effect of this was the (rather disorderly) collapse of the Bretton Woods fixed exchange rate agreement in 1972/3. Historical exchange rate series at this point changed from being straight horizontal lines with the odd discontinuity up or down, to the wobbly lines that look like the FX prices of today. The collapse also heralded the final demise of any practical link between the monetary system and gold, although formal arrangements lingered on, and are still highly visible 30 years later in the very large (but completely pointless) official reserves of gold held by the major central banks.[2]

What in practice happened was that offshore (i.e. Euro) trading of pairs of non-domestic currencies became the price-setting mechanism, and domestic spot exchange rates had to follow suit. If they did not, qualified economic agents like domestic banks who bridged the domestic/Euro divide could otherwise exploit the arbitrage. A few tightly controlled anomalies remained [like the sterling/dollar pool for external capital flows (abolished in 1979)], but generally the free markets dominated.

The subsequent 30 years have seen the explosive growth of the FX market, and the domination of this global free market model in the price-setting mechanism. One by one country-specific protections have been dismantled, and most developed countries now have an exchange rate that is widely traded without restriction in this market. The US and EU economies have gone the farthest in embracing the global FX market, the Far East economies the least far. There remain pockets of resistance to this model, and at the most extreme (say in mainland China or Malaysia[3]), the local currency is effectively shut out of the global market by tight domestic legal restrictions on permitted trading. See Section 4.4.1.

---

[1] The use of the word 'Euro' in this context is unrelated to the new euro currency. It was coined initially by American bankers in the 1960s who realised that trading US dollar-denominated securities and foreign exchange in London circumvented the regulatory and tax hurdles erected at that time by the US government.

[2] For those interested in the role of gold in central bank intervention, see Record, N. P., *Central bank intervention: a new approach*, Centre for the Study of Financial Innovation, London, Working Paper Series, November 1996.

[3] Malaysia is an interesting case because prior to September 1998 the ringgit was a widely traded and largely uncontrolled currency. Exchange controls were reimposed as a political and economic response to 'speculation' in the ringgit depressing its value. The implications of exchange controls on an economy are far-reaching, and beyond the scope of this book.

Box 4.2   Currency unions

Currency unions are the adoption of one currency by more than one sovereign country. They have a long and somewhat chequered history, the most successful being unions between countries at least one of which was not fully sovereign. In the last 200 years – a period sufficiently recent to have some meaningful parallels with the current unions – there have been several currency unions, all of which have failed.

The Latin Union of 1865 was an attempt by France to create a common currency in the 'Latin' trade area (France, Italy, Switzerland, Belgium, Greece). It faded after the First World War, and was formally abandoned in 1927. Sweden, Denmark and Norway formed a similar union in 1870, and this also failed after the First World War. The US, with its strong federal bias, did not establish a federal currency until 1863, in the middle of the Civil War, when there was arguably not a single state. The dollar has endured – a reflection perhaps of the overarching power of the federal government over individual states of the US.

A feature of all these unions, however, is that they came at a time when the gold standard held sway. The gold standard, in a way a global Exchange Rate Mechanism, was the mechanism by which governments guaranteed the convertibility of their paper currency (i.e. bank promises) into an incorruptible and absolute commodity – gold. The gold standard had one fundamental feature which rendered it unsuitable for the currency platform after the first half of the twentieth century – it was inflexible. It did not allow individual countries suffering different economic conditions from their economic partners to alter domestic monetary conditions or devalue or revalue their currencies. See also Section 4.1.5.

4.1.5   The euro

Until the end of 1998, most EU member states tied their currencies more or less loosely together in the ERM (Exchange Rate Mechanism), an exchange rate system that had been in force in one form or another for over 20 years. The ERM was an anomaly in the general development of the FX market because it clearly represented a throwback, in concept if not in execution, to the old controlled-rate parities in Bretton Woods. It had suffered badly from successful market pressure for realignments; twice in serious attacks, 1992 and 1993, and on several lesser occasions (mainly involving the French franc/Deutschmark parity) in the 1980s and 1990s.

The ERM was replaced in January 1999 by the euro, a new currency which replaced 11 currencies[4] in the EU in an unprecedented experiment in monetary union. Whatever the merits or otherwise of such a major and untested step in monetary arrangements between states, the effect on the FX markets was to eliminate the last vestiges of the Bretton Woods legacy, and to create a new, fully liquid and uncontrolled free market in a large new currency. By the time of writing (2002), the euro has emerged as the uncontested 'second' currency behind the US dollar, and despite some 'unexpected' and persistent weakness in the four years since it was created, the introduction of the euro into the wholesale markets has been a technical success.

---

[4] Now 12 – Greece joined in January 2001.

4.1.6 Instruments

The dominant role of the banking sector in the development of the foreign exchange market has to a large extent determined the development of the instruments available. As we have seen above, the key instruments in the currency markets are spot and forward contracts; bilateral instruments which are designed to facilitate the management of cross-border transfers of cash. These instruments remain the backbone of the currency market, despite the fact that the majority of the users of the forward foreign exchange market are using these instruments to hedge currency exposure, not to plan ahead the exchange rates at which they are actually going to exchange cash.

New types of instruments have only been introduced in the past 15 years. Currency futures are the largest volume of these new instruments – and the design of currency futures is explicitly to hedge currency risk, not to facilitate its transfer. Currency futures, as we have seen, are dependent on the massive volume and liquidity of the interbank market for their pricing, and while nominally outside the control of the banking sector, have nevertheless been annexed to a significant extent by the futures broking arm of major banks.

The other significant new instruments are currency options. These are more a class than a single instrument, since the nature of the instrument allows almost infinite diversity. They are heavily promoted by banks, particularly in their less plain vanilla forms, as they represent an opportunity for more opaque pricing, and therefore more profit potential, than the 'commoditised' spot and forward markets.

4.2   BASIC STRUCTURE

The foreign exchange (FX) market is by far the largest market in the world, with unparalleled liquidity and natural two-way trading. Information flows almost instantaneously through the market, and there are no insider trading laws and no common taxation regime to distort market-clearing prices. There is no brokerage commission on wholesale trading, and the only form of payment to banks for market-making is the difference between their quoted buying and selling prices – so-called 'bid/offer' spreads. The number of participants in the market is huge – measured in hundreds of millions if direct and indirect players are included. All the ingredients, one would imagine, for an efficient[5] market if ever there was one. Figure 4.1 illustrates the core structure.

The diagram has been pared down to avoid confusion – in practice FX customers are highly varied, and very numerous. They will typically have dealing arrangements with a number of banks. The banks shown in this diagram are market-making banks – this is explained in detail below – and they communicate with each other to 'clear' the balance of positions they cannot eliminate through customer orders through the interbank network.

Although the network is shown as a concrete entity, in reality the network is a series of bilateral relationships between the market-making banks – their communication is generally by screen-price and telephone. The CLS Bank (see Box 4.5) is not included in this diagram (and would not be even when it is up and running), because it has no role in the price-setting and position-clearing process.

---

[5] *Efficient* in the academic sense of the word. This is to be distinguished from execution efficiency, in which the currency market is the unchallenged world leader. Efficiency is discussed at length in Chapter 9.

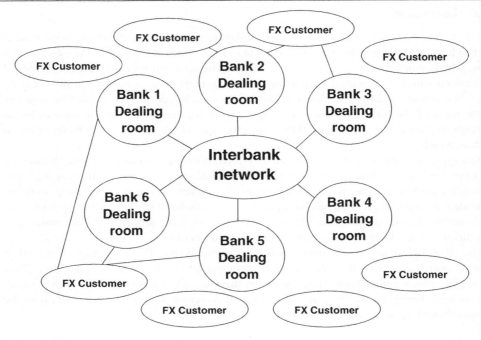

Figure 4.1 FX market structure

4.2.1 Market size

Because the market is informal, with no central clearing or exchange, market-wide data has been in short supply. However, in March 1986 four major foreign exchange centres were surveyed for the first time by their central banks under the auspices of the BIS[6] in an effort to redress this balance. It was decided to establish a regular triennial survey, and the number of foreign exchange centres surveyed has grown dramatically. In April 1989, 21 countries were surveyed; in the latest BIS Survey preliminary results, published in 2002 but referring to April 2001, 48 countries were surveyed. In summary, the volume of FX dealing in April 2001 was $1.2 trillion *per day*.

The first thing to remark about this number is how high the transaction volume is. Contrast daily London Stock Exchange (*c*. $10bn) or NYSE (*c*. $50bn) figures to see how high. The second thing to note is that although the survey compilers have tried to eliminate straight double counting (i.e. buyer and seller both reporting the same transaction), the nature of the foreign exchange market means that customer orders 'echo' through the interbank system to find a counterparty customer. The survey reports that non-financial customer deals account for only 13% of the total turnover, with financial sector customers another 28%. We will return to this point later.

While the BIS survey tells us much about the size of the market and the nature of the transactions, it tells us nothing of the motivation and goals of the participants.

---

[6] The Bank for International Settlements in Basle.

Box 4.3   Netting

'Netting' is a process established between counterparties in the FX market to reduce the risk from FX deals. There are commonly two types of netting: settlement netting and forward contract netting.

Settlement netting
In active foreign exchange dealing organisations, there may be multiple deals with given counterparties that mature on the same day. For example, Bank A may have many out-standing deals to sell dollars (versus a number of currencies) with Counterparty B, and which require the delivery in total of, say, $100m. However, they may also have several outstanding deals with Counterparty B to buy dollars which imply the receipt, in total, of $200m. Under netting arrangements, these two payments will not be made: instead one payment of $100m from Counterparty B to Bank A will be made. The same calculation is made for all currencies, with net payments only being exchanged. This netting is bilateral – multilateral netting is now the province of the CLS Bank (see Box 4.5).

Forward contract netting
Many of the maturing obligations of Bank A and Counterparty B on the day in question above would have been the result of forward deals conducted many months earlier. Some of these forward deals may have the same currency pairs, and the same amount of one currency, but one purchase and one sale. This is typically described as one deal followed by a 'reversing' deal. In contract netting, the gross exposure of either party to deliver currencies to one another is eliminated, and replaced by one contract for the payment of the difference account (i.e. profit and loss). This is also called 'netting by novation', implying that the obligation to only deliver the difference is 'new' (novation), and not simply the two old deals put together.

The risk that netting is designed to eliminate is theoretical rather than practical – the possibility that a receiver of an insolvent counterparty 'cherry picks' the contracts that are favourable to the receiver, and reneges on the unfavourable.

4.2.2   Banks – the market-makers

At the market's core are the banking sector's foreign exchange dealing rooms. Their key role is to make prices. For this service, the sector is paid, and the payment comes in the form of spreads: quoting a lower price for buying than selling. This is the only source of FX earnings for the bank; as mentioned above, there are no commissions in the wholesale FX market. While it is true that an individual bank may not make money on a single customer transaction, the banking system, taking the generality of deals, will.

4.2.3   Customers

Customers are, by the conventional definition of foreign exchange dealing rooms, those counterparties who are not expected to make prices, only take them. In layman's terms, customers

Box 4.4   Market-makers

The currency market is not based in one geographical location or in any legal entity. It is composed of a network of market-making banks linked to customers via both the telephone direct, and also via a range of intermediaries. A common price is established and maintained by means of continuous price-screen information. This global network deals only in the main traded currencies (see Box 5.7); smaller and controlled currencies fall outside this market.

The primary market-makers in the currency market are the 'money centre' banks which form the core of the global foreign exchange network. They are market-makers in the sense that they deploy risk capital to allow them to run unmatched currency positions within the working day. With this ability, they make 'two-way' prices, that is transparent pricing at which they will either buy (lower price) or sell (higher price) a currency. These are called bid/offer spreads (see Box 3.3).

Unlike market-makers in many other markets, banks do not have to hold an 'inventory' of currency, or 'borrow' it from existing holders at premium rates. The depth and liquidity of the cash markets and their associated derivatives (forward currency market) mean that the mechanics of market-making are symmetrical whether long or short.

Market-makers in currency need two-way volume to make consistent profits. Since currencies are zero-sum instruments in the hands of the private sector, there is no net return to expertise for the market-making other than bid/offer spreads. Competition between the main global money centre banks has forced bid/offer spreads to be the lowest in any market.

Within the market-maker banks, specific individuals are assigned to 'run the book' in specific currency pairs. While there is an extensive folklore in the scalp-hunting exploits of these individuals ('I knew he was coming, so I tipped it a bit left, and when he took the bait I stuffed him with half a bar I bought 20 points cheaper' – a 'bar' being market slang for a billion), the evidence is that the consistently profitable market-makers are those with the best distribution (branch networks, wholesale customers, captive customers like investment custody), and that market-making itself is a clearing function which could (and probably will) be automated.

ring bank dealers and ask them to do a deal, not the other way round. Customers are in practice a very varied collection of organisations. They include: financial institutions like (smaller) banks and insurance companies; the other divisions of the bank market-makers themselves (i.e. retail banking, credit cards, investment banking, FX option writers); active investment trading houses like hedge funds and proprietary traders; industrial and commercial companies (ICCs); oil and commodity dealers and merchants; central banks; and investment managers and currency overlay managers acting for their (mainly) pension fund clients. The reader can probably think of more categories not explicitly identified here.

'Trade', as generally understood by the man in the street, is only conducted by two of these counterparty sectors (ICCs and oil and commodity merchants). And the total amount of 'trade' conducted per year (i.e. world imports and exports) could be accommodated in four or five days of foreign exchange trading annually. The remaining sectors are more or less trading on capital account, and their motives range from outright defensiveness (a pension fund hedging 100% of a foreign bond purchase) to outright speculation (a hedge fund taking a forward short position in a currency seen as vulnerable).

The next section analyses customer behaviour in some detail. In summary, a very large proportion of the players in the FX market are not profit-seeking and/or not price-sensitive.

Box 4.5   CLS Bank

The CLS Bank began operation in 2002, after many years in gestation. The idea behind it is to reduce the foreign exchange market's exposure to daylight settlement risk. In a nutshell, all currency transactions, which are bilateral and privately arranged, require the simultaneous transmission of money by both parties to the other. Because both cannot wait until the other has paid (because then no money would ever flow!), payments are made with no security that the counterbalancing receipt will arrive on time, or at all. This puts each party at risk of the potential default by the other. It is called 'daylight' risk, because the amount at risk is the amount paid out during a working day which is not yet settled with a payment in during that day.

CLS Bank is a co-operative bank set up by the banking industry to centralise the settlement process. In a nutshell, individual CLS settlement members (large commercial/FX banks who are also shareholders) will pool all their commitments to pay other CLS settlement members. These funds will be paid to CLS, who will release them on receipt of the funds of all the other settlement members. This is known as a Payment-versus-Payment (PVP) system, and the whole CLS 'system' is a Continuous Linked Settlement (CLS) system.

The system works by linking the real-time gross payments systems of the seven central banks of the currencies to which this system initially applies (US, ECB, UK, Japan, Switzerland, Australia and Canada). It operates on a daily cycle, with a 5-hour common window for settlement, 7am to noon Central European Time. During this period CLS gathers funds from its settlement members (via the central banks), and then subject to receipt of funds, pays out funds to settlement members. All settlement members maintain sufficient liquidity at CLS to cover failed trades and other contingencies. However, the volume of gross settlements that are made via CLS will be 80–90% smaller than the equivalent settlements made in the conventional bilateral settlements procedures.

This opens up the opportunity for a small group of players with the necessary characteristics to exploit the constraints of the majority for gain.

Since the only medium through which this can happen is the FX price through time, we will try to discover whether the structural characteristics of the FX market indeed feed through to 'inefficient' price behaviour.

4.2.4   Clearing mechanism

In contrast to 'customer' behaviour, which is enormously varied, unpredictable and highly disaggregated, foreign exchange dealer behaviour – the remaining 59%[7] of turnover – mostly represents the 'clearing' of deals through the FX market. Let's give an example. A customer rings a bank and buys $10m vs. yen forward for six months, a typical wholesale customer deal. To avoid running overnight risk, which is risky and regulatorily expensive, the bank will need to unwind its short dollar/long yen position before the end of the day, if possible at a profit. The

---

[7] 59% is the residual from the 13% + 28% of customer deals in the BIS Survey above.

methods by which it does this are two-fold – it can either hope that a customer or customers will ring and ask to buy yen/sell dollars on their quoted prices, or it can go to other banks asking for prices to sell yen/buy dollars. In a multi-dealer system, the likelihood of the right customer coming to that specific bank at the right time by chance is slim – but in the countless thousands (probably millions) of wholesale deals done each day, there will be customers around the world taking the positions that our bank desires to square its book. The 59% of interbank deals therefore represent the 'clearing system' for exposure to 'find' another customer.

4.2.5   Turnover excluding 'clearing'

If there were only one global bank (but still the same number of customer deals) there would be no clearing, since it would be done by the global bank's internal system. Reported foreign exchange volume would therefore fall by over half, although in reality nothing would have changed. Interbank dealing does not 'make' or 'lose' money. For the banking sector as a whole, it is, by definition, a non-profit activity. Conducting foreign deals in a closed loop cannot generate net income inside the loop. Therefore customer deals (41% of turnover, or $485bn per day[8]) pay all the costs of the market.

4.3   CUSTOMER TYPES

In this section I look at the customer participants in the foreign exchange market, their behaviour, and the constraints under which they operate. In attempting to describe the behaviour of hundreds of thousands of different entities (taking all participating organisations together), or hundreds of millions of individuals (taking individual decision-making into account), I am inevitably forced to make broad generalisations which may not in every case be defensible. The reader will have to forgive me for this.

4.3.1   Industrial and commercial companies (ICCs)

4.3.1.1   Profit-seeking

There are a number of types of market behaviour subsumed within this category. Most obvious is the treasury department given leeway to take positions in forward currency contracts, derivatives, capital instruments or cash. These decisions could be model-driven (technical, fundamental, option replication, hybrid); they could be the result of a 'currency committee' deciding to extend or reduce coverage of key variables (import/export exposure); they could be a capital event (bond issue, swap, foreign asset purchase) which is explicitly or implicitly chosen to be hedged, partially hedged or unhedged; or they could be the discretionary undertaking of financial contracts or derivatives[9] which open, close or modify currency exposure.

This is a very large category of decision-making processes, but they are all characterised by a lack of systematic nature, by fundamentally differing perspectives (importer/exporter, dollar-based/euro-based/yen-based/sterling-based), and almost universally by a lack of clear benchmark against which to measure success. They are also carried out by employees of ICCs

---

[8] See BIS Press Release, 9 October 2001, Table 2.

[9] Some of these can be surprising. Some years ago I was an expert witness in a case of 'mis-selling' of an unusual derivative to a European food processor. The client thought that it was a $50m deposit contract. In fact, the contract was the sale by the client of a currency option with a principal value of more than $1.6bn. The loss in dispute was over $100m.

with no general access to close or inside information on the FX market, and with less analytical resources than professionals in financial organisations.

4.3.1.2   Non-profit-seeking

In contrast to the above behaviour, which is profit-seeking, much of the day-to-day transactions of ICCs are simply automatic responses to contracts, deliveries, invoices or other underlying business events. A typical example of this category is where (say) an importer takes delivery of some goods from a foreign supplier, and is presented with an invoice for payment of a foreign currency amount due on a particular day. Just prior to the payment date, the importer rings his bank, and undertakes a spot FX deal to buy the required amount of foreign currency. The importer is almost completely impervious to movements in the spot rate or the rate achieved; he has to do the deal, so he does.

The behaviour can apply to forward rates just as much as to spot rates. On placing a firm, fixed price order for (say) a consignment of oil, the customer may execute a forward contract to 'lock' in the cost in his home currency. The customer will have no leeway over whether or not to execute the deal, it will be done if the overall package of the foreign currency and the spot rate at the time is acceptable.

4.3.2   Oil and commodity dealers and merchants

This sector is very active in the FX market because of the nature of their business. Even quite modest merchants can conduct very large and frequent FX deals, as each supplier and customer contract is risk-matched in every aspect. The vast bulk of this volume is not profit-seeking; the answer from a merchant as to why he bought $100m for sterling this morning will almost always be 'because I was simultaneously selling a crude contract to a UK customer priced in sterling and covering it on the Rotterdam market', or similar. It will not be because he thinks the dollar will on balance go up.

There will be smaller net amounts of profit-seeking behaviour, say from the well capitalised merchants, and this can be categorised in exactly the same way as the equivalent behaviour from the ICC sector.

4.3.3   Financial institutions (banks and insurance companies)

These two entities are rather different: banks will usually be acting as intermediaries for an underlying customer order or request, and in effect are part of the clearing network. They will earn a fee by charging their customers a wider bid/offer spread than they are charged by the FX market. They are put in the 'customer' rather than the 'market-maker' category because generally they take the prices that are given to them by the FX market, and pass them on to their customers without taking price risk on their own account. To the extent that they make fixed prices to their customers prior to covering their risk, they slide over into the market-maker category.

Insurance companies are very different. On the one hand, non-life insurance companies have a plethora of cross-border transactions arising from premium, underwriting and claim payments. In this they will behave like ICCs. On the other hand, life companies are pools of capital, and will generally behave in a similar way to investment managers (see below), subject to the following exceptions.

Many insurance companies have fixed liabilities (say annuities), and little room for manoeuvre in their asset allocation, which will be largely domestic fixed income. The pool of unitised or 'with profit' (UK only) assets which tend to attract an equity allocation also tend to be largely domestic to the country concerned. Where either insurance companies or banks act as gatherers of defined contribution funds (personal and stakeholder pensions in the UK; 401(k) in the US), the extent to which the managers of these funds can take currency positions for profit will be largely determined by their prospectuses. A brief survey of these reveals almost none that offer fully currency-hedged products, or claim to be able to add value by taking bets in currency. FX market evidence also shows that this sector generates relatively small volume.

4.3.4   FX option writers

This is a little understood, but quite important, category. There is now a well-developed FX option market, and the technology and software exists for uncovered option writers to hedge their resultant currency exposure in the cash (spot and forward) markets. This technology is now pretty standard, and it requires option writers to vary the proportion of their forward cover in a process called delta hedging. Any regulated bank that holds a balance of uncovered 'delta' will be active in this category, not least because their regulator will demand it.

It is very difficult to categorise this behaviour into either the non-profit-seeking or profit-seeking pot. It is profit-seeking in that the bank involved will seek to make a profit out of the totality of the options book (i.e. premiums charged) and the related hedge. However, the immediate behaviour in the market is largely mechanistic. This sector increases its delta as a currency strengthens and reduces it when a currency weakens; this means buying currencies as they go up, or having what an economist would describe as an 'upward sloping' or perverse, demand curve. Such a demand curve is destabilising to markets in the short-term.

At particular times, delta hedgers can become quite dominant in the market. That was true in 1985, when high currency volatility and a period of rapid growth and new technology in the FX option market meant that they generated large and destabilising FX volumes. This effect was self-correcting as the high option premiums, and losses incurred by the delta hedgers, quickly removed both option demand and option writing capacity from the market. Exactly the same phenomenon was seen again in 1992 in the successful speculative attack on sterling. It is likely that the sum of the net sales of sterling by delta hedgers in the run-up to the ERM exit was much greater than the legendary $10bn bet by George Soros (see below). Ironically, however, option writers over this period would have lost significant amounts of money (despite the fact that their hedges made money), as they would have sold options at low 'implied volatilities',[10] and hedged them in the very volatile subsequent market behaviour. This is borne out by statements made by the major FX option-writing banks in the aftermath. There was also a similar period in October 1998 in the yen exchange rate crisis (see below).

4.3.5   Investment pool traders in FX (hedge funds, proprietary traders)

This category is the only category whose involvement in the FX market is almost wholly profit-seeking. The typical customer description is of a hedge fund. Such a fund may have an absolute return target, with very wide discretion as to the instruments and markets that the fund can invest in.

---

[10] An 'implied volatility' is the standard deviation of annualised changes in the underlying FX market that is implied by the Black–Scholes (or similar) option pricing formula from the option premium traded in the option market. This rather complicated concept is very important in all option markets. Indeed, many option traders will claim that they 'trade implied volatilities'.

These players' entry into (and exit from) the FX market has developed into a pattern over the years, and two distinct styles can be distinguished. One is the attack on artificial prices maintained by central banks or their governments. These attacks can only take place when a rate is being defended, and also only tend to take place in a herd manner at particular times of stress. The most famous attack was by George Soros on the UK pound in September 1992. This was successful, and by repute Mr Soros's Quantum hedge fund made £1bn out of the trade. The success of the attack was predicated on two key elements: weak political will and a large herd attack. It is likely that the weight of 'speculative' attack was an order of magnitude larger than the $10bn principal value that Soros reputedly put at risk. Much of this will have been essentially defensive in nature (see Sections 4.3.4 and 4.3.6). It is worth noting that speculative attacks are not always successful. A sustained and large attack on HK$/US$ parity at 7.80 was mounted in 1998, and the Hong Kong government, clearly demonstrating the will to defend this level, mounted a successful campaign of interest rate rises together with some physical intervention to maintain the parity level. The cost to the unsuccessful attackers (which included a significant number of hedge funds) was high – a US/HK adverse 1m interest rate differential which rose to 11% p.a., paid by the attackers.

The other style is the 'macro' style, which does not require defensive levels to attack. Hedge funds also tend to hunt in packs in this approach, but they usually have an 'obvious' play which becomes popular. The most notorious of these was the so-called 'carry' trade of 1998 against the yen. In the popular language of the time, speculators were being 'paid' to 'short' the yen, since borrowing yen short-term cost about 0.5% p.a., and lending US dollars paid about 5.5%. This thinking, combined with a long period of yen weakness which had started in 1995 following a period of yen strength, led hedge funds to believe that there was a free lunch. For several months in 1998 there was. Then in October 1998, a rally in the yen prompted the hedge fund sector to reduce their short positions. The scale of these was such that it created a sharp upward price movement of the yen, which prompted more buying to cover remaining short yen positions. The outcome was an exceptionally large movement in the yen/$ exchange rate (around 11% depending on the time reference of consecutive days), the largest one/two-day movement seen in any of the major traded currency rates in 30 years. This experience (which was very painful for the hedge funds, and which invalidated many of their risk models) largely removed the macro hedge funds from the FX markets, and there is little evidence of their return at the time of writing (2003).

4.3.6   Investment managers and currency overlay managers

This group is roughly homogeneous in structure, in that they manage on a more or less discretionary basis the assets (and in this context cross-border assets) of the world's funded pension schemes. These are principally schemes located in the US, UK, Switzerland, Netherlands and Japan. From national estimates,[11] these pension systems account for about 95% of the roughly $8.6 trillion of global funded DB pension assets. From the same estimates, about $1.2 trillion of assets is held cross-border. This creates a pool of $1.2 trillion in the hands of this group of investment managers and currency overlay managers which can be moved across the exchanges, or hedged using forward contracts, either for profit or as a result of non-currency-led policy decisions.

---

[11] *Source*: Watson Wyatt and OECD, Sep 00 (updated to Dec 02 with market valuation changes). Note that Germany and France have very small funded pension sectors.

The behaviour of this group in the FX markets is better documented than most of the customer groups in the FX market. Most cross-border (or 'international') fixed income mandates are established with a fully hedged benchmark. This means that no economic exposure generally flows across currencies – when foreign bonds are purchased, the currency exposure is simultaneously sold forward. This sector (which is small compared to internationally held equities) is therefore characterised by small and selective profit-seeking bets, often more or less loosely based on the 'forward rate bias' theory,[12] or on opportunistic 'plays'.

In international equity mandates, our research indicates that between $80bn and $130bn of international equities have fully or partially hedged benchmarks or have active currency mandates associated with them. Of this total, probably around $80bn have active currency management mandates. Active currency mandates will generate variable hedge ratios (generally but not universally between 0% and 100%), and these variations will be entirely profit-seeking.

Currency overlay managers, as distinct from investment managers, generally have more systematic or model-driven approaches. Investment managers (whose principal responsibility is to manage the underlying assets) tend to undertake more opportunistic 'bets' on currency. Many (but not all) currency overlay managers, but few investment managers, exploit a well-known inefficiency in the currency market – that of 'trends'. Without going into details, this exploitation tends to make the currency overlay sector as a whole a perverse trader just like option hedgers – they buy when currencies are going up and sell when currencies are going down. While this behaviour is destabilising, the effect on the market (if any) clearly depends on the relative scale involved. Other management styles tend to be more heterogeneous (and therefore harder to summarise), although the forward rate bias, technical indicators[13] and fundamental forecasting all play a part.

4.3.7 Central banks

Central banks have a strategic position in the currency markets, and over the years have had a significant effect on it. Their principal role is that of executor of government foreign exchange policy. Over time their policy environment changes, and therefore their behaviour changes along with it. Their behaviour can be categorised into three types.

(1) *Declared target exchange rate defence*. This is the Hong Kong model, and the ERM prior to 1992/3. In this behaviour, the central bank has an absolute requirement to ensure that the spot exchange rate trades within more or less narrow bands. In earlier environments (say Bretton Woods 1948–71), this effort scarcely involved domestic interest rates, direct use of foreign exchange reserves was enough. However, with the scale of private capital stock and flows hugely outgunning the relatively modest official foreign exchange reserves, exchange-rate-defending central banks, particularly the successful ones, have marshalled domestic interest rates to the defensive armoury. This involves using domestic-monetary-policy muscle to raise domestic interest rates when the currency is under external attack. The downside of this policy

---

[12] The forward rate bias theory stipulates that the average mean appreciation of the low interest currency in a currency pair is less than the full interest rate differential. It obviously applies vice versa to high interest rate currencies.

[13] Technical trading is a long-established approach designed to capture movements generated by 'market dynamics' (often the relative behaviour of differing horizon moving averages). I place Chartism (where the shape of time series price charts is seen to be important) as a subsection of technical trading. Like all active approaches, there is an underlying assumption that markets are not random-walk.

is that unless Euro-interest rates[14] are separated from domestic rates by exchange controls (as they were in France in 1982[15]), then the domestic economy is put through the mill for the sake of the defence of an arbitrary external exchange rate.

(2) *Tactical intervention.* Many OECD countries, while not maintaining a fixed exchange rate policy, have not abandoned their ability to intervene in their own and others' exchange rates to further economic or political policy. The timing, size and stated reason for interventions of this type are very widely varied, from a smoothing operation to calm the market (perhaps in the wake of an external shock), to an organised and concerted attempt to move the equilibrium market exchange rate or trend. Examples of this are numerous in the recent history of the yen, and also in the failed attempt by the ECB to stem the fall of the euro in autumn 1999 through the psychologically important level of 1.00 dollar/euro.

(3) *Rejection of FX intervention.* The UK has largely pursued this policy in the last 10 years, as has the US. Both governments regard the external value of the exchange rate as a matter for the markets.

The overriding common characteristic of the behaviour of central banks, whatever their policy framework, is that they are not profit-seeking. Generally, although not universally, they are designed to act in a 'smoothing' capacity, and tend to buy weaker currencies and sell stronger currencies.

All of the above is designed to demonstrate that the structure and participants in the FX market are very different from other markets, are unique to this market, and mean that profit-seeking behaviour is a relatively small proportion of the overall volumes in the market.

4.4   PHYSICAL AND REGULATORY ISSUES

As mentioned above, the foreign exchange market is physically highly disaggregated. Unlike many regulated markets (stock and futures markets, for example), there is no 'place' that it can be said that the foreign exchange market resides. This disaggregation has led to a number of notable effects unique to the foreign exchange market.

4.4.1   Exchange controls

The foreign exchange market is not one market in the physical sense, nor is it one market in the conceptual sense. In the physical sense its networked multi-centre basis means that different centres, which operate under different political and legal frameworks, are treated differently by their governments. In the conceptual sense, there is one global market, and many local markets, which are largely or totally disconnected from the global market. Currency overlay inhabits the former almost exclusively, but an understanding of the latter is useful for a complete picture of the foreign exchange world.

The key to understanding those foreign exchange markets outside the global market is understanding what governments do, and why.

---

[14] 'Euro' used in its old meaning here – not the single currency but the 'black' or 'uncontrolled' foreign market in domestic interest rates.

[15] In 1982 (and again in 1983) the markets attacked the FRF/DEM parity in ERM. The French defended with intervention and domestic interest rate rises (to about 18%). However interest rates in the 'Euro-franc' (uncontrolled francs owned offshore) rose to peak overnight interest rates of 3000%. The French lost the fight and devalued 8% (one day's worth of 3000% interest rate differential!).

4.4.1.1   Controlling domestic currencies – why do it?

Let us begin by listing the main policy objectives that governments claim to target by exchange controls on their own currency:

1. To prevent or deter capital outflows (and sometimes inflows)
2. To 'protect' the exchange rate (i.e. to keep it high, except see 4 below)
3. To ration imports (protect domestic producers or control the trade balance)
4. To encourage exports (i.e. to depress the exchange rate)
5. To isolate the economy from (undesirable) external market factors

Not all countries aim to achieve all these objectives (2 and 4 are mutually incompatible). However, exchange controls will not be maintained by a government unless at least one of the above are publicly espoused. There may, in addition, be hidden motives that no government will publicly admit to. Three candidates stand out:

1. To deter emigration/immigration (mainly the former)
2. To levy hidden 'export taxes'
3. To control foreign currency reserves and the (corrupt) sales of import licences

The motivation behind most of these objectives is self-evident. Once a government has gone down the exchange/price control route, how do they typically execute them?

4.4.1.2   Physical controls

Physical controls (commonly called exchange controls) can be applied to residents (preventing them acquiring foreign currencies) and to non-residents (preventing them acquiring the local currency, and maybe preventing them buying foreign currencies once they have acquired the local currency). The level and mechanisms of control vary widely across countries.

Whatever the mechanics of controls, and they are too numerous to mention here, the intention of the government is the same: to limit by law the ability of residents to sell their own currency in favour of a foreign currency.

4.4.1.3   Price intervention

In the absence of physical controls, or in concert with them, governments have another option. They can choose to use their considerable resources to buy their own currency when it falls below a reference price of their choice, or sell it when it rises above. The detailed way they can approach this intervention was laid out in the previous section. If their resources are sufficient, this can be a powerful tool; flexible and adaptable, unlike exchange controls. The resources in question are not just the inevitable financial clout wielded by every government, but something much more tangible: foreign currency (and gold) reserves. High levels of reserves, expressed both in absolute terms and as a percentage of that country's GDP, can give a government effective control over the floor at which its own currency will trade. Or can it? I will argue later that the size of reserves is only one factor when we come to evaluate the ability of a government to defend, or otherwise manipulate, its currency exchange rate.

Box 4.6   Exchange controls

Both active and passive management of currency risk may be difficult or impossible if the target country maintains exchange controls.

Exchange controls' purposes are various, and there is probably a gap between the declared purposes (protecting the exchange rate, protecting the reserves, preventing speculation) and the actual purposes (retaining control over import/export resource allocation, keeping imported goods cheap for the urban/elite population, hidden tax on exports, corrupt use of import/currency licences, supply of foreign currency to be stolen and sent to Swiss bank accounts).

Exchange controls come in a variety of forms. The most stringent types (e.g. PR China) do not permit foreigners or residents to buy or sell spot or forward currency without a permit. All transactions have ultimately to be routed through the central bank. The next level down of stringency (e.g. South Africa) controls residents' ability to buy or sell the currency, but allows foreigners to exchange offshore currency between themselves, and allows direct investment flows in and dividends/earnings out. The lightest types of control involve controls mainly on forward contracts (to prevent 'speculation'), and on residents.

For those countries with exchange controls but substantial capital markets and trade, offshore commercial banks have developed a contract called the Non-Deliverable Forward (NDF). NDFs are priced and traded like forward contracts as bilateral arrangements, but the mutual delivery of the currencies is not contemplated – instead a cash payment in an uncontrolled currency is made to compensate for the change between the contract rate and the actual spot rate at maturity. NDFs tend to be illiquid and therefore expensive to trade. They are unlikely to be suitable as part of a currency overlay portfolio.

Where there are substantive exchange controls or highly illiquid forward markets in a country in a hedged index, most currency overlay managers will argue that the costs of hedging outweigh the benefits, and leave that exposure unhedged.

4.4.1.4 Conditions for currency market liquidity

We have seen that the FX market developed as something of a 'black market' in London. It did so because exchanging one currency for another, particularly if neither of the transaction participants was a resident of either of the countries of the currencies of the transaction, was best carried out outside the legal grasp of the 'country owner' of the currency. This tendency of the FX markets to flee taxation and regulation created, by a process of natural selection, a remarkably elegant, liquid, low-cost and reliable market. Once, and this only finally occurred in the mid- to late 1990s, OECD (i.e. developed) countries recognised that they could not control the nature and manner of currency exchange, they finally abandoned all efforts at doing so. Most developing economies have yet to take this step; indeed, many retain legal (exchange control) powers over their own currency which make even offshore trading between offshore parties difficult or impossible.

For countries that have abandoned exchange controls completely, FX market liquidity is dependent on the scale of the country's economy, the country's external trade as a percentage of GDP, the extent of overseas ownership of the country's assets or debt, and the extent of ownership by the country's residents of overseas assets or debt. With a large, open economy, with no exchange controls, an FX market and related hedging products will naturally develop without any official assistance. Australia is a good example of a country whose increasing openness, and abandonment of exchange controls, transformed the FX market into the modern, low-cost, flexible market that it is today. For developing countries that have not yet taken the step of abandoning exchange controls, the extent of liquidity depends on the detailed nature of the exchange controls, and the extent of fulfilment of the other conditions above.

4.4.1.5   Symptoms of controlled currency economies

Given the myriad of factors affecting economic performance across sovereign states, it is very hard to directly isolate, at least by examining only the economic data, the impact of exchange controls on an economy. The following are my list of key areas of importance and their impact:

(a) **Net capital outflows**. Governments want to 'keep capital in the country'. A simple enough idea, but not easily achieved with exchange controls. Here's why. There is ample evidence that the existence of, or threat of, exchange controls strongly inhibits *inward* capital flows, because foreign investors are frightened that their money will be 'locked up'. Since net capital outflows are the sum of both inward and outward flows, the outward would have to be reduced for the balance just to remain stable. Capital outflows are likely to be inhibited to some extent by exchange controls, however, they are unlike capital inflows in that physical investments (land, buildings, plant) cannot be unbolted and carried off. Portfolio investment is in theory more vulnerable to capital flight, but if a foreign investor wants to sell equity or bond holdings, he must find a buyer. His desire to sell may push the price down, but if the buyer is also foreign, then there remains a foreign owner, and if the buyer is local, then capital ownership is actually repatriated. So 'capital flight' is not always what it seems.

(b) **'Protecting' the exchange rate**. As long as the controls are draconian enough, a country may choose its own exchange rate and maintain that rate indefinitely. If, as is almost always the case, that rate is higher than the 'free market' rate, then an unofficial or 'black' market will emerge. At its most extreme, the formal exchange rate might effectively exist in name only, with virtually every currency deal being done at 'special' rates. Whether maintaining appearances like this constitutes success is a moot point; it certainly has severe, often devastating consequences in the real economy.

(c) **Rationing imports**. A universal characteristic of exchange controls is that they restrict the ability of residents to acquire foreign currency. This rationing can take many forms, but it will always give the government power to allocate import/currency licences as they choose. Such choices are by definition motivated by political considerations, and regrettably but naturally are often accompanied by corruption in the form of personal payments for licences. There is no denying that imports are controlled by this process, but the same effect could be achieved by simple price rationing with free access to foreign exchange at an open market price. The advantage of the latter is that the motivation which determines the scale and mix of imports is entirely economic, not political. Rationing imports is usually, and explicitly, a device to promote domestic employment, and to (slightly circularly) 'protect the exchange rate'. They fit comfortably with the gamut of state intervention in a state-run economy; they do not in a market-price-led economy.

(d) **Monetary isolation**. At its extreme, monetary isolation is born of economic xenophobia such as held sway in China and the former Soviet Union until the beginning of the 1990s. By rigidly preventing access to roubles or yuan by foreigners, and preventing access to

---

Box 4.7   Exchange controls – UK case study

Amongst the most bizarre, and possibly cynical, of the exchange control regimes in recent history is that of the UK, home to the currently dominant FX market location, London.

Between the Second World War and 1979, i.e. some 40 years, the UK maintained remarkably strict exchange controls on its citizens. UK resident companies had to receive permission from the Bank of England to conduct foreign exchange transactions on current account (i.e. for imports and exports); UK resident investment institutions (i.e. pension funds and life insurance companies) had to buy and sell their non-UK investment through an arrangement known as the 'dollar pool' – which was a fixed pool of external currency, and which traded at an exchange rate premium, reflecting the excess demand for dollar investments. UK individuals even had to take their passports to the bank to get foreign exchange for spending abroad. Amazingly, the annual limit was £50 a year, raised only in the 1970s to £200 a year.

All this time, London was carving out its position as the pre-eminent location for the foreign exchange market. Non-residents were completely free from exchange controls; they were reassured by the highly creditworthy UK government, effective but informal banking regulation (by the Bank of England), transparent and fair legal structure, skilled and educated workforce, and convenient time zone. It is hard to think of another democratic jurisdiction which so penalised its own population, while so effectively promoting the operation of a free market right in its midst.

---

dollars, yen and Deutschmarks by residents, the authorities effectively cut off their domestic economies from the outside world. Inflation rates and exchange rates, and in fact all prices, were set by government planners to fulfil political objectives. In centrally planned economies like these, exporting is not an economic activity measured (or measurable) by profit or loss, but by the needs of the planners to acquire hard (i.e. uncontrolled) currencies to spend on imports to keep the economy functioning. The case against monetary isolation is not that it cannot be achieved – it certainly was in these countries for decades – but that it does not allow international price signals to filter through to the domestic economy. And the poor historical growth record of the centrally planned economies in the 1950–90 period is a testament to the effects of this isolation.

4.4.2   Taxation

Most markets around the world are taxed. The taxes fall on transactions (stamp duty), on the profits made by participants (capital gains taxes), and on the income from investments (withholding tax/income tax/ACT/dividend taxes).

The global foreign exchange market is, broadly speaking, not taxed. This is not the benevolence of governments, rather it is a reflection on their inability to do so. For the free-marketeer, the inability of national governments to reach the global foreign exchange market is a wonderful thing. The very mobility of the markets, and their ability to migrate away from difficult or taxing environments to liberal, welcoming ones is as close to a process of natural selection both of the location and of the market structure as one is likely to get.

As we have seen above, the locations in which the global foreign exchange market has flourished are those which are welcoming, legally and politically secure, and with a regulatory 'light touch', without being casual about the stability of the banking system. Whenever a jurisdiction has imposed transaction or withholding taxes, or excessive regulation or control, the foreign exchange market has promptly moved to alternative locations.

4.4.2.1 Tobin tax

In 1978, James Tobin, an American economist (and later a Nobel Laureate), made the suggestion[16] that all foreign exchange transactions worldwide should be taxed at a low rate (say 0.1% per deal) to 'throw some sand in the wheels of speculation'. Whatever the merits or otherwise of his arguments, the fatal flaw in his proposal is its sheer unworkability – it would be impossible to get all the possible jurisdictions in the world to agree to such a tax, and its enforcement would spill over to derivatives and futures, and then to domestic money markets. Even if it were possible to raise the tax, the division of the proceeds (which would be a great deal smaller than its proponents imagine) would be a further major obstacle, with competing claims coming from the owners of the currencies in question, the jurisdiction of the transaction, and all the other jurisdictions without major market places.

Interestingly, the Tobin tax has more recently attracted a significant lobby following. There are a number of campaigning websites, including a number of anti-poverty charities, devoted to putting pressure on politicians to impose the tax.

4.4.3 Financial regulation

Regulation of the markets under the jurisdiction of each of the major foreign exchange centres is a different matter to taxation. All governments, but particularly business-friendly ones, wish to preserve the integrity of FX market-makers, and to protect their domestic banking systems against any knock-on effects of problems in the foreign exchange market, and vice versa. This has meant that in almost all the major centres of the FX market, banking regulations with respect to foreign exchange (capital requirements, risk management processes) have been consistently tightened over the years. This systemic regulation is regarded by investors as positive up to a point – excessive regulation, particularly that which seeks to regulate areas that are not seen as a risk, is seen as negative. Most national regulatory environments of the major centres have not sought to provide major consumer protection. This is largely because private investors are only indirect users of the market, and then generally on a small scale, and to fund overseas travel and expenditure. Foreign exchange 'mis-selling' would in normal circumstances have a minimal effect on individual consumers' wealth, so governments have wisely decided to leave well alone.

4.4.3.1 Argentina – a case study

There is, however, a recent case, that of Argentina, in which consumers were a very major casualty of a currency debacle.

Argentina had established a peg between the Argentinian peso and the US dollar. The peg was established after many years of endemic inflation and devaluation, and was intended to provide a base of stability and external discipline. The peg was underwritten with a currency board – in which central bank peso liabilities were matched one-for-one with US dollar monetary assets

---

[16] Tobin, J., 'A proposal for international monetary reform', *Eastern Economic Journal* **4** (1978) 153–159.

held at the central bank. The government made much of the immutability of this arrangement, and the superior security gained from the currency board underwriting, and the population, who (rather surprisingly) believed the government, went out and borrowed money (mainly in the form of mortgages) in US dollars. They did so because US dollar interest rates were significantly lower than peso rates.

This alone should have rung alarm bells. Interest rates between two currencies that are irrefutably pegged will converge to (close to) zero, otherwise there are risk-free arbitrage profits to be made. If interest rates demanded by savers were higher than US dollar rates, it could have been regarded as compensation for the exchange rate risk. Alternatively, if peso interest rates were higher than US rates because Argentina was pursuing its own monetary agenda, then that should also ring alarm bells. How can two countries with very different monetary policies maintain a constant exchange rate? History is littered with examples of the answer – they can't in the long-term.

Unfortunately, the Argentinian government found itself, in January 2002, unable to defend the peg any longer, and chose to end the convertibility of the peso, blocking residents' dollar deposits, ultimately forcing their conversion to pesos. The abandonment of the peg left the peso (by mid-2002) at about 30% of its former value against the dollar, and millions of Argentinians owing massively more than they had borrowed, with no commensurate increase in the value of their assets. The knock-on effect of the devaluation has had a catastrophic effect on consumer spending and business confidence, and also brought many banks to their knees, sending the economy into a 'post-peg devaluation winter'.

The Argentinian experience is a warning, if one were needed, of the dangers in attempting to control exchange rates while maintaining a broadly market-based economy. Fortunately, most of the currencies subject to overlay are not controlled in this way.

5

Theory of Currency Hedging of
International Portfolios

This chapter will deal with the theory of currency hedging in international portfolios or, put simply, why hedging is a good idea, other things being equal. Of course, other things are never equal, but that issue will be dealt with extensively in the succeeding chapters which look at the practicalities of currency hedging. As a precursor to this discussion, I will visit the issue of measuring risk and return under the lognormal assumption (see Chapter 3). The chapter will then cover in some detail those arguments, both theoretical and practical, that can be brought to bear.

5.1 LOGNORMAL RANDOM WALK RETURNS

I will adopt an assumption that runs through most modern investment theory, namely that the behaviour of currency exchange rates over time (like that of equity and bond returns) follows a lognormal random path. This is to say that if we take the natural log of the change in currency rates expressed as a percentage over a unit time period (say one day), then these are normally distributed, with an observable mean and standard deviation. This amounts to saying that the random linkage from one time period to the next is multiplicative, not additive. This assumption is the same as that made in the Black–Scholes model; assumptions which I expended some energy on refuting in an earlier chapter. However, the sharp-eyed reader will note that the lognormal assumption did not bear the brunt of my previous attack – in fact it remained largely unscathed. Later in the book, I will be looking in more detail at the lognormal random walk assumption, and while its random walk credentials will come under attack, its lognormality assumptions will not.

Percentage changes in currency rates I will call *currency returns*. However, these are calculated not by reference to spot exchange rates, but by reference to currency surprise (see Chapter 3). In summary, currency returns are the difference between the forward rate at the end of the prior period, and the spot rate at the end of the current period, expressed as a percentage of the spot rate at the end of the prior period. The name 'currency returns' is something of a misnomer, it derives from the algebra of conventional assets (equities, bonds) and implies that such returns are independently investible. As discussed in the currency surprise section, they are not investible without a 'carrier' asset.

5.1.1 Measurement

The lognormality assumption for financial markets, including currency markets, is very fundamental. We need to reflect this fundamental nature of the markets by using accurate measurements for the key variables – return and risk – which match the assumptions we are making. The two matching measures are 'annual return', in which returns are measured at an annual frequency and compounded at any other frequency, and 'annualised volatility', in which the standard deviation of the unbiased normal distribution of the return series is measured.

5.1.2   Returns

There is no debate in investment circles about annual return methodology. When we say that the return of an investment is 10%, we mean that an asset value of 100 at one year end becomes 110 at the next year end.

Box 5.1   Convexity

Convexity is a term that turns up a lot in investing. At its most general, it means that 'X can go up more than it can go down', or 'if I invest $100, I can only lose $100, but I can make an unlimited amount'. Graphically, it can be represented something like this:

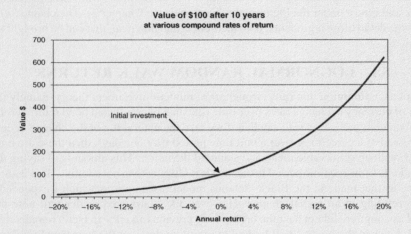

**Value of $100 after 10 years
at various compound rates of return**

Convexity also turns up a lot in currency analysis. The most obvious feature is that if I sell a foreign currency forward, then I can lose a potentially unlimited amount of money, whereas if I buy a foreign currency forward, I can only lose the cost of the purchase.

Interestingly, this statement is only true if I express my gains and losses in my home currency. If I express them in the foreign currency, then the converse is true; a forward sale of the foreign currency can be restated as a forward purchase of the home currency, with unlimited gains and limited losses expressed in the foreign currency.

A further source of convexity can arise from the way in which currencies are expressed. If I am dollar-based, then expressing the sensitivity of my pounds sterling investments using a $/£ exchange rate (i.e. the value of the foreign currency (£)) produces linear valuations. However, expressing my yen investments using a yen/$ exchange rate (i.e. the reciprocal of the value of the foreign currency (yen)) produces convex valuation curves.

Convexity arises out of the expression of multiplicative (or logarithmic) processes over time (i.e. investment returns, currency movements) in absolute asset values or currency amounts. It is important because while investment theory teaches us to think and analyse in annualised return terms (i.e. multiplicatively), we actually consume absolute cash in our everyday lives, and our utility functions are more likely to be 'wealth-based' than 'return-based'.

We link period returns geometrically, so that they compound. To annualise compound returns for periods other than one year, we use the following formula:

$$AR = [(TR_{t,t+n} + 1)^{(f/n)}] - 1$$

where

AR = annualised return (%)
$TR_{t,t+n}$ = total compound return (%) (% of value at end-period t)
between the end of period t and the end of period $t + n$ (i.e. n-periods' return)
f = frequency of period in a year (e.g. monthly = 12, quarterly = 4, etc.)

Compound returns are simply geometrically linked period returns, as follows:

$$TR_{t,t+n} = [(1 + PR_{t+1})(1 + PR_{t+2})(1 + PR_{t+3})(1 + PR_{t+4}) \cdots (1 + PR_{t+n})] - 1$$

where PR_t = return for period t expressed in % of value at $t - 1$.

This methodology is fully consistent with lognormal returns, and no errors (not even second-order) arise as long as these are the consistent definitions and methodology. However, note that 'annual return' is not the same thing as the rate of return in continuous-time maths. See Appendix 2 for details.

Box 5.2 Central Limit Theorem

The Central Limit Theorem (CLT) is a statistical law that is widely (if unknowingly) used in investment management analysis. In essence it states that if a number of observations of an independent random variable are taken, then the standard deviation of the resulting sample mean is the standard deviation of the underlying population divided by the square root of the number of observations. Furthermore, even if the underlying distribution is non-normal (even strongly so), the distribution of the sample mean tends to normality as the number of observations in the sample grows. For most independent variables, a sample size of 10 is getting pretty normal.

The CLT is the basis for all conversion of standard deviations across different frequencies of data. The logic is as follows (note that *returns* below are the natural log of (1+percentage monthly return)) (see Appendix 2).

Suppose we measure returns monthly. To calculate annual returns we sum the monthly returns. This represents the sum (i.e. 12 × mean) of a sample of 12 observations. The standard deviation of the average monthly return in this sample under the CLT will be (Monthly SD)/(Sq. Root 12). But we are interested in the annual sum, not the monthly mean. This is 12 times as large as the monthly mean, so we have to multiply the expression above by 12:

Annual SD = (Monthly SD)/(Sq. Root 12) × 12 = (Monthly SD) × (Sq. Root 12)

Hence the special case of annualising volatilities requires us to *multiply* by the root of the number of observations in a year.

While the Central Limit Theorem is very effective at converting any old distribution into normal, it only works if the variables in the sample are independent. Therefore it remains a strong theoretical possibility that currency and other markets are not normal at one-year horizon if the constituent variables (daily, weekly, monthly returns) are serially correlated in some way.

A worked example of return methodology is given in Table 5.1, taking one year's worth of monthly return data. The reader might like to satisfy himself that the annual return (which in this case is the same as the annualised and the total return) is 24.02%.

Table 5.1   Example asset returns

Period	% Returns
1	2.4142%
2	4.9287%
3	1.3992%
4	2.5029%
5	−1.4179%
6	6.6249%
7	5.5299%
8	4.4657%
9	2.9206%
10	0.1610%
11	−3.5356%
12	−3.6404%

5.1.3   Volatility

I have slightly laboured the return point to make a much more telling one about volatility. I give a full explanation of the following argument in Appendix 2, but the summary is as follows. The returns above are not normally distributed. They are not because we have assumed that the generator of period returns is a lognormal process. Percentages are not logs. We can convert the series in Table 5.1 into a log series by taking the natural log of each (1 + period return %). This gives us the series in Table 5.2. Just to be clear, these values are the logs of 'one plus the percentage returns' – that is they are the 'linking' values for each period of the asset. Because they are logs, they are additive, and because they are logs (and we assume a lognormal distribution), they are normally distributed. This is the series we need to measure for volatility, not the percentage returns series.

Table 5.2   Log asset returns

Period	Log returns
1	0.023855
2	0.048110
3	0.013895
4	0.024721
5	−0.014281
6	0.064147
7	0.053824
8	0.043688
9	0.028788
10	0.001609
11	−0.035997
12	−0.037083
Sum of logs	**0.215276**

To confirm the additive nature of these log returns, the reader should take the exponential (or 'anti-log') of the sum (0.215276), and he will find that it equals 1.2402. Take away 1 and you have the annual percentage return of 24.02% – an illustration that the return methodologies (log and percentage) are (exactly) the same.

What about the volatility calculation, though? The conventional volatility (standard deviation) calculation for the return series is (in words) to take the root of the [(sum of the squares of the percentage returns' differences from the mean)/$n - 1$], or in algebra:

$$SD = \sqrt{\frac{\sum_{i=1}^{n} (r_i - \bar{r})^2}{n - 1}}$$

where

r_i = percentage return for period i
$\bar{r}_i$ = mean percentage return (from sample)

This calculation produces a volatility at the horizon of the period's frequency, so in this case it is the monthly volatility. If we want to annualise it, we use the Central Limit Theorem, which tells us that if the period returns are statistically independent from each other, the volatility at any horizon is $\sqrt{[(\text{desired horizon})/(\text{period horizon})]}$ measured in consistent time units (days, months, years). As an example, annualising monthly volatility would mean multiplying the above formula result by $\sqrt{(12/1)} = 3.464$. See Appendix 2 for fuller details on using the Central Limit Theorem for annualising.

So with this information and a calculator, we can calculate the monthly volatility of the above series as 3.40%, and the annualised volatility as 11.79% ($=3.40\% \times 3.464$). However, this will be taking data that we know to be non-normal (percentage returns). Non-normal data is likely to give us unpredictable and unexpected results, and is not amenable to the series of statistical tests that makes normal distributions so helpful – and, surprisingly, the Central Limit Theorem is not going to help us 'make the distribution normal' (again see Appendix 2).

Box 5.3   Siegel's paradox

Siegel's paradox was proposed by Professor Jeremy Siegel in 1972. His basic proposition is that when exchange rates move, the returns when viewed from both bases currency perspectives sum to greater than 0:

	US perspective $/£		UK perspective £/$		
	Rate	Returns	Rate	Returns	Total returns
Period 0	1.5000		0.6667		
Period 1	1.0000	−33.33%	1.0000	50.00%	16.67%
Period 2	1.0000	0.00%	1.0000	0.00%	0.00%
Period 3	1.6000	60.00%	0.6250	−37.50%	22.50%
Period 4	1.5000	−6.25%	0.6667	6.67%	0.42%
	Sum of				
	returns	20.42%		19.17%	39.58%

I have used extreme exchange rate moves to illustrate the effect. Siegel's paradox is caused by the inappropriate mixing of multiplicative and additive environments. Geometrically linking the returns (rather than adding them) from each currency's perspective over time will eliminate the positive sum of returns, but not the positive sum across base currencies (i.e. the right-hand column). However, taking logs of the returns will allow the elimination of errors both over time and across base-currency perspectives. The table below illustrates:

	US perspective $/£		UK perspective £/$		
	Rate	Log returns	Rate	Log returns	Total returns
Period 0	1.5000		0.6667		
Period 1	1.0000	−0.4055	1.0000	0.4055	0.0000
Period 2	1.0000	0.0000	1.0000	0.0000	0.0000
Period 3	1.6000	0.4700	0.6250	−0.4700	0.0000
Period 4	1.5000	−0.0645	0.6667	0.0645	0.0000
Sum of returns		0.0000		0.0000	0.0000

5.1.4 Normally distributed period returns

Why don't we instead take data that we know (from our assumptions) to be normal, namely the log returns?

In this case we apply exactly the same SD algebra, but this time to the log return series. The monthly SD is 0.0336, and the annualised SD is 0.11655. But what units is 0.11655 in? It is in logs[17], and we do not easily think in logs. So we could convert it back into a percentage by the reverse of the route taken above, namely $\exp(0.11655) - 1 = 12.36\%$. So by this calculation the volatility of this very simple data set is a full 0.5% higher than the conventionally accepted method. Which is right?

Box 5.4   Fat tails

'Fat tails' is an expression used in financial markets when 'rare' events appear to happen more often than 'expected'. The 'expected' likelihood of large movements in financial markets is most commonly derived from the normal distribution, and the appearance of extreme events more frequently than the normal distribution would predict is evidence that the normal distribution may be an inappropriate distribution to use for price change prediction. Why should this be so?

The normal distribution is computationally very convenient, and is also commonly observed in many 'natural' processes (see Box 3.6). However, price movements in currency and other markets are not 'natural processes', they are the result of the behaviour of numbers of market participants.

---

[17] In fact, of course, 'log returns' are 'continuous time' returns. Using these routinely is very difficult (since the real world of investment is measured in discrete time, not continuous time), and would mean that an annual 10% return in continuous time (i.e. '0.1' expressed in logs) has an asset value of 100 becoming 110.52 is a year's time, rather than 110. Not intuitive, and indeed not the industry standard.

Students of market behaviour will explain that very large market movements can occur when there is a positive feedback from market prices to participants (falling markets ➔ sell; rising markets ➔ buy), reinforcing the price movement. While this behaviour is unstable (i.e. it may not always be present), it may appear strongly at times of market stress.

Long-Term Capital Management, a large hedge fund relying on sophisticated statistical arbitrage, was brought to its knees by its reliance on classical assumptions (i.e. normal distributions) even though two Nobel Laureate economists on its Board of Directors would have ensured that the maths applied to these distributions would have been right. Applying a fat-tailed (rather than normal) distribution would have lowered their (statistical) confidence in their processes, and thereby probably saved them from near collapse.

The answer is that the log approach is right. I have already demonstrated the mathematical and statistical basis for preferring this approach, but we can demonstrate it with a Monte Carlo analysis.

5.1.5 A simple test

According to the normal distribution function, an observation drawn from a normal distribution falls outside $1.96 \times SD$ of the distribution 2.5% of the time. This is the test:

1. We generate a long series of random returns from a lognormal random walk generator. The generator will be genuinely random, with a constant SD and mean return of zero (to reflect the fact that we will be dealing with currency surprise). The random number generator has a monthly volatility of 0.040345798, which is that monthly log volatility which would produce a 15% annualised volatility if correctly calculated via logs. The series is 12 000 monthly returns.
2. Measure the annualised volatility the conventional way, and measure the number of years the annual returns fall outside $1.96 \times$ the measured SD. Record this as a percentage of years tested.
3. Repeat step 2), but measuring the annualised volatility using logs as above, and applying the 1.96 test on the log returns, not the percentage returns.
4. Repeat both processes 100 times.
5. Record the average of the percentage occurrence for both methods (2 and 3).

The results of the test are given in Table 5.3. They clearly show that the conventional volatility measure (and annualising methodology) is seriously skewed, and that the log volatility measure produces answers almost exactly in line with theoretical expectation.

Table 5.3 Monte Carlo test results – 100 runs, each run 1000 years

	Percentage below $1.96 \times SD$	Percentage above $1.96 \times SD$
Conventional percentage volatility measurement	1.08%	4.13%
Log volatility measurement	2.49%	2.48%

5.1.6 Relevance to currency hedging

Why is this so important in a currency context? All of the above is relevant to the theory of currency hedging because we will be examining the impact of currency exposure, and its removal, by reference to historical volatility. Unless we can be confident in our volatility calculations, and our annualising processes, which will all be annualised from high-frequency (monthly or daily) data, then we run the risk that the results will be tainted.

There is another feature of volatility calculations which are unique to currency calculations. The reader may think that the result above, namely that negative returns are under-represented (or over-predicted) in the conventional percentage volatility calculation, is not a problem, or perhaps that it is a 'nice' problem to have. But currency returns do not have a natural 'way up'. I can represent the monthly currency surprise for, say, $/£ as either the value of the pound versus the dollar, or the value of the dollar versus the pound. This means that we can reverse the return series at will, depending on the base currency perspective, and that one person's positive return is another's negative.

This brings out the fundamental inconsistency of the conventional volatility measurement, the same exchange rate series can generate returns whose distribution depends on the 'way up' the exchange rate is represented. So extreme performance can at the same time be both under- and over-represented, depending on this choice. The log approach completely eliminates these errors.

I will avoid all of these measurement difficulties because throughout this book I will measure volatility using the log method. I will, however, always convert any resulting logs back to percentages, so as to remain consistent with the return conventions in investment management. If at any stage we use logs in algebra, I will represent them using x.xxxx notation. Similarly, I will always represent return percentages as x.xx%.

One final note of caution. Combining period returns of the various investment classes that make up a portfolio requires that we add weighted percentage returns together, including the contribution from hedging of hedged assets or currency overlay. We cannot add log returns since this is, in effect, multiplicative combination.[18] However much we may wish to the contrary, a rise in equities by 10% will not make the simultaneous return on bonds increase by 1%! However, we will continue to treat combined series (including whole portfolios) as if they are lognormal, and measure them as such.

With this mathematical and measurement background in place, we can move on to the substantive issues in currency and international investment.

5.2 THE 'FREE LUNCH'

The expression 'free lunch' in currency hedging was coined by Perold and Schulman[19] in 1988. What they were referring to was their observation that when currency hedging is applied to international portfolios, the volatility of the historical hedged return series goes down, but (excluding any bid/offer spreads in the hedging contracts) the return remains constant. This is similar to the volatility effect seen from diversifying a portfolio by adding additional, uncorrelated, equal-return stocks. Any portfolio whose expected volatility can be reduced

---

[18] The only relationship that is multiplicative is the effect of spot exchange rate movements on asset returns. Since spot rates are not investable stand-alone, this is not a particularly useful observation.

[19] Perold, A. F. and Schulman, E. C. 'The free lunch in currency hedging: implications for investment policy and performance standards', *Financial Analysts Journal* May/June (1988) pp. 45–52.

without reducing the expected return is not lying on the 'efficient frontier', or can be said to be an 'inefficient portfolio'.

Let me start the explanation of this phenomenon by looking at the theory of diversification.

5.2.1   Which way up?

Please note that I will refer in this chapter to currency returns expressed as the return of the foreign currency with respect to the base currency. So this means that if we have a USD base currency, and we are looking at the behaviour of Japanese equity returns, positive currency returns mean the yen is going up against the dollar, negative returns mean the yen is going down against the dollar. From a mathematical point of view, this will mean representing the yen/$ exchange rate as dollars per yen, or 'upside down' from the conventional measurement of yen per dollar. I will refer to correlation between currency returns as positive if equity returns move with currency returns, and negative if equity returns move opposite to currency returns.

Note that if world equity markets are highly correlated, then if we see negative correlation from one perspective (say German equity and currency from a US perspective), then we are highly likely to see positive correlation from the mirror image relationship (i.e. US equity and currency from a German perspective). This implies that while it is possible for currency hedging not to be risk-reducing from one base currency perspective, this is likely to make the case for hedging stronger from the counterparty currency perspective.

5.2.2   Adding 'moving parts'

In conventional investment decision-making, the addition of more 'moving parts' (individual securities, sectors, countries, asset classes) is seen as naturally adding diversification. It is also generally understood that the effect of diversification is diluted if the new moving parts are positively correlated with the existing moving parts. But as long as the underlying volatility of the new moving parts is not materially higher than that of the existing ones, then the overall volatility of the portfolio will at worst remain constant, and at best fall substantially.

The mechanics of diversification in underlying assets are straightforward. If an investor holds one stock (or index) and wishes to diversify into another, he sells (say) half his holding in the original stock and buys the new stock with the proceeds. Each stock's contribution to the overall volatility of the portfolio is then only half that of each stock on its own. There is some reasonably straightforward maths associated with diversification. If a second stock (or index) is introduced into a one-stock portfolio, and the volatility of the two stocks is the same (at, say, 16% p.a.), and the stocks are held at 50% weight each in the portfolio, then the volatility of the resulting portfolio will depend on the extent of correlation of the two stocks as shown in Figure 5.1. The maths of this effect can be computed from a statistical theorem that determines the volatility (standard deviation) of the sum of distributions A (returns from Stock 1 as a percentage of the whole portfolio) and B (returns from Stock 2 as a percentage of the whole portfolio) as follows:

$$SD(A + B) = \sqrt{Var(A) + Var(B) + 2Cov(AB)} \qquad (5.1)$$

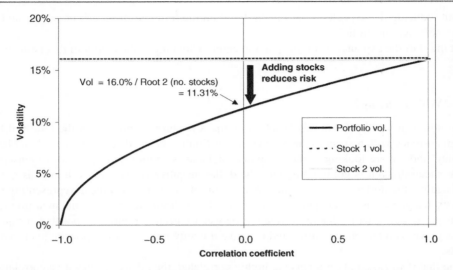

Figure 5.1 Portfolio volatility versus stock correlation coefficient – equally weighted two-stock port-folio, both stocks 16% volatility

where

$$\text{Var(A)} = \frac{n \sum A^2 - \left(\sum A\right)^2}{n(n-1)} \tag{5.2}$$

$$\text{SD (A) or Volatility (A)} = \sqrt{\text{Var(A)}} \tag{5.3}$$

$$\text{Cov(AB)} = \sqrt{\frac{\sum\limits_{i=1}^{n} \left(A_i - \overline{A}\right)\left(B_i - \overline{B}\right)}{n}} \tag{5.4}$$

A and B are the series of returns from each stock as a percentage of the whole portfolio and $n =$ number of observations (i.e. months of returns).

Covariance can only be calculated on identical sample sizes, so in the context of asset returns, they are computed for the length of the shorter return series if return series are of different lengths. To derive the diversifying value of adding an uncorrelated stock (i.e. portfolio volatility being reduced from 16% to $16\%/\sqrt{2} = 11.3\%$), we can substitute the numerical values into equation (5.1) above. Note that the volatility of both A and B as a percentage of the whole portfolio is $16\%/2 = 8\%$, because each stock is 50% of the portfolio. The lack of correlation assumption means that $\text{Cov(AB)} = 0$.

$$
\begin{aligned}
\text{Portfolio volatility} = \text{SD(A+B)} \quad &= \sqrt{8\%^2 + 8\%^2 + (2 \times 0\%)} \\
&= \sqrt{2(8\%)^2} \\
&= \sqrt{(\sqrt{2} \times 8\%)^2} \\
&= \sqrt{2} \times 8\% \\
&= 16\%/\sqrt{2}
\end{aligned}
$$

For n stocks and for the generalised non-zero correlation case:

Portfolio volatility $= SD(A + B + C + \cdots + n)$

$$= \sqrt{\sum_{i=A}^{n}[Vol(i)]^2 + \sum_{i=A}^{n}\sum_{j=A}^{n}[Cov(ij)], i \neq j}$$

where $Vol(i) = SD(\text{asset } i) \times$ weight of asset i in the portfolio.

Returning to the two-stock model example, if the two stocks in question have the same expected return, then the argument for adding stocks to create diversification is indisputable. Even if all the stocks (indices) are highly correlated with each other, the volatility of the portfolio can still be reduced. We will return to this graph later when we consider international diversification, and equity index correlation.

5.2.3   Currency exposure is different

Suppose an investor holds one international stock (or index) as his entire portfolio, and no currency exposure. He will hold the stock hedged back into his base currency,[20] and currency fluctuations will have no effect on the performance of his portfolio. Suppose he is then encouraged by the logic above to diversify by holding currency exposure. He removes the hedge on his stock, and he has two 'moving parts', not one. However, he does not have to sell any of this original stock to do this, and so all of the currency volatility he accepts is *in addition* to the existing stock volatility.

In mathematical terms, this alters one key component: the SD of each asset in this example is not weighted by its proportion in the portfolio because both of the weights are 100%. We can produce a graph similar to that of Figure 5.1, but this time continuing to hold one (international) stock and adding currency exposure. Again I have assumed that both the international stock volatility and the currency volatility are 16%. Figure 5.2 illustrates the impact of the stock:currency correlation coefficient on portfolio volatility.

The maths of this effect closely follows the maths above. Let's repeat the worked example above, but with the new asset and currency mix. From the basic two-stock formula:

$$SD(A + B) = \sqrt{Var(A) + Var(B) + 2Cov(AB)}$$

Substituting values:

$$\begin{aligned}
\text{Portfolio volatility} = SD(A+B) &= \sqrt{16\%^2 + 16\%^2 + (2 \times 0\%)} \\
&= \sqrt{2(16\%^2)} \\
&= \sqrt{(\sqrt{2} \times 16\%)^2} \\
&= \sqrt{2} \times 16\%
\end{aligned}$$

It is clear from this analysis that unless there is strong *negative* correlation between the stock price and the foreign currency, the volatility of the portfolio will go *up* when currency exposure is added. The break-even for the negative correlation required for currency to reduce volatility is -0.5 in this example. This value is not fixed, it depends on the relative volatilities of the

---

[20] I will use *hedge* throughout this chapter to mean rolling one-month forward contracts to sell the foreign currency in which the foreign asset is denominated. The amount of the hedge is adjusted monthly to accommodate changes to the value of the assets. This is a passive hedge, no attempt is made to analyse the success or otherwise of active currency managers.

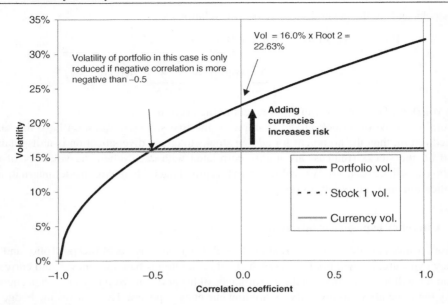

Figure 5.2   Portfolio volatility versus stock : currency correlation coefficient – one stock/one currency portfolio, both 16% volatility

stock and currency concerned. We will return to this later. If there is either no correlation, or alternatively positive correlation, then the volatility of the portfolio must go up – this is a mathematical certainty.

It is worth remembering that the sequence of events in international investment (particularly equity investment) is usually the reverse of this. The first decision is to invest abroad, this brings both international equity and currency exposure (i.e. 22.63% volatility in Figure 5.2). The second (and usually secondary) decision is to hedge (remove) the currency exposure, reducing the equity portfolio volatility in this example to 16%.

5.2.4   Correlation of asset classes

One of the most apparently compelling arguments for retaining currency exposure in international investments is that the unhedged foreign indices (i.e. with currency exposure) almost always have a lower correlation with domestic equities than hedged foreign indices (i.e. without currency exposure). This observation implies that currencies bring diversification. I want to take the elements of this argument to pieces very carefully, and I will demonstrate that it implies no such thing.

I start with the theoretical case. Let's make the following assumptions. A fund is invested only in domestic equities (Index 1) with volatility 16%. On offer are unhedged international equities (Index 2), also with volatility 16%. Currency surprise has a volatility of 11%. The expected returns of both equity indices are the same, and the expected return of currency is zero. There is no correlation between currency and hedged international equities, and 0.5 positive correlation between domestic and unhedged international equities. What do the correlation curves look like, and what is the optimum investment strategy?

Firstly, we can calculate the volatility of hedged equities. Currency surprise methodology tells us that unhedged returns = hedged returns + currency surprise. Statistical theory tells us the variance of the sum of two distributions is as follows:

$$Var(A + B) = Var(A) + Var(B) + 2Cov(AB) \tag{5.5}$$

so in this context:

$$Variance\ (unhedged) = Variance\ (hedged) + Variance\ (currency)$$
$$+ 2\ Covariance\ (hedged:\ currency)$$
$$Covariance = 0\ because\ correlation\ currency:\ hedged\ asset$$
$$= 0\ (by\ assumption)$$

Therefore:

$$Volatility\ (hedged) = \sqrt{Variance\ (unhedged) - Variance\ (currency)}$$

since $\log(1 + 16\%) = 0.1484$ and $\log(1 + 11\%) = 0.1044$. Then:

$$\log[1 + Volatility\ (hedged)]^{21} = \sqrt{0.1484^2 - 0.1044^2} = 0.10553$$

And so:

$$Volatility\ (hedged) = \exp(0.10553) - 1 = 11.13\%$$

So the volatility of the hedged foreign index is lower than the unhedged at 11.13%, compared to 16% for the unhedged equity. We had already found this in the example above, although the use of logs is more accurate.

The correlation coefficient, R, is a measure of the correlation between the two series. Its value can only lie between $+1$ (perfect correlation) and -1 (perfect negative correlation). Pairs of series with a correlation coefficient of zero are said to be 'statistically independent'. R, the correlation coefficient between Index 1 and Index 2, is defined as:

$$R = Cov\ (Index\ 1:\ Index\ 2)/[Vol(Index\ 1\ ) \times Vol(Index\ 2)]$$

For domestic : unhedged equities we know (from our assumptions) that the correlation is 0.5. From this information we can calculate the correlation of domestic : hedged equities.

$$Hedged\ equities = unhedged\ equities - currency$$

The correlation coefficient R for domestic : hedged equities is:

$$R = Cov(domestic:hedged)\ /\ [Vol(domestic) \times Vol(hedged)]$$

A little maths will show that as long as Cov(hedged : currency) = 0 (which it is because we have assumed $R = 0$), then:

$$Cov(domestic:hedged) = Cov(domestic:unhedged)$$

---

[21] I am adding log returns in this equation. Adding log returns means multiplying percentage returns. As discussed elsewhere in this book, this is a complex question when it comes to currency. Unhedged returns *are* a multiplicative relationship between local returns and spot returns, but hedging eliminates currency exposure at the additive level, leaving the multiplicative residual term unhedged. The shorter the rebalancing period, and/or the lower the two constituent volatilities, the smaller this residual term. The effect is material in this context of correlation calculation.

We can now calculate Cov(domestic : unhedged):

$$\text{Cov(domestic : unhedged)} = 0.5 \times \text{Vol(domestic)} \times \text{Vol(unhedged)}$$
$$= 0.5 \times 0.1484 \times 0.1484$$
$$= 0.011014$$

Therefore:

$$R = \text{Cov(domestic : hedged)} / [\text{Vol(domestic)} \times \text{Vol(hedged)}]$$
$$= \text{Cov(domestic : unhedged)} / [\text{Vol(domestic)} \times \text{Vol(hedged)}]$$
$$= 0.011014/(0.1484 \times 0.10553)$$
$$= 0.70$$

(We do not need any conversion back to percentages because this is a ratio.) So we can demonstrate that under these assumptions the apparent correlation between domestic equities and international equities rises from 0.50 to 0.70 when international equities are hedged.

However, this is *only* because the volatility of hedged international equities is lower, and for no other reason. Just to recap this point: correlation coefficients are calculated as the covariance of the two series divided by the product of their respective volatilities. The covariance of domestic equities and international equities is the same (on the above assumptions) whether or not they are hedged or unhedged. But hedged international equities have lower volatility than unhedged equities, therefore the denominator of the correlation calculation will be lower and the correlation coefficient will be higher. So it is only the (desirable) reduction in volatility through hedging international equities that increases the correlation coefficient. This, then, is a spurious basis on which to claim that currencies bring diversification.

Figure 5.3 shows the trade-off from hedging between portfolio volatility and correlation (between domestic and international) as the hedge ratio rises (i.e. as currency is progressively

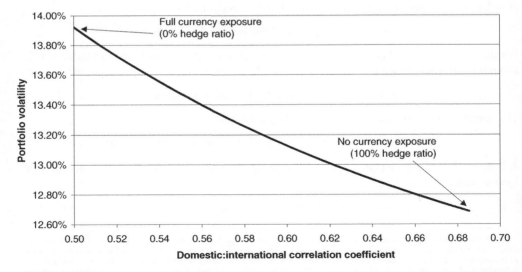

Figure 5.3 A spurious effect-scattergram of portfolio volatility and domestic : international correlation versus currency exposure

removed from the portfolio). It shows a portfolio consisting of 50% domestic and 50% international, and it uses the assumptions above.

This graph emphasises the apparently counterintuitive relationship between domestic : international correlation and portfolio volatility. In this example *all* of the increase in correlation is accounted for by the reduction in volatility of the international assets as they are hedged. So rising domestic:international correlation coefficients are a 'good thing' in this context!

5.3   HEDGING AND THE EFFICIENT FRONTIER

The analysis and graphs above are not commonly found in the investment literature, they are peculiar to currency. However, it is possible to look at the impact of hedging in a more conventional framework, that of the mean-variance optimiser. There is, however, a technical issue which has made this analysis difficult and slightly inflexible – most proprietary optimisers are designed to operate with assets which 'use up' capital and have a positive expected return. Passive currency overlay does neither – it requires no capital, and it has an expected return of zero. Active overlay may have a positive expected return, but it also uses up no capital. However, modern optimising software, particularly if it uses iterative rather than Markowitz maths, is capable of incorporating currency overlay as well as other 'non-funded' activity, like futures-based equitisation and tactical asset allocation.

Box 5.5   Mean-variance optimisation

This technique was first developed by Nobel Laureate Harry Markowitz, and developed by many other economists and financial engineers subsequently. His thesis was that investors will by nature seek higher rather than lower returns, and take less rather than more risk, which he chose to measure by the standard deviation (or volatility) of returns. He showed the mathematics by which investors could maximise the expected return of a portfolio subject to a given risk, or minimise the expected risk of a portfolio subject to a given return. He demonstrated that the correlation of returns between asset classes was a key input into the solution.

Portfolios created by this method, and for which no increase in return was possible without an increase in risk (and no reduction in risk was possible without a reduction in return), were known as 'efficient portfolios' (a subset of Pareto optimality).

Modern software can compute optimums for large numbers of asset classes very easily, which was not the case when Markowitz wrote his paper. See also Box 5.6.

5.3.1   Constructing an optimiser including currency

There are three key variables that need to be established to conduct a mean-variance optimisation. For each asset class that is going to be included, you need:

- Expected return
- Expected volatility
- Correlations with the other asset classes

The choice of these values is the subject of intense academic and practitioner debate, and space does not allow us to join that debate in any detail here. However, to give a flavour of some of the issues, it is crucial to the assumptions whether or not the whole exercise is conducted in 'real' (i.e. index-linked) terms, or in nominal terms. If it is the latter, then a critical assumption of expected future inflation needs to be made. In addition, is the analysis going to be conducted as returns and volatility relative to liabilities, or in current terms? If the former, then the discounting methodology of the liabilities becomes the driver of the risk-neutral portfolio.

Let me give an example. If a pension fund has made a fully inflation-proofed promise to its employees, and it discounts its liabilities at the risk-free index-linked bond rate, then investing in matching-maturity sovereign bonds is essentially risk-free – i.e. relative volatility is zero. However, if the fund discounts its liabilities using the arcane equity-linked methods embedded in the UK's Minimum Funding Rate (MFR) calculation, then index-linked bonds will be far from risk-free. So in this case the chosen liability discount rate is the driver of the whole asset allocation process.

For the example below, I have chosen to define expected return and volatility as risk relative to the discount rate embodied in the new UK accounting standard, FRS17. This requires UK companies to discount their liabilities (and publish the resulting present value in their report and accounts – see FRS17 section (p. 21) for more details). In Table 5.4 I set out these estimates for a UK investor.

Table 5.4   Assumed asset characteristics

	Expected return over liabilities	Expected volatility
Domestic equities	2.00%	16%
International equities (unhedged)	2.00%	16%
Passive currency overlay	0.00%	10%
Bonds	0.00%	2%
Private equity	5.00%	30%
Active overlay	0.75%	6%

I have put in passive and active overlay, rather than the more conventional 'hedged international equities', so that the optimiser is not necessarily constrained to 0–100% hedge ratios. I have assumed 0.75% value added p.a. for active overlay, and zero for passive. We can vary these values later if required (particularly to test sensitivity to transactions costs). The volatilities for the overlays have been taken from 20 years' history of 'World ex-UK' portfolios. The active overlay is Record Currency Management's proprietary process – my guess is that other proprietary processes would produce similar numbers. The lower volatility for active overlay is explained by a lower average hedge ratio (around 50% vs. 100% for passive hedging).

To complete the information needed to run an optimiser, we need a correlation matrix. In Table 5.5 I have used some educated guesses based on 20-year historical averages between the classes. Private equity does not have good marked-to-market information, so these guesses are more guessed than educated! The reader may have good reason to question some of the assumptions; this is to be expected. The principle at stake here is not the assumptions, but the methodology by which assumptions are turned into an asset allocation.

5.3.2   Optimiser methodology

Markowitz's genius was in devising not only the principles of portfolio optimisation, but also the mathematical solution. However, in this era of high-speed data processing, we do not

Table 5.5   Correlation matrix

	Domestic equities	International equities	Passive currency overlay	Bonds	Private equity
Domestic equities					
International equities	0.6				
Passive currency overlay	−0.1	−0.5			
Bonds	0.2	0.1	0.0		
Private equity/alternatives	0.3	0.4	−0.2	0.1	
Active overlay	−0.1	−0.4	0.8	0.0	−0.1

need his mathematics,[22] just the principles. In the following optimisation, I use an iterative numerical solution (that is, trial and error) with many iterations to 'home in' on the optimum solution[23].

Box 5.6   Modern portfolio theory

The father of modern portfolio theory, as it is now retrospectively called, is Harry Markowitz. Markowitz was a young mathematical economist in Chicago in the 1950s, and wrote a paper in 1952 ('Portfolio selection', *op. cit.*) in which he set out for the first time the mathematics of portfolio risk and return – defining the concept of portfolio optimisation. Markowitz's innovation was to show how, with three pieces of information about each component of the portfolio (expected return, expected volatility and correlation with other assets/stocks), an 'efficient frontier' of portfolios could be constructed for which, at each level of return, risk was minimised, and at each level of risk, return was maximised. This process was christened 'portfolio optimisation'.

The next innovation was the introduction of the concept of the risk-free asset. A risk-free asset in this context is, contrary to popular opinion, not a monetary asset with nil probability of default; it is rather an asset with zero volatility of return (and hence zero correlation with any other equity). Sharpe showed that adding the possibility of a risk-free asset to a portfolio could only improve its performance. He also derived the counterintuitive finding (under the 'classical' assumptions of these theories) that *one* optimal asset mix prevailed whatever the investor's risk/return preferences, the only variation being the extent of risk-free asset/borrowing. This led to the concept of the Capital Market Line, the efficient (and linear) risk/return trade-off.

To round up this group of theories, the Capital Asset Pricing Model extends this concept to a valuation model for individual securities. This establishes the individual security equivalent of the Capital Market Line – the Security Market Line. This is the (linear) relationship between the expected return of a security and its covariance with the market's returns. A stock's beta (covariance between stock and market/market variance) is, under this theory, the sole determinant of its expected return.

Although all three of these theories only hold under assumptions that are violated in practice, nevertheless they form a framework for quantitative analysis which has endured.

---

[22] Markowitz optimisation maths is still widely used, but it is not the only method available.
[23] Microsoft Excel does this very efficiently for us using an add-in called 'Solver'.

The constraints I apply to the first result are that no asset class can have negative allocation (i.e. no borrowing), no asset can have more than 100% of the assets, private equity/alternatives has a maximum allocation of 10%, and neither of the currency overlays uses up any capital (i.e. they do not require any initial capital allocation), nor can they have a combined hedge ratio on international equities of greater than 100%.

The results of running this optimiser are shown in Table 5.6, with maximum portfolio volatilities as shown in the columns (5%–15%). In this case, the optimiser favours international equities over domestic for two reasons:

Table 5.6 Asset allocation from optimiser (active overlay permitted)

% of portfolio	Maximum relative portfolio volatility				
	5.0%	7.5%	10.0%	12.5%	15.0%
Domestic equities	0.0%	1.7%	3.0%	4.8%	0.0%
International equities	26.9%	40.3%	53.6%	70.1%	90.0%
Passive currency overlay	0.0%	0.0%	0.0%	0.0%	0.0%
Bonds	68.4%	50.5%	33.4%	15.1%	0.0%
Private equity/alternatives	4.7%	7.5%	10.0%	10.0%	10.0%
Active overlay	26.9%	40.3%	53.6%	70.1%	73.9%
'Optimised' relative portfolio return	**0.97%**	**1.52%**	**2.03%**	**2.52%**	**2.85%**

(a) The assumption that their volatility is the same (both 16%) hides the fact that the currency-hedged volatility of the international equities is lower than domestic (this is borne out in the historical data in all cases except the US as base currency).
(b) Active currency overlay adds value, but can only be overlaid on international assets under the constraints of this optimiser. Hence the optimiser boosts the proportion of international to catch the overlay added value.

Active overlay is strongly negatively correlated with international, but much less negatively correlated with domestic (as is in fact the case). The strong negative correlation with international is always true – the currency exposure inherent in unhedged international being offset by the 'negative' currency exposure in overlay. Active is preferred in the optimiser over passive because it is almost as negatively correlated with international equities as passive is (about 0.1 less, again borne out in the historical data), but yields value added.

If we do not allow active currency overlay (which might be the case for an investor who is not convinced there is active value added available in the currency markets), and re-run the optimiser with otherwise the same assumptions, we get the results in Table 5.7. This portfolio cannot get more than 2.30% excess return, irrespective of volatility, given the constraints imposed. The 15% volatility column is a volatility constraint that is not biting. The mix between domestic and international equities is therefore random, as is the currency overlay proportion.

We can impose transaction costs on passive hedging, keeping active currency overlay prohibited. For this exercise, I will use passive costs of 0.20% p.a. – a cost level provision that is very generous in my experience (see Chapter 6 for more details). Table 5.8 shows the results. Again, in the 15% volatility column, the volatility constraint is not biting. This means that

Table 5.7   Asset Allocation from optimiser (active overlay prohibited)

	Maximum relative portfolio volatility				
	5.0%	7.5%	10.0%	12.5%	15.0%
Domestic equities	6.3%	12.1%	19.5%	26.5%	22.2%
International equities	18.5%	29.4%	43.2%	56.0%	67.8%
Passive currency overlay	18.5%	29.4%	43.2%	56.0%	1.4%
Bonds	68.1%	48.5%	27.3%	7.5%	0.0%
Private equity/alternatives	7.1%	10.0%	10.0%	10.0%	10.0%
'Optimised' relative portfolio return	**0.85%**	**1.33%**	**1.75%**	**2.15%**	**2.30%**

Table 5.8   Asset Allocation from optimiser (active overlay prohibited, passive costs 0.2%)

	Maximum relative portfolio volatility				
	5.0%	7.5%	10.0%	12.5%	15.0%
Domestic equities	0.0%	16.0%	24.3%	32.3%	71.6%
International equities	21.5%	25.0%	37.7%	49.2%	18.4%
Passive currency overlay	17.0%	20.3%	27.7%	34.7%	0.0%
Bonds	70.4%	49.0%	28.1%	8.5%	0.0%
Private equity/alternatives	8.1%	10.0%	10.0%	10.0%	10.0%
'Optimised' relative portfolio return	**0.80%**	**1.28%**	**1.68%**	**2.06%**	**2.30%**

passive overlay is abandoned, since its risk-reducing appeal (which in this case is its only appeal) is lost. At the lower volatility constraints, the optimised hedge ratio varies between 70% and 81%. This illustrates that even where there is performance drag from passive overlay, the optimiser regards this as a price worth paying to get the benefit of the risk-reducing properties (i.e. negative correlation) of currency overlay.

5.4   IMPLICATIONS OF TRANSACTIONS COSTS

We can extend this analysis on the impact of passive overlay transaction costs. In Chapter 6 we will examine in detail how passive overlay costs arise, in which categories, and estimate their likely averages and ranges. However, the result can be expressed in summary as a performance 'drag' on the passive overlay assumption of zero expected return. Keeping all the other assumptions intact, we can vary the annual costs of passive overlay assumed within the optimiser. In Figure 5.4, I show the result of this exercise for three of the lower portfolio volatilities (5–10% volatility), and graph the hedge ratio versus the cost.

We can see from this graph that the optimiser remains keen to include a proportion of passive overlay even at very high annual cost drags. How can the optimiser want to include an overlay (which does not displace any other asset class) if it is such a drag on performance? In summary, the optimiser seeks to maximise return subject to the portfolio risk constraint (and any other

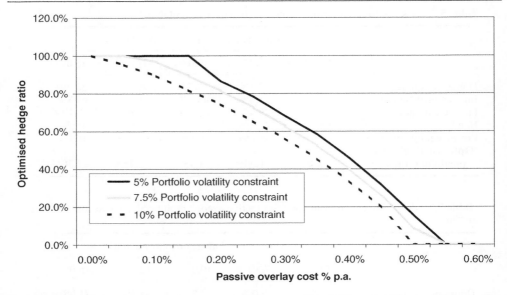

Figure 5.4   Optimised hedge ratio versus passive costs (5%, 7.5% and 10% portfolio volatility constraints)

constraints we have imposed). Equities are the core strategic 'added value' asset, and the optimiser will seek to add these with as little additional risk as possible. Hedged international equities are lower risk than domestic equities, and even though (with positive passive costs) hedged international equities will have lower return than domestic equities, they nevertheless remain the most efficient way of adding expected return within the constraints.

Portfolios with lower volatility constraints will pay a higher return premium than those with higher volatility constraints, hence the higher passive costs the portfolio will tolerate before the passive overlay is reduced. Once the volatility constraint is eliminated (as is the case with the 15% volatility portfolio), passive overlay becomes irrelevant, and will not be included in the optimiser even if the passive costs are zero. (Strictly speaking, the optimiser is indifferent to overlay under these conditions, so the hedge ratio is indeterminate.)

5.4.1   Expected portfolio added value from passive hedging

While the curve in Figure 5.4 looks quite smooth and well-defined, at high levels of overlay cost, and low volatility constraints, the hedge ratio becomes relatively immaterial, that is it does not affect expected portfolio returns very much. Similarly with high volatility constraints – in this case passive overlay will be ignored.

How can we get a feel for the improvement in a portfolio's return given a fixed level of portfolio risk? And how does changing that fixed level affect the expected value added? In Figure 5.5, I have run the optimiser at each risk level to show the difference in expected annual portfolio return of optimally hedged versus unhedged. I assume a passive cost of 0.1% p.a. – a level of passive costs which has been achieved in practice.

The 'random' variations in the curve are the result of the 'coarse' nature of the optimisation, and the small numbers involved. While the absolute values of the value added might appear

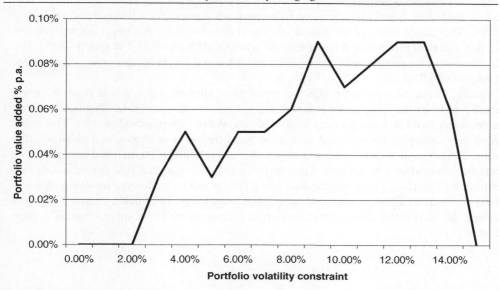

Figure 5.5 Optimum portfolio value added from passive hedging (0.1% p.a. hedging costs, 2% equity risk premium)

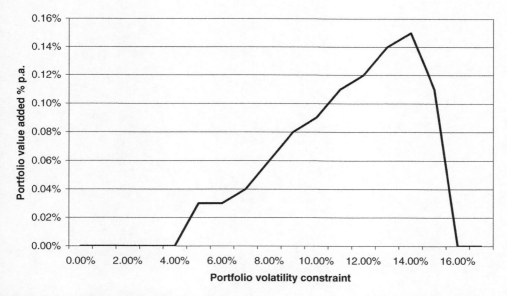

Figure 5.6 Optimum portfolio value added from including international (2% equity risk premium, equal volatilities for domestic and international equities)

quite small, nevertheless we are measuring the effect of passive hedging at portfolio level, while the proportion of the portfolio that overlay covers (i.e. international equities) might be, say, in the high 30%s. This means that a passive overlay that costs 0.1% p.a. might generate a gross 0.30% or so in effective value added through risk reduction and asset reallocation. Where do I get the 0.30% from? The allocation to international equities for a 10% portfolio volatility is 40%. The 'added value' of the passive overlay is therefore 2.5 times larger when expressed as a percentage of international rather than the whole portfolio (=0.23% = 0.09%/40%). The passive overlay has an (assumed) cost associated with it of 0.1%, hence the gross 'value added' of passive of 0.33%.

Finally, to put in context the effect of other asset allocation changes at portfolio level, Figure 5.6 shows the value added from releasing a 'no-international' rule. That is, I have run the optimiser (with no overlay of any kind) with and without international equities. The 'value added' from allowing international equities in the optimiser is as shown, and illustrates that a quite fundamental asset allocation change – that of prohibiting international equities in the portfolio – only affects the optimised returns by up to 0.15% p.a. At a 10% portfolio volatility restriction (a 'normal' risk portfolio with some 28% bonds), disallowing passive hedging is as expensive as disallowing international equities completely. This makes passive hedging a strategic decision in the same order of magnitude of importance as the international allocation decision.

6

Passive Currency Overlay

In the preceding chapter we saw that passive currency overlay produces a stream of returns (which I have called 'contribution from hedging'). We saw that this stream is always negatively correlated with international equities, has an expected return of zero, and does not employ any capital (i.e. does not use up any asset allocation in the 100% available). This chapter investigates exactly how this stream of returns is generated, and the consequences of passive hedging on the structure and returns on the portfolio.

6.1 MECHANICS

Let us start with the mechanics of passive hedging. A fund with a base currency of US dollars has an international portfolio invested abroad. For the purposes of this example (Table 6.1) it does not matter whether the assets are equities, fixed income or any other asset capable of regular valuation. Suppose the asset mix is as shown. This is a not untypical mix of assets

Table 6.1 Example asset mix

Country/currency bloc	Asset value (foreign currency)	Spot rate (foreign currency per dollar)	Asset value (USD)	Proportion of international
UK	20.00	0.6250	32.00	32.0%
Japan	24.00	120.00	20.00	20.0%
Euro	35.00	1.0000	35.00	35.0%
Switzerland	7.00	1.4000	5.00	5.0%
Other			8.00	8.0%
Total			**100.00**	**100.0%**

from a currency perspective. What does an overlay (or investment) manager do when asked to provide, say, a 100% passive hedge for this portfolio?

Let us suppose that the benchmark is one month, and that the fund is seeking a 25 bp p.a. tracking error limit. This will prompt a number of decisions from the overlay manager. The detailed reasoning behind these decisions need not be the concern of the reader yet. We will discuss these in more detail later, and in Chapter 7. A summary list of decisions is shown in Table 6.2. I will take each of these in turn, grouping related decisions where relevant.

6.1.1 Original maturity of forward contracts

This is one of the key decisions to be taken. The default position of an overlay manager is to use a maturity of contracts that matches the benchmark, since otherwise tracking error between the actual portfolio and the benchmark will be created for no expected return. Most published hedged benchmarks use one-month original maturity contracts, and so one-month contracts in the portfolio are common. Maturities of less than one month are rare.

Table 6.2 Passive overlay decision list

Decision to be made	Manager's choice
Original maturity of forward contracts	1 month
Frequency of cash flows	Monthly
Currencies to be hedged	GBP, JPY, EUR, CHF, AUD, SEK, HKD
Benchmark or actual asset weights to be hedged?	Benchmark
Denominator of 'contribution from hedging'	All international assets
Frequency of asset valuation	Monthly
Frequency of rebalancing	Monthly
Rebalancing buffer (Y/N? Size)	Yes – 1% of total overlay size
Delay in rebalancing	4 working days
Instantaneous absolute hedge ratio limitation?	No
Valuation rates	Reuters/WM London Close

As an aside, why do I use the expression 'original maturity'. The answer is because hedging contracts are only one-month maturity on the day they are initiated. They naturally decline in maturity with the passage of the month, and their average maturity is therefore two weeks.

What might lead an overlay manager to adopt a contract maturity different from the benchmark maturity? There are several possible reasons:

1. He may determine that the overlay transactions costs over time are lower with an original maturity other than one month.
2. One-month maturities will produce cash flows of at least once a month – this may be too frequent for the fund, and/or create too much short-term volatility of cash flows.
3. If the benchmark maturity is long (which is not the case in this example), the overlay manager may choose to hedge at shorter maturities to get better liquidity. (It could be argued that liquidity is a subset of a costs argument, but on occasion it may not directly be costs but ability to execute that is the key.)

6.1.2 Frequency of cash flows

It may appear at first glance that this is the same as the first question. However, forward contracts do not necessarily have the same 'roll-over' dates – they could be staggered for smaller 'tranches' of each currency, or by currency. In the above example, there could be maturities every week or every fortnight, creating twice or four times as many cash flows. This choice may be occasioned by practical needs (resources required to undertake roll-over deals), by risk-reduction arguments (reducing the impact of one roll-over price), or by a desire to reduce or smooth the impact of cash flows.

6.1.3 Currencies to be hedged

This is always an awkward problem whose solution is always a compromise. Almost all international portfolios have a small proportion of their assets held in currencies that are not easily or cheaply hedgeable, or indeed not hedgeable at all (see Box 6.2). In our sample portfolio, we are (typically) given an 'other' category which is 8% of the portfolio by

Box 6.1   Tracking Error

Currency overlay managers, like all active managers, can be measured according to relative performance versus a benchmark return. If actual portfolio returns and benchmark returns are recorded (say monthly), the difference between the two series will produce a monthly series of relative returns. These relative returns will have measurable characteristics – a standard deviation (or relative volatility) and average return. When annualised, the standard deviation is called 'tracking error' and the average return is the manager's value added or 'alpha'.

Tracking error is a measure of the deviations of the manager's return from the 'neutral' benchmark position. It is a measure of the actual risk that the manager has taken relative to the benchmark. In overlay mandates, tracking error is often specified in the manager's investment guidelines. This allows the client a further means of checking that the manager is operating his process in the way agreed prior to the start, and at a level of risk that is acceptable to the client.

Currency overlay has some active management styles which are designed to be asymmetric in their return patterns. These styles, especially if they are being implemented effectively, can lead the tracking error to be wider than desired, but only on the upside – i.e. when added value is positive. This has led to alternative tracking error measures (particularly 'downside only' standard deviation) being considered for this type of mandate. Despite the obvious appeal in not penalising a manager when performance is good, nevertheless most tracking error tests have remained as a simple standard deviation.

value. In the example I have assumed that a proportion of this 8% is in Australian dollar and Hong Kong dollar, but that there are a number of other currencies (Taiwanese dollar, Korean won, Malaysian ringgitt to name a few) which are not practicably hedgeable at reasonable cost. What to do with these currencies, when the benchmark is hedged?

It is worth examining the detail of the construction of the benchmark before making a decision, but generally it is simply not cost-effective to include these and similar currencies in a hedging programme.

Most overlay managers will adopt a pragmatic stance towards this question. They may proxy hedge (see Box 6.3) if the correlations with another currency are thought good enough (e.g. proxy hedge the Hong Kong dollar with the US dollar for a UK, euro or Japanese base currency), but generally they will simply leave the exposure unhedged. If a manager leaves a currency unhedged, it will create an unrewarded tracking error versus the benchmark. However, it is reasonably arguable that the benchmark is uninvestible if the minor currencies, assumed by the benchmark to be investible, in fact are not.

This leads many managers to request that their benchmark only include hedgeable currencies, and that benchmark performance is calculated only including these currencies, and using only assets invested in hedgeable currencies as the denominator. This eliminates spurious tracking error, but it also means that the benchmark becomes custom, rather than published. Many fund clients find this awkward, and will resist pressure to adopt this route. In practice, my experience is that most mainstream (pension fund) portfolios have less than 10% of their assets invested in unhedgeable currencies. For many it will be less than 5%. This means that the materiality of this question can be quite small in relation to other sources of tracking error and other issues.

Box 6.2   Tradeable currency

In the context of currency overlay, a tradeable currency is a matter of opinion, rather than fact. The key requirement for a currency overlay manager is to deal in currencies which do not undermine the rationale for the overlay. This essentially means dealing at low transaction costs.

The key criteria for a currency to be tradeable could therefore be characterised as follows:

- No exchange controls preventing purchase or sale
- A well-developed spot market
- A well-developed forward market
- Adequate liquidity (ability to trade at least $10m a time)
- Acceptable bid/offer spreads (say <0.20% for outright forwards in active overlay; <0.50% for outright forwards in passive overlay)

One further criterion is sometimes applied to very weak/high interest rate currencies in passive overlay. That is, the interest differential with the home currency has to be ≤10% for the currency to be 'tradeable'. Very high levels of anticipated depreciation (which hedging locks in) begin to undermine the rationale for hedging – spot depreciation is not eliminated by such hedging, it is merely delayed.

At 30 September 2002, the following 19 currencies satisfied the active and passive criteria respectively, and 152 currencies did not:

Active		Passive
Hong Kong dollar	UAE dirham	Czech koruna
Euro	Danish krone	Mexican nuevo peso
Japanese yen	Norwegian krone	Polish zloty
British pound	Swedish krona	Slovak koruna
Swiss franc	Australian dollar	
Singapore dollar	New Zealand dollar	
Canadian dollar	Thai baht	
US dollar		

6.1.4   Benchmark or actual asset weights to be hedged?

This is an interesting and somewhat philosophical question. Let me give an example. Suppose the sample portfolio above is the benchmark weights at a particular period, and that the active equity manager is overweight euro by 5% of the portfolio (i.e. 40% allocation vs. benchmark 35%), and underweight Japan (i.e. 15% vs. benchmark 20%).

If the equity manager has an unhedged benchmark (as would be common if the passive hedging is separately executed by an overlay manager), then:

(a) If the currency overlay manager hedges the benchmark weights, and the equity manager is not permitted to currency hedge, all equity bets will include a currency bet which will be the responsibility of the equity manager. This nails responsibility for performance onto those who will have to account for it, but limits the equity manager's freedom to bet on the euro equity market without betting on the euro.

Box 6.3   Proxy hedge

Proxy hedging is the practice of using one currency to hedge a different currency's exposure. Let me give an example. Suppose a euro-based fund has an exposure to the Taiwan dollar. The Taiwan dollar is not a hedgeable currency, but the fund may wish to go some way towards reducing the currency volatility of its exposure to Taiwan. Taiwan has had a series of exchange rate arrangements, and for most of the relevant history it has closely tracked the US dollar. The Taiwanese government exerts strong control over the exchange rate via a structural surplus and very large foreign currency reserves.

The following is a graph of spot exchange rates of the Taiwan dollar (TWD) versus the USD and the euro (pre-1999, rebased Deutschmark):

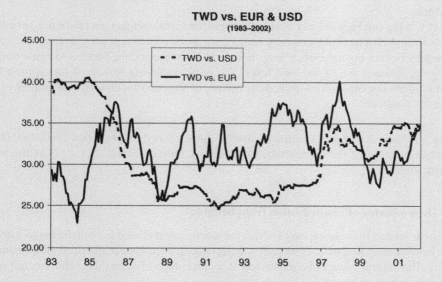

In the short-term, the TWD is much more volatile against the euro than against the dollar. Its annualised volatility against the euro is 12.3%, versus 5.5% against the dollar. From a euro perspective, the dollar accounts for some 79% of the variance of the TWD versus the euro, and using the US dollar as a proxy currency to hedge the Taiwanese dollar will reduce the volatility associated with currency risk to around 5.5%.

Proxy hedging was very common for USD and GBP-based investors in Europe pre-euro. The Deutschmark and the French franc were commonly used as representatives of 'strong' and 'weak' European currencies, respectively. However, the advent of the euro has eliminated the need for European proxy hedging of this nature. Unhedgeable Pacific Rim, Eastern European and Latin American currencies now constitute the bulk of the currencies substituted by proxy currencies for hedging purposes.

(b) If the currency overlay manager hedges the benchmark weights, and the equity manager is also allowed to tactically currency hedge back to the benchmark weights (i.e. if he wants an equity bet but not a currency bet), then equity bets do not automatically include a currency bet. This gives the equity manager more freedom, but also allows the equity manager to make tactical currency decisions separately from equity decisions. However, the fund client may feel this gives a specialist currency decision to the wrong manager.

(c) If the currency overlay manager hedges the actual weights, and the equity manager is told this, and not permitted to currency hedge, the equity manager needs ideally to have his performance adjusted for the performance of the tactical hedges (i.e. the difference between the benchmark weight hedge and the actual weight hedge), otherwise he will be held responsible for currency bets (in this case overweight euro/underweight yen) which are not actually taking place (because the currency overlay manager has neutralised them), and which have been excluded from the responsibility of the equity manager. This is probably too complicated in practice. If the equity manager does not have his performance adjusted for the tactical currency hedges, there is a misalignment of responsibilities and powers.

(d) Finally, if the currency overlay manager hedges the actual weights, and the equity manager is also allowed to tactically currency hedge back to the benchmark weights (i.e. if he wants an equity bet but not a currency bet), then there is a real conflict. This could cause double hedging, creating risk at the fund level. The only redeeming feature of this approach is that it aligns responsibility for the performance of the equity manager with control of his hedging contracts.

Of these alternatives, (b) gives partial control of currency hedging to a non-specialist, (c) is unattractive because of the complexity, (d) is fatally flawed, which leaves (a) as the most appealing route.

6.1.5 Denominator of 'contribution from hedging'

This issue is related to the question of which currencies are included in both the passive hedge and the benchmark. 'Returns', expressed as percentages, are the meat and drink of investment reporting. But returns have to be expressed as a percentage of something, and this question asks: 'a percentage of what?'

If the answer is 'all international equities', then the 'contribution from hedging' will be diluted by the inclusion of assets in currencies which are not being hedged in the denominator of the calculation. If the answer is 'hedgeable currencies only', then the resulting percentage returns will not be comparable with any published benchmark, nor will the 'contribution from hedging' be able to be added to anything other than the returns of the hedgeable currency assets.

6.1.6 Frequency of asset valuation

This is important only because the rebalancing frequency cannot be higher than the underlying asset valuation frequency. In most institutional asset management environments, valuation frequency is monthly. In pooled vehicles, the frequency can be higher, often daily. Asset valuation is usually provided to overlay managers by the (global) custodian (if there is one) or by the equity manager. The speed of valuation, and its consolidation into the custodian's database, is important for the mechanics of rebalancing (see below).

6.2   REBALANCING

Rebalancing is the process by which the amount of currency exposure hedged is adjusted to take account of subsequent changes in the value of the underlying currencies in that currency. Rebalancing in passive overlay, unlike rebalancing in asset allocation, is not a 'strategic' decision. Let me explain.

Suppose a fund has determined a strategic asset allocation process of, say, 60% equities and 40% bonds. Let us also suppose that equities outperform bonds over a particular period, so that the fund proportions change to 65:35. The design of the process by which the proportions are rebalanced back to 60:40 is of strategic importance, and will have a material impact on the performance of the fund. Asset rebalancing limits the compounding, or 'convexity' (see Box 5.1), in a portfolio by selling highly performing assets, and buying lower performing assets with the proceeds. At the asset allocation level, it is a form of 'value' investing (i.e. selling 'expensive' stocks and buying 'cheap' ones). Rebalancing in passive currency overlay, however, does not have this effect, nor the same cause. The engine of currency overlay rebalancing is the performance of the underlying asset expressed in the foreign currency, not the performance of the foreign currency (and therefore the overlay). We can conduct a worked example on the basis of the portfolio shown above (which is a USD base). Table 6.3 takes the original portfolio asset mix (from Table 6.1) and shows an example of its development over time.

Table 6.3   UK asset valuations over time

UK assets (one period = one month)	Asset value (£)	Spot rate (foreign currency per dollar)	Asset value (USD)
End period 0	20.00	0.6250	32.00
End period 1	22.00	0.6250	35.20
End period 2	22.00	0.6452	34.10
End period 3	19.00	0.6061	31.35

Suppose overlay starts at the end of period 0, with (as mentioned above) a hedge ratio of 100%. The first thing to note is that consideration of the passive hedge is an individual currency-specific question, and that (with the exception of any proxy hedging) each currency's hedging is entirely independent of the others'.

So, concentrating on the pound sterling hedge, at the end of period 0, the overlay manager will sell £20m versus dollars one-month forward. I have not included the forward rate in Table 6.3, as it is not relevant to this discussion. If the rebalancing frequency is monthly, then at the end of period (month) 1, the overlay manager will increase the hedge from £20m to £22m because the underlying asset has increased from £20m to £22m. The calculation is always performed with the amount of the foreign currency (in this case pounds sterling) as the determinant of the size of the forward contract, and any profits or losses that might arise on the forward contract when it is closed will be paid or received in the home currency (in this case US dollars). Attempting to calculate the size of the hedge required by reference to dollar amounts (rather than foreign currency amounts) creates a series of complexities which are completely avoided if we always use the foreign currency amount as the size determinant. Note that between period 0 and period 1, the spot exchange rate did not move. In the next period, we have the opposite effect – the spot rate moves, but the asset value in sterling does not. In this case, at the end of period 2, no rebalancing is necessary. The hedge remains at £22m, despite the movement of the spot rate. Note that the dollar valuation of the sterling asset has gone down in period 2 – this is not relevant for rebalancing, and indeed the hedge will have thrown up a profit to offset this loss. Finally, at the end of period 3, the asset valuation has fallen to £19m. This would require a reduction in the hedge to this amount.

What is clear from this example is that strong performance from an asset class is not 'penalised' (as it would be in a conventional asset rebalancing exercise) by a sale of the stronger performing asset and a purchase of the weaker performing asset. At the end of period 1, when the UK asset is strong in sterling terms, it is not the asset that is sold, it is an increased amount of currency. The currency has been neither strong nor weak in period 1. In period 2, the dollar is strong (vs. the pound), and the overlay will have produced a profit to offset the loss of dollar value resulting from this, but because the asset value of the UK asset has not changed in sterling terms, the size of the currency hedge is left unchanged at the end of period 2. This illustrates the mechanics of rebalancing, and shows that it does not act as an inhibitor of 'convexity'.

6.2.1 Frequency of rebalancing

One of the key decisions to be made is the frequency of rebalancing. There are competing pressures (for both higher and lower frequency), which makes the question a pragmatic one. The first point to note (as made in Chapter 3) is that the value of foreign assets expressed in dollar terms is a multiplicative relationship between the asset and the spot foreign currency, and also between the asset returns and the spot foreign currency returns. Simply put, this means that a 10% increase in both the value of an asset in foreign currency terms, and a 10% increase in the foreign currency spot, will mean a 21% rise in the asset value in dollar terms, not a 20% rise.

For currency overlay to replicate (and therefore fully neutralise) this multiplicative relationship, the size of the passive hedge must be continuously adjusted. 'Continuous adjustment' means just that – the adjustment has to happen in infinitesimal size, infinitely frequently. If there were a 'no-cost' trading environment, then in theory (although not in practice, since how does one trade infinitely frequently?) it would be possible to completely neutralise all the impact from currency exposure. However, the trading environment required for this is the 'classical market assumptions' – exactly the same behaviour as is assumed in the Black–Scholes model and in Chapter 3. I have taken some time and effort to argue that these assumptions must always be materially violated in practice. Human beings, and indeed computers, respond and operate in discrete time, not in continuous time. If the 'ideal' is to be approached, it will be an approximation in which rebalancing takes place at very high frequency.

In passive hedging in the real world, approaching the ideal (continuous rebalancing) has to be weighed up against the transaction and other costs associated with high-frequency transactions. This calculation is heavily influenced by the observation that rebalancing is created by the movement of underlying assets, not the movement of currency, and so the strong presumption is that higher frequency adjustment will not improve (or reduce) returns, only marginally reduce the residual currency error inherent in the asset valuation.

There is a further, and important, point. A manager is generally required to minimise tracking error versus the benchmark, other things being equal. As we shall see below, any good benchmark must have a transparent calculation methodology, and this will include a discrete rebalancing period (since continuous rebalancing is not replicable and uninvestible). If the benchmark has a rebalancing period of t, what incentive is there for a manager to deviate from that, except on grounds of cost? Certainly there is no incentive to attempt higher frequency rebalancing than the benchmark; there may be some incentive to adopt a lower frequency if the costs of dealing are material.

Can we make some estimate of rebalancing costs at different frequencies? If we assume a lognormal random walk distribution for (equity) asset returns with 16.3% annual volatility[1] (and remember it is the asset volatility, not the currency volatility, which is the 'generator'), and assume a 6.5 bp bid/offer spread (the average of the 1m outright spreads from Table 3.3), we can estimate the annual cost of rebalancing at each frequency using a statistical property (not derived here) that the mean absolute outcome of a normal distribution with $SD = x$ is $0.796x$.[2] (This means that (speaking loosely and not adjusting for the log element) a 10% annualised vols return series has an average absolute annual movement of $10\% \times 0.796 = 8.0\%$.) Since mean absolute movements are the determinant of rebalancing costs, and the properties of lognormal random walk returns allow us to calculate these for any horizon, we can produce an (amusing) theoretical table (Table 6.4).

Table 6.4   Rebalancing costs at various frequencies

Frequency of rebalancing	Average size of deal (% of exposure)	No. deals per year	Total cost p.a. (bp)
1/1000000th sec	0.0000025%	2.26368E + 13	1 858 613
1/1000th sec	0.00008%	22 636 800 000	58 774
1/100th sec	0.00025%	2 263 680 000	18 586
1 sec	0.003%	22 636 800	1858
1 min	0.020%	377 280	239
1 hr	0.152%	6288	31
6 hr	0.37%	1048	12.6
1 day	0.75%	262	6.3
2 days	1.06%	131	4.49
1 week	1.68%	52	2.84
2 weeks	2.39%	26	2.02
1 month	3.5%	12	1.38
3 months	6.2%	4	0.81
6 months	8.9%	2	0.58
1 year	12.8%	1	0.42

This tells us that rebalancing frequencies of anything less frequent than 1 day are manageable if measured purely in terms of annual transactions costs. If we try to go close to the theoretical continuous-time model, the costs explode out of control.

In practice, rebalancing is unlikely to be less frequent than once a month, and is virtually certain to be no more frequent than once a day, since virtually no benchmark will have higher than daily frequency. This puts the cost range between 0.7 and 3.2 bp p.a. on the assumptions.

---

[1] The 22-year historical hedged average of four: US, UK, Germany, Japan – a close approximation to the local return vols.
[2] Brenner & Subrahmanyam, *Financial Analysts Journal* **45** (Sep/Oct 1988).

6.2.2   Rebalancing buffer (Y/N? size)

For practical management, rather than the construction of a benchmark, it is possible, and may be desirable, to insert a buffer into the rebalancing decision. Any transaction, however small, attracts a fixed cost. This will consist, at the very least, of the labour involved in agreeing the deal and the confirmation process. This makes very small deals increasingly expensive, even if that expense is not necessarily visible.

To avoid very small deals, a buffer (expressed either as a percentage of the particular currency exposure concerned, or as a percentage of the total currency programme) will reduce the volume of transactions, and on average increase their size.

We can rewrite Table 6.4, inserting a buffer of, say, 1% of the particular currency involved, and the results are given in Table 6.5. We can play with these variables endlessly; the maths for buffers gets hard very quickly – Table 6.5 was calculated using Monte Carlo analysis. However, it is clear that buffers are useful where the rebalancing frequency is potentially very high.

Table 6.5   Rebalancing costs with buffer

Frequency of rebalancing	Average size of deal (% of exposure)	No. deals per year	Total cost p.a. (bp) with buffer	Total cost p.a. (bp) without buffer (from Table 6.4)
1hr	1.113%	177.6	6.43	31
6 hr	1.266%	132.2	5.44	12.6
1 day	1.548%	86.2	4.33	6.3
2 days	1.786%	62.0	3.60	4.49
1 week	2.389%	33.3	2.58	2.84
2 weeks	3.043%	19.1	1.88	2.02
1 month	4.155%	9.8	**1.32**	1.38
3 months	6.720%	3.6	0.78	0.81
6 months	9.236%	1.8	0.55	0.58
1 year	12.702%	0.9	0.39	0.42

Finally, we can add in a *de minimus* fixed cost per deal. I have used $8.33 per deal (based on 10 min labour at $50/hour). Table 6.6 shows the effect of this on a $10m single currency exposure (i.e. quite small). Assumptions are otherwise unchanged.

Table 6.6   Rebalancing with a fixed cost per deal

Frequency of rebalancing	Total cost p.a. (bp) (inc. fixed deal cost) with buffer	Total cost p.a. (bp) (inc. fixed deal cost) without buffer
1 hr	7.9	83.4
6 hours	6.54	21.4
1 day	5.05	8.5
2 days	4.11	5.59
1 week	2.86	3.27
2 weeks	2.04	2.23
1 month	1.40	1.48
3 months	0.81	0.84
6 months	0.57	0.59
1 year	0.40	0.42

6.2.3   Buffer – 'percentage of what?'

Finally, in this section, the denominator of the buffer can be the total underlying currency exposure of the overlay programme rather than the individual currency exposure. This would be logical where there is a fixed cost per deal, since it equalises the importance of each deal to the fund – even if the buffer could be 10% of a very small currency, or 1% of a large currency.

Just to elaborate on this point. A rebalancing buffer can be calculated on each individual currency, and expressed as a percentage of the currency exposure related to that currency alone. This is a common approach, that has the merit of making each currency's hedge portfolio behaviour independent from each other currency.

But there is a significant drawback to this approach. A European (euro-based) fund might have $100m in US dollars, and $1m in Swedish krone, both of which it is hedging passively. This means that the size of the buffer might be $10 000 in SEK, but $1m in USD, and that deals in SEK are a hundred times less material than deals in US dollars. This creates an execution inefficiency – a common effort (dealing time, back office usage) has a hundred times the importance when applied to the US dollar compared to the Swedish krone.

The solution is to base the buffer on a common denominator – say the total currency exposure. Under this example the buffer might be 0.25% – and let us suppose the total currency exposure overlaid is $250m. This would mean that whenever there was a US dollar exposure change of greater than $0.625m (0.2% × $250m), the amount of the US dollar hedge would be altered to re-establish the hedge ratio back to benchmark. This equates to 0.625% of the dollar exposure, so this is a smaller buffer for the dollar portfolio. However, if the same criterion ($0.625m exposure change) is applied to the SEK exposure, this represents 62.5% of the Swedish exposure. This could mean in theory that the SEK exposure could fall by 60% from $1m to $0.4m, and no action would be taken. A 100% SEK hedge ratio could become a $1m/$0.4m = 250% hedge ratio.

Many investors would find it hard to swallow a hedge ratio at such variance with the benchmark, and some operate in regulatory regimes where hedge ratios over 100% are not permitted. However under this regime, each deal will have the same economic impact on the overall portfolio, and virtually the same impact on tracking error.

Some investors will adopt a combination of the two denominators, or impose a minimum deal size on the single-currency denominator to eliminate spurious dealing. These choices are a matter of expediency rather than of great strategic importance.

6.2.4   Delay in rebalancing

In an ideal world, there would be no delay between the valuation of the underlying international assets, and the execution of hedging contracts to rebalance the hedging according to the guidelines agreed. In particular, any benchmark calculation will assume that there is no delay, and therefore delays will appear as a source of tracking error.

In practice, however, an overlay manager will need to put in place, and agree with the client, a timetable for this process. This will give the manager a framework within which to operate, and the client confidence that the rebalancing process is timely and effective. A typical timetable might go as follows for a monthly rebalancing procedure:

Last business day of month (LBDM):	Date for asset prices to be collected by custodian
LBDM + 3:	All prices required are captured by custodian

LBDM + 5:   Custodian produces asset valuation
LBDM + 6:   Overlay manager receives asset valuation
LBDM + 7:   Overlay manager conducts rebalancing trades

While in theory the price collection, capture and valuation could be virtually instantaneous, in practice new assets, erroneous prices, questionable prices, mistakes in data entry and so on make the valuation process neither automatic nor particularly timely. In the above example, an overlay manager would plan to rebalance on LBDM + 7, and this will build in a small, but irreducible tracking error versus benchmark. We can quantify the tracking error that delays in rebalancing will create, and this is done in Section 7.6.

6.2.5   Valuation rates

The decision of which valuation rates to use is a matter of convenience and convention. Unlike other markets, where prices are of varying quality and liquidity, there is rarely any issue over the liquidity or tradeability of prices in the major foreign exchange markets. A commercial service provider – WM/Reuters – now provides a wide range of daily prices, spot and forward, for London closing prices, which are defined as 4pm London time. These have very quickly become the market standard in the investment industry, and are now the valuation rates of choice for custodians, investment managers and currency overlay managers. They are available in mid-price form (which is the arithmetic average of the bid and offer prices), and in bid and offer form. There is a range of forward horizons up to one-year maturity to allow the accurate interpolation of rates for intermediate forward contracts. Most custodians use mid-exchange rates in conjuction with mid securities prices for their valuations of pension fund and investment trust portfolios, and while these are not strictly realisable values, the very narrow bid/offer spreads make this approximation acceptable. For the valuation of unit trusts, bid and offer exchange rates are normally used in conjuction with bid and offer securities' price in an effort to obtain more exact Net Asset Values for dealing in the units.

6.3   CASH FLOW

All currency hedging and overlay produces cash flow. This is the settlement, in cash, of the profits and losses of the forward FX contracts that comprise the overlay or hedge. Cash flow arises at the maturity of forward contracts.

Let us first examine the likely scale and pattern of cash arising from the model portfolio above. Figure 6.1 shows the monthly cash flows for a market-cap-weighted EAFE portfolio over the past 20 years: the asset weights shown in the model portfolio are quite close to market cap weights, and rather than assuming fixed weights, I have assumed these have changed in line with asset valuations over history.

The first thing to notice about Figure 6.1 is how large the monthly cash flows are: the average absolute monthly value is 2.06%. Figure 6.2 shows the cumulative annual rolling cash flow; it illustrates the scale of the cumulative cash flow – the average absolute annual rolling average annual cash flow is 8.8%.

Cash flow is an inevitable concomitant of currency hedging or overlay. Changing the original maturity of the hedging contracts can change (and delay/advance) the cash flow, but the cumulative cash flow over time will be very similar irrespective of the maturity of the

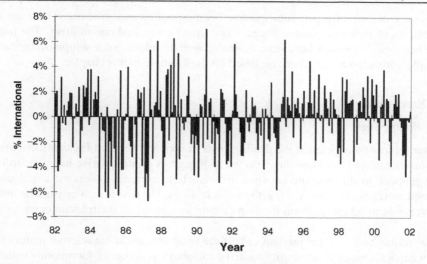

Figure 6.1 Passive hedging monthly cash flow (USD base, EAFE weights, Sep 82–Sep 02, 100% hedge ratio)

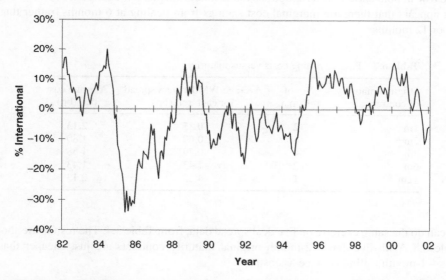

Figure 6.2 Passive hedging 1-year cumulative cash flow (USD base, EAFE weights, Sep 82–Sep 02, 100% hedge ratio)

contracts. It is, after all, the cumulative cash flow from hedging contracts which form one of the key contributors to the volatility-reducing properties of hedging/overlay – the other being the marked-to-market valuation of the unmatured forward contracts.

6.4   COSTS

The costs of passive hedging are a key determinant of the strategic decision of whether to hedge international assets or not. It is therefore important that we know, or can calculate, what the expected costs are of a particular passive hedging policy and structure. There are three main elements of cost in a passive hedge – two direct costs, and one indirect. The indirect costs are less straightforward, but can be estimated with the additional assumptions below. The assumptions for the costs are otherwise based on the example in this chapter.

6.4.1   Direct costs

6.4.1.1   Rolling costs

In Chapter 3 I looked in detail at the dealing costs of spot and forward FX contracts. We can use this information to calculate the expected rolling costs of any passive hedging structure. I do not propose to differentiate between different base currency investors: I will use the unweighted averages of dealing costs in these calculations. The reader with a particular investor base currency in mind can perform his own calculations based on the relevant currency pairs only.

Annual rolling costs are the product of half the swap spreads at the relevant maturity, and the frequency with which that maturity has to be rolled in a year (i.e. 12 for monthly maturity). Using the WM/Reuters averages from Table 3.3, the rolling costs can be deduced (see Table 6.7; the row in bold shows the assumptions made in this chapter's model portfolio). From this data, it appears that there are marginal cost savings from dealing at 6 months, rather than 1 month or 12 months.

Table 6.7   Passive rolling costs versus maturity

Original maturity of contract	No. of rolls p.a.	Average WM/Reuters spread for each roll (bp)	Average cost p.a. (bp)
1m	**12**	**0.35**	**2.13**
2m	6	0.60	1.80
3m	4	0.79	1.58
6m	2	1.43	1.43
12m	1	4.25	2.13

We can do the same exercise on live deal spread data, from Table 3.4. The results are shown in Table 6.8. With live data, 12-month original maturity contracts are just cheaper than 6 months – 1-month rolling is twice as costly.

Table 6.8   Passive rolling costs (live spreads)

Original maturity of contract	No. of rolls p.a.	Average live spread for each roll (bp)	Average cost (bp) p.a.
1m	**12**	**0.46**	**2.77**
2m	6	0.68	2.03
3m	4	0.81	1.61
6m	2	1.54	1.54
12m	1	2.86	1.43

6.4.1.2   Rebalancing costs

Rebalancing, as discussed above, is the process by which the amount of currency hedged is adjusted to remain in line with the valuation of the underlying assets. It can be conducted at any frequency, independently of the original maturity of the hedging contracts.

Rebalancing requires outright deals, i.e. spot and forward, to increase or reduce the hedge in line with the new asset values. Table 6.9 is a cut-down version of Table 6.5, showing the effect of the frequency of rebalancing on costs. The WM/Reuters cost column shown is the 'with buffer' column in Table 6.5. I have also added a cost column which uses the live deal data rather than the WM/Reuters data, to illustrate the cost savings possible by competitive quoting. Because the model portfolio in this chapter is one-month maturity contracts, I have assumed that deals are conducted at one-month outright spreads.

Table 6.9   Rebalancing costs-WM/Reuters vs live spreads

Frequency of rebalancing	Total cost p.a. (bp) WM/Reuters	Total cost p.a. (bp) live deals
1 day	4.33	2.20
2 days	3.60	1.83
1 week	2.58	1.31
2 weeks	1.88	0.96
1 month	**1.32**	0.67
3 months	0.78	0.40
6 months	0.55	0.28
1 year	0.39	0.20

6.4.2   Indirect costs

There are some possible indirect costs associated with passive overlay. There is one – cash flow management – which has the potential to be high, higher than the costs shown in Section 6.4.1. There is a second – overlay manager fees – which although apparently transparent, may in some circumstances generate opaque costs (and income for the manager/manager's bank) from the bid/offer spreads in the FX contract pricing.

6.4.2.1   Cash flow management

As we have seen in Section 6.3, passive hedging produces cash flow. This is not, of itself, a source of cost, but the consequential management of the cash can be. The management of cash flow is not directly the responsibility of the currency overlay manager, but the policies adopted by the client can materially affect the costs they suffer. The key requirement is the minimisation of transactions in underlying securities.

We can categorise (Table 6.10) the range of policies from most to least potentially costly. Option D is costless if it results in no changes in either asset allocation or any securities transactions. Option C will be very low cost if properly structured. The cost of option B depends on the size of the cash buffer. Finally, we can cost option A as follows:

$$\text{Annual cost}\% = \text{Average cash flow per maturity} \times \text{Number of maturities} \times \text{Underlying security transaction costs}$$

Table 6.10 Cash from management choices

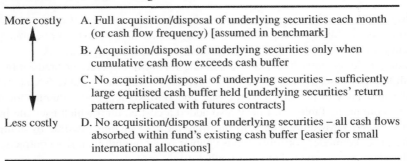

More costly   A. Full acquisition/disposal of underlying securities each month
                  (or cash flow frequency) [assumed in benchmark]

               B. Acquisition/disposal of underlying securities only when
                  cumulative cash flow exceeds cash buffer

               C. No acquisition/disposal of underlying securities – sufficiently
                  large equitised cash buffer held [underlying securities' return
                  pattern replicated with futures contracts]

Less costly   D. No acquisition/disposal of underlying securities – all cash flows
                  absorbed within fund's existing cash buffer [easier for small
                  international allocations]

We know the first two values for the model portfolio from the above data. Average transaction costs for securities, however, are notoriously variable. Table 6.11 is a very rough guide (it is expressed in 'round trip terms' (like bid/offer spreads) and so has to be divided by two to get the single transaction cost).

Table 6.11 Estimated asset transaction costs

Security type	Transaction cost range
OECD government bonds	2–15 bp
Lower sovereign + high quality corporate credit	15–50 bp
Large cap OECD equities/lower quality corporate credit	50–80 bp (+50 bp UK)
Small cap OECD equities/large cap emerging	80–200 bp
Other emerging equities, etc.	200+ bp

From this data we can create a similar table (Table 6.12) of the overall expected cost of hedging cash flow management for the top three securities categories using the most costly option A. Again the costs are basis points of the international allocation. For a one-month original maturity passive hedge, the calculation is as follows (values from data given): annual cost $\% = 2.06\% \times 12 \times$ underlying security transaction costs/2.

Table 6.12 Estimate costs from cash flow

Security type	Estimated annual costs from cash flow transaction costs p.a. (bp)
OECD government bonds	0.6
Lower sovereign + high quality corporate credit	3.7
Large cap OECD equities/lower quality corporate credit	9.9

Finally, we can show the effect of adding a cash buffer (option B). The maths is quite complicated, but Figure 6.3 shows the impact of adding a cash buffer with the following rules:

- A cash buffer defined as '$x\%$' (say 2%) will be held initially.
- When it falls to zero through cash outflows, securities disposals will be made to restore the buffer to $x\%$.
- When it rises above $2x\%$, security acquisitions will be made to reduce it to $x\%$.
- The acquisition and disposal rules are therefore symmetrical, and a 2% buffer can allow cash to move between 0% and 4% without underlying securities transactions.

Figure 6.3 shows the transactions costs compared with the buffer (expressed as the $x\%$ above) for a buffer size of 0–40%. The base case transaction cost is 9.9 bp – final row of Table 6.12 – i.e. buying and selling large cap equities.

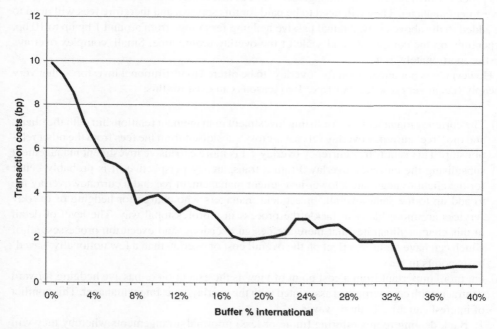

Figure 6.3 Transactions costs from currency hedging cash flow (1982–2002 data, USD base, 100% passive hedge)

The graph shows that there are significant marginal cost savings for a buffer of up to 8% – thereafter the rate of marginal cost reductions begins to reduce.

6.4.3 Summary on costs

From this detail, we can summarise (Table 6.13) the expected total costs of a standard USD-base passive 100% hedging programme expressed as basis points of international exposure hedged. I have assumed that large cap equities are the main security class transacted to provide cash.

Table 6.13 Passive hedging costs p.a. (bp)

Cost category	No cash buffer	4% Buffer
Rolling cost	2.1	2.1
Rebalancing cost	1.3	1.3
Cash flow transactions costs	9.9	6.3
Total	**13.4**	**9.8**

6.5   POSTSCRIPT ON COSTS – CONFLICT OF INTEREST

Finally, it is worth mentioning that currency overlay management, even passive management, is a process which requires the management skill of an overlay firm or the currency team of an investment manager. They will need to be paid for this service, and therefore fees will need to be added to the above costs. Annual passive hedging fees range from around 1 bp up to 10 bp, depending on the complexity and scale of the overlay programme. Small, complex overlays cost proportionately more.

However, it is not uncommon for 'overlay' to be offered to institutional investors either very cheaply (i.e. at very low fees) or free. Two reasons can exist for this:

(a) The currency manager has an existing investment management relationship with the client, and the 'free' currency overlay service is cross-subsidised from the fees from the other relationship. This is not 'free currency overlay', it is more expensive investment management subsidising the currency overlay. From a transparency perspective, it is probably better for the client to negotiate a lower investment management fee and a currency overlay fee to add up to the same overall. Investment managers who charge for hedging or overlay services are more likely to tackle the process in a professional way. The level of detail in this chapter illustrates that there are design decisions, and execution processes, all of which can have far more effect on the overall cost of overlay than a few notionally 'saved' basis points in fees.

(b) Far more important from a cost point of view is the execution of passive hedging forward contracts with counterparties associated with the overlay/investment manager. This conflict of interest can arise in three ways:
    1. Bank dealing rooms offering (more or less) informal arrangements whereby they will take responsibility for executing deals on behalf of the customer in line with the customer's orders. This kind of activity has had a long history, and is part and parcel of the bank FX sales team's effort to generate customer volume for their dealers. It can be evidenced in 'limit' orders (where the bank agrees to 'watch' a particular exchange rate, and execute a deal on behalf of the client when the market rate reaches a specified limit), in 'rate matching' orders, where for example a bank agrees to execute a deal at WM/Reuters London Close prices, or simply in having control over the orders given to the interbank dealers, and the decision-making process once the price comes back.
    2. It can also arise when investment managers (or custodians) are part of an organisation which maintains an FX business, and an FX dealing room. If an investment manager or custodian undertakes an FX deal with their own organisation, it creates a very fundamental conflict of interest:

- It is the job of the investment or overlay manager to act on behalf of the client and in the client's interests.
- It is the job of the dealer in a bank dealing room to get the best possible price for the bank, which means the worst price for the customer (there is nowhere for deals that are good for the bank to go – they have to go to the customer!).
- If the manager is able (under the terms of the contract and regulatory arrangements) to deal with another part of the same organisation (as well as external bank dealing rooms), then he will naturally come under pressure to do so.
- There may be arrangements under which the investment manager is obliged to deal with the in-house bank. This will yield the most damaging conflict and be the most expensive solution.

3. Finally, it can arise that an investor has negotiated arrangements with the custodian for the custodian's FX dealing room to have a monopoly on the FX transactions arising in the fund. This obliges investment managers and overlay managers to utilise the custodian's FX rates (whether they are competitive or not). This is not so much a conflict of interest as a waste of money. The investment or overlay manager may be fully aware of the problem, and complain at poor rates, but be powerless to change them. In these circumstances, the cost-conscious investor should re-negotiate the arrangements to unwind the custodian's monopoly.

In all these situations, the investor client can experience costs way above those cited here. It is almost universal in these situations (except 3 above) that the 'manager' will not seek to charge the client fees: this often acts as a magnet to the client, since fees are a visible overhead.

The scale of the cost implications arising from conflict situations can be startling. The author's firm has audited the foreign exchange transactions for a number of pension funds. In a particularly bad example, a large public sector pension fund was found to have been suffering executions on spot trades (with the custodian as the captive FX provider) at single-sided transaction costs of 58 bp, compared to 3 bp indicated by WM/Reuters spreads (half of the values in Table 3.3), and 1.4 bp by the author's firm (Table 3.4). Over the 6-month period in 2001 that this report covered, there were 1378 FX deals reviewed, so this was not an accidental 'one-off'.

Costly pricing on this scale can have a dramatic impact on investors' returns, and the costs are almost completely invisible. They arise out of pricing, not out of commissions, fees or brokerage, and it requires expert analysis to establish that mispricing is taking place.

This makes it all the more imperative that investor's Investment Management Agreements (IMAs) with managers for overlay or hedging include the provision that the manager is prohibited from dealing with any affiliated or associated bank FX dealing room, and that the manager has the freedom to choose a range of banks (subject to client veto on credit grounds) which will be assessed principally on deal execution pricing.

7
Currency Overlay Benchmarks

The theory and practice of investment benchmarks, and particularly currency benchmarks, has undergone a huge revolution in the last few years. I do not propose to reinvent the wheel in this chapter's discussion, but rather I will adopt the basic principles and methodology recommended by AIMR in the AIMR Benchmarks and Performance Attribution Subcommittee Report of August 1998 (the 'AIMR Report') – reproduced here as Appendix 3.

7.1 WHAT IS A CURRENCY BENCHMARK?

Currencies and currency returns and currency benchmarks are not as intuitively easy to understand or conceptualise as other asset classes. I will start by describing currency benchmarks using equities as an analogy.

Box 7.1 Benchmarks

Benchmarks perform two purposes in modern portfolio management. Firstly they set out the strategic exposure which the investor wishes to embrace, and secondly they act as a reference point against which the investor can judge the performance of his investments (or investment manager). Occasionally there are benchmarks which fulfil only the latter purpose – the most obvious example being peer group benchmarks popular in the UK in the 1980s and 1990s.

An investor wishing to hold a high proportion of equities in his portfolio might adopt a strategic portfolio benchmark which includes, say, 70% equities. This choice establishes a basis for allocating specialist mandates, and it is taken as the 'neutral' position. The performance of the investor's equity managers will be judged against the performance of an equity index acting as an equity benchmark. Similarly with currency benchmarks.

An investor wishing to hold no currency exposure in his strategic benchmark will set a *fully hedged benchmark* – i.e. a strategic position that eliminates all currency risk. An investor who wishes to hold all the currency exposure that comes with his international exposure will choose an *unhedged benchmark*. Choosing to strategically hold half the currency exposure would imply a *50% hedged benchmark*. The decision of which currency benchmark to adopt is commonly made by default. The default benchmark (when the issue is not thought about or analysed) is always unhedged – i.e. to accept full currency exposure.

When either an active or a passive currency manager is engaged, he will be judged by reference to a benchmark portfolio. That portfolio will include passive hedging at the same hedge ratio (proportion hedged) as the benchmark.

Suppose an investor wishes to invest in equities. The investor may wish to provide a guide to the equity manager as to the returns, and asset mix, he expects. Let us suppose the investor wants the manager to invest in US equities, weighted by market cap. He may well specify the S&P500 index as a benchmark. The manager then knows that if he holds the stocks in the S&P500 in the index weights he will have established a riskless (as well as a no-value-added) portfolio. A well-constructed benchmark will be such that if the manager adopts the riskless portfolio, the manager's relative performance (i.e. versus the benchmark) will be close to zero. There will almost inevitably always remain a small tracking error; it may be marginally negative through transactions costs, it may be marginally positive if the tax treatment of dividends is more favourable in the live portfolio than the benchmark assumptions. The investor will use the relative performance of the manager as his guide to the manager's performance.

Now let us translate this into a currency context. An investor wishes to know what contribution (and risk) currency exposure is making to his international returns. He may wish to alter his currency exposure in some way, and he needs objective information on which to base his judgements, and to measure his currency overlay manager.

7.1.1   Misleading currency attribution

A popular but misleading way for this to be done in the past was for the investor to break down international returns between the 'local' equity return and the spot currency return. The 'local' return is the return of the asset expressed in local currency. The spot return is the change in the spot exchange rate. Geometrically link the two returns and you have the return in the investor's currency – the unhedged return.

We have already seen how this method was misleading because neither the local returns, nor the spot returns, are independently investable by the investor. Dividing a return series between two component returns is not a useful exercise if neither of the components is independently investable. By naming the two components 'equity return' and 'currency return', the investor is encouraged to believe that the returns are truly individually available from these assets. For many US investors, this meant that they saw that 'currency returns' were positive, and therefore jumped to the conclusion that hedging would be loss-making. These two statements do not follow on from each other, as we shall see.

7.1.2   Benchmark as portfolio

A currency benchmark is a portfolio. In calculating benchmark returns, the constituents of this 'benchmark portfolio' must be enumerated, and the constituents' behaviour, their characteristics and their pricing must be defined. Unlike, say, an equity portfolio, the constituents of a currency benchmark portfolio are not straightforward assets. They are concepts like 'currency surprise' (see Box 2.2 and fuller description in Chapter 3) and 'contribution from hedging'. This makes currency benchmarks particularly difficult to understand and to maintain an intuitive grasp over.

7.1.3   Benchmark mechanics

What the investor can do is eliminate the effect of spot exchange rates by hedging the currency risk – selling currencies forward using forward contracts. What this does is to divide the two components (currency, equities) on quite different lines – *hedged return* (instead of local return) and *currency surprise* (instead of spot return). These two components *are* investable, and they will form the basis of a currency benchmark construction.

Currency differs from equity in two further important ways. Firstly, an equity investor will wish his manager to broadly *replicate* an equity index, while an international investor is more likely to ask his currency overlay manager to *neutralise* currency surprise – in effect holding a currency hedging portfolio exactly opposite to the underlying currency portfolio. Secondly, currency exposure comes 'by accident' along with holding international assets, it is almost never constructed deliberately.

Going back to the equity analogy. The investor who wishes to know his returns from currency can calculate a 'currency only' benchmark (see below). This will set out accurately the 'voluntary' exposure to currencies that the investor is accepting, and make no reference in its returns to the underlying asset returns. However, the 'currency only' benchmark is almost always calculated in the context of some hedging activity. It is possible (although rarely done) to calculate a 'currency only' benchmark without any associated hedging programme or currency overlay.

Of more practical interest is to define a benchmark in terms solely of the currency hedging activity rather than a combination of the underlying currency and the hedging activity. I will define a benchmark which looks only at the hedging activity as a 'currency overlay only' benchmark, and that which looks at strategic currency exposure as an 'embedded currency plus currency overlay' benchmark (and this will include both the strategic currency returns and any 'contribution from hedging' from overlay. I will discuss the concept of 'contribution from hedging' in more detail below.

Alternatively, the investor may want to know how his underlying international investments would perform if currency exposure were eliminated, but the exposure to international equities (or whatever his chosen asset class) is retained. In this case we can define the benchmark as an 'asset plus currency overlay' benchmark (see below).

7.2   INVESTABILITY

The investability of a benchmark is one of its most important characteristics. Currency benchmarks rely on forward contracts for their execution, and these have certain characteristics which make the investability test a little different from most asset class benchmarks.

The two key points about investability are that the calculations performed are:

- On instruments which are available in the quantities required
- At prices which are available in the market to investors at the date/time specified

To enable us to examine benchmark investability, we need to understand the investment process that currency benchmark construction implies. Section 7.3 will spell out the full detail, but the steps below illustrate the issues we have to contend with.

7.2.1   Forward currency prices

Most published benchmarks have now adopted WM/Reuters London Close as the pricing source. This source is calculated at 4pm London time from the screen quotes of a pre-selected range of money centre banks.

7.2.2 WM/Reuters rates[1]

7.2.2.1 WM/Reuters closing spot rates

Since 1993, WM has calculated daily standardised spot rates for global foreign exchange transactions, using rates provided by Reuters. The service covers quotes for 103 currencies against the USD, GBP and EUR. Bid, offer and mid rates are available.

7.2.2.2 WM/Reuters closing forward rates

Since January 1997, the WM/Reuters closing forward rates have been calculated and published to complement the WM/Reuters closing spot rates. Nine time periods (ON, TN, SW, 1m, 2m, 3m, 6m, 9m and 12m) for 41 currencies are quoted against the USD, GBP and EUR. Bid, offer and mid rates are available daily and are used in portfolio valuations, index compilation and performance measurement.

7.2.2.3 WM/Reuters intraday spot rates

In June 2001, the WM/Reuters intraday spot rates service was launched. This service provides hourly spot rates from 6.00am to 10.00pm (UK time), covering Asia close throughout the global day to US close. 103 currencies against the USD, GBP and EUR are quoted. Bid, offer and mid rates are available.

7.2.2.4 Cross rates

The WM spot rates reconcile when crossed, as long as the 'direction' of the cross is correct, i.e. the rates used to cross are the 'primary market' rates. For example, crossing JPY/USD with USD/GBP gives exactly the same JPY/GBP cross rate as quoted by WM. The primary market for JPY and GBP is USD.

However, crossing DKK/USD and USD/EUR to obtain the DKK/EUR cross rate produces a spread on the DKK/EUR spot rate that is much greater than the DKK/EUR rate quoted directly, but crossing DKK/EUR and USD/EUR gives exactly the same DKK/USD cross rate as quoted by WM. This concurs with the fact that the primary market for DKK is EUR-based.

The forward rates do not reconcile exactly to cross forward rates, but the difference is usually no more than a fraction of an FX point and can be attributed to rounding in the calculations.

7.2.2.5 Bank holidays

WM rates are published on every day where at least two from the following four financial centres are open: UK, US, Japan, Germany. In practice, this means that the only days on which WM rates are not published tend to be Christmas Day and New Year's Day.

---

[1] The interested reader can find out more about WM/Reuters rates on https://www.wmcompany.com/page.php?page_id=market_data_currency_service&cat=vrmds.

7.2.3   Contract rolling

Many asset class benchmarks are calculated on mid-prices. For a static basket of securities in a benchmark, the benchmark would not outperform a live static portfolio, since little or no transactions are required – only valuations. Currency benchmarks are different. Forward contracts are for fixed maturity dates, and in the benchmark, as in the actual portfolio, they must be closed out for cash settlement, and re-opened for a new maturity date. This process is known as 'rolling'.

Rolling forward contracts requires regular transactions in the currency market – and for most published benchmarks, this is monthly.

7.2.4   Scale of contracts

The author's firm has conducted surveys over the years of the quoted prices for various sizes of currency contract. It is clear that Reuters/WM prices are applicable to individual contracts of around USD50m or less – larger contracts will suffer wider bid/offer spreads. While USD50m is substantial in most market contexts, for currency benchmarks we have the whole portfolio to contend with – and for many overlay clients this can be a billion dollars plus.

The relevance of scale is not that the FX market is illiquid – far from it – but that violation of the 'no-cost' assumption for most benchmarks becomes less important with time, however large they are. This is because there are only two material deals in a typical equity portfolio – buying at the start and selling at the end. In FX, this buying and selling happens every month. This means that a large portfolio ($100m+) is likely to show significantly more drift from both the costed and costless benchmark than a small one.

7.2.5   Rebalancing

At the end of each reporting period, the size of the currency contracts needed to hedge an international portfolio will need to be changed, because the size of the assets, expressed in the foreign currency, will have changed. This process is known as rebalancing, and in practice (as well as in benchmark assumptions) it requires that not only are existing contracts rolled, but in addition a spot (reducing the size of the hedge) or forward (increasing the size of the hedge) deal is executed to bring the new hedge size in line with that required. These may be calculated either from the relevant bid or offer prices (costed) or mid-prices (costless).

7.2.6   Geometric linking

It is now universal to link period returns geometrically (i.e. by multiplication rather than addition – see Appendix 2 for details). For currency benchmarks, this requires the assumption that, whether or not the benchmark currency prices are costed or costless, the underlying assets can be costlessly dis- or reinvested in the underlying (international) securities to neutralise the cash flow arising from the settlement of maturing forward contracts. The mathematics of the benchmark methodology makes this assumption implicitly, as we shall see.

The practicalities of the market mean that this is likely to be by far the worst violated assumption in benchmark construction since the bid/offer spreads and other transactions costs of the underlying securities are an order of magnitude higher than that of the currency markets. This is fully explored in Chapter 6.

In theory, a benchmark could be constructed which included an allowance for this cost drift. I have never seen this done, and I regard it as unlikely to be done in the future. This drift is also largely invisible. The very act of geometric linking – applied to both the live portfolio and the benchmark portfolio – excludes it by assumption. However, just because standard methodology does not highlight a cost does not mean the that cost disappears. Cash flow management and sensible investment guidelines are two of the key skills required of the overlay manager and client to minimise this cost.

7.3   DESIGN

The AIMR Report specifies, amongst other things, that effective benchmarks should be:

- Investable
- Constructed in a disciplined and objective manner
- Formulated from publicly available information (i.e. transparent), and
- Consistent with underlying investor status (e.g. regarding regulatory restrictions, time horizons, etc.)

AIMR also specifies that when reporting actual portfolio results against benchmarks, returns should be calculated to include both realised and unrealised gains/losses; that rates of return should be time-weighted, with revaluations at least at every 'cash flow' (created, *inter alia*, by forward contract maturities – see more on this below); and that returns in one period should not be affected by returns in another period, or by the start date of the analysis.

The following section sets out three possible benchmark methodologies which are in line with AIMR principles, and based on essentially the same philosophy and mathematics. These are the 'asset plus currency overlay', 'embedded currency plus currency overlay', and 'currency overlay only' methodologies.

As its name suggests, the asset plus currency overlay methodology produces a benchmark which is made up of changes in underlying (unhedged) asset values and a contribution from currency hedging. Periodic returns of this benchmark can be geometrically linked to create multi-period and/or annualised returns of hedged assets. These can be compared with 2 the out-turns from an overlay programme (based on the same underlying asset returns as the benchmark) to assess the effectiveness of the currency management, whether passive or active. In addition, the volatility of this benchmark and of its unhedged 'underlay' can be compared with that of the overlay programme to assess the effectiveness of overlay as a risk reduction strategy.

The embedded currency plus currency overlay methodology produces a full 'carve-out' of all the currency exposures incurred (and hedged) by an international investor.

The currency overlay only methodology produces a benchmark without underlying asset returns, and is made up of the same contribution from currency hedging as is used as an input into the asset plus currency overlay benchmark. Currency overlay only period returns cannot be geometrically linked without a 'carrier asset', but are not influenced by the returns on the underlying assets. They can be used to assess the effectiveness of currency management by looking at the average periodic performance of the benchmark and overlay, and by looking at the tracking error of the overlay relative to the benchmark.[2]

---

[2] 'Tracking error' is throughout defined as the annualised standard deviation (volatility) of the difference between two return series (usually between a benchmark and actual returns). All these measures are calculated via logs (see Appendix 1).

The algebra of each of these methodologies are set out below: numerical worked examples are shown in Section 7.5. We also set out below brief details of certain other methodologies, and the reasons why these have been rejected as models for benchmarks.

7.3.1   Asset plus currency overlay methodology

The asset plus currency overlay methodology defines the benchmark return for each period t as:

$$\text{Benchmark returns}_t \% = \text{Hedged returns}_t \% \qquad (7.1)$$

where

$$\text{Hedged returns}_t \% = \text{Unhedged returns}_t \% + \text{Contribution from hedging}_t \% \qquad (7.2)$$

where all these terms are expressed as % of the unhedged asset value at the start of the period. The hedged return is in other words the return of the hedged asset expressed in the investor's home currency.

Regular period returns calculated in this way are then geometrically linked to create an index over time, as follows:

$$\text{Hedged index}_t = \text{Hedged index}_{t-1} \times (1 + \text{Hedged returns}_t) \qquad (7.3)$$

For the purposes of this example, I will assume that the investor is USD-based and the investment is denominated in EUR. The component pieces of this structure are derived as follows:

$$\text{Unhedged returns}\% = \left[\frac{\text{Foreign currency portfolio value}_t \times \text{Spot rate}_t}{\text{Foreign currency portfolio value}_{t-1} \times \text{Spot rate}_{t-1}} \right] - 1 \qquad (7.4)$$

where the spot rate is expressed as USD/EUR.

$$\text{Contribution from hedging}_t \% = \left[\frac{\text{Contribution from hedging USD}_t}{\text{USD amount of exposure}_{t-1}} \right] \qquad (7.5)$$

where

$$\text{Contribution from hedging USD}_t = [\text{Hedge valuation USD}_t + \text{Cum cash flow USD}_t] $$
$$- [\text{Hedge valuation USD}_{t-1} + \text{Cum cash flow USD}_{t-1}] \qquad (7.6)$$

and

$$\text{USD amount of exposure}_{t-1} = \text{Valuation of overlaid international assets}_{t-1} $$
$$\text{converted to USD at spot rate}_{t-1} \qquad (7.7)$$

Hedge valuation USD is the marked-to-market valuation (MMV) of all the outstanding unmatured forward contracts (or other instruments) in the benchmark hedge structure, and *Cum cash flow USD* is the simple cumulation over time (with no allowance for interest or return on capital) of the realised cash from maturing benchmark hedges.

7.3.2   Special case – monthly benchmark calculation

If the hedge maturity is equal to the reporting period (i.e. if the benchmark hedges are put in place at point $(t-1)$ with a maturity at point t), the hedge MMV is zero and the end-month cash flow *is* the contribution from hedging.[3] Under these particular circumstances we can express the contribution from hedging in exchange rate terms. In this equation, we deal with one currency (say EUR) for a USD-based currency:

Contribution from full hedging EUR %

$$= \frac{(\text{EUR portfolio value}_{t-1} \times \text{Fwd rate}_{t-1}) - (\text{EUR portfolio value}_{t-1} \times \text{Spot rate}_t)}{\text{EUR portfolio value}_{t-1} \times \text{Spot rate}_{t-1}} \quad (7.8)$$

where the exchange rates are expressed as USD/EUR and the 'Fwd rate' is the one-month forward. Note that if the foreign currency is the denominator of the exchange rate (say JPY/USD), then the portfolio values are divided by the exchange rates, not multiplied.

We can eliminate the EUR portfolio value from the equation, to get the neat:

$$\text{Contribution from full hedging EUR\%} = \frac{\text{Fwd rate}_{t-1} - \text{Spot rate}_t}{\text{Spot rate}_{t-1}} \quad (7.9)$$

The sharp-eyed reader will note that this is the negative-signed currency surprise (see Chapter 3). If the benchmark hedge ratio is less than 100%, then the value from equation (7.9) will be multiplied by the BHR.

This formula determines the 'contribution from hedging' from one currency (EUR). The total contribution from hedging all the currencies in the portfolio is therefore simply:

$$\text{Total contribution from hedging \%} = \sum_{i=1}^{n} w_i \, (\text{Contribution from hedging}_i \%) \quad (7.10)$$

where

n = no. of currencies hedged
i = currency
w_i = weight of currency i in the total international portfolio (all measured at $t-1$)

Note that it is quite possible that the sum of the weights (w) add up to less than 100%. The residual will be unhedged or unhedgeable currencies. The denominator of the percentage on the LHS of equation (7.10) is the total international portfolio$_{t-1}$, which is also the denominator of the asset return calculations for the portfolio. This common denominator means that percentages can be added across each period.

---

[3] The inquiring reader may wish to understand why the cum cash flow is cumulated without interest. Simplifying away some details, this is because the 'contribution from hedging' measure we need is the change in value of the currency overlay portfolio (expressed as a percentage of the end-prior-period international assets) assumed to be PV'd to the period end. In all major published benchmark calculations, the cash flow from the overlay is simultaneous with the period end. This means that outstanding MMVs are always zero, and we do not need any cash cumulation, we can simply take the cash as the numerator in the 'contribution from hedging' return calculation. However, if we chose to construct, say, a 3-month maturity benchmark, and value it monthly, we would need to calculate the change in MMV plus (the PV of) any cash that has flowed in the month (i.e. the change in the cum cash flow). However, once the return calculation has been made, any cash that has flowed will be caught up in the geometric linking process (which assumes that all the currency overlay return in a period is then invested in the underlying asset in the next period). To uprate the cash with any interest or return would mean double counting returns on the cash.

7.3.3   Valuation of unmatured contracts

The above case is the special (but common) case of monthly reporting and one-month hedging. In more general terms, the MMV of the hedges will be the value of the outstanding hedges, evaluated based on a publicly available pricing source. In a published benchmark, relevant foreign exchange rates would almost certainly be the relevant WM/Reuters closing prices (spot and forward points, with intermediate dates determined by straight-line interpolation between forward points). The question of whether the MMV should be calculated with or without discounting of future cash flow is considered further below.

7.3.4   Benchmark hedge ratio

I have not until this point mentioned the benchmark hedge ratio in detail. This is a critical element in the strategic currency decision, but where does it fit in the above maths? The answer is that the benchmark hedge ratio can be expressed as follows:

$$\text{Benchmark hedge ratio } \% \text{ (BHR)} = \left[\frac{\text{Contribution from hedging}_t}{\text{Contribution from full hedging}_t} \right] \qquad (7.11)$$

And in practice, the size of the hedges to match the underlying embedded currency exposure will be BHR% × size of underlying exposure.

This approach to benchmarking currency overlay is widely used. Its advantages are that it allows the investor to see the return of his underlying international assets with all or part of the currency returns removed. It can be geometrically linked without difficulty, and it allows the volatility-reduction properties of currency overlay to be directly observable in the benchmark returns. The key disadvantage is that, for benchmark hedge ratios of 1–99%, when the benchmark returns are being increased by currency returns, there are negative returns and negative cash from the 'contribution from hedging'. While this is not a problem in principle, it does give investors a headache!

A worked example (with numbers) of the asset plus currency overlay methodology is set out later (Table 7.3).

7.3.5   Embedded currency plus currency overlay methodology

This section deals only with the 'embedded currency' plus overlay methodology. The overlay only methodology is set out in Section 7.3.6. The benchmark return is defined as follows:

$$\text{Benchmark return}_t \% = \text{Currency surprise}_t + \text{Contribution from hedging}_t \% \qquad (7.12)$$

This is because currency surprise represents the embedded currency return in an international portfolio. In what may seem rather a circular calculation, we reach the currency surprise as follows:

$$\text{Currency surprise}_t \% = \text{Unhedged returns}_t \% - \text{Fully hedged returns}_t \% \qquad (7.13)$$

But we know from equation (7.3) that:

$$\text{Hedged returns}_t \% = \text{Unhedged returns}_t \% + \text{Contribution from full hedging}_t \%$$

Therefore substituting:

$$\text{Currency surprise}_t \% = -\text{Contribution from full hedging}_t \% \qquad (7.14)$$

So the only way we can calculate the currency surprise is to take the negative of the contribution from full hedging. This leads us to:

$$\text{Benchmark return}_t \% = \text{Contribution from hedging}_t \% - \text{Contribution from full hedging}_t \%$$

$$(7.15)$$

If there is an overlay programme in place, then the returns of the combination of the embedded currency and the overlay are the sum of the two. Taking the three main benchmark hedge ratios:

Benchmark hedge ratio	Currency only benchmark (embedded currency + overlay)
0%	−100% × contribution from full hedging
50%	−50% × contribution from full hedging
100%	Nil

This approach is not widely used. It does, however, have the merit of fully expressing the currency risk and returns that an investor is running, and of spelling it out independently from asset returns. But it has two important disadvantages:

1. Because currency surprise is not an asset, returns generated under this regime cannot be independently geometrically linked. Instead, they have to be attached to an asset (the 'carrier asset') to make geometric linking possible.
2. The returns under this regime are precisely negatively correlated with the cash flow arising from hedging contracts. This is because this benchmark is always 'long' of currencies (as the fund is), but any cash flow arising from a hedge is 'short' of currencies. So for a 50% benchmark hedge ratio, the benchmark will show positive returns when the hedge cash flow is negative, and vice versa. While this is not a fundamental investment problem, in my experience it gives investors a great deal of intuitive trouble.

7.3.6   Currency overlay only methodology

The currency overlay only methodology requires the separation of currency return from asset returns, like the currency only methodology. However in this regime, we ignore the embedded currency exposure, and report the benchmark returns purely as the 'contribution from hedging' component. Alternatively or additionally, the currency overlay only methodology can generate a benchmark as a *cash* amount (rather than a percentage return), as in equation (7.6). Cash benchmarks are unsuitable for mainstream benchmarking, but for active currency management programmes, they may help the investor 'keep a handle' on what is going on.

A worked example (with numbers) of the currency overlay only methodology is set out later in Table 7.9, and the (very simple) maths is shown here:

$$\text{Benchmark return}_t \% = \text{Contribution from hedging}_t \% \qquad (7.16)$$

where 'contribution from hedging' is derived as shown in equation (7.5).

7.3.7   Other methodologies

There is a range of methodologies which, although sometimes used and intuitively simple, violate AIMR principles. I highlight two of these here, but will not consider them in detail further as they are not compatible with the AIMR compliance criterion required. One such methodology is the 'cumulative cash' approach. This approach takes the cash flow generated by hedging and accumulates it, earning interest and contributing to future performance. The algebra is as follows:

$$\text{Value of hedged portfolio} = (\text{Value of unhedged portfolio}) + (\text{Marked-to-market} \\ \text{value of hedge programme}) + (\text{Cum cash incl.} \\ \text{cum interest}) \tag{7.17}$$

The return for a period is then given as:

$$\text{Return}_t \% = \left[\frac{\text{Value of hedged portfolio}_t}{\text{Value of hedged portfolio}_{t-1}} \right] - 1 \tag{7.18}$$

The difficulty with this methodology lies in the fact that the returns for any period are dependent on the start date of the history. In addition, the cumulative cash can grow to such an extent that the cash and the interest on it comes to dominate the returns from hedging. It is also impossible to analyse volatility on the basis of this return series, as the denominators of the unhedged returns and hedged returns are different.

The other methodology to note here is a non-investible version of the currency overlay only methodology (see above). In this approach, hedged currency return is arrived at by adding the contribution from hedging, equation (7.4), to the unhedged currency return. 'Unhedged currency return' is defined as the percentage change in the spot exchange rate over the period:

$$\text{Unhedged currency return}_t \% = \left(\frac{\text{Spot rate}_t}{\text{Spot rate}_{t-1}} \right) - 1 \tag{7.19}$$

While this term is intuitively understandable, it is not investible, as there is no way in which one can invest in spot rate change. Consequently, this methodology violates a core AIMR principle, and will not be considered further.

7.3.8   A currency benchmark with or without asset returns?

The dominant distinction to be drawn between the three methodologies outlined above relates to the calculation of multi-period returns. In the case of asset plus currency overlay, this can be done in the standard manner used for other asset classes – multiplicative 'geometric' linking. In the case of the other two, this is not appropriate, and other multi-period measures need to be considered.

The algebra of geometric linking of the asset plus currency overlay period returns is straight-forward, and is set out in equation (7.3). It assumes that the contribution from hedging in each period is reinvested in (or disinvested from) the underlying unhedged asset pool at the end of the period in which it arises. This impacts upon a range of other issues highlighted further below, but it is also the reason why it is inappropriate to apply geometric linking to the methodologies without asset returns included.

Even though it is not possible to generate meaningful performance measures for such a benchmark independently of another return series, it is possible to generate meaningful *relative* performance measures such as tracking error and average periodic out- or underperformance. The measures which can be generated are further explored later in this chapter.

7.3.9   Pricing/costs

Whichever benchmark methodology is chosen, a decision will need to be taken as to whether the benchmark is to be 'costed' or not (i.e. whether it is to include bid/offer costs of trading). In the case of conventional equity instruments, standard convention now is to use mid-market prices, resulting in 'uncosted' benchmarks. This is accepted as the standard convention for equities as no transactions are necessarily taking place at each period or subperiod end, and as the benchmark needs to be unbiased with respect to buyers' and sellers' perspectives. This is not the case in currency hedging. The forward currency contracts which are the basic instrument of currency hedging are fixed-term instruments, and require to be rolled over at maturity to maintain a hedged position/benchmark. These transactions cannot be executed mid-price, and therefore for the index to be investable it should be priced and valued at the appropriate side of the market relating to the hedge.

   However, all published hedged indices use mid-prices for their benchmark calculations. While these are uninvestable, nevertheless they are an objective measure, and therefore we have no objection if a client chooses this convention, although this benchmark will consistently overstate achievable returns.

7.3.10   Prices, not interest rates

Certain published methodologies[4] suggest that currency benchmark calculations be based on spot currency moves plus interest rate differentials, rather than on currency forward prices as actually available in the markets and as applicable in practice to overlay portfolios. There are two types of interest rate methodology, one based purely on interest rate differentials, and one based on notional lending and borrowing. Let's take them in turn.

7.3.10.1   Interest rate differentials

In the earlier days of currency overlay, one of the most common benchmark methodologies was as follows:

$$\text{Benchmark return}_t \% = \text{Asset return}_t \% \text{ in local currency} + \text{Interest rate differential}_{t-1} \%$$

$$(7.20)$$

This is obviously designed to produce an 'asset plus overlay' benchmark return. How does it compare with our calculations of the same benchmark in equations (7.1)–(7.10)? Omitting for brevity the detailed algebra (the mathematically-minded reader might like to do this independently), equations (7.2) and (7.20) produce different results – and only the returns in equation (7.2) are achievable. The difference between equations (7.2) and (7.20) [that is (7.2)–(7.20)] is (for the EUR example above):

$$\text{Error}_t \% = \frac{(\text{Spot rate}_t - \text{Spot rate}_{t-1})}{\text{Spot rate}_{t-1}} \times \frac{(\text{EUR portfolio value}_t - \text{EUR portfolio value}_{t-1})}{\text{EUR portfolio value}_{t-1}}$$

$$(7.21)$$

Or, in words: the error from equation (7.20) is the product of the percentage change in the spot rate and the percentage change in the underlying EUR portfolio value (i.e. local asset return).

---

[4] Notably Karnosky and Singer, 'Global Asset Management and Performance Attribution', published by the Research Foundation of The Institute of Chartered Financial Analysts, February 1994.

If the spot rate moves up by 1%, and the asset in foreign currency terms moves up by 3%, the error is $1\% \times 3\% = 0.03\%$, or 3 bp.

7.3.10.2   Notional borrowing and lending

The basic principle of this method of constructing a benchmark is that it is possible to eliminate currency risk by borrowing money in the foreign currency (in which the investor has equity investments), converting the proceeds to the home currency, and on-lending the proceeds. The two legs of the transaction attract interest – payable in the foreign currency and receivable in the domestic currency. The net effect is that the investor pays or receives an interest rate differential, and has to revalue his debt each period, which acts as a hedge to the revaluation of his (equity) assets.

A correctly constructed interest-rate-based hedge will be different from the conventional forward-contract-based benchmark. With one modification it can be identical as long as the forward rate conforms exactly to the interest rate arbitrage or (which is the same thing) the same interest rates are used for the forward rate pricing and the lending and borrowing calculations. This modification is that the forward hedge has to be for (1 + (foreign interest rate × year fraction)) times the foreign asset value (or, by analogy, the foreign debt has to be [1/(1 + (foreign interest rate × year fraction))] times the foreign asset value). I will let the reader work through the maths if he wishes to prove that this is the case.

This methodology is perfectly acceptable from a mathematical perspective, but I would question why anyone would want to use it. Forward rates are expressed in FX terms, and valuations are made by managers and custodians on the basis of forward rate calculations. Interest rates are neither independently collected for the FX market, nor are money market rates (exactly) the same as the implied interest rates from FX forward rates. Perhaps most importantly, no single institutional portfolio investor that I have ever come across has hedged their foreign portfolio by borrowing the foreign currency, and re-depositing it in the home currency. That has been the preserve of corporations, individuals, and the odd hedge fund.

The 1998 AIMR benchmarks paper (Appendix 3) recommends forwards-based benchmarks – although it too recognises that interest-rate-based methodologies are valid if properly used.

7.3.11   Rebalancing

Rebalancing frequency in the benchmark can only be equal to a fund's benchmark reporting period. This is because different frequency rebalancing would create a path- or history-dependent benchmark – breaching the principle of transparency and replicability.

The choice of rebalancing frequency will be influenced by a variety of factors, of which the two most important are:

- Regulation relating to permissible foreign exchange exposures;
- Cost (as each benchmark rebalancing will incur costs involved with the bid/offer on the contracts inherent in the benchmark).

Benchmarks cannot include rebalancing buffers: i.e. benchmark rebalancing is triggered by the passage of a pre-set amount of time, and is not triggered by investment or currency exposure-related factors. This is because any trigger related to investment matters will result in the benchmark performance being path-dependent.

The overwhelming frequency of rebalancing for published benchmarks is monthly.

7.3.12   Original contract maturity

The maturity of the benchmark is an important decision. We have called it 'original contract maturity', because while forward contracts have a maturity date that progressively approaches with the passage of time, nevertheless at initiation they have an original maturity, and this defines them.

Where the original maturity of the benchmark contracts is equal to the reporting and rebalancing frequency (all monthly in the case of most hedged indices published by external providers), there is zero MMV included in the rebalancing process[5] (almost zero, and not exactly zero, because of roll-over costs). This has one significant advantage: it avoids a potential source of tracking error between the reported performance of the benchmark (and of the actual portfolio), and the cumulative value of the actual portfolio.

This source of tracking error arises because the algebra of geometric linking assumes that cash actually flows at the end of each period in the amount of the hedges' value at that time, and that it is reinvested in or disinvested from the underlying (unhedged) assets at the closing asset prices. The next day the new denominator relating the new period is the MMV of the unhedged assets (including any assets assumed to have been acquired or sold as a result of the previous day's 'cash flow'). However, if the value of the hedges at the end of the previous period does not actually flow as cash (as it would not if the contracts have not yet matured), then this portion of the hedge return will still be MMV or 'notional' cash, and will on the face of it not be capable of being reinvested in the underlying hedged assets. This will create a tracking error between the cumulative returns calculated from both the benchmark and actual overlay on the one hand, and the actual cumulative asset value observed in the fund on the other.

7.3.13   Constant maturity benchmarks

This is a special case of the maturity decision. If we take as an example a constant maturity 3-month benchmark, this could be constructed, if the reporting frequency was daily, by daily closing out the 3-month original maturity contract one day after it is initiated, and re-establishing a new contract with an original maturity of 3 months. The 'closing out' at a maturity of 3 months less a day would require interpolation of 2- and 3-months forward pricing data.

The 'sawtooth' pattern of maturity can be no finer that the reporting frequency. So if the reporting frequency is daily, then the variation in maturity can be limited to one day. However, if the reporting frequency is monthly, then the variation in the maturity would be a minimum of one month.

A constant maturity benchmark has a very high transaction turnover – in the above example 26 000% p.a. The costs of this high turnover would not appear in a benchmark if it was calculated at mid-prices, but would make close tracking with an actual portfolio expensive.

---

[5] Only exactly zero if the benchmark is costless. If it is costed, then the newly rolled contract will have to be valued, and this will be negative because of the bid/offer spreads.

7.3.14 Discounting

Related to the original contract maturity issue discussed above is the question of whether or not to use discounting in the MMV of unmatured hedge contracts[6]. In situations where the reporting frequency and hedge contract maturity are the same, MMV is immaterial to the benchmark calculation as MMV will be nil at each period end (and the cash flow is likely to arise at or near the reporting date). In situations where there is a mismatch, by contrast, MMV will be much more important, and will grow in importance with the length of the mismatch.

The non-discounted approach is usually acceptable on the basis that the expected long-term effect of discounting on returns is zero, and that discounting would add very significantly to the algebraic complexity (and hence opacity) of the benchmark calculation. However, in the case where the asset plus currency overlay methodology is being applied and there is a reporting/original contract maturity mismatch, discounting will have a greater and longer-term impact on benchmark performance, and may even be necessary to achieve investibility (because margining is normally done at discounted MMV – especially if it is two-way).

Either way, each fund will need to decide whether or not discounting is to be applied in their benchmark calculations. Obviously, whatever is decided in relation to the benchmark should be reflected in the management of the MMV of contracts actually traded. Only one major index provider – JP Morgan – discounts the valuations of forward contracts in hedged index calculations.

7.3.15 Benchmark hedge ratio – strategic considerations

A key benchmark decision is the BHR. Typically, a hedge ratio is specified as the percentage of the value of international assets to be hedged, but this is not a universal or necessary way of specifying it. It would be equally possible (although rare) to specify, for example, that the benchmark should always be rebalanced such that a fixed percentage of a fund's whole portfolio value (rather than just the international) remains unhedged (or hedged).

The important point here is that the benchmark's hedge ratio needs to be specified and constant – its denominator can change with the value of the underlying assets and/or with investment/disinvestment, but the ratio must remain constant from period to period. A constant BHR does not mean a completely immovable one, any more than an international equity allocation has to be fixed for all time. Rather, the BHR has to be an anchor against which to measure any currency overlay portfolio, and from which the strategic currency position is measured. An investor is quite entitled to change the BHR from time to time, as indeed would be natural given the evolving appetite for risk of a maturing fund. The implications for active currency management evaluation may also need to be considered. If an active mandate's guidelines restrict an active manager to hedge ratios between 0% and 100%, then a 50% hedge benchmark has the merit of allowing an active manager to outperform in all market conditions (i.e. foreign currencies either strong or weak). By contrast, an unhedged benchmark (0% hedge ratio) does not allow an active manager to outperform when foreign currencies are strong (because 0% hedged is the best possible position), and a fully hedged benchmark (100% hedge ratio) does not allow a manager to outperform when foreign currencies are weak (because 100% hedged is the best possible position). Over a full cycle, a manager can expect to add equal

---

[6] Custodians typically generate marked-to-market valuation of forward currency positions by calculating the expected cash flow on a forward contract (based on the contract's price and the price of a reversing contract in the market at the time of the valuation). They do not discount this cash flow back to present value.

value against any benchmark, but for the reasons given above, the manager's tracking error for 'polar' benchmarks (0% and 100%) will be wider (and more episodic) than his tracking error for a symmetrical (50% hedged) benchmark.

Chapter 8 has a very full discussion on hedge ratios and their role in risk-reduction.

7.3.16 Currency coverage and denominator calculation

The final benchmark decision to be made relates to which currencies are to be included in the benchmark currency hedge, which to be proxied, and which omitted. This is partly a cost issue, as many currencies are capable of being hedged only at significant cost (relative to the more liquid currencies), and partly an investibility issue, as although it is possible to construct a theoretical hedge price for certain currencies, trading this may in practice be impossible.

The question to resolve is whether only hedgeable currencies, or all foreign currencies in the exposure aggregate, should be used as the denominator in the benchmark returns calculation. Typically, the all-country aggregate is used as the denominator of benchmark (and actual overlay) returns, but the benchmark returns should not include any 'hedge' of unhedgeable currencies. In these cases, unhedged returns should be used. However, there are other ways of tackling this issue, although it will be necessary to ensure that whatever approach is adopted is also replicable in practice.

Related to this issue will be specification of the benchmark hedge ratio – if it is expressed as a percentage of international assets, is it to be a percentage of hedgeable values only, and if not, how is the benchmark to deal with the overweighting which will be required in relation to the hedged currencies? Typically, benchmark hedge ratios are expressed as percentages of exposure to particular currencies, but again this is not the only way of expressing them. Again, whatever approach is adopted will need to be replicable in practice to maintain the benchmark's investibility.

7.3.17 Underlay

A related issue is that of the 'underlay' for the currency benchmark. This is the question of what is being hedged/overlaid – is it to be an asset benchmark (e.g. MSCI EAFE or Salomon World Government Bond Index), or is it to be the assets actually owned by the investor?

Subject to any regulatory requirements to limit actual currency exposures, this issue relates to where a fund wishes to place responsibility for the investment decisions being taken. Is an equity manager who decides to underweight Japan, for example, taking a stock market only position (which would be the case if the currency benchmark has actual assets as its denominator), or a stock market and a currency position (which would be the case if the currency benchmark has the equity benchmark as its denominator)?

As above, this question has no theoretically correct answer, but will need to be resolved as part of the benchmark construction, and its resolution will need to be communicated to the managers of the relevant portfolios.

7.3.18 Benchmark performance

The benchmark created after considering the issues outlined above will have its own characteristics in return and volatility terms. These will differ depending upon the specification developed within the above methodologies. To illustrate this, Figure 7.1 plots a comparison

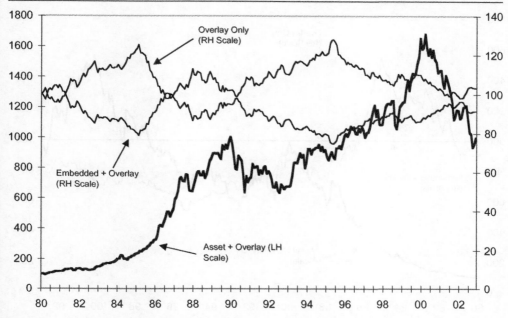

Figure 7.1 Performance of alternative benchmarks (index Jan 1980 = 100, USD base, EAFE weights, 50% BHR)

of the rolling annual returns of three different benchmark methodologies' returns for a 50% hedged BHR over the last 20 years. The figure shows the completely divergent nature of the different benchmarks.

Figure 7.1 compares the three acceptable benchmarks that we have discussed, and illustrates that the choices made in benchmark construction will have significant impact on the returns (and potentially the volatility) of the benchmark. The two 'no-asset' benchmarks are mirror images in this example; they lose that mirror-image characteristic when the BHR is not 50%. At 0% or 100% one of the two becomes a nil return (i.e. a flat line). Figure 7.2 shows the same graph with 100% BHR.

In view of the wide choice available, and the hugely different profiles of the alternative benchmark choices, it is important to ensure that the investor understands how the fund will use the benchmark information, and therefore the implications of the final choice.

7.3.19   Benchmark cash flows

It is clear from the above that if a benchmark is established which involves passive currency hedging, then the benchmark will generate notional cash flows. Figures 7.3 and 7.4 plot the monthly cash flow and the rolling 12-month cash flow arising from a 100% BHR 1-month rolling hedge of MSCI EAFE – effectively World ex US. The alert reader will hae seen these graphs before (Figures 6.1 and 6.2).

Clearly, this benchmark generates substantial cash flows, and all other benchmark structures will also generate cash flows of comparable size (depending on hedge ratio and base currency). It may seem odd to say a *benchmark* generates *cash flows*: let me explain. A benchmark is a portfolio that produces the benchmark return. A benchmark portfolio of, say, equities will

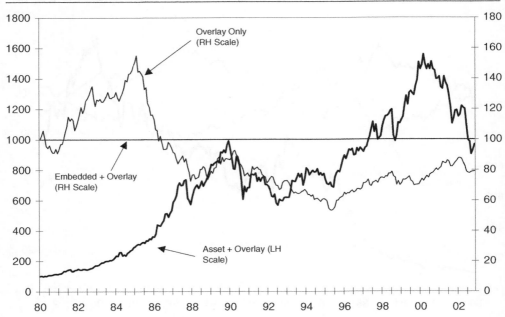

Figure 7.2   Performance of alternative benchmarks (index Jan 1980 = 100, USD base, EAFE weights, 100% BHR)

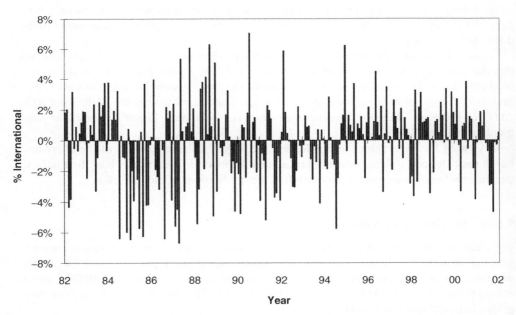

Figure 7.3   Passive hedging monthly cash flow (USD base, EAFE weights, Sep 82–Sep 02, 100% hedge ratio)

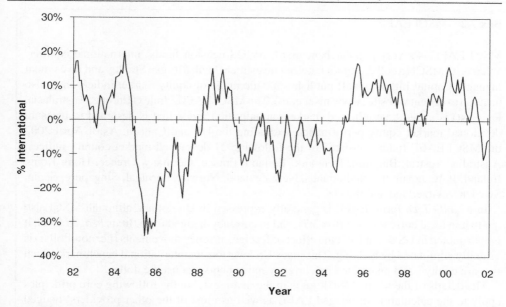

Figure 7.4   Passive hedging 1-year cumulative cash flow (USD base, EAFE weights, Sep 82–Sep 02, 100% hedge ratio)

produce, for example, dividends, which have to be reported and treated in a particular way. An equity benchmark return calculation cannot ignore dividends if it is to be a relevant comparator for an actual equity portfolio. Similarly, a benchmark portfolio of passive currency overlay is comprised of a rolling series of forward currency contracts. When these contracts mature they produce cash flows, and these have to be dealt with in the benchmark return process just like dividends from equities.

Where a fund has selected the asset plus currency overlay methodology, benchmark cash flows will need to be incorporated into the benchmark return calculation. This arises because (as explained above) geometric linking requires that the 'contribution from hedging' is reinvested in or disinvested from the underlying assets at the end of each period. In all the published hedged asset plus currency overlay benchmarks this reinvestment/disinvestment is not costed – i.e. it is assumed to take place without incurring bid/offer spread costs in the equity market. This is in line with the general benchmark practice of valuing all assets at mid-prices.

Valuing long-held assets at mid-prices (on the basis that most investments are held for indeterminate and long periods) is a minor violation of the real world (since only the entry and exit prices are affected). But (again as mentioned above) forward contracts need to be rolled at (monthly) frequency, and the resulting cash flow has to be raised or invested in underlying equity markets. Section 6.4 illustrates that this will cost around 0.15% p.a. if efficiently executed.

There is nothing that can be done to avoid these cash flow issues completely, but a great deal that can mitigate the effects and the associated costs. Certainly, an assessment of cash flow impact should be included in the consideration of the options when selecting a currency benchmark. It is simply necessary to be aware that these issues are present, and to take account of them when designing asset management structures and evaluating performance.

Box 7.2   MSCI EAFE

MSCI EAFE is a very popular benchmark for US pension funds' international equities. What is it? MSCI (a collaboration between investment bank Morgan Stanley and investment manager Capital International) publishes a wide range of equity market indices, and also hosts an excellent website (www.msci.com). The MSCI EAFE® Index (Europe, Australasia, Far East) is a free float-adjusted market capitalisation index that is designed to measure developed market equity performance, excluding the US and Canada. As of April 2002 the MSCI EAFE Index consisted of the following 21 developed market country indices: Australia, Austria, Belgium, Denmark, Finland, France, Germany, Greece, Hong Kong, Ireland, Italy, Japan, the Netherlands, New Zealand, Norway, Portugal, Singapore, Spain, Sweden, Switzerland and the UK.

In its *unhedged* form, EAFE is generally expressed in US dollars, although MSCI also quote it in local currency (see Box 3.7), and in currency-hedged form. In its *hedged* form, it is also quoted in US dollars, but the effect of foreign currency movements (i.e. non-dollar) is virtually eliminated by hedging. This gives US investors an international benchmark which is 'pure equity', and unaffected by currency movements against the dollar.

The details of the maths MSCI use is in the main text, but the following core principles apply to the calculation of hedged EAFE as well as most of the other providers' hedged indices:

- Hedging is conducted using forward currency contracts to sell the foreign currencies one month forward.
- The amount sold in the benchmark calculation is the value of the equities in each foreign currency at the start of each month. The size of the forward contract does not vary intra-month, even if there is a large movement in equity prices and the amount of the hedge is therefore too large or too small.
- When the contract matures at the end of the month, the profit or loss it has generated is settled for cash, and a new contract for the new asset amount is taken out.
- The foreign exchange rates at which this settlement is made, and the new forward contract taken out, are at WM/Reuters end-month London closing mid-prices. The price used for the closing price is spot, and the cash is assumed to flow immediately, even though spot deals settle two days later in reality.
- The cash received/required from the maturing contract is invested/disinvested from the underlying equity markets in proportion to their index weights. That is, the index weights of the equity index are unhedged, not hedged.
- This investment/disinvestment takes place at the equity closing mid-prices for the month, i.e. reinvestment/disinvestment is instantaneous and costless.

7.4   CURRENT PRACTICE

Table 7.1 sets out a brief summary of the hedged currency benchmark methodology of some major international index providers. Please note that all providers geometrically link their monthly returns (which is the same as costless (dis-) investment), but those providers that can supply daily hedged index valuations do so by geometrically linking to the prior end-month index value, not the prior day. Prior day returns are then derived from the change in the daily

Table 7.1 Hedging methodology by index provider

Provider/index	Equities/bonds	Maturity of hedging contracts	Correct (investable) methodology?	Comments
MSCI – EAFE plus other global indices	Equities	1m	Yes	WM/Reuters mid-price; daily valuation available
FTSE World Indices	Equities	No hedged indices – 'currency-stripped-out' indices are based on local currencies, and are not investable			
Lehman Bros. Fixed Income Indices	Bonds	1m	Yes	Mid-price spot; forwards derived via interest rates
Salomon Bros. Bond Indices	Bonds	1m	Yes	Estimated end-month values hedged; WM/Reuters mid-price
Merrill Lynch Bond Indices	Bonds	1m	Yes	Mid-prices; daily valuation available
JP Morgan Bond Indices	Bonds	1m	Yes	Daily valuation available; discounted daily valuation

index values. Daily returns thus produced are not 'genuine' daily returns, but interim values of a monthly process. The key to this is the denominator – it remains the prior-end-month value.

Two index suppliers – Salomon Smith Barney and JP Morgan – do not base the value of the hedge on the end-prior-month value. Instead, they estimate the end-current-month value from the end-prior-month value and the current yield (SSB) and current coupon (JPM), and base the size of the hedge on this. For bonds this is likely to create a better hedge than the end-prior-month value methodology, although it does create another level of complexity that reduces transparency. For equities, a sophistication like this would be unlikely to be sufficiently material (since yields are so low) to warrant the additional complexity.

One index provider (JPM) discounts daily valuations of monthly forward contracts.

7.5   WORKED EXAMPLES

In the following pages, I have set out worked examples of the algebra for the three main types of benchmark discussed in this chapter. Each column has algebra showing how the numbers presented are calculated. Each cell value has a column reference, and a t subscript. The use of t means the current period; the use of $t - 1$ means the prior period value, and so on. If I omit the t subscript, then I am referring to the current period values.

7.5.1   Asset plus currency overlay methodology

I have chosen a fictitious two-asset/two-currency international portfolio. We have a EUR base currency investor, and the two target currencies are USD and JPY. So, in lay terms, a Eurozone investor has invested in only two assets, one in the US and one in Japan. Thinking of the assets as stock indices makes this a more intuitive benchmark (although of course they could be any type of asset).

We are required to calculate hedged returns for a benchmark for this portfolio. We are given the values of the assets at the end of each period, and the relevant exchange rates. Table 7.2 shows the portfolio assumptions.

Table 7.2 Portfolio information (EUR base)

	JPY asset			USD asset		
Period end	End-period JPY asset value (JPYm) A	End-period spot rate JPY/EUR B	End-period forward rate JPY/EUR C	End-period USD asset value (USDm) D	End-period spot rate USD/EUR E	End-period forward rate USD/EUR F
0	1000.00	115.7013	115.368240	15.00	0.9011	0.899940
1	1021.00	115.9451	115.610410	15.10	0.9343	0.933060
2	931.20	118.3738	118.033330	14.84	0.9876	0.986280
3	950.30	117.4127	117.066370	14.61	0.9804	0.979070

Table 7.3 shows the calculation for a fully (100%) hedged benchmark. In the 'total return' row, the calculation uses geometric linking for unhedged return and hedged return. I have noted that we do not use geometric linking for the 'contribution from hedging' since we cannot reinvest in stand-alone currency overlay, which is the implicit assumption of geometric linking.

Table 7.3 Asset plus currency overlay benchmark (100% BHR)

	EUR asset value at spot rates	Unhedged benchmark return	Benchmark contribution from hedging $[BHR\{(A_{t-1}/C_{t-1} - A_{t-1}/B_t) + (D_{t-1}/F_{t-1} - D_{t-1}/E_t)\}]/G_{t-1}$	100% hedged benchmark return
Column Formula:	$(A/B) + (D/E)$	$(G_t\text{-}G_{t-1})/G_{t-1}$		$H + J$
Period end	G	H	J	K
0	25.29			
1	24.97	(1.27%)	2.59%	1.32%
2	22.89	(8.31%)	4.41%	(3.90%)
3	23.00	0.45%	(0.58%)	(0.13%)
Total return		**(9.07%)**	**6.31%** *	**(2.76%)**

* 6.31% = (2.76%) − (9.07%). The geometrically linked return of 'contribution from hedging' is 6.50%, but this is not investable.

Table 7.4 shows the relevant additional columns to calculate a 50% hedged benchmark, and Table 7.5 the same working for an unhedged benchmark. I have included the 0% hedge benchmark working for completeness – but of course the contribution from hedging is zero, and the benchmark return equals the unhedged return.

Finally, I have added two tables (Tables 7.6 and 7.7) which are not strictly a benchmark calculation. They show how an actual overlay portfolio's returns relative to benchmark would be calculated under this methodology. The marked-to-market valuations (MMVs) of an actual portfolio at the end of each month are illustrated in Table 7.6, but they are not derivable from information presented here – they come from the (assumed) valuation of the individual manager's currency positions. I show how overlay performance could be calculated from this information.

Table 7.4   Asset plus currency overlay benchmark (50% BHR)

	Benchmark contribution from hedging $[BHR\{(A_{t-1}/C_{t-1} - A_{t-1}/B_t) +$	50% hedged benchmark return
Column formula:	$(D_{t-1}/F_{t-1} - D_{t-1}/E_t)\}]/G_{t-1}$	H + L
Period end	L	M
0		
1	1.30%	0.03%
2	2.20%	(6.11%)
3	(0.29%)	0.16%
Total return	**3.14%** *	**(5.93%)**

* Total resulting from the subtraction or addition of other totals, not geometrically linked.

Table 7.5   Asset plus currency overlay benchmark (0% BHR)

	Benchmark contribution from hedging $[BHR\{(A_{t-1}/C_{t-1} - A_{t-1}/B_t) +$	0% hedged benchmark return
Column formula:	$(D_{t-1}/F_{t-1} - D_{t-1}/E_t)\}]/G_{t-1}$	H + N
Period end	N	P
0		
1	0.00%	(1.27%)
2	0.00%	(8.31%)
3	0.00%	0.45%
Total return	**0.00%**	**(9.07%)**

Table 7.6   Additional portfolio information – actual overlay portfolio MMV and cash flow (50% BHR)

Period end	End-period EUR valuation of actual overlay (MMV) Q	Cash flow from overlay in period (EUR) R	Cum cash flow EUR S
0	0.000	0.000	0.000
1	0.282	0.000	0.000
2	0.937	0.000	0.000
3	(0.024)	0.891	0.891

7.5.2   Embedded currency plus currency overlay methodology

Keeping the same portfolio information, Table 7.8 sets out the workings for an 'embedded currency plus currency overlay' benchmark. I have not included a total return row, since none of these returns contains the 'carrier' asset that allows geometric linking. I have also only included a 50% BHR calculation – the reader can work through other hedge ratios if required.

Table 7.7   Actual portfolio and performance calculation (50% BHR)

	% Return from overlay	Portfolio return**	Relative performance of overlay portfolio vs. benchmark
Column formula:	$[(Q_t - Q_{t-1}) + (S_t - S_{t-1})]/G_{t-1}$	$H + T$	$U - M$
Period end	T	U	V
0			
1	1.12%	(0.16%)	(0.18%)
2	2.62%	(5.69%)	0.42%
3	(0.31%)	0.14%	(0.02%)
Total return		**(5.70%)**	**0.23%****

* Total resulting from the subtraction or addition of other totals, not geometrically linked.
** Column U is not the actual portfolio return. It is the *benchmark* unhedged asset return (column H) plus the *actual* currency overlay return. The *actual* unhedged asset return would not normally be used in currency overlay benchmark calculations.

Table 7.8   Embedded currency plus currency overlay benchmark (50% hedged)

	Embedded currency (= currency surprise) $-\{(A_{t-1}/C_{t-1} - A_{t-1}/B_t) +$	Benchmark contribution from hedging $[BHR\{(A_{t-1}/C_{t-1} - A_{t-1}/B_t) +$	50% hedged return
Column formula:	$(D_{t-1}/F_{t-1} - D_{t-1}/E_t)\}/G_{t-1}$	$(D_{t-1}/F_{t-1} - D_{t-1}/E_t)\}]/G_{t-1}$	$W + X$
Period end	W	X	Y
0			
1	(2.59%)	1.30%	(1.30%)
2	(4.41%)	2.20%	(2.20%)
3	0.58%	(0.29%)	0.29%

In essence, this benchmark clearly shows that a 50% BHR eliminates half of the embedded currency exposure in an international portfolio. This is much clearer under this methodology than under the 'asset plus currency overlay' methodology in Section 7.5.1.

7.5.3   Currency overlay only

This is the easiest methodology to calculate, and to conceptualise. Only the overlay return is recorded in the benchmark – there are no elements from the underlying portfolio. Table 7.9 shows the calculations for a 50% hedged benchmark, along with actual overlay returns and relative performance. None of the values in this table is investable back into the return series from which they emerge, and so none is geometrically linked. Total or annualised returns will be approximations – as long as this is recognised, the method of totalling or annualising is not critical.

7.6   TRACKING ERROR

This section brings together this chapter and Chapter 6. Tracking error in this context is the annualised standard deviation of the percentage differences (usually monthly) between actual

Table 7.9   Currency overlay only benchmark (50% BHR)

	Benchmark contribution from hedging	% Return from overlay	Relative performance of overlay portfolio vs. benchmark
Column formula:	L	T	AA − Z
Period end	Z	AA	AB
0			
1	1.30%	1.12%	(0.18%)
2	2.20%	2.62%	0.42%
3	(0.29%)	(0.31%)	(0.02%)

returns and benchmark returns. We use logs for all the volatility calculations (see Appendix 2), but percentages for the arithmetic required to calculate the tracking error. Columns V in Table 7.7 and AB in Table 7.9 above are examples of the relative return series which generate the tracking error measure.

7.6.1   Passive hedging

Tracking error arises in passive hedging because the actual overlay portfolio is not identical to the benchmark portfolio, and is not identically valued. We can list (more or less exhaustively) the possible sources of tracking error:

- Interest rate differential duration
- Dealing prices/benchmark prices mismatch
- Valuation rates for outstanding forward contracts
- Hedge ratio variations
- Rebalancing trades – buffer and timing
- Discounting methodology on valuations

We take each source in turn.

7.6.1.1   Interest rate differential duration

If the actual portfolio contains forward contracts with different maturities to the benchmark, then variations both in the absolute size and shape of the term structure of interest rates, and variations in the term structure, will generate deviations between the actual portfolio and the benchmark. We can calculate the size of this effect from historical data. Figure 7.5 shows the tracking error purely from this effect for horizons of 2m, 3m, 6m and 12m (versus a 1m benchmark), for a three-currency hedge (JPY, EUR, GBP) for a USD-based investor.

It is clear from Figure 7.5 that this source of tracking error is relatively important – certainly at contract maturities over 3m. For example, the 6m basket tracking error is 29 bp. However, unlike many sources of tracking error, which are the result of continuous small discrepancies, this source is a direct function of whether or not there are large swings in interest rate differentials, whether the differentials are wide, and whether the term structure of interest differentials is sloping rather than flat.

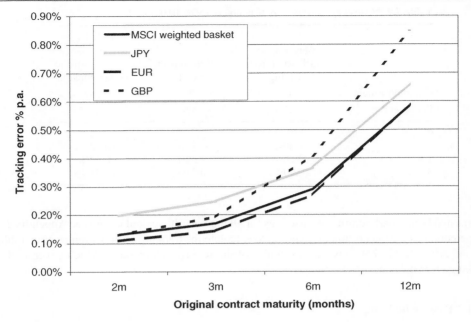

Figure 7.5   Tracking error versus 1m benchmark (USD base, overlapping roll-over, variable contract maturity, 1983–2002, three currencies)

There were several periods in the 1980s and 1990s when these conditions obtained, but less so in recent history. If we only use the last five years' data (Nov 1997–Nov 2002), we can reproduce Figure 7.5 but with the shorter data, and find much lower tracking errors. Figure 7.6 illustrates this. In this period, the 6m basket tracking error is 14 bp.

The tracking errors in Figures 7.5 and 7.6 are compiled from an overlapping roll-over process, rather than a bullet process. An overlapping rolling process is where, for example, in 3-month original maturity hedging, one-third of the exposure matures each month, and the maturing contract is rolled 3m at the end of each month, rather than 100% of the exposure being rolled 3m every three months. For a 6-month original maturity hedge, the contracts are divided into units of one-sixth of the total hedgeable amounts, and one-sixth is rolled each month, for six months. Likewise for all the other original maturity lengths.

This smoothes the effect of the interest rate differential 'snapshot' at roll-over, and creates a hedge closer to constant maturity than the very jagged saw-tooth interest rate differential duration that a 'bullet' roll-over creates. It also significantly smoothes cash flows.

We can chart the two tracking errors (overlapping and bullet), and compare them graphically. Figures 7.7 and 7.8 show the 20-year and 5-year data, respectively. Again, the tracking errors for the most recent period (1997–2002) are much smaller.

7.6.1.2 Dealing prices/benchmark prices mismatch

Even if there was sufficient information to allow rebalancing and rolling trades to be executed at precisely the time that the feeds for the valuation rates for the benchmark are taken,

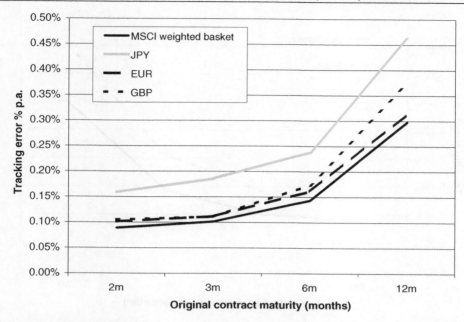

Figure 7.6 Tracking error versus 1m benchmark (USD base, overlapping roll-over, variable contract maturity, 1997–2002, three currencies)

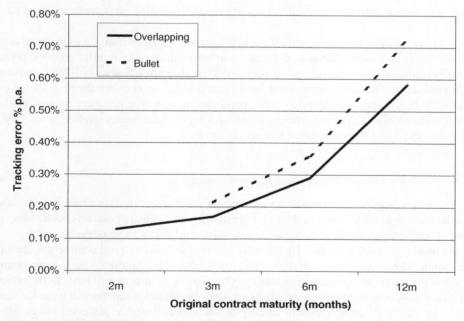

Figure 7.7 Tracking error versus 1m benchmark – overlapping versus bullet roll-over (USD base, variable contract maturity, 1983–2002, three-currency basket)

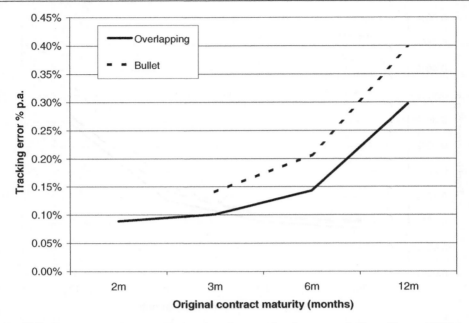

Figure 7.8 Tracking error versus 1m benchmark – overlapping versus bullet roll-over (USD base, variable contract maturity, 1997–2002, three-currency basket)

nevertheless there would still be a difference between the valuation rates, and the actual rates dealt.

There are two elements at work here. If the benchmark is based on mid-prices (as most are), then at each roll, and each rebalance, the actual portfolio will receive slightly less good prices than the benchmark. This will generate a very small tracking error, and a small but consistent underperformance. Secondly, there is a natural (small) variation between the prices used for 'deals' in the benchmark, and the prices that a particular manager can negotiate for a particular live deal in the market. Given the efficiency and liquidity of the currency market, this is likely to be a very small (<1 bp) contributor to tracking error.

7.6.1.3   Valuation rates for outstanding forward contracts

Most 1-month rolling benchmark calculations use only the end-period spot rate to value (and close) the maturing hedge. All actual passive portfolios will maintain contracts outstanding at the end of a reporting period, and they will require forward prices to value them.

At the most obvious level, a live 1m maturity passive portfolio will roll contracts at the end of the month. This means that at all times there are contracts outstanding – there is never any time when there are no contracts outstanding. Outstanding contracts will have to be valued (even if they have only just been executed). Most portfolio valuation reports will value forward contracts at 'dealable' rates; this will usually be the appropriate (i.e. adverse) bid or offer prices. If mid-prices are used, then this will minimise (but not eliminate) the tracking error versus benchmark.

Where forward prices include bid/offer spreads, the side of the market (LHS/RHS) of the spot price off which the forward FX swaps are priced will depend on whether the simultaneous rebalance is an asset rise (sell more foreign currency – so the foreign currency bid price is used) or an asset fall (buy back foreign currency – so the foreign currency offer price is used). This switching of the spot reference price can be responsible for a tracking error of around 10 bp p.a. – although since it is only 'shifting' of return between one month and the next, it will cumulate over time to zero.

7.6.1.4   Hedge ratio variations

A difference between the benchmark hedge ratio and portfolio hedge ratios for each currency in the benchmark can occur for a variety of reasons. Among the most common are:

- Not hedging a very small currency allocation for reasons of materiality
- Not hedging a currency for reasons of liquidity or pricing
- Overhedging a currency because it is acting as a proxy for a currency in the categories above
- Changing a hedge mid-month because of, say, an absolute limitation of max 100% hedge ratio
- Holding hedge ratios at levels other than benchmark because of rebalancing buffers or timing

The tracking errors generated by these mismatches are proportional to the size of currency movements. For a USD-based investor with market cap equity weights, an across-the-board 1% hedge ratio mismatch will produce an annualised tracking error of about 10 bp. This makes hedge ratio mismatches quite an important source of tracking error.

7.6.1.5   Rebalancing trades – buffer and timing

This tracking error source is dealt with in some detail in Chapter 6. There is a cost/tracking error trade-off between close adherence to benchmark methodology, and rebalancing costs arising from spot deals. The costs issues were dealt with earlier; the tracking error issues are dealt with here.

Rebalancing buffer: Rebalancing buffers are used by passive overlay managers to reduce costs. Table 6.7 to 6.13 set out costs for some key variables under the control of the manager. However, in choosing to use buffers for rebalancing, a manager also accepts a trade-off in terms of tracking error.

We can calculate the tracking error resulting from the use of buffers. For a US investor, with market cap weights, and a buffer policy expressed as a percentage of the amount of each currency exposure, we can calculate the approximate tracking error as set out in Table 7.10. The maths for this calculation gets quite complicated, so the table has been put together with numerical analysis and a Monte Carlo simulation.

This tracking error table can be represented in conjunction with the costs table. Figure 7.9 is an 'XY graph'.[7] We can see that we have reached a depth of analysis in which we are measuring costs in fractions of a basis point p.a. The graph indicates that, in spite of the popularity of buffers, in fact they contribute very little to cost reduction. In return, they generate relatively

---

[7] An XY graph is a scattergram which joins the lines between dots. Scattergrams like this can curve in any direction, even 'backwards' on themselves, round in circles, and the line crossing itself. Figure 7.9 happens to be rather conventional in shape.

Table 7.10 Tracking error vs
rebalancing buffers

% Buffer size	Tracking error (bp)
1%	1.5
2%	4.4
3%	7.4
4%	10.9
5%	14.1
6%	17.5
7%	20.1
8%	23.5
9%	26.0
10%	29.0

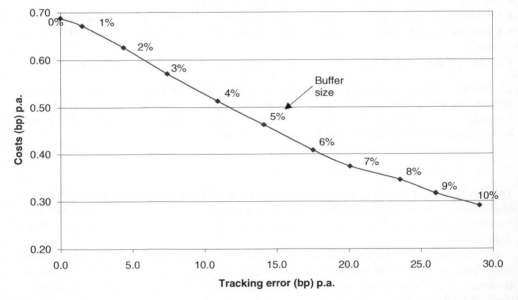

Figure 7.9 XY Chart of costs and tracking error versus rebalancing buffer size (monthly rebalancing, nil delay)

wide tracking errors for fractional changes in cost levels. This would mitigate against their use for any but the most cost-dominated clients.

Rebalancing timing: To calculate this we first calculate the average size of rebalancing required for a monthly rebalance. The average rebalancing size (3.5%) comes from the '1 month' row in Table 6.4. Then we calculate the volatility of currencies, calculated from the observed average historical volatilities. This average is the unweighted average of the MSCI weighted currency surprise volatility for the four major base currencies 1980–2002, and comes out at 10.2%. The formula for the tracking error from delays is then (ignoring logs for simplicity):

$$\text{Tracking error} = \text{Annual currency vols} \times \sqrt{\text{Days delay/Days in month}}$$
$$\times \text{Average size of rebalance}$$

I have not derived this equation here – the interested reader should either apply standard statistical rules to derive this, or confirm its accuracy with numerical testing. This equation produces a tracking error with a root function of the length of the delay, and the resulting tracking error values are shown in Table 7.11.

Table 7.11 Tracking error vs rebalancing delay

Delay in rebalancing	Tracking error (bp)
1 day	7.4
2 days	10.0
3 days	12.5
4 days	14.5
5 days	16.5
6 days	18.1
7 days	19.8
8 days	20.9
9 days	22.1
10 days	23.2

It is clear from this table that delay in rebalancing can be a quite significant source of tracking error. Since there are no dealing-cost consequences from reducing the delay – only administrative effort – currency overlay managers should press clients and their custodians hard to produce timely asset valuations.

7.6.1.6 *Discounting methodology on valuations*

This is likely to be a very minor source of error, particularly at the current (2003) low level of interest rates. It is also a completely artificial one. It will only arise if the benchmark uses discounted valuations of the MMVs of the overlay programme, and the manager's or custodian's valuation does not, or vice versa. It can be completely eliminated by a common reporting methodology across service providers.

7.6.2 **Summary on tracking error**

Tracking error attribution is like performance attribution for bonds. Each element can be separately analysed, but their contribution to total tracking error is not a simple sum of parts; rather, it is a calculation based on the standard rule for combining series:

$$
\begin{aligned}
\text{Variance (combined)} = {} & \text{Variance Series } 1 + \text{Variance Series } 2 + \text{Variance Series } 3 \\
& + \cdots + \text{Variance Series } n + 2\text{Cov}(\text{Series } 1, \text{Series } 2) \\
& + 2\text{Cov}(\text{Series } 1, \text{Series } 3) + \cdots + 2\text{Cov}(\text{Series } n - 1, \text{Series } n)
\end{aligned}
$$

and

$$
\text{Tracking error} = \sqrt{\text{Variance (combined)}}
$$

So for n tracking error contributors, there are $n + [n(n - 1)]/2 \ [= (n^2 + n)/2]$ terms in the equation. The 'difficult' terms are the covariances – they are not 'intuitively' easy to guess or hypothesise. They may be negative or positive, depending on a variety of factors. The interested reader (and he/she would have to be *very* interested to go into this level of detail!) might like to conduct their own experiments to determine the covariances of these tracking error series.

I would like to conclude this chapter with an approximate combined tracking error table. For the purpose of this exercise, I will assume that all the covariance terms are zero – i.e. that none of the contributors to tracking error are correlated (positively or negatively) with each other. This means that the total tracking error is the root of the sum of the squares of the constituent parts. I have included three types of passive mandate in the table (Table 7.12) to give a flavour of the range of costs possible. I have 'guessed' some of the more opaque values, but generally speaking heroic efforts to minimise tracking error will be increasingly expensive. Similarly, a determination to minimise costs will inevitably mean the appearance of more tracking error.

Table 7.12   Passive tracking error for three strategies

Source of tracking error	Passive strategy 1 – benchmark hugging (bp)	Passive strategy 2 – cost minimising (bp)	Passive strategy 3 – error/cost compromise (bp)
Interest rate differential	0	14	10
Valuation rates	3	9	5
Hedge ratio variations	2	8	5
Rebalancing timing	10	14.5	12.5
Rebalancing buffer	0	0	0
Miscellaneous	3	8	3
Total tracking error	**11.0**	**24.8**	**17.8**

One point remains: tracking error is a relative concept. There is no compulsion for a client to adopt one of the published benchmarks as their benchmark. Many will not because the benchmark asset allocations do not match their chosen strategic allocations. This leaves open the possibility of designing a benchmark methodology which is lower cost to execute, to match in a passive portfolio, than the published benchmarks. This allows the client to reduce passive hedging costs (which is a real gain), while not generating tracking error – which is a relative (and therefore somewhat artificial) measure. The contents of this and the two preceding chapters should help benchmark designers in this task.

Overlaying Different Asset Classes

This chapter develops the theoretical arguments made in Chapter 5 into the real world of actual assets. Currency overlay is most commonly associated with cross-border equity holdings. Accordingly, equities, and equities' return behaviour, will comprise the bulk of this chapter.

There are two reasons why equities have dominated bonds in currency 'underlay'. The first is that there is much more cross-border equity investment than cross-border bond investment. The overall weight of equities in pension funds (the main cross-border investors) is much higher than the overall weight of equities, and the proportion of that higher weight is also much higher. The second reason is a little perverse. It has long been accepted that cross-border bond investment does not make economic sense (or at least sense in modern portfolio theory) unless the bonds are fully currency hedged. Leaving bonds unhedged increases their volatility from $c.$ 6% to $c.$ 12%, without increasing their expected return. This simple observation has meant that almost all international bond mandates are benchmarked against hedged benchmarks.

This, in turn, has meant that hedged mandates have been handed out, and that international bond managers have been expected to hedge as a matter of routine. This has meant that currency hedging expertise has been developed in bond management firms, and the conditions for the development of stand-alone overlay in this asset class have been absent. Interestingly, however, the style of active currency management adopted by bond managers has been very different from the styles adopted by overlay managers. Bond managers typically take opportunistic decisions to lift currency hedges in ad hoc decision-making processes. Overlay managers have developed more structured processes.

8.1 EQUITIES

8.1.1 Correlation – the historical evidence

The discussion in Chapter 5 has been largely theoretical. However, it established that the critical relationship needed for us to be able to determine the effect of hedging on international portfolios is the correlation (if any) between currencies and equities. I want to turn now to the historical evidence to test this relationship.

What relationship to test? We have assumed in all of the above theory that there is no correlation between currency returns and equity returns. We need to examine the extent to which this assumption is satisfied, or violated, in practice. It is important to understand why the correlation between *hedged equities* and *currency surprise* is the right one to test.

What we are trying to do is to assess whether 'equity returns' and 'currency returns' are correlated. But what are 'equity returns'? For a domestic market, this is easy: the returns of the chosen equity index. For an international market, what do we do about the currency issue? Clearly if we measure the correlation between currencies and unhedged international equities, we are highly likely to get a strong positive correlation. This is because the international asset is having the currency return added to it; and then we are measuring the correlation between this measure and the foreign currency. If there was not a strong positive correlation, it would be indicative of a strong negative correlation between hedged international equities and currency.

But why have I not mentioned 'local' returns in equities? The reason is that local returns are not investable for anyone other than a local investor. Correlations between currencies and an uninvestable index may be academically interesting, but are not useful in determining asset strategies. What we need to do is analyse what is actually available to international investors. What is available, and looks very like 'local' returns in correlation if not in absolute returns, is 'hedged international'. This is the only way that an investor can access international markets without accepting currency risk, and therefore this is the measure we are interested in.

We could look at hedging in a slightly different way which might help intuitive understanding. Because, for the reasons above, we expect unhedged equity:currency correlations to be strongly positive, undertaking hedging (whose returns are the negative of currency surprise) alongside unhedged international is like investing in an asset class negatively correlated with an existing class (good), but with an expected return of zero. 'Shorting' equities cannot perform the same function because of the expected negative returns (i.e. negative because of the positive expected equity risk premium for long equity positions).

8.1.2   Correlation evidence

How do historical currency:hedged asset correlations compare to the assumptions in the above example? Taking the nearly 20-year period Jan 80–Sep 00, I have set out in Figure 8.1 the correlations for four major investor base currencies (USD, EUR, JPY, GBP). The measure is the correlation coefficient between the hedged returns of the international equity market expressed in the base currency, and the returns of a weighted basket of the relevant currencies.[1] So for example under 'USD base', the graph shows the correlation coefficient between hedged EAFE and EAFE-weighted EAFE currencies.

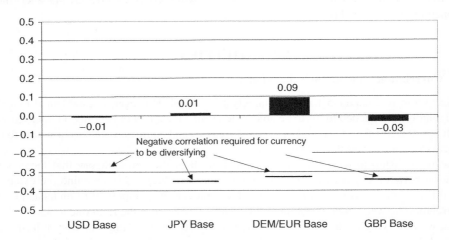

Figure 8.1   Correlations between currencies and equities – correlation between hedged equities and currency surprise of the same market (market cap basket wieghts 1980–2002)

[1] The currency series is the market-cap-weighted sum of the one-month currency surprises of three currencies versus the base currency. The equity weighting is from MSCI, and the currency data is from Record Treasury's database. The equity return series are country indices from MSCI (including net dividends). The EUR is DEM prior to 1999.

I have also shown the negative correlations that would be required for the addition of currency surprise (i.e. holding the equity unhedged) to be diversifying.[2] These are different for each base currency and international asset pair because the underlying volatilities are different. If the currency and hedged equity volatility are identical, then the break-even is –0.5. The reader can see from the formula in the footnote that there is a linear relationship between this value and the relative volatility of the currency and equity.

8.1.3   Individual currency:equity correlations

Figure 8.1 shows the 'rest of the world' correlations for four base currencies. But what do individual currencies:equities look like? Figure 8.2 shows the 12 relationships (four base currencies each with three 'foreign equity markets'). It is notable that the individual country correlations are more variable than the 'World ex domestic' baskets. In particular, the German equity market has a negative correlation with the DEM from two base currency perspectives – USD base and GBP base. As we saw above, this will mitigate the additional risk from holding German equities unhedged, and reduce the impact of hedging. I will look into this more deeply below.

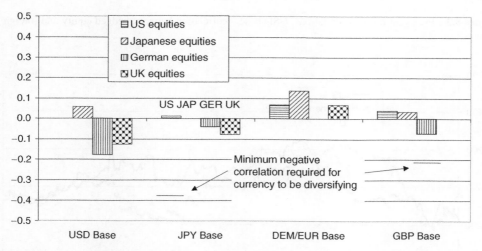

Figure 8.2 Correlations between currencies and equities – correlation coefficients between hedged foreign equities and same-country currency surprise for each base currency (1980–2002)

In Figure 8.2, two examples of break-even values for currency exposure to become diversifying are included. For EUR equities/currency from a GBP base, the value is significantly less negative than –0.5 (at –0.23) because this currency relationship is less than half as volatile as German equities. In contrast, the value for US equities and currency is –0.38 from a JPY base. The dollar is nearly as volatile a market as the hedged US equity market when looked at from a Japanese point of view.

---

[2] For the mathematically minded, currency exposure becomes diversifying (i.e. reduces volatility) when the correlation coefficient is more negative than –(SD currency surprise)/[2 × (SD hedged equity)].

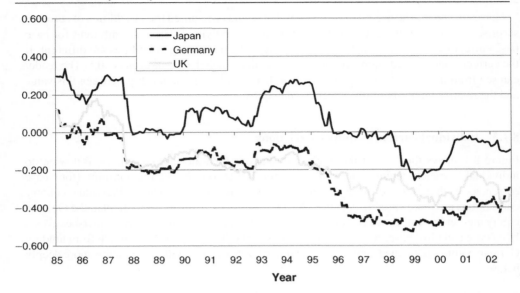

Figure 8.3 Five-year rolling correlations, USD base – correlation between hedged equity and foreign currency

Figure 8.4 Five-year rolling correlations, JPY base – correlation between hedged equity and foreign currency

8.1.4 Stability of correlations

Figure 8.2 shows that equity:currency correlations are close to zero, and certainly far from the level of negative correlation required for currencies to be diversifying. Is this a stable finding,

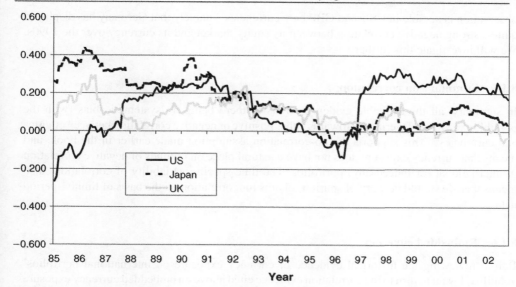

Figure 8.5 Five-year rolling correlations, DEM/EUR base – correlation between hedged equity and foreign currency

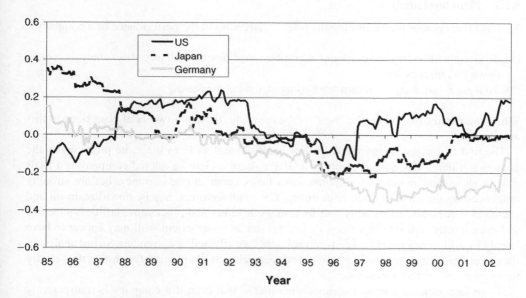

Figure 8.6 Five-year rolling correlations, GBP base – correlation between hedged equity and foreign currency

or do correlations vary? Figures 8.3 to 8.6 show the 5-year rolling correlations for the same 20-year period for each of the currency bases.

It is clear that correlations are not very stable over time, and we should be wary of constructing models, hypotheses or strategies which are sensitive to specific correlation assumptions. One observation is notable in USD and GBP base currencies – namely that Germany has displayed quite a strong negative correlation between its equity market and its currency over the 1990s. We will investigate this further.

8.1.5   Summary on correlation

In summary, all the available evidence points to there being no systematic bias (with the possible exception of Germany) towards either positive or negative correlation between equities and currencies.[3] This supports the no-correlation assumption made earlier in the book, and means that currency exposure does not have a natural place on grounds of negative correlation in international (or indeed any) portfolios. The time-specific variability of correlations also means that we should be wary of spurious claims for correlation on the basis of limited-period data.

8.1.6   Embedded currency

Before reviewing the historical evidence of currency exposure on international portfolios' volatility, I want to turn to the correlation evidence cited above on embedded currency exposure in international equities – what has been coined the 'BP'[4] problem.

8.1.7   Firm level analysis

We have two choices for examining the role of currencies in the performance of a company:

(a) To attempt an individual corporate income/expenditure and balance sheet analysis broken down by currency, or
(b) To tease it out at equity return level using statistical measures.

While the former may seem the 'best' or 'pure' route, there are two fatal objections to this approach.

The first is that the 'corporate cash flow analysis' suffers from the same problems as the assumption that a UK-quoted equity is a GBP risk, or a German-quoted company is a EUR risk. A significant number of corporate cash flows occur in one currency, but are strongly influenced by the level of another currency. Car manufacturers, hotels, downstream oil and chemical processors, commodity and food manufacturers and processors, utilities, telecoms and even farmers fall into this category to a greater or lesser extent – all may appear to have largely local currency payables and receivables, but are affected by currencies. So just analysing the currency of denomination in payables and receivables is likely to confuse rather than clarify the corporates' currency exposure.[5]

If one fatal objection wasn't enough, the other is that even if a company is transparently exposed to a particular currency or currencies, it is irrelevant if the market valuation of the

---

[3] The other exception is Canada. In Canada, there is sufficient negative correlation between non-domestic (i.e. US equities) and USD/CAD to render hedging USD from a CAD base ineffective for volatility reduction.

[4] So called because of the uncertainty as to whether BP is a sterling-based company (currency of accounts, head office, main quotation) or a dollar-based company (head office of two large acquisitions, Amoco and Arco, and currency of denomination of oil, its dominant product).

[5] The author has over 20 years advised many multinationals on these issues, and indeed pioneered in the early 1980s the hedging of 'invisible' exposures not accounted for by foreign currency payables and receivables.

Box 8.1   Embedded currency exposure

Currency exposure conventionally arises from investment in securities of different currency denomination from the home currency. So UK pension fund investing in US Treasury bonds is unequivocally a denomination-based exposure.

Let us suppose, however, that a UK pension fund invests in a US oil company. Ostensibly a US dollar investment, complete with currency exposure. If this company is taken over by a UK oil company, and the denomination of the share quote changed to sterling, has all the currency risk been eliminated?

The answer is more complicated than at first might appear. It is possible to determine how much 'foreign currency' content any security has by analysing the 'elasticity' of the price (expressed in the home currency) with respect to currency movements. A 'pure' dollar investment (say US T-bond) would show 100% elasticity of sterling price movement with respect to the dollar. However, the oil company in the example above might show 50% elasticity with respect to the dollar (reflecting the strong US dollar earnings stream).

This exercise can be conducted at index level, rather than at individual security level, and can determine whether classes of equities have any foreign currency exposure embedded in them. A 20-year study (Diversification – *op. cit.*) shows that the UK equity market has about 19% US dollar content. The German equity market has about 40% US dollar content, and rising. The US equity market has no foreign currency content. Bond markets have no foreign currency content.

This raises the questions of whether, for example, German investors in their domestic equity market should hedge their embedded currency exposure, and whether US investors investing in UK stocks should hedge only 80% of their value. In practice, the concept of embedded currency exposure has only been adopted by isolated investors and corporations, and not generally.

business does not respond in a systematic way to changing currency values. There is little evidence that valuation processes are that consistent – and anyway the way to test this is to conduct a statistical test on equity market returns, which is what we will do – i.e. option (b).

At the company level, it means that there are businesses which are notionally UK- and sterling-based, such as BP, which deal in international markets (mainly priced in dollars), which in the BP case are comprised of significant portions of fully US businesses (Arco, Amoco). It is reasonable to assume that these businesses will have a positive correlation between their profits (expressed in sterling) and dollar returns versus sterling. Strong dollar, higher profits; weak dollar, lower profits.

From an investment perspective, however, the level of profit is not a direct determinant of equity returns. In determining hedging strategy, we must concern ourselves with equity returns, not with corporate profits. So the question is: is there positive correlation between equity returns for BP expressed in sterling, and dollar returns versus sterling? If there is a correlation, how much of BP profits are 'really' dollars?

We can test this proposition, and the rolling 5-year correlation graph of Figure 8.7 is the result. This shows a surprisingly stable result, and implies that there is a consistent (but quite small) 'dollar content' in the BP sterling share price.

We can test the same data series using a different approach, which will indicate the proportion of BP returns that are dollar-denominated (rather than the proportion of the volatility which

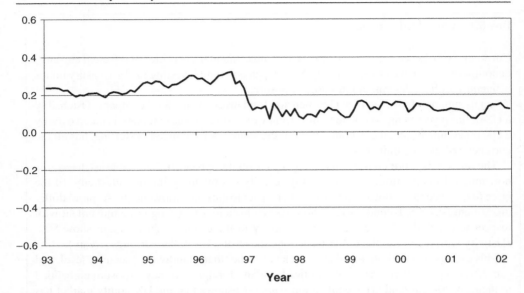

Figure 8.7 Five-year rolling correlation between BP £ share price returns and dollar surprise (1988–2002)

is explained by exchange rate volatility). Firstly, we hypothesise the existence of a particular currency embedded in an equity's return. For example, we would hypothesise quite naturally that BP £ equity returns had USD embedded in them. We then apply an overlay to neutralise this currency exposure, and we can examine a range of hedge ratios from 0% to 100%. For the avoidance of doubt, the overlay in this example would be for the UK investor to sell USD vs. GBP forward, the amount being a proportion (between 0% and 100%) of the value of the UK equity valuation. This forward sale, in common with all passive currency overlay, would be rolled at the maturity of the forward contract. This process would produce a series of profits and losses, or 'currency overlay returns', which would be added to the returns of the underlying assets. The question of whether there is any embedded USD exposure could then be observed by measuring portfolio volatility (the portfolio equals UK equities plus overlay returns) in relation to the 'hedge ratio'. Note that this process is applied if our hypothesis is that BP *earn* USD net; we might think that other UK companies, for example, *pay* USD (or another currency) net.

The 'low point' of the curve in the graphs that follow will indicate the optimum proportion of dollars to be hedged from a UK perspective, and therefore give an indication of the proportion of 'embedded dollars' in the equity return series.

Figure 8.8 shows that the optimum hedge ratio is around 40% – implying (very loosely) that 40% of BP's investment returns are dollar-denominated. It should be emphasised that currency surprise only accounts for some 2.5% of the total volatility of the BP share price, so the importance of this effect should not be overestimated.

There is an interesting question (although largely academic) as to whether the key driver of the 'dollar content' (or any other currency) of equity prices is:

(a) The equity-market-wide response to exchange rate moves
(b) The domicile mix of ownership

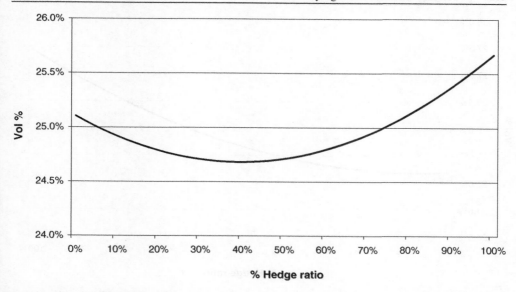

Figure 8.8 Volatility of BP share price versus hedge ratio – BP £ returns 'hedged' with a short dollar overlay versus sterling (1988–2002)

(c) The trading 'weight' in different share listing environments (e.g. UK listing vs. NYSE listing), or
(d) The genuine economic impact of exchange rates on a business.

Because the question is interesting rather than critical, I will not devote a significant amount of time trying to ascertain the importance of each of these elements. However, we can conduct a couple of simple tests which might help to eliminate one or more of these elements.

I will examine the behaviour of a widely held, large cap UK stock, but this time with no ostensible US dollar income or expenditure. I have chosen Tesco, a UK supermarket chain with little international activity. Figure 8.9 shows the same measure as that above: the volatility of the 'hedged' return series versus the hedge ratio (remember that the hedge is to sell dollars vs. sterling – eliminating any 'embedded dollar exposure' if there is any). The result is pleasingly intuitive. The graph shows that Tesco shows no embedded dollar returns in its equity returns – any addition of a dollar 'hedge' increases the volatility of the Tesco equity return series.

These two graphs might lead us in the direction of thinking that it is the underlying economics of a business that are the main determinant of the equity returns' sensitivity to exchange rate movements. However, if we look at a third stock, HSBC – the banking group – we get a confusing message. Using the same analysis and graph design, we get Figure 8.10. This shows a continuous reduction in equity volatility with increasing hedge ratio. It implies that all of HSBC's profits (and more (actually 150%) if we extrapolate the curve) are derived from dollar-based sources. It may be plausible that a significant proportion of HSBC's profits are dollar-related, but given its substantial interests in the UK and non-dollar locations elsewhere, it is implausible that it is exposed to the dollar to more than 100% of its profits.

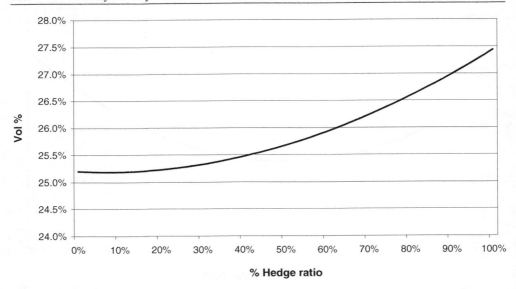

Figure 8.9   Volatility of Tesco share price versus hedge ratio – Tesco £ returns 'hedged' with a short dollar overlay versus sterling (1988–2002)

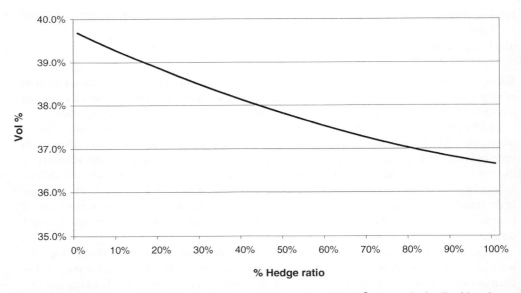

Figure 8.10   Volatility of HSBC share price versus hedge ratio – HSBC £ returns 'hedged' with a short dollar overlay versus sterling (1988–2002)

It seems more likely, therefore, that some of the explanation of this apparent exposure to the dollar lies in the other three reasons. We could continue the exercise *ad infinitum*, with each stock generating a different profile. But of more value for our purposes is to move on to the equity returns at the country level.

8.1.8   Country index equity returns

I would remind the reader that we assumed that all these companies *earned* USD net. As it turned out from the result, it was not an unreasonable assumption to make. However, we might think that there are UK companies (say net importers) which *pay* USD net. In this case we might like to test an overlay which had rolling *purchases* not sales of USD against GBP.

We should perhaps allow for this eventuality by allowing the hedge ratio to vary from –100% (100% purchases of USD vs. GBP) to + 100% (100% sales of USD vs GBP). We have conducted this test on the UK, and Figure 8.11 shows the UK market/embedded USD example described tested over 22 years (1980–2000).

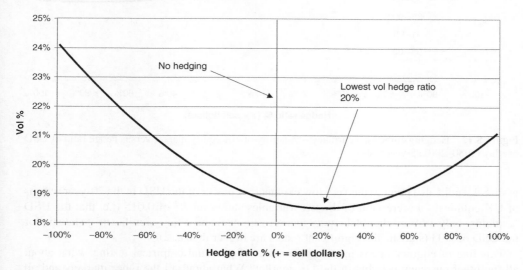

Figure 8.11   Hedging embedded currency, GBP base – volatility of UK equity market versus hedge ratio of USD overlay (1980–2002)

It shows a small reduction in overall portfolio volatility (compared to 'unhedged') with the minimum volatility at around 20% hedge ratio. This might be thought of as the amount of the embedded net USD exposure in the UK equity market being around 20%,[6] or alternatively it might well be a spurious result (particularly given the small volatility reduction achieved). How can we tell the difference?

One way is to look at stability. Figure 8.12 shows the same graph for four non-overlapping 5-year periods (I have normalised the absolute start level of volatility to make the graph more readable). This shows a significant apparent increase in the 'USD' content over the past 20 years. In the last 5-year period, the low point of volatility is at a hedge ratio of 74%, compared with a 'lowest volatility' hedge ratio of −15% for 80–85. There is probably not much point 'overmodelling' beyond what we have. We can easily *ex post* rationalise that the world has got more 'global'; that the USD has increasingly become the *numeraire* of international business; that the US pension fund perspective dominates global equity market behaviour; that the UK businesses that now dominate the UK indices (TMT, oil, financial) are global in nature, and 'dollarised' in outlook. However, I suggest that however plausible all these are, they are still *ex post* rationalisations, and the firm evidence supporting a large USD content in the UK market

---

[6] It also implies that the optimum hedge ratio for hedging UK equity exposure from a USD perspective is 100% − 20% = 80%.

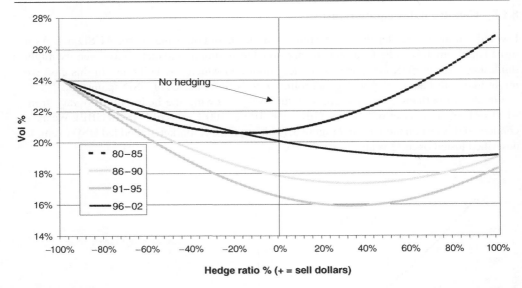

Figure 8.12   Hedging embedded currency – volatility of UK equity market versus hedge ratio of USD overlay (1980–2002, 5-year tests)

is slim. I would also point to the very low explanatory power of the USD in the 20-year returns of UK equities – a regression of the two variables shows an R^2 of 0.015 (i.e. that the USD 'explains' only 1.5% of the total equity market variance) and a 'just significant' t-statistic for the USD of 2.03 (statistically significant t-stats are higher than c. 2).

This line of enquiry opens up a huge amount of potential empirical testing: what about all the other currency weights in the UK market? What about all the other markets and all their foreign currency weights. Regression, a (rather abused) statistical technique, allows us to test whether any number of independent variables (in this case currency returns) provide any explanation for one dependent variable (in this case domestic equity returns). The results of the regression can estimate both the size of the effect, and its statistical significance. We have performed single regressions[7] for each of our four major base currency equity markets (US, UK, Japan, Germany), and the results are summarised in Table 8.1.

Regression results always need to be treated with caution, and these results particularly so. There appear to be only three currency:equity relationships with any explanatory power at all:

(a) A weight of 19.5% of dollars in the UK equity market
(b) A weight of −25.7% of euros in the Japanese equity market
(c) A weight of 31.7% of dollars in the German equity market

---

[7] In conventional (econometric) modelling, *multiple regression* is the standard approach to estimating variable signs, weights and significance. However, where the explanatory power of the independent variables (in this case individual currency surprises) is low, and the independent variables are significantly correlated with each other (which they are in this case), multiple regression can throw up spurious results. One way round this problem is to perform separate regressions for each single independent variable (single regression), and I have chosen this technique. The reader may like to note that the (currency) weights of the variables in the regression results are very close to the hedge ratios that give minimum volatility (compare Figure 8.11 and the weight of USD in the UK market in Table 8.1).

Table 8.1 Embedded currency weight and sign
(*t*-stats in brackets) – regression coefficients
monthly data (1980–2002)

Equity market	Embedded currency			
	USD	GBP	JPY	EUR
US		Neg	Neg	Neg
UK	19.5% (2.0)		Neg	Neg
Japan	Neg	Neg		−25.7% (2.4)
Germany	31.7% (2.8)	Neg	Neg	

Note: A *t*-stat greater than approximately 2 is statistically
significant. Where the regression that produces these values
has an R^2 of less than 1%, I assign 'Neg' = negligible
impact.

We have discussed item (a) at some length earlier. The effect is weak, but it is plausible. We know the relationship to be unstable, currently with rising dollar weights, and with a number of different possible explanations. My favourite explanation is that rising dollar weights indicate a combination of the internationalisation of some of the heavyweights of the UK indices (BP, Vodafone, HSBC), together with a rising weight of international (particularly dollar) investors in the UK market. It is notable that on current (December 2002) market capitalisation and exchange rates, the UK is easily the largest equity market outside the US. This makes it the number one target of US investors, the largest group of international equity investors.

Item (b) indicates that the Japanese equity market returns are negatively correlated with the DEM/EUR. This is a bizarre finding, implying, *inter alia*, that the companies making up the Japanese equity market are net importers of euro-denominated goods (which they are not). It is hard to find other plausible explanations, and frankly I suspect that this finding may be spurious (i.e. chance). This feeling is supported by the split test: the relationship is strong for the 1980–1991 period, and absent for the 1991–2002 period. I would therefore suggest that the null hypothesis embedded in the assumptions for the theoretical case made above – namely no correlation - is maintained intact.

Item (c) appears to be a more secure finding. It implies that there is a significant weight of dollar returns in the German (and by association, European) equity market. The effect appears to have increased over the past 20 years, and it is highly plausible that this has come about through the same influences as the dollar impact on the UK market. The strength of the relationship, however, may be greater than the UK's because there is little in the way of German (or indeed European) institutional investment; the dominant investors (and at the margin) in the German equity market are US investors.

8.1.9 International equity correlations

We have spent a considerable amount of time examining the question of currency:equity correlation, since our theoretical model earlier in the chapter assumed a currency:equity correlation of zero. We have uncovered scant evidence to abandon that hypothesis. But what about the historical evidence as it applies to our theoretical analysis of international equity correlations?

We set up a theoretical example above, in which we assumed that domestic equities had an annualised volatility of 16%, unhedged international equities had a volatility of 16%, and currency surprise had a volatility of 11%. We assumed that domestic and unhedged international had a correlation of 0.5, and we predicted that domestic and hedged international would have an 'apparently higher' correlation of 0.69, despite the fact that the covariance was unchanged. We saw that this was due entirely to the reduction in volatility of the international assets through hedging, and not through any loss of 'diversification'. How does this theoretical prediction match up with the historical evidence?

In Figure 8.13 we show (for 1980–2002) the actual historical correlation for domestic:unhedged international equities for each of four base currencies versus the 'World ex domestic index.' From this information, we make a theoretical prediction of the expected correlation for domestic:hedged international equities, and show the actual observed correlation for comparison. The graph also shows the average correlations for all currency bases.

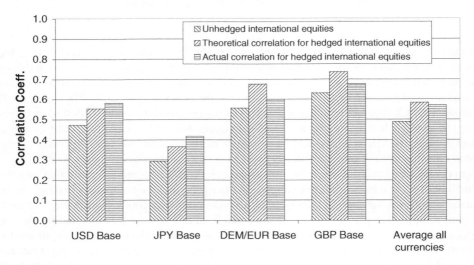

Figure 8.13   Correlations between domestic and international equities – international equities unhedged and hedged ('World ex domestic' weights, 1980–2002)

The graph illustrates that the increases in correlation are close to what we would have predicted. The middle (upward striped) bar shows the increase expected purely from historical volatility reduction, and the right (horizontal striped) bar shows the actual historical correlation. The average of all currency bases shows that there is little overall difference in the theoretical and actual correlation values.

8.1.10   Volatility reduction – the historical evidence

In this section we will examine the volatility of portfolios containing international equities (both hedged and unhedged), and compare theoretical expectations with actual observed. We have established that, broadly speaking, equity:currency correlations are zero. We therefore expect that currency exposure will always increase volatility, and conversely that hedged international equities will always have lower volatility than unhedged international equities. On the basis of the historical volatilities of equities and currency, we can theoretically predict the volatility increase from taking currency risk (see Chapter 5 for the theory), or expressed another way, the reduction in risk for eliminating currency risk. Figure 8.14 shows the results for 'World ex domestic' for the four base currencies and the average. Note that all the hedges are 100%, despite the fact that we have identified above that hedge ratios less than 100% may be optimally risk-reducing.

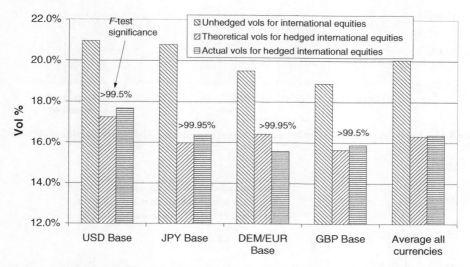

Figure 8.14 Volatility reduction from hedging – market cap international equity weights (1980–2002)

The results are ringingly clear – currency exposure is always risk-increasing,[8] and currency hedging is always risk-reducing. The volatility reductions available from eliminating it are large, and in line with the theoretical predictions based on no correlations between equities and currencies. The result is robust over different time periods. Figures 8.15 to 8.18 show the three 5-year and one 7-year time periods 80–85, 86–90, 91–95, 96–02.

The only exception to the risk-reduction hypothesis from all the time periods is the USD base for 1996–02. The evidence we have already seen shows that the dollar has become increasing positively correlated with German and UK equity markets (we have earlier called this 'embedded currency'). This means that the DEM/EUR is negatively correlated with the German equity market, and the pound is negatively correlated with the UK equity market, both from the US dollar perspective.

If this relationship persists, it may prove an argument against the risk-reduction properties of currency hedging these markets from a dollar perspective. In the absence of a satisfactory explanation for the 'embedded dollar' phenomenon, we cannot be confident of the stability of this relationship.

---

[8] I have shown the F-test results in Figure 8.14. An F-test shows the likelihood that the two samples (unhedged returns and hedged returns) are not drawn from populations with the same variance. The results in Figure 8.14 are very significant indeed; i.e., it is proof that hedging reduces risk.

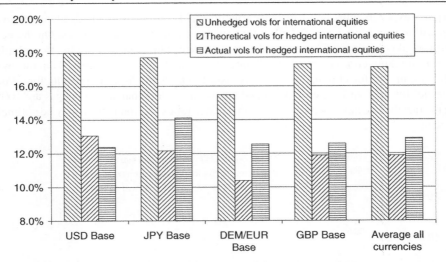

Figure 8.15   Volatility reduction from hedging – market cap international equity weights (1980–1985)

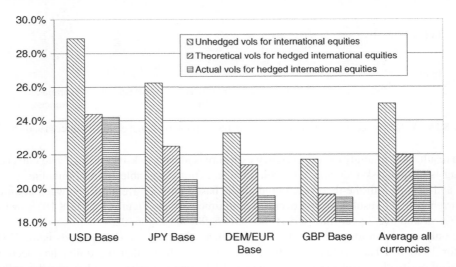

Figure 8.16   Volatility reduction from hedging – market cap international equity weights (1986–1990)

8.1.11   Effect of hedging on portfolio risk

Finally, we can add the reduction in international equities' volatility to domestic equities to give the effect on portfolio volatility. Figure 8.19 the average (across all four currency bases) of equity portfolio volatility as the proportion of international equities (hedged and unhedged) in total equities rises. The X-axis of the graph is the proportion of international in the total (0% = fully domestically invested; 100% = fully internationally invested, with no domestic equities), and the Y-axis of the graph is equity portfolio volatility. The graph illustrates two non-base-currency-specific findings: that the risk-reduction properties of hedging are disproportionately valuable at high international allocations, and that hedging moves the optimum percentage

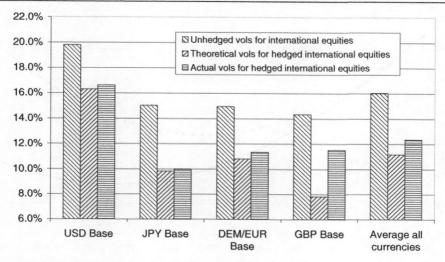

Figure 8.17 Volatility reduction from hedging – market cap international equity weights (1991–1995)

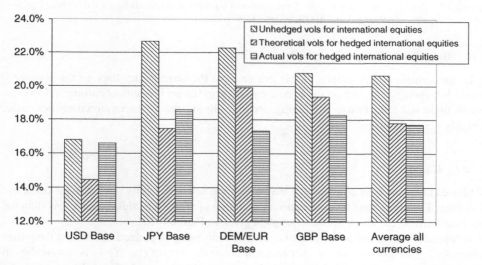

Figure 8.18 Volatility reduction from hedging – market cap international equity weights (1996–2002)

allocation to international up about 20%. In the four-base-currency average, the optimum moves up from about 55% to about 75% international. However, the absolute levels of the optimum proportions of international are very dependent on the base currency, as we shall see.

Expressed in words, the graph shows that, on average, hedging is immaterial at international allocations of less than 10% – although note that the proportion is international equities/total equities. For an Anglo/American pension fund with a typical equity allocation of, say, 60%, this is an international equity allocation of only 6% of the fund – much lower than both the US and UK averages.

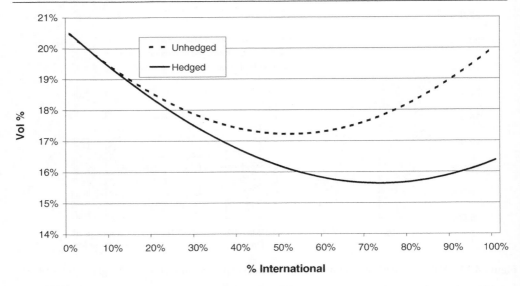

Figure 8.19   Portfolio volatility versus % international equities average, all bases – domestic equities, international equities unhedged and 100% hedged (1980–2002)

8.1.12   Base-currency-specific graphs

All the individual country graphs of this design have the same basic shape as the average – indeed it is a universal finding for every base currency and target investment currency. However, the scale of the risk reduction from hedging, and the optimum mix of international and domestic, are highly country-specific.

8.1.12.1   US base

USD-based investors have a large, well-diversified and low-risk equity market in the domestic US market. The arguments for international investing are therefore significantly less than for other base currencies. The USD-base graph is given in Figure 8.20.

The 'optimum' international mix for US investors investing in hedged international equities is about 48%. Not coincidentally, this residual domestic weight (i.e. 52%) is reasonably in line with the weight of the US in the global equity market (currently 59%; 20-year average 45%). Hedging shifts the optimum proportion of international about 15%, from around 33% to about 46%.

8.1.12.2   Japanese base

The same graph from the Japanese perspective is given Figure 8.21.

Here the effect of hedging is immaterial up to the comparatively high proportion of 30% of international. However, hedging becomes very important for risk reduction at higher levels of international, and the optimum for hedging international equity is about 72%. This implies a weight of domestic (28%) again quite close to the average 20-year weight of Japan in global equity market cap (24%).

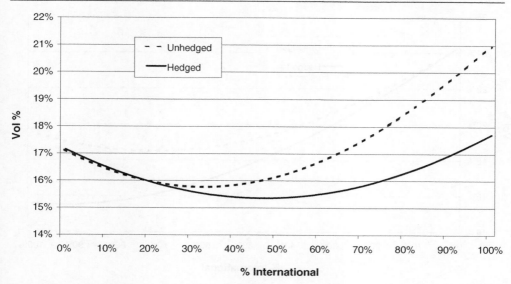

Figure 8.20   Portfolio volatility versus % international equities, USD base – domestic equities, international equities unhedged and 100% hedged (1980–2002)

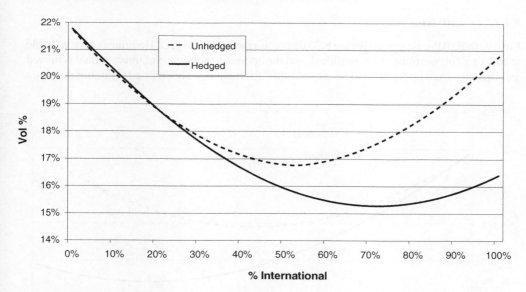

Figure 8.21   Portfolio volatility versus % international equities, JPY base – domestic equities, international equities unhedged and 100% hedged (1980–2002)

8.1.12.3   German/euro base

The story is now reasonably self-explanatory (Figure 8.22). Hedging is very valuable at almost all proportions of international, and the optimum proportion of international is around 95% – again implying a proportion of domestic (5%) close to the 20-year average German equity market cap weight (4%).

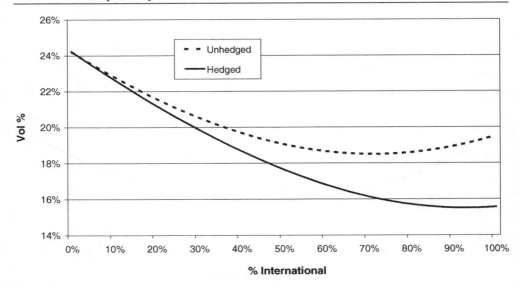

Figure 8.22   Portfolio volatility versus % international equities, DEM/EUR base – domestic equities, international equities unhedged and 100% hedged (1980–2002)

8.1.12.4   GBP base

Finally, the GBP-base graph (Figure 8.23) is much as we would expect. Hedging is very valuable at almost all proportions of international, and the optimum proportion of international is moved significantly from about 50% to about 78% through hedging. The implied optimum domestic

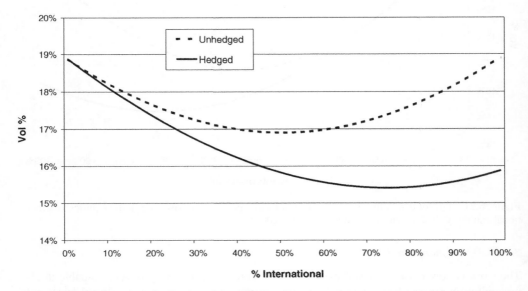

Figure 8.23   Portfolio volatility versus % international equities, GBP base – domestic equities, international equities unhedged and 100% hedged (1980–2002)

allocation (at 22%) is a little higher than the long-term UK market cap (10%). There is no immediately obvious explanation for this. Nevertheless, for all the base currencies, the rule of thumb that equity market investment should be in proportion to market caps if currency hedged, but home-biased if unhedged, is attractive and plausible.

8.2   HEDGE RATIOS

Optimisers have a particular use in strategic asset allocation. They are very good at handling multiple, interrelated and simultaneous asset allocation decisions (how much in equities?, how much in international?, how much to hedge?). However when all of the variables can move, it can be difficult to pin down what is moving and why. I therefore propose to abandon the optimiser approach in looking at the last question in this chapter – that of hedge ratios.

8.2.1   Current debate

There is a live debate on the general question of an 'ideal' hedge ratio for internationally invested portfolio. Different commentators have drawn different conclusions. Summarising the range of opinions, Perold and Schulman (1988) have concluded that passive currency hedging offers a 'free lunch' in reducing the volatility of returns, even though the expected long-term return from currency hedging is nil or marginally negative (transactions costs). Following on from this conclusion, Perold and Schulman recommend a 100% hedged benchmark for non-domestic equities.

Taking the middle ground, a number of commentators have sought to define optimal hedge ratio benchmarks at values between 0% and 100%. One approach has been to define an *efficient* (in mean/variance terms) hedge ratio. Black (1989) proposes a fixed ratio (a universal hedge ratio at less than 100%); both Nesbitt (1991) and Jorion (1994) link hedge ratios to whole-portfolio risk, not just international exposure. All conclude that hedging is justified under certain combinations of international allocation and hedging transaction cost, and at hedge ratios of less than 100%. By contrast, Gardner & Wuilloud (1994) approach the problem from the point of view of minimising 'regret'. This approach favours a 50% hedge ratio, which, not surprisingly, turns out to minimise regret. Some writers, although the minority, have concluded that currency hedging is sub-optimal at observed transaction costs, and therefore to be avoided.

All researchers in this area agree, however, that empirical evidence is in general inconclusive in determining final or firm answers. Correlations between currency movements and other asset classes are highly unstable over time, exhibiting alternatively positive, insignificant and negative correlations.

In the limited space available, can we make an assessment of hedge ratios and their impact on portfolios? We have already done so for limited hedge ratios (0% and 100%) but we can extend this analysis to the full range of hedge ratios. I will concentrate on the effect of hedging on equity portfolios. I choose to ignore (at least in this section) the impact on whole portfolios (i.e. including bonds, property, alternatives) because the range of possible portfolio combinations becomes too numerous to handle. Domestic fixed income returns are not highly correlated with either equities or currency returns, and so most of the conclusions drawn from an equity-only analysis are likely to apply to whole portfolios.

The methodology I will use is identical to that just conducted on four base currency perspectives above (USD, EUR, JPY, GBP), but both the hedge ratio and the proportion of international equities (as a percentage of total equities) will be varied simultaneously. As a start, we can pick an arbitrary domestic:international mix, say 50:50, and show the effect of varying the hedge ratio from 0 to 100%. Figure 8.24 shows the effect on equity portfolio volatility of this varying hedge ratio from the four different base currency perspectives.

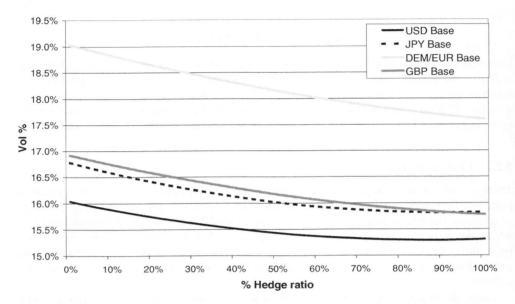

Figure 8.24   Equity portfolio volatility versus hedge ratio (MSCI indices, 50:50 domestic: intenational, 1980–2002)

The graph shows clearly that raising the hedge ratio from zero is always risk-reducing in this 50:50 mix of domestic:international equities. For all of the base currencies except USD, the fall in volatility as the hedge ratio is raised is continuous. For the US, the fall stops at a hedge ratio of 86%, and then rises very slightly. It is likely that this is because of the 'dollar' content that we identified in German and UK equities, which means that at high hedge ratios the USD investor is selling too many euros and pounds.

This graph could be construed as a two-dimensional representation of a 'cross-section' of a three-dimensional surface. We have fixed the proportion of international equities in total equities (i.e. 50%), and varied the hedge ratio from 0% to 100%. In theory we could vary both variables, and represent the result in a three-dimensional 'surface' graph. Although three-dimensional graphs are quite difficult to read, I have nevertheless completed this exercise for the four base currencies, and Figures 8.25 to 8.28 show the results.

8.2.1.1   USD base

The graph for the USD base is shown is Figure 8.25. Firstly, how to read this graph? The values on the 'back wall' of the graph are the values in the unhedged line from Figure 8.20. The values at the front of this surface are the same as the '100%' line from the same graph. The USD line hedge ratio graph (Figure 8.24) shows the 'slice' going from back to front in the middle of Figure 8.25, starting at the 50% point on the back wall. To 'see' it as shown in

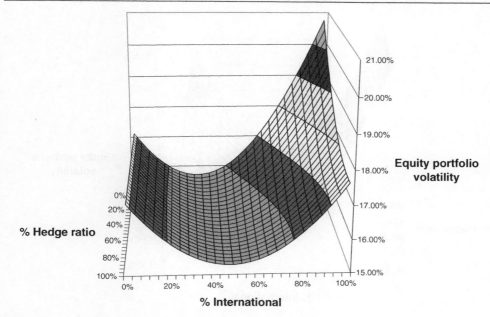

Figure 8.25   USD base 'hammock' (MSCI indices, 1980–2002)

Figure 8.24, you would have to look from the left-hand side at this cross-section. Note that the 'front' axis shows the proportion of international equities in total equities, not in the total fund. For a fund with 50% of its assets in bonds, and the rest in equities, the 40% international level would be an asset allocation of 20% international in the fund.

In summary this graph tells us that international diversification with unhedged foreign equities can reduce equity portfolio volatility by about 1.25% (and that the optimum international proportion is about 30% in international). If a full hedging policy is adopted, the optimum international mix rises to about 45%, and the volatility falls about a further 0.5%. The benefits of international diversification and hedging for US equity investors are there, but they are not overwhelming. In particular, the strategic benefits of hedging are modest. As we shall see, the US is a special case. The other three base currencies that we look at display very strong risk reductions from both international diversification and from hedging.

Why is the US special? The evidence points very strongly to two causes: the 'embedded dollar' content in the UK and German (European) equity markets, and the sheer size and diversification of the US market in comparison with the international alternatives.

Let's look at the other base currencies.

8.2.1.2   JPY base

The JPY base shows a very different pattern (Figure 8.26). For the yen investor, international diversification is hugely risk-reducing (by a nearly 5% volatility reduction), with the unhedged optimum at about 55% international, and the hedged optimum at about 70%. Hedging is also very strongly rewarded, with a nearly 2% further fall in portfolio volatility.

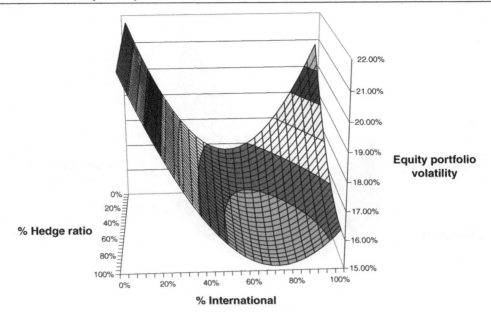

22.00%
21.00%
20.00%
19.00%
**Equity portfolio
volatility**
18.00%
17.00%
16.00%
15.00%

% Hedge ratio

0%
20%
40%
60%
80%
100%

% International

0%   20%   40%   60%   80%   100%

Figure 8.26   JPY base 'hammock' (MSCI indices, 1980–2002)

8.2.1.3   DEM/EUR base

The DEM/EUR investor (Figure 8.27) shows a similar pattern to the yen investor, except that the optimum domestic equity proportion is much smaller, and the gain from hedging is greater. Here the optimum mix of international is even higher (70% unhedged), and fully hedged is about 90%. The combination of international diversification and hedging is, again, extremely risk-reducing, with the combination reducing overall equity portfolio risk by a massive 9%. Euro investors ignore both international diversification and hedging at their peril.

8.2.1.4   GBP base

Finally, the graph from a UK investor's perspective is shown in Figure 8.28. Again, both international diversification and hedging are very risk-reducing for the UK investor. Hedging is particularly valuable – diversification and hedging contribute equally to the nearly 4% reduction in portfolio risk.

It is worth re-noting an observation that I remarked on earlier – namely that the proportion of domestic equities which gives the lowest risk when combined with hedged equities is, for all base currencies, very close to their average historical weight in the world market caps. This is not true where the equities are left unhedged: unhedged international equities are under-represented in optimising any equity portfolio from the historic data, and such portfolios will display home bias and higher-than-necessary volatility.

It is possible that this is one area where financial theory and actual outcomes match. In the world of classical markets, all equities, whatever their base currency, will be arbitraged

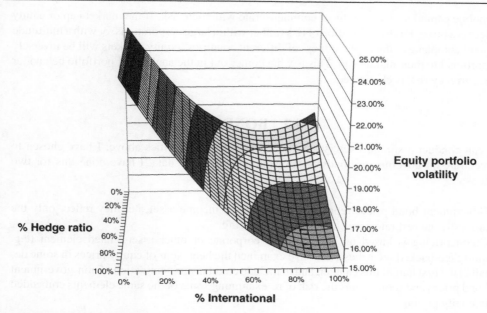

Figure 8.27   DEM base 'hammock' (MSCI indices, 1980–2002)

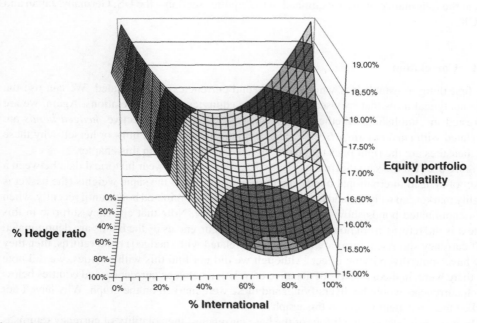

Figure 8.28   GBP base 'hammock' (MSCI indices, 1980–2002)

by mobile capital to deliver returns commensurate with their risk. If the market cap of equity indices is a proxy for diversification of risk (either within large corporations, or with a multitude of small companies), then the riskiness of different countries' equity markets will be inversely proportional to their market cap. This is what comes out in the analysis of portfolio behaviour once currency risk is eliminated.

8.3   BONDS

We can conduct a similar exercise to that conducted with equities above. I have chosen to concentrate on government bonds in the examination of the data. I have done this for two reasons:

1. Government bond prices represent a 'pure' fixed income asset, i.e. they reflect only the domestic interest rate curve, and not credit pricing.
2. Credit pricing is based on an individual corporate or other asset-related element (e.g. mortgage-backed securities). We have examined the behaviour of equity prices in some detail in the first half of this chapter, and to include credit in an examination of non-government bond prices and returns runs the risk of re-examining some of the same elements embedded in equity pricing.

Much of the analysis of currency:asset correlations (particularly with individual stocks), however, will be superfluous. Accordingly, I will concentrate on national bond indices, and look at the four main countries examined in the equities section – the US, Germany, Japan and the UK.

8.3.1   Correlation

The first thing to establish is whether bonds and currencies are correlated. We can use the same analytical tools that we used in examining equity:currency correlations. Again, we are interested in establishing whether, from each base currency perspective, *hedged bonds* are correlated with *currency surprise*. The reader might like to remind him- or herself why these two measures are the right ones to look at by reference to p. 215 in this chapter.

Figure 8.29 (in the same format as Figure 8.1) shows the 17-year historical data between a basket of hedged international bonds and currency surprise in the same weights (the basket is roughly market cap weights, and is dominated by USD-denominated bonds until recently, when JPY-denominated bonds show a strong weight increase). Note that currency surprise in this context is the returns from holding the same foreign currencies as the bonds are denominated in. If currency surprise returns are negatively correlated with (hedged) bond returns, then they may have some diversifying effect. Although we did not find this with equities, we did note that there were, in theory, levels of negative correlation between currencies and equities below which currencies would be diversifying, and these were marked on the graph. Why have I not marked the equivalent levels on this graph?

The answer is because in all four of the base currencies, the volatility of currency returns is more than twice as high as the volatility of hedged bond returns. The figure 'twice as high' is important. I explain in footnote 2 of this chapter that the formula for calculating the negative

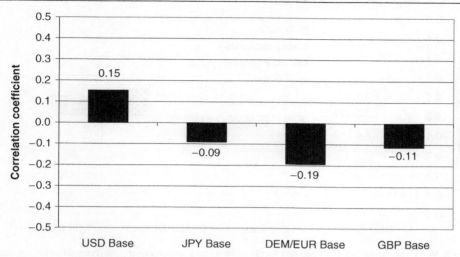

Figure 8.29   Correlation between hedged bonds and currency surprise of the same market basket weights (1985–2002)

correlation required to make currency exposure diversifying is:

$$-(SD\ currency\ surprise)/[2 \times (SD\ hedged\ bonds)]$$

It does not need more than a cursory glance to see that if the volatility of currency surprise is more than twice the volatility of hedged bonds, then it would need a correlation of less than −1 to produce diversification. Correlation coefficients are bounded by −1 and 1, so it is impossible, under any circumstances, for currency exposure to be diversifying when the volatility of currency returns is more than twice as high as the volatility of bond returns. This does make the case for currency hedging for international bonds rather compelling, if the case for hedging international equities was not compelling enough!

Just turning to Figure 8.29 for a moment. It is interesting that the correlations are, if anything, rather stronger both ways (i.e. more distant from zero) than in the equity case. I suspect that this is for two reasons. Firstly, we know there is a relationship between bond returns and domestic monetary conditions. There is a looser, rather unstable, relationship between domestic monetary conditions and currency returns. This implies that correlations might not be zero between the two. Secondly, government bond indices are effectively one asset. While there are typically scores (but not hundreds) of securities in a government bond index, they all move in tandem as the yield curve moves, and only break away from each other when the slope or shape of the yield curve changes. This makes the possibility of a common causal link more likely.

As well as the weighted average of bond and currency returns, we can show the correlations of the individual country indices (Figure 8.30 mirroring Figure 8.2). The pattern of correlations for bonds is quite different from the pattern for equities. In particular, it appears from the consistent pattern here in relation to the USD base that US dollar currency returns are negatively correlated with US bond returns, and that US bond returns are positively correlated with the other country bond returns.

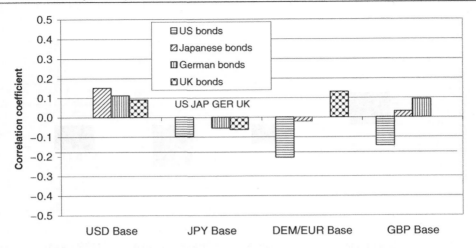

Figure 8.30   Correlation between hedged foreign bonds and same-country currency surprise for each base currency (1985–2002)

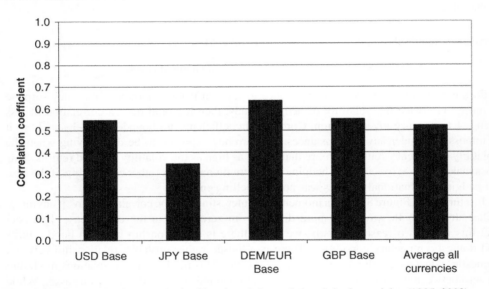

Figure 8.31   Correlation between hedged bonds and domestic bonds basket weights (1985–2002)

The intuitive explanation of the first point is that US bond returns are strong when US rates are falling. When US rates are falling, this depresses, at least under this theory, US dollar currency returns – not just spot, but currency surprise. A falling Dollar means a rising foreign currency. But does a rising US bond market mean a rising foreign bond market? As for the latter point, we can check it: Figure 8.31 shows correlation coefficients between hedged foreign bond returns and domestic bond returns.

Certainly it appears that there are quite strong positive correlations between the international government bond markets – perhaps surprisingly high. But this observation supports the contention made above to explain the USD bond correlations.

8.3.2   Stability of correlations

The above explanation is not an attempt to provide a forecasting mechanism for the US dollar, and the following rolling correlation graphs show why. Figures 8.32 to 8.35 show the 5-year rolling correlations (monthly data) of hedged bond returns and currency returns of the same

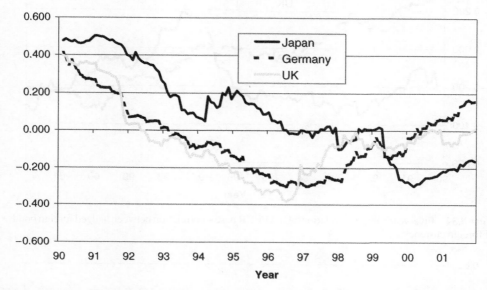

Figure 8.32   Five-year rolling correlations, USD base – correlation between hedged foreign bonds and foreign currency

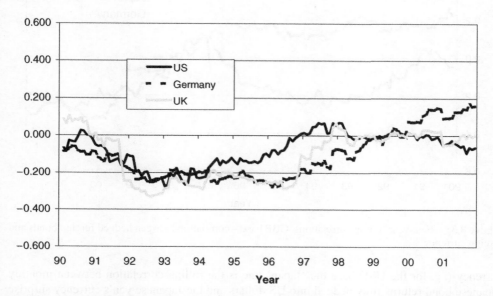

Figure 8.33   Five-year rolling correlations, JPY base – correlation between hedged foreign bonds and foreign currency

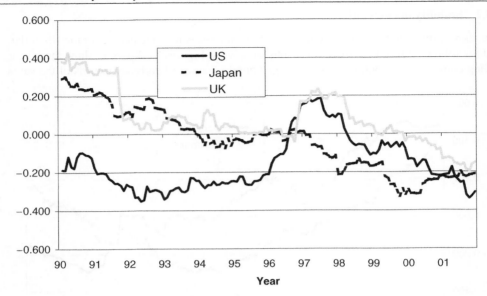

Figure 8.34   Five-year rolling correlations, DEM/EUR base – correlation between hedged foreign bonds and foreign currency

Figure 8.35   Five-year rolling correlations, GBP base – correlation between hedged foreign bonds and foreign currency

currency (i.e. for the USD base the 'Japan' line is the rolling correlation between monthly Japanese bond returns fully hedged into US dollars and the Japanese yen's currency surprise versus the US dollar; a strong yen gives a positive currency surprise).

The USD base graph (Figure 8.32) shows that the overall positive correlations shown in Figures 8.29 and 8.30 do not translate into a systematic effect. Indeed, the most recent 5-year period has correlations on average negative. Similar stories of instability apply to the other base currencies (Figures 8.33–8.35).

All of these correlations exhibit instability in both size and direction. Since we have established above that there is no chance, even in theory, of negative correlations undermining the rationale for hedging international bonds, then we can move on to look at the historical data in relation to risk reduction.

8.3.3 Volatility reduction from hedging bonds – the historical evidence

In Figure 8.36 I have compiled the effect on hedging on the volatility of international bonds baskets from the four currency bases we have been dealing with. There is no doubt whatever that currency hedging of international bonds is massively risk-reducing. I have conducted an F-test on the two series (monthly unhedged returns and monthly hedged returns); the F-test tests whether two series are samples drawn from a population of the same variance. The F-test result for all four of the base currencies is 100% – namely we can be 100% confident that the samples are drawn from different-variance populations. The 100% remains at 100% even if we expand it to 46 decimal places! I think we can be confident that hedging reduces bond volatility.

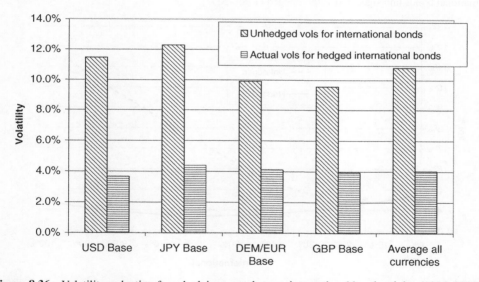

Figure 8.36   Volatility reduction from hedging – market cap international bond weights (1985–2002)

8.3.4 International diversification

Similarly to our equity analysis above, we can look at the effect of diversifying a bond portfolio internationally, with both hedged and unhedged international bonds. Figures 8.37 to 8.40 show this from the four main base currencies' perspectives. These graphs are similar in axes to Figures 8.20 to 8.23 and, to recap, they show the effect on bond portfolio volatility (Y-axis) of increasing the proportion of bonds in international (X-axis). The two lines are for unhedged international bonds and fully hedged international bonds respectively. It is immediately clear from the graphs what we have already discovered earlier in this section, namely that without

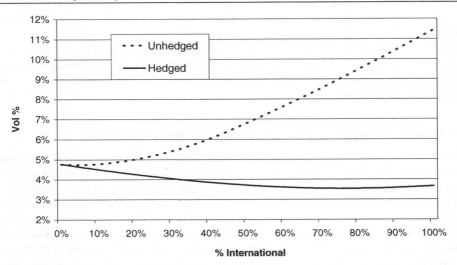

Figure 8.37 Bond portfolio volatility versus % international bonds, USD base – domestic bonds, international bonds unhedged and 100% hedged (1985–2002)

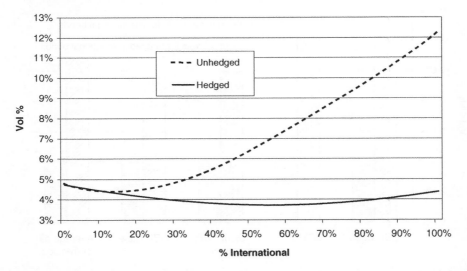

Figure 8.38 Bond portfolio volatility versus % international bonds, JPY base – domestic bonds, international bonds unhedged and 100% hedged (1985–2002)

currency hedging, international diversification of bonds has no attraction. With hedging, the attraction is varied – for UK investors, diversification is very valuable; for DEM/EUR investors, less so.

There are two reservations I would have about these graphs. The first is that bond investment for pension funds and insurance companies is in many cases designed to match liabilities – obligations to pay fixed amounts of pensions for long periods. Many will therefore regard a long bond exposure in their assets as the least-risk asset, and may even measure volatility against long bond straight or index-linked returns. Under these circumstances a reduction in nominal return volatility may not be an attractive goal.

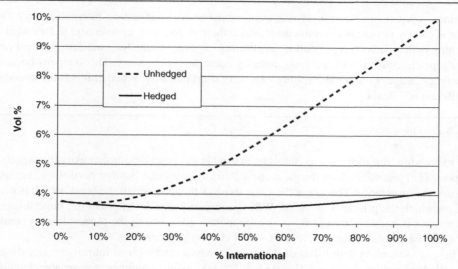

Figure 8.39   Bond portfolio volatility versus % international bonds, DEM base – domestic bonds, international bonds unhedged and 100% hedged (1985–2002)

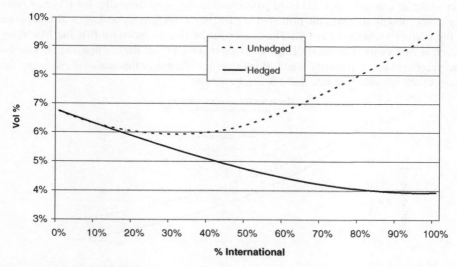

Figure 8.40   Bond portfolio volatility versus % international bonds, GBP base – domestic bonds, international bonds unhedged and 100% hedged (1985–2002)

The second reservation is that these graphs only show the effect of diversification in the government bond universe. Sovereign debt (at least from OECD countries) is as near risk-free as possible, and indeed is treated as completely 'risk-free'[9] for most purposes. Under risk-free

---

[9] The academic literature generally refers to risk-free interest rates as those with zero volatility (and therefore zero volatility with other asset classes). By contrast, the practitioner community usually refers to risk-free as meaning sovereign debt of any maturity (which may or may not be zero volatility, depending on the horizon of the analysis). Note that only the sovereign debt of a country issuing debt in the currency of its own denomination is generally accorded risk-free status. The case of the euro and its constituent countries is currently puzzling the more thoughtful practitioners.

conditions, what diversification of risk is being achieved by investing internationally? The answer is clearly not credit diversification, since there is no credit to diversify. In fact what is happening is that each foreign bond is substituting exposure to the long maturity interest rate curve domestic country with the long maturity curve foreign country. This happens because the currency hedge is one-month rolling – i.e. very short maturity. Whether this is the intended diversification, I doubt.

Box 8.2   Duration

The expression 'duration' is a technical term used in the bond investment world to express the point (i.e. years ahead) on the yield curve that any particular bond or portfolio of bonds exposes the investor to. This is *not* the same thing as the maturity of the bond, which is the date on which the principal is repaid. Why are maturity and duration not the same thing? The answer is because, except for a zero-coupon bond, some of the money from a bond will come earlier than maturity, in the form of coupon payments.

There are two main definitions of duration – we will start with an intuitively appealing one called 'Macaulay duration'. This (in words) is the average number of years ahead of all the cash flows, with the cash flows weighted by their present value using the current yield to maturity of the bond as the discount rate.

Let's take an example. A USD bond pays 6% p.a., say semi-annually, for 10 years from today's date, and then repays the principal at $100 per $100 face value. Let us also suppose that the current yield curve is 6%. The reader might like to ascertain that the Macaulay duration is 7.67 years. This maths leads us to see that the higher the coupon, the shorter the duration relative to the maturity. The following graph illustrates this trade-off, showing the curves at both 6% discount rate and 1% discount rate:

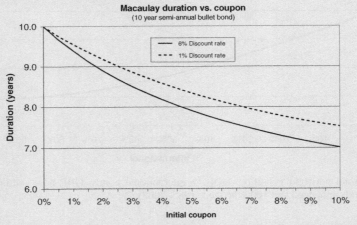

Macaulay duration vs. coupon
(10 year semi-annual bullet bond)

A small modification to Macaulay duration leads to a definition called 'modified duration'. Modified duration equals Macaulay duration/[1 + (discount rate/number of coupon payments p.a.)], where the discount rate is the yield to maturity of the bond. The appeal of the modified duration measure is that even though its unit is years, it is used as an elasticity – a modified duration of 7 means that for every 1 bp change in the yield curve, there is a 7 bp change in the value of the bond.

For those investors who wish to hold the long end of the domestic yield curve, it is possible, although rarely done at the moment, to extend the maturity of the foreign exchange hedge using interest rate and/or currency swaps. It is possible (indeed straightforward given the certainty of bond maths and the liquidity of the swaps) for, say, a UK investor to eliminate the (say) US yield curve inherent in US bonds, fully hedge the currency risk, and 'go up' the UK yield curve as far as at least 30 years. The diversification argument for this structure becomes strong when the bond portfolio contains credit, not just sovereigns.

8.4 PROPERTY

Using currency overlay for property portfolios is rare, but not unheard of. However, very little of the foregoing analysis which we used for equities and bonds has any application to property portfolios. The reason is simple: property cannot realistically be marked-to-market every month with prices that are either traded or tradeable. This means that the size of the currency hedge needed is likely to be a crude 'current value' approximation, or another alternative, like cost.

However, just because valuation prices are not easy to obtain, or frequent, does not mean that currency exposure has gone away, or is irrelevant. Foreign property portfolios generate currency risk without any expected return, and therefore the same arguments that can be demonstrated in support of currency hedging in the case of marketable assets apply here. Where property is held corporately (for example in property investment companies or investment trusts), then it is quite likely that part of the initial cost would be financed by borrowing. Many companies would borrow in the currency of the residence of the property to hedge the currency risk and, incidentally, give the lender better security.

Interestingly, some years ago, one large UK property investment company with substantial foreign property holdings, Hammerson, polled its large investors as to whether they would prefer the company to currency hedge their non-sterling assets and income, or not. Surprisingly, a majority of the larger investors (presumably professional institutional fund managers) responded by saying that they would prefer the company to remain unhedged, supposedly to retain the diversification of foreign currency exposure. Perhaps they would have answered differently had they read this book!

8.5 OTHER CLASSES

It is possible for currency overlay to overlay any asset, assuming it has some foreign currency content. Possible candidates include private equity, hedge funds, commodities, synthetic assets constructed with swaps, futures and options, rights of various kinds (copyright, media rights), non-bond monetary obligations such as cash, deposits, T-bills, commercial paper, mortgages and bilateral debt.

For liquid assets, the investor determines the optimum policy for currency hedging using similar analysis to that shown in this chapter. Illiquid assets cannot be analysed using quantitative methods; the decision of whether to hedge, and the benchmark hedge ratio, must be taken on general policy grounds.

9

Is the Currency Market Efficient?

For an active manager to make money consistently over time in a particular market, then that market must be *inefficient*. The use of this word originated in academic financial theory,[1] and means only that the market price does not always reflect the information then available. If, by contrast, a market price does always represent all the information available, then it is called 'efficient'.

9.1 TYPES OF INEFFICIENCY

The academic literature[2] has highlighted three (rather arbitrary) levels of efficiency.

Weak form efficiency is where past prices are not predictors of future prices. This means that any model (equation, chart, mechanistic trading process) that uses past prices of that market as the only input will not be found to have predictive power – i.e. future price movements will not be provably different from random for any price-only-based model.

Semi-strong form efficiency is where all public information about a market is already in the price, and models that use public information to predict that market's future prices will not have predictive power.

Strong form efficiency is where all information about a market, private and public, is already in the price. Under this, strongest, form of inefficiency no model, process, information, expertise, insider status, or indeed anything can improve the predictability of prices above random. Strong form efficient markets would not reward active managers, or hedge funds, with added value, however expert they were.

I mention it elsewhere, but it is vital that the reader understands that calling the currency market 'inefficient' is not the same thing as questioning the efficiency of its operation. In Chapters 3 and 4, I have explored in some detail the extraordinary size, diversity and liquidity of the foreign exchange market, and in Chapter 6 I have shown the extremely narrow bid/offer spreads (i.e. transaction costs) that can, and have, been achieved in executing currency contracts. All of this information, and comparative information from the other main financial markets, leads us to conclude that the foreign exchange market is the most *transactionally* efficient market in the world. This meaning of the word 'efficient' is not related in any way to the question I want to address here.

Concepts of efficiency are very 'pure' concepts, and in reality markets are the result of constant human activity, motivations and necessity, and these are not 'pure' processes. There are probably no markets in the real world that correspond to the strongest efficiency model, although this is a highly contentious subject. I will stick to the currency markets, and argue below that currency markets are certainly not efficient in at least one sense.

---

[1] See Fama, E.F., 'Random walks in stock market prices', *Financial Analysts Journal* **Sept/Oct** (1965).
[2] See also two surveys by Fama: Fama, E.F., 'Efficient capital markets', *Journal of Finance* **46** (1991) 1575–1617 and Fama, E.F., 'Market efficiency, long-term returns and behavioural finance', *Journal of Financial Economics* **49** (1998) 283–306.

9.2   MAKING THE CASE FOR CURRENCY MARKET INEFFICIENCY

To make the case that active currency management with a well-founded expectation of success is possible, I first have to demonstrate that the currency markets are inefficient at some level. Fortunately, I do not have to enumerate all the myriad possible ways in which inefficiency may exist; I only have to describe or demonstrate one convincingly, and I will have disproved the efficiency hypothesis. I will start with a somewhat anecdotal description of one of the functions of currencies and exchange rates, and go on from there to test a hypothesis that flows naturally from the description.

9.2.1   Cyclical behaviour

Currency exchange rates perform a fundamental function in the global economic system – that of a negative feedback loop for the current account performance of individual countries. Let me elaborate.

Suppose an individual country, for whatever reason, begins to run a current account deficit – i.e. its imports are greater than its exports (including invisibles). This means that there is an excess supply of that country's currency which will have to be mopped up by capital account transactions – foreign borrowing, asset sales to foreigners or inward foreign investment. While the capital accounts of most advanced economies are well developed enough to cover many years of normal deficits, in the end the appetite for this 'surplus' currency will run out. When this happens, the currency will fall as sellers of excess currency fail to find buyers, and they press the need for sales by offering the currency at lower prices. A falling currency will raise the domestic price of imports, and cheapen exports when viewed from abroad. This will stimulate the latter and inhibit the former, although with a potentially long and variable lag.[3]

None of these adjustments happen quickly, and the depth of capital markets now means that this adjustment process can be delayed for years. However, *in extremis*, currency weakness (or strength, the argument vice versa) is ultimately the author of a fundamental rebalancing of an economy back towards equilibrium. The buffer effect of the capital account is further strengthened by the long lags in the real economy in response to price changes. As an example, the US steel industry, decimated by the strength of the US dollar in the mid-1980s, started seriously closing plant and cutting capacity in 1984/5, almost at the high point of the dollar, and five years into the dollar bull run. Two years later, the dollar had fallen far enough to make US steel competitive again – but too late.

This is what engineers call a negative feedback loop with a lag. Any competent school physics student will tell you that negative feedback loops with lags (and without dampers) can create oscillation. The evidence is that the frequency of exchange rate oscillation is variable, but measured in years not months.

9.2.2   Lack of statistical arbitrage

Oscillations which evolve over time with smooth price adjustments create profitable opportunities for active currency participants. Under these conditions, simple trend-following models will be profitable – but the behaviour of these profit-seeking participants will tend to eliminate

---

[3] The lag is the origin of the 'J' curve of economics textbooks.

such trends. They will buy appreciating currencies (and vice versa), which will tend to increase their price and reduce the expected gain. In a market which is dominated by profit-seeking participants, such behaviour would be expected to completely eliminate any opportunity for consistent gain. This is what happens in most securities markets where inefficiencies begin to emerge.

But the currency market is not dominated by profit-seeking participants, and therefore this arbitrage is not fully eliminated. The currency market is dominated by highly constrained (but active) players like the ICCs, fund managers, portfolio investors and central banks (see Chapter 4). To exploit this particular inefficiency, profit-seeking participants need to have a key characteristic: a long horizon. A long horizon because the inefficiencies I have described are likely to emerge over a full currency cycle, and may be unreliable at shorter horizons. The horizons could be five years or more.

There is a shortage of long-horizon risk capital for this arbitrage, and not surprisingly. The opportunity is not self-evident; the appropriate method of exploiting it is not universally agreed; many former active participants have failed to capture the opportunities because of overconfidence and a misunderstanding of the nature and role of modelling in this context (the hedge funds 'yen-carry trade' of 1998 stands out). And, most importantly, it is a zero-sum game in a world where the creation of wealth through equity appreciation is positive-sum. This makes it a poor cousin of the simple expedient of taking long (not necessarily active)-positions in equities.

9.3   EMPIRICAL EVIDENCE FOR MEDIUM-TERM TRENDS

If the currency market is inefficient by the nature of its structure, do we have firm evidence of this in the evolution of prices over history? The answer is yes, and Figure 9.1 illustrates one particular way of presenting the evidence. The vertical axis shows the volatility of the

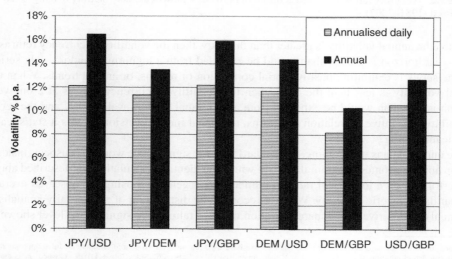

Figure 9.1   Volatility measured at different horizons – volatility of currency surprise 1981–2002, daily volatility annualised and annual volatility

historical series. The hatched bars show the annualised volatility[4] calculated from daily prices, annualised by the standard $\sqrt{262}$ multiple.[5] The black bars show the annual volatility calculated from observing the one-year forward price on one day, and the spot price (for delivery on the same day) one year later. This test is repeated daily for the 22 years of historical data (i.e. 5455 times, ignoring the first year of daily vols to avoid possible data bias), and the volatility of the resulting return series is measured using standard statistical techniques.

We can present the same data in a different way. For each currency, the annual volatility can be represented as a ratio to the annualised daily volatility. Because all the annual volatilities are larger than the annualised daily, all the ratios will be higher than one. Figure 9.2 shows the data presented in this way.

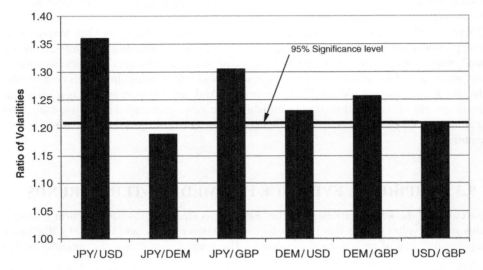

Figure 9.2   Volatility ratios measured at different horizons – ratio of annual volatility to daily volatility annualised (1981–2002).

When the annual volatility is greater than the daily, then the volatility of currency returns at a one-year horizon is greater than would be expected from a lognormal random walk series, and the series is exhibiting positive serial correlation of returns, or annual trends. When the annual volatility is less than the daily, then the volatility of currency returns at a one-year horizon is less than would be expected from a lognormal random walk series, and the series is exhibiting negative correlation of returns, or annual mean reversion. Is this a statistically significant finding?

The annual data is overlapping, so standard tests for significance would be suspect. Instead, we can apply a Monte Carlo simulation, in which the identical calculations as described above are performed on a lognormal random number series generated using the observed average 22-year daily historic volatility. We have recorded the distribution of ratios (daily annualised to annual), and derived a standard deviation of these ratios. The significance level shown in

---

[4] Volatility is the standard deviation of price changes. We have used log-transformed data to eliminate additive approximation errors. [Using Excel notation: if $r = (p_t/p_{t-1}) - 1$, then annualised vol $= \text{Exp}(\sqrt{262}(\text{Stdev}(\ln(r+1)))) - 1$, where p_t is the FX market rate on day t.]

[5] 262 is the number of weekdays in the year. The Central Limit Theorem tells us that we annualise volatility using the root function.

the graph is the 95% confidence level from this distribution. Figure 9.2 tells us that all of the currency pairs shown have exhibited annual trends over 20 years of data, and all but one are individually significant at the 95% confidence level. But taken together, are these results really statistically significant?

Using the Central Limit Theorem, we can test whether the average of the sample of six currencies lies outside the range contemplated by a random generator. The average ratio of the six currencies is 1.26. The SD of the average of six randomly generated ratios is 0.052. The mean ratio of randomly generated series is 1.00. This makes the average of the six currencies $(1.26 - 1)/0.052 = 4.99$ SDs away from the mean. This is significant at the 99.99997% level.

I will refer to the most obvious hole in this analysis – the choice of currencies. The first point is that the reader will recognise the four main currencies (USD, JPY, DEM, GBP) from

---

Box 9.1   Trends

It is commonly asserted, and not only in relation to the currency markets, that there are 'trends' in markets. But what are trends, and how can we identify them?

Let's start by stating what kinds of markets do not exhibit trends. These are the theoretical constructs of classical finance theory. Under these assumptions, markets exhibit 'lognormal random walk'. This means (roughly) that the percentage change in the market each period (say one day) is normally distributed, with a mean of the expected market return. (For the exact description, see Appendix 2.) Under these assumptions, each daily (weekly, monthly) movement is independent of every other, and indeed independent of any other variable. This market will not exhibit trends.

If, then, we can establish from the historical record sufficiently consistent data to reject the classical hypothesis, we can say that a market exhibits trends. Mathematically, we can express period return with the equation:

$$\text{Return}_t = \alpha + \beta(\text{Return}_{t-1}) + \varepsilon$$

where 'Return' is the currency surprise in the period and ε is a random normal variate.

If we can demonstrate that β is positive and significantly different from zero, then we can reject the 'no trend' hypothesis. If β is negative and significantly different from zero, then the market can be said to be mean-reverting. Note that in reality, relationships may be unstable, and changing the periodicity of the data (daily, monthly) may change the results of the tests. This test is conducted in Chapter 10.

There are other, more sophisticated and sensitive ways of establishing trending behaviour. One of these is the volatility/horizon analysis conducted here.

---

all the other chapters in the book. These currencies were chosen not because they 'trend', but because they are the largest in the world. The six pairs are just all the possible pair combinations of the four.

The other possible attack from a statistical point of view is that currency pairs are not independent (i.e. USD/GBP is not statistically independent from USD/DEM), and therefore if one or more are trending, it is more likely that they all will be. There are two points here. The first is that while returns from the two pairs (like the two cited) may be correlated, that does not imply that the ratios of daily annualised to annual SD must be correlated. Secondly, since we are trying to identify inefficiencies, the fact that these inefficiencies arise in a group is largely irrelevant – if they are there they can be identified and exploited. However, while the scale of the confidence (99.99997% level) is undoubtedly overstated by my simple maths, even if there was 100% correlation between currency return series, the average ratio of 1.25 would still be significant at the 98% level. The truth is somewhere in between.

While it is possible for a purist to pick these kind of holes in this 'proof', the length of the data, and the strength and consistency of the effect, must force us to abandon the efficient market hypothesis. But we will not have to rely on this observation alone.

9.4   FORWARD RATE BIAS – ANOTHER INEFFICIENCY

What is the forward rate bias (FRB)? The FRB is the name given to the collective observation that, on average, the spot rate of a currency whose forward rate is at a discount (higher interest

---

Box 9.2   Forward rate bias

The 'forward rate bias' is a theory rather than a fact. It hypothesises that where a pair of currencies have a liquid forward market, the forward rate of higher interest rate currency is a biased estimator of the future spot rate. The bias in this theory is one-way, the higher interest rate currency is expected to show a positive currency surprise. In other words, the forward discount of the higher interest rate currency is too large: the spot rate will not depreciate as much as predicted by the forward rate.

The forward rate bias theory has firm support from the historical price record. We can, however, only reliably test about twenty years' data. Longer periods of data run into problems of illiquid forward markets, and of fixed exchange rates.

There are three plausible explanations for its hypothesised existence. The first is the idea that the higher interest rate currencies are 'less attractive' or 'lower quality' than the lower interest rate currencies. Under this theory, these currencies would offer a 'risk premium' to persuade international investors to hold them rather than lower risk currencies. The risk premium cannot just be higher interest rates – international investors' exposure to a currency is a combination of the interest rate and the movement of the spot rate. Hence the forward rate bias theory.

The second explanation is the domestic monetary policy argument. High interest rate countries are often those where domestic monetary considerations overwhelm all others. A high interest rate country's government may choose to hold rates higher, and for longer, than international economic considerations may warrant.

Finally, there is a school of thought that says that currency market participants suffer from 'nominal price illusion'. This says that, for example, a period of price stability (i.e. the spot rate remaining unchanged) is seen by the market as just that, whereas in fact a period of price stability for a high interest currency is a period of currency surprise appreciation, and vice versa.

---

rate currency) does not depreciate as much as the forward rate predicts. This also means that the spot rate of a currency whose forward rate is at a premium (lower interest rate currency) does not appreciate as much as the forward rate predicts. Currency forward discounts and premiums are always relative to another currency – so the FRB phenomenon is always about currency pairs.

9.4.1   What is the evidence for the FRB?

Numerous studies have found evidence of bias. Simply presented, in the equation:

Currency surprise $= a + b$ (previous period forward discount/premium) $+ e$ (error term)

we must reject the unbiasedness of the forward rate if we can show that b explains a significant proportion of the currency surprise. We measure significance with a 't-stat' for the coefficient b – over 1.96 means we are more than 95% confident that the forward discount/premium has genuine explanatory power for the currency surprise.

If we take monthly data, Table 9.1 shows the extent of the bias based on 1980–2002 exchange rates. The row and column headers define the pairs of currency that relate to the t-stats, and the 'P' value in brackets is the confidence we can have that the effect is genuine. From this table we can see that the FRB is reliable across major currencies, and has remained valid for 22 years of data. Although this test is crude, and only tests the FRB at one horizon (monthly), despite this we have good evidence to abandon again the efficient market hypothesis.

There are a number of explanations that have been put forward to explain the FRB.

Table 9.1   Significance (t-stats) of forward rate bias regression variable b

	USD	JPY	DEM/EUR
JPY	3.9 ($P > 99.99\%$)		
DEM/EUR	2.7 ($P > 99.3\%$)	2.7 ($P > 99.2\%$)	
GBP	4.1 ($P > 99.99\%$)	3.5 ($P > 99.95\%$)	2.7 ($P > 99.2\%$)

9.4.2   Risk premium

The most common explanation, which is also widely used to explain the excess return of other asset classes (equities, credit), is that the FRB is a payment to investors for their accepting additional risk. The argument runs: high interest rate currencies are high interest rate because they are risky (i.e. volatile and more likely to suffer spot depreciation). Investors recognise this, and demand an expected return premium to hold these currencies – and this is the FRB.

The strength of this argument is that it fits in with modern portfolio theory and investors' risk/return trade-off. Its weaknesses, and they are serious weaknesses, are: (1) that currency rates are not dominated by international investors (trade and current account transactions have much larger volumes); (2) that in the forward market, half of the transactions are short positions not long positions, and for these investors the FRB becomes a cost, not a return; and (3) that investors in each country have different perspectives dependent on their base currency, and they will regard their home currency as riskless, even if it is a high interest rate currency.

Box 9.3 Currency risk premium

At the core of modern portfolio theory (see Box 5.6) is the concept that investment risk is rewarded. Investors will only hold more risky investments if they expect to receive, on average, a higher return from these. Does the same hold for currencies?

On the face of it, the market assigns a 'risk' rating to each currency in the form of the interest rate (which in turn implies a forward discount or premium in the currency). 'Risky' currencies (say the South African rand) have high interest rates; safe currencies (say the Japanese yen) have low interest rates.

This is a pleasing description, but does it stand up to inspection?

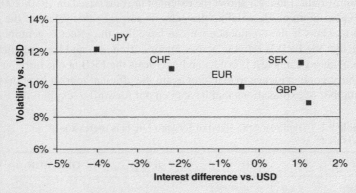

10-Year data, USD base

We need to establish what 'risky' means for currencies. For investments, the most common measure is volatility of return. But if we apply this to currencies, from what perspective do we measure volatility? Suppose we take the US dollar as the base, we can graph the relationship between historical currency volatility historical average interest rates. The graph above makes it plain that if we compare 10-year volatility and 10-year average interest rates among five major currencies, we find a negative relationship, rather than a positive one. The same relationship holds for 5-year and 20-year data. We will clearly have to abandon the naive risk premium theory.

However, we may also have to abandon the concept of volatility as the relevant measure of risk. It may be that the yen is volatile for a US investor, but the dollar is, by the same measure, volatile for the Japanese investor. On the basis of the graph above, the yen had a negative premium, but therefore by definition the dollar had a positive premium for the Japanese investor. Since all currency relationships can be inverted, we are going to get zero net risk premiums if all currency bases are taken into account. We are now left without risk premium theory for currencies.

However, one final possibility is that high interest rates are seen by the market as a proxy for risky (i.e. potentially weak) currencies. The risk premium argument could be reinterpreted as claiming that high interest currencies are more likely to have positive currency surprise (i.e. the high interest rates on average more than compensate for the expected spot devaluation). This is a subset of the forward rate bias theory, which is discussed elsewhere (see Box 9.2).

In summary, the expression 'currency risk premium' should be used with care!

9.4.3 Monetary policy and inflation

A different explanation lies in the relationship between monetary policy and inflation. It runs as follows. It is governments, not markets, that set short-term domestic interest rates. They do this in pursuit of their monetary policy objectives – generally the control of inflation. Forward rates in currencies reflect these short-term interest rate differentials, and are therefore politically controlled.

Governments who maintain higher-than-average interest rates in a particular period will do so to fight inflation and inflation expectations. To reduce both of these requires higher-than-equilibrium real interest rates (i.e. after adjustment for inflation expectations). This will tend to create a forward rate bias, since the subsequent movement of the spot rate will reflect the actual (lower) inflation. The same effect will also happen in reverse – countries pursuing low interest rate policies do so to stimulate demand, potentially raising inflation above expectations.

The weakness in this explanation is that the relationship between short-term interest rates, spot rate movements and inflation is highly unreliable, and a poor basis for a stable phenomenon like the FRB.

9.4.4 Nominal rate illusion

An explanation which does not suffer from the same shortcoming as the two above is the nominal rate illusion argument, which runs as follows. Markets are dominated by the behaviour of their players, and therefore by their perceptions and expectations. Currency markets are reported and traded in spot rate terms, and 'currency surprise' is a little known concept. However, all profits and losses in the forward market in currency arise out of currency surprise, which, to recap, is the result of currencies not ending up where their forward rate predicts they will. This dissonance between profits and losses actually experienced (currency surprise), and the direction of the market and its 'pressure points' as actually reported and understood, means that FRB can flourish. How is it that this is not arbitraged away by the force of the market recognising the profit opportunity?

Currencies are not principally investment instruments, and the vast majority of players in the currency markets are not 'investing' in currencies. This means that not just the perception, but the reality, is different for different players.

Currency exchange rates have always attracted the attention of central banks. They are often charged with defending particular (spot) exchange rates, and will 'smooth' extreme (spot) movements by intervention. They are not profit centres, and therefore they have a political imperative to perpetuate the 'nominal price' illusion by their behaviour. A significant proportion of market participants are corporations, and many of these will have target exchange rates expressed in spot terms, and the movement of the spot rate will be a critical determinant of their currency transaction behaviour. This emphasis on spot rates is extremely widespread. Major commodities are priced around the world by conversion of their 'core' currency (mainly dollars) into the users' currency at the spot rate. When a German oil company is buying Rotterdam crude in dollars, it is the spot euro/$ that determines the oil price in euros – and ultimately the price of petrol at the pumps in Germany and the rest of Europe.

Similarly, when a company has multiple production facilities in different currency blocs, it is the spot rate that is the determinant of the lowest cost producer. To a great extent for corporations, the nominal price illusion is not an illusion – nominal prices are hard reality. Corporations inhabit the 'current account' world, and they have to respond to immediate opportunities and threats arising from exchange rate movements, not to notional accumulation of 'currency surprise' (which calculations are irrelevant).

But the scale and importance of the 'irrelevant' calculations is significant. As an example, the yen was on a downward path in 1995 (from a high of 82 yen/$), and in October crossed the 101 yen/$ level and continued down (i.e. the number rising). It reached a low of 144 in July 1998, and then promptly recovered its poise, to rise all the way to 101 in December 1999. It then turned round and fell again. It looks at face value as though the 101 in 1999 was the 'same level' as the 101 in 1995. From the point of view of the 'exchange rate charts', the market-watchers, the competitiveness of Japanese goods, the price of oil in yen and the opportunities for exporters to sell to Japan, this is true. But the JPY/USD currency surprise index which was 101 in October 1995 was *126* in December 1999. So some 25% of yen weakness in the currency surprise was concealed in the nominal price illusion, and any market player who maintained a short position in yen throughout this period (exploiting the forward rate bias) would have made a 25% cumulative profit, as opposed to nothing measured by the spot rate.

9.4.5   Other inefficiencies

I have demonstrated the evidence for, and some possible explanations for, two well-established and widely accepted inefficiencies. There are more inefficiencies, although perhaps none as readily demonstrable and as transparent as trends and the forward rate bias.

Active currency overlay managers have successfully exploited more inefficiencies than just trends and the forward rate bias over the past 10 years, and have as a manager group added value (see Chapter 11). This observation itself is unusual and needs elaborating.

9.5   A SUCCESSFUL UNIVERSE?

How can a universe of managers add value versus an objective benchmark? In a market where the universe of managers in a survey constitutes all the managers in the market, then it is logically impossible for the universe to outperform the index (which is the objective benchmark), since the universe being tested is itself the complete constituents. Since managers incur costs and indices don't, then managers as a group will not just not outperform, they must underperform. All the available studies of active management that I have seen, where the active manager universe is a significant proportion of the market (which is most equity and bond markets), illustrate the reality of this finding: that active managers as a class do not (and cannot) add value.

The best analogy for this comes from sport. While the absolute skill in the UK Soccer Premiership[6] is undoubtedly very high, the inescapable fact is that the average final position of the teams in this league is 10.5. The interesting question then becomes 'are there any individual teams which have a consistent record of success' (i.e. consistently higher than 10.5th place)? In the active manager context, this is a question about individual management firms (or possibly even individuals within firms) – not about the universe. The average score of the universe is always 10.5.[7]

---

[6] The top UK soccer league, which has a fixed membership of 20 teams.

[7] The analogy can neatly be extended to survivor bias as well. Since the lowest three teams are relegated each season, the average 5-year premiership position of teams currently in the premiership must be a lower (i.e. better) number than 10.5 (and cannot be higher) as some teams will have less than a full 5-year record.

What is different about currency? From the foregoing sections on the structure of the currency markets it is clear that the active money available to exploit the persistent inefficiency identified above, and any others, is inadequate to fully eliminate them. On very rough guesstimates based on the volume of cross-border assets, and the constraints on asset managers, I estimate that the total of long-term active money directly available for this purpose is less than 1% of FX market turnover.[8]

With this very small active, profit-seeking component, it is entirely consistent with logic that an identifiable sector of active managers (currency overlay managers), who all exploit one or more persistent inefficiencies, can outperform an objective benchmark or market index. The corollary of this is that the remaining 99% non-profit-seeking sector must lose money against the same benchmark. Why don't they notice or mind?

They don't notice for three reasons. Firstly, the amounts involved are tiny, and get 'lost in the wash'. Secondly, many participants have to trade in the FX market to cover international payments, so they do not have the choice to withdraw even if they thought they were losing an unidentifiably small amount in their trading activities. Finally, the measurement of performance in FX is fundamentally dependent on the customers' perception of the benchmark, and their base currency. This means two participants can simultaneously think they are making money. Section 9.5.1 gives a simple example of this phenomenon.

9.5.1   An example of different perspectives in the FX market

Customer 1 buys $1m dollars with euro from the bank, and simultaneously another customer (customer 2) sells $1m to the bank for euro. The bank charges 0.05% difference between the two prices, and it is profitable (and happy). Suppose the market rates were (in $/EUR) 0.9000 and 0.9004 respectively. Let us suppose the rate then moves to 0.9500 over the next few weeks. Customer 1 is a euro-based importer, and is delighted that his imports for next month and subsequently will be cheaper. He plans to reduce his prices (which will stimulate demand) and simultaneously increase profits because of the 5% input price reduction. He may take more forward currency cover at these levels to lock these new rates in. Customer 2, a US-based investor, congratulates himself on the timing of his unhedged euro investment – it has already gone up 5% in value. In these complex and varied circumstances, it is easy to see that very small and unidentifiable amounts of 'losses' will get lost.

9.6   SUMMARY ON EVIDENCE FOR INEFFICIENCY

9.6.1   Weak form efficiency

I have presented here two independent pieces of evidence that give very strong support for the contention that currency markets are not even weakly efficient. Both of these pieces of evidence refute the weak form of the efficiency model, namely that prices are not predictable from historical prices or price patterns.

If weak form efficiency is refuted, does this mean that semi-strong and strong form efficiency are refuted as well? This is an interesting question, to my knowledge not examined widely in the literature.

---

[8] Currency overlay = $110bn; cross-border portfolio assets = $1.5trn; 10% asset manager hedging leeway = $150bn. Hedge funds = $100bn of risk. Total active = $360bn. T/O 3× value p.a. Therefore long-term active turnover = $1.08trn p.a. Total FX turnover = 260 × $1.2trn × 41% (customer proportion) = $128trn p.a. Therefore active proportion = 1.08/128 = 0.84%. All 2000 estimated values, various sources.

9.6.2   Semi-strong form efficiency

This form of efficiency states that all public non-price information is already in the price, but private information is not. To refute this form requires evidence that there is public non-price information not in the price. This in turn requires evidence that non-price-based models (i.e. fundamental models) can be constructed which give us predictions about future prices in which we can have (statistical) confidence. So this boils down to the question 'do fundamental models or forecasting work?'. We will explore this question further in Chapter 10.

9.6.3   Strong form efficiency

In the mainstream developed currency markets (which includes probably 15 currencies, and therefore 105 pairs $[=(15 \times 14)/2]$), there is virtually no availability (and little concept) of private information. Currencies are not like equities or other corporate securities: they are not 'owned and controlled' by any one individual or group of individuals. Whereas a disappointing trading statement, composed by the CEO and CFO of a quoted company, will almost certainly cause a fall in the price of the company's share price, a piece of 'bad news' about an economy may not necessarily cause a fall in the exchange rate. For example, 'weak demand' may be interpreted by the markets as reducing the possibility of a rate rise (probably bad for the exchange rate), or as reducing the demand for imports (probably good for the exchange rate). In addition, the length of time that price-sensitive information remains in the private domain is very limited. Most statistics are published very quickly after they emerge from compilation – often within 24 hours.

This combined with the paucity of such information remaining in the private domain makes strong form efficiency in the currency markets hard either to prove or disprove – in fact probably irrelevant.

9.6.4   Transactional efficiency

As mentioned above, all of this makes no statement about the transactional efficiency or otherwise of the currency market. The evidence presented elsewhere in this book is strongly supportive of the argument that the currency market is extremely efficient from the perspective of transactions and liquidity. The evidence presented shows that the depth of liquidity is the deepest, and the cost of transactions is the lowest, of any of the global markets. This low cost of transactions does not sit at all uncomfortably with the informational inefficiencies identified in this chapter. In fact, as one consultant specialising in the currency market says: 'wouldn't you expect active managers to be able to make money if over 90% of assets were indexed, transactions costs were 5 bp or less, there were no taxes, duties, or other frictional costs, and daily turnover was over $1trn per day?'

10
Active Currency Overlay – Management Styles

In this chapter I will look at two main issues – *how* active currency managers come to design the active processes that they do, and *what* those processes are. To use an architectural analogy, this is the same thing as firstly looking at *how* architectural styles developed (the cultural, technological and artistic background) and therefore why an architect designed in the way that he did. Secondly, again using the architectural analogy, *what* the styles are (i.e. a description of classical, gothic, modernist, etc.).

10.1 THE PROBLEM

The problem that all active currency managers (or potential active currency managers) face is how to use information available today to predict with a measure of success (at least a measure

---

Box 10.1   Cross hedging

Cross hedging is where a currency overlay manager undertakes a forward contract or hedge between two currencies, neither of which is the home currency of the investor. Such activity either passes risk from one currency to another, or creates new currency risk; it does not by itself hedge or reduce it.

Under what circumstances is cross hedging likely to be used? Firstly, there are circumstances in which the owned (i.e. the target of the underlying investment) currency is relatively illiquid and expensive to trade, but closely associated, either formally or informally, with another foreign currency. An example for a European investor might be a Latin American currency, with the US dollar being the associated currency. It would be quite possible to passively hedge the target currency back to US dollars (i.e. cross hedge), and then run an active overlay between the US dollar and the home currency.

Secondly, the overlay manager may wish to exercise more freedom to choose the currency pairs on which he is likely to add value. With the client's agreement, he may release the restrictions on (i) the client's base currency always being one half of the traded currency pair; and (ii) the weights of the active bets being determined by the underlying asset allocation. In theory cross hedging could have any number of legs. (Currency A hedged to B; B hedged to C; C hedged to D; D hedged to home currency, etc.). However, active cross hedging is a form of gearing. It allows more active bets on the same asset base; it will engender a higher tracking error, higher expected value added and a higher potential downside.

There are few circumstances in which cross hedging would be a valid strategy for passive hedging. Only if the currency market was quoting irrationally (bid/offer spreads for currencies A:C being wider than the sum of bid/offer spreads for currencies A:B and B:C) would passive hedging have a financial incentive.

more than random) what will happen to exchange rates in the future. This is a problem simply stated, but extremely difficult to solve. I should state here that there will be a group of readers who will believe that the problem does not have a solution. Such a belief will be founded in their own experience, and based perhaps also on what they see as inconclusive evidence to the contrary.

My goal is to present the relevant information clearly and with insight to both sceptics and believers. I will also declare my beliefs so that the reader can gauge the position from which I am speaking:

> The evidence from over 20 years' experience of analysing and trading in the foreign exchange markets has convinced me that highly sophisticated managers can consistently beat the market (and therefore add value) over time. However, doing so is difficult (much more difficult than it might appear), requires time and patience as well as expertise, and will be a great deal more anticipated than achieved by those managers who try.

It is worth stating at this point that most active overlay mandates will constrain the active manager to vary hedge ratios between 0% and 100%, irrespective of the benchmark. It is within this constraint that the following discussion takes place.

10.2   MODELLING AND FORECASTING

Faced with the problem above, almost all currency managers turn to historical data, and quantitative modelling, to assist them in unravelling the mysteries of the currency market. If they do not do so, what is their guide? They may have some anecdotal or period-specific experience of a particular currency move or moves, but without mathematical support, any views or beliefs they may have are untested and unverifiable. So how do they go about modelling?

10.2.1   Modelling – Occam's razor[1]

Many professionals in currency management, particularly in stand-alone currency overlay, use mathematical models to analyse and exploit historical inefficiencies in price movements, and to determine (more or less formally) their active positions for their clients. The advantage of models is that they allow scientific methodology to be applied to the process of active management. A hypothesis is established – say that currencies have medium-term trends, or that volatility in a period is positively influenced by a decay in volatility in previous periods. A model is built to test the hypothesis or hypotheses, and the model is tested on historical data. Modern computers and statistical techniques are now very sharp tools for conducting this analysis, and it is not difficult to get statistically significant results out of this process. Statistical significance means abandoning the efficient market hypothesis, and accepting that the chosen model has explanatory power.

However, there are significant pitfalls in applying naive modelling processes. The first one is that a competent modeller can get very high levels of explanatory power modelling many data series.[2] Increasing model complexity, and relaxing the 'intuitive tests' that good models satisfy, can allow explanatory power to rise almost without limit, to the point where information

---

[1] Occam's razor states that where there is a choice between two equally valid explanations or approaches to a problem, you should choose the simplest. William of Ockham (Occam) (1285–1349) was a medieval English philosopher. Einstein had a similar view – 'theories should be as simple as possible, but no simpler'.

[2] This also unfortunately applies to data series which have no genuine explanatory variables. It is frequently possible to get significant explanatory variables by modelling randomly generated series with enough different 'explanatory' series.

ratios[3] apparently exceed 1. Increasing model complexity increases the historical fit, but the evidence is that it also increases the gap between history and the future: as the explanatory power increases, the relative predictive power decreases. The intuitive explanation for this is as follows.

Historical price patterns in history are the distillation of the almost infinite variety of human behaviour, economic conditions and chance. When presented with a price series, and other economic variables (relative interest rates, inflation rates, economic data, flow data), a modeller will design a mathematical model to 'explain' the movements. The model may have a variety of intuitive bases, but can only capture, at best, a tiny subset of the actual forces which 'really' applied to the historical price series. There will be a huge amount of unexplained price movement. The temptation will be to try to 'explain' the unexplained movement, and modern modelling techniques will allow the modeller to do this by adding autoregressive terms, non-linear functions, and almost limitless exogenous variables. The explanatory power can only go up when this complexity is added. But unless this added complexity is genuinely capturing underlying behaviour, the added complexity is just 'curve fitting' – that is it 'explains' the historical movement by nature of identifying particular correlations and relationships that are supported only by the data – not by any *ex ante* intuitive beliefs. It is only a short step from this to *ex post* rationalisation of the chosen model, and we have the makings of a very unsuccessful model.

In reality, there is a continually varying combination of generators of currency returns which include long-term structural elements, and shorter term factors which will create a great deal of noise if ignored, but by contrast will lead to disappointment and failure if modelled. The yen hedge fund debacle of 1998 was a classic case of a large amount of money temporarily behaving in a particular way, and thereby moving the market. Modellers were faced with a dilemma (which faces them less obviously all the time): either this behaviour creates a lot of 'errors' in models which ignored this factor, or it is captured and 'explained' by new complex model features. Unfortunately, the causative factors for this behaviour, namely a herd play on the 'yen carry', evaporated in a few days in October 1998 with a massive fall-out for the hedge fund players, and a failure of the new 'explaining' elements of the model.

This feature of model building is very difficult to guard against in inexperienced hands, since enthusiastic exponents will always be looking for 'best fit' models, and will be under commercial pressure to present them with short (or 'theoretical') track records. It takes a very experienced modeller to reject models with good fit and good 'stats' (split-test results, etc.) because he does not believe them to be capturing a stable non-random characteristic of the market.

With all these caveats, is there a role for modelling in active management?

10.2.2   Can models work?

The answer is yes they can – but it doesn't mean they all do. Models of physical processes are the life-blood of technological advance, and many model the real world near perfectly. However, as the explanatory power of models decreases with increasing 'random' elements, their validity is increasingly hard to be sure about. You only need to think about weather forecasting to understand some of the problems.

---

[3] Information ratio = annual value added %/annualised tracking error %. Annualised tracking error is the annualised standard deviation of the differences between manager performance and benchmark performance. Successful active managers (currency or any other asset class) tend to deliver live information ratios in the 0–0.5 range. It is rare (although not impossible) to find long live track records (which haven't been 'cherry picked') with information ratios higher than this.

Models of financial market behaviour are bound to have large unexplained elements, and they also have a further, logical problem already referred to above. In most financial markets (e.g. equities and bonds), if a model is used to observe a market inefficiency (i.e. explain a proportion of the returns), and then used to exploit it, the very act of exploiting it will (if done in sufficiently large volume) change the market's behaviour and thereby undermine the model. However 'reflexive' and 'clever' a player – perhaps calculating the extent of a particular model's use and predicting how its use will subsequently affect the markets – nevertheless in all markets in which objective benchmarks can be established, one player's outperformance will be another's underperformance.[4] It is quite hard to imagine a model sufficiently reflexive and 'game theory' orientated to be reliably successful in such an environment. Hence the relatively small proportion of purely quantitative houses in active management of equities and bonds.

Box 10.2   Alpha

The expression 'alpha' means 'value added' or 'excess return' over and above the market return available for that asset class. The use of the greek letter α arises from an equation in the Capital Asset Pricing Model (CAPM) that describes the pricing of an actual portfolio in relation to its riskiness, namely:

$$\text{Portfolio return} = \alpha + \beta(\text{market return}) + \varepsilon$$

where 'return' is the return in excess of the risk-free rate, β is the elasticity of the portfolio return with respect to market return, and ε is a random error term with a zero mean.

Put into words, alpha is the additional return in a portfolio over and above the return expected from a passively managed portfolio of a certain riskiness. The expression 'alpha' is often used as shorthand for the 'skill' of a manager.

The expression 'alpha' was popularised by Michael Jensen, then a Chicago PhD student, who studied (in 'The performance of mutual funds in the period 1945–64', *Journal of Finance*, 1968) the performance of actively managed mutual funds compared to the performance of market indices. He suggested that 'alpha' was an effective measure of stock-picking ability in such mutual managers, although he found a disappointingly small proportion (a minority) of his subjects did outperform the market index.

In the context of currency overlay, 'alpha' is universally used to mean the value added of the currency manager versus the benchmark. Since there is no concept of 'beta' in currency management, alpha is a measure of skill. It does not, however, say anything about the non-systematic risk that a manager is taking to achieve his alpha – this is commonly measured by the information ratio.

What about active currency models? As described above, there is a very large, active (in the sense that they are dealing), but non-profit-seeking customer sector in the currency market. If this sector behaves in a stable way (because of its sheer size and diversity, and because it doesn't have a choice about a lot of its deals), then in logic it should be possible to build a model which

---

[4] This is only true if *all* the players in the market are represented in performance measurement, and the benchmark represents the whole relevant universe of investments. Under these conditions, the universe must underperform the benchmark – because the former have costs and the latter does not. However this does not imply that active management cannot make money – just not all active managers.

exploits the inefficiencies which this behaviour throws up without the model being self-limiting or self-destroying. However, stable features are likely to be few and rather general (trending market, forward rate bias), so such a model will have to successfully contend with a great deal of noise. The level of noise may make the process of creating a successful track record quite long-drawn-out, but if the model is genuinely exploiting a stable market feature, which is not submerged by transaction costs, then it will slowly haul ahead of a passive benchmark. Section 9.2 tells us that this can happen at active manager universe level as well.

Box 10.3   'Star' investors

'Star' investors are a modern, and interesting, phenomenon. They exist in many active investment management firms, and they are believed by clients and their employers alike to possess exceptional investment skills which translate into exceptional investment performance. How far are these perceptions based on reality, and how much are they created and promoted by the investment firm and the stars? There are two obvious tests to apply to answer these questions. The first is to ascertain whether the firms in question are able, with any consistency or reliability, to beat the benchmarks against which they are measured. The second is whether this performance is portable with respect to the stars – that is, if they move firm does their performance move with them?

Both of these questions are hard to answer, but the first is easier. Most active equity managers do not have records of consistent outperformance. There is an active debate whether US equity managers are, as a group, so sophisticated and so dominant in the US equity market that all inefficiencies have been removed. This would both undermine the case for the 'star' system and for active managers in general. American investors would argue that active outperformance is still possible in the 'less sophisticated' foreign equity markets, although such evidence as there is appears to point to country (and currency) selection as being the greatest contributors to outperformance.

The evidence for 'portability' of performance is almost impossible to establish. Firms do not provide performance by portfolio manager; much of the support for the 'star' system is therefore anecdotal, or explainable by chance and survivor bias. Hedge funds are a potential source of evidence in this area, since they are often linked to (or founded by) particular investment stars. However, the hedge funds with long track records are so few, and the benchmarks against which to measure them so debatable, that it is impossible to abandon the hypothesis that active equity outperformance is the result of chance.

In currency overlay management the star system does not really exist. Most overlay managers have adopted highly quantitative approaches to active management, and it is the reputation of the quality of the analysis and modelling process, rather than reliance on a 'star', that is the key distinguishing feature of overlay managers.

10.2.3   What about active management without models?

Successful active managers are like successful chess players. They need to be clever, knowledgeable and resourceful, and be able to respond to new situations in an effective way, and ultimately, they need to beat their peers. It is therefore likely in many markets that personal knowledge (knowledge of target companies, knowledge of market behaviour) is the best route to beating the other market participants. However, even a game-theory-driven game like chess can be codified. With modern computers, all but the very best players are now being routinely beaten by computer models. Even the best player in the world was beaten by a computer model in the celebrated 1997 series.[5]

Very good players, in markets as much as in chess, operate in a non-random way which could in theory be codified into a model. Arguably the most successful living investor, Warren Buffet, has publicly set out his criteria for investment in the stock of a company. He has (largely) stuck to his 'model' despite it looking poor in some circumstances (e.g. the Internet bubble). The criteria are simple, and in theory easy to copy. They have not been widely copied for many reasons, the most pressing being that those asset managers with enough money under management to be able to take strategic stakes in top-of-sector companies are required by their clients to deliver index-like returns. Warren Buffet-like investing is inconsistent with index-like returns.

Models only codify consistent ways of behaving, however complex the thinking and the input data. In the currency market 'personal' styles of active management have been less popular and successful than more quantitative approaches because the levels of noise are high, the horizons long, the quantity of data high, the 'inside information' scarce or non-existent, and the 'reflexive' element quite low. The latter is a consequence of the huge size and diversity of the market. However, the previous section explained that the most likely long-term winners in active currency will have relatively simple models, and these do not necessarily need to be formally codified as long as their rules are consistently applied.

10.2.4   Dealing and practical execution

The best models in the world are no good unless an active currency manager has a well-designed process for converting model output (or indeed discretionary judgement) into live deals. This is no easy task, the difficulty of which is much underestimated.

Let us suppose that a manager is developing or refining a model. The inputs to the model will include the current exchange rate (spot and forward), a variety of historical rates (spot and forward), and an array of other, exogenous variables. To be effectively tested, the testing procedure must exactly match the live procedure to be adopted once the model is live. Otherwise it's like testing a new car on a smooth, flat, test-track, and the customer taking it out on real (rough and hilly) roads, expecting it to perform to test-bed specification, and being disappointed.

10.2.5   Timeliness of inputs

For all modellers with an eye to forecasting, a firm understanding of the timeliness of inputs is critical. Let us suppose that one of the exogenous input variables is (say) balance of payments data. This data may be released regularly at, say, 10.00am local time once a month. Whatever use the model makes of this data, it must always ensure that it uses it (and only contemporarily available information) after this date and time. If the announcement also includes revisions of past data (as is common), then only those contemporary revisions are capable of being used. It is common for economic data to have a series of revisions; and unless each of

---

[5] Kasparov vs. IBM's Deep Blue.

these is independently stored as the latest information on a particular date, then the model is in danger of targeting post-dated data. If only (finally) revised data is stored in one time series, then the model will be anachronistic – using data at time t that was only available at time $t + 1$.

Similar problems occur with price data. If the technical component of an active currency management model uses contemporary prices, exactly what prices are these, and how are they reflected in the live execution process? Let us suppose a technical model is designed with, and runs on, daily prices. It assumes (not unreasonably) that it can execute deals at the stored historical daily price, with an adjustment for bid/offer spreads. Does the execution process only run on daily prices, or does the dealer have a price-level signal stored in the computer ready to deal at any time once the level is breached? If the latter, then this is a significant deviation from the model, and either the model should be revised to use higher-frequency prices, or the execution should be amended to deal at only once-daily price 'fixings'. Maintaining a gap in execution process between the model and live dealing significantly reduces the quality of the model, because the model has no information about higher frequency data.

10.2.6 Judgement and modelling

The exercise of discretion in the execution of a quantitative model in the currency market sits very uneasily with the concept of the scientific method in modelling.

Let us suppose a model generates a signal. The signal is passed to the portfolio manager, who then exercises his judgement as to the timing and manner of the execution (and indeed the advisability of the deal at all). The question that needs to be answered of such a process is this: does the discretion of the portfolio manager improve the operation of the process?[6] To answer this, the firm will need accurate record-keeping of the tradeable prices at the time the model's signal is issued, and of the final (judgement-influenced) deal. If this data is available, then the portfolio manager's input can be analysed, and value-added and risk measures applied to determine its success or otherwise. The model's live track record (which is the non-judgement-influenced trades) can be analysed and compared to the simulations on which the model was constructed. Quite separately, the portfolio manager's deals (the gap between the model's deals and actual execution) can be analysed. If the portfolio manager is consistently successful, then he is a generator of currency 'alpha',[7] and not dependent on being 'given' trades by the model. It may also be worth the firm trying to understand what (further) inefficiency the portfolio manager is exploiting (not being fully exploited by the model) that allows this value added. Finally, the firm might consider whether this skilled input from the portfolio manager can be codified, and itself turned into a model.

If the portfolio manager is not consistently successful, then there might be good reason to eliminate this source of uncertainty from the firm's process. If the data for this 'alpha attribution' is not available to the firm (or the client), how can either be sure that the discretionary exercise by the portfolio manager is worth doing? Clients who get the opportunity should ask a firm with discretionary override to justify its policy with data.

---

[6] This section refers to value-added processes in currency markets, but not necessarily to other, less liquid markets. Because of the liquidity of currency markets, model-generated deals do not need to be 'finessed' to get good execution. The quoted price is in most instances instantaneously tradeable at narrower than quoted spreads. See Chapter 4 for more on this.

[7] 'Alpha' is commonly used to denote 'value added' versus a benchmark.

10.2.7 Deal execution

Currency managers will be judged on their 'after-dealing-costs' performance. While this should prove a strong spur to ensure that their deals do not attract excessive bid/offer spreads from the foreign exchange market, there may be some factors which influence an overlay manager's choice of counterparty for his client. The most obvious factor (and potential conflict) is where an overlay manager is owned by a bank with an active FX dealing room. Deals undertaken by the overlay manager with his parent will always create an element of uncertainty – and probably the most transparent solution is for such a manager to forbid themselves deals with their parent.

Box 10.4   Active currency styles

Currency overlay managers are commonly categorised into three styles: fundamental, technical and dynamic. There is a fourth, option-based, which in many ways (but not all) is a different manifestation of dynamic hedging.

Fundamental managers believe they can exploit price inefficiencies using models and processes in which economic and financial data is used as the 'exogenous' variables. Examples of such data include balance of payments, capital flows, relative price levels, relative monetary conditions, etc. Fundamental managers have to accept that there may be quite long lags (measured in years not months) where their models may not work effectively, and this has reduced to a handful the number of overlay managers who use exclusively fundamental techniques.

Technical managers are philosophically the 'opposite' of fundamental managers. They tend to ignore completely external economic variables, and argue that price and price history provide the most effective mechanism for exploiting inefficiencies. Their typical approach would be to model price history to determine successful trading rules – say like buying a currency when its 5-day moving average price crosses its 25-day moving average. Good technical managers in currency overlay have added value over time.

Dynamic managers are a group that aims to create an asymmetric return – running profits and cutting losses. Many dynamic managers use currency option technology to do this. Most use forward contracts for this process, but a smaller group use option instruments (see below).

Option-based managers' approach is to exploit what they see as systematic differences between implied and actual future volatility. In many ways the inefficiencies they exploit, and the pattern of excess returns, are similar to dynamic managers'.

There is a live debate as to whether these categories are accurate or appropriate. Few of the overlay managers active at the time of writing would fully subscribe to these descriptions.

10.3   ACTIVE MANAGEMENT STYLES

I want to turn next to the common styles in active currency management. The naming of styles in asset management is always a little contentious – each style is named by its proponents in such a way to make it attractive or 'natural'. Two popular styles in active equity management are 'growth' and 'value'. Both sound good. But they are simply two halves of the spectrum of one particular value or group of values – essentially price/earnings ratios. High ratio = growth stock; low ratio = value stock. They can't both simultaneously outperform the combination of the two (which is the whole market).

Active management styles are in reality a reflection of the types of model and model input that a manager chooses to employ. Once a manager chooses to accept a particular relationship as having predictive power, it will determine his 'style' as seen by the outside world. The most common categories in active currency overlay (see Box 10.4) are as follows:

- Fundamental
- Technical
- Dynamic
- Option-based

I will take each in turn, although I will look at option-based styles before dynamic hedging, since this gives the introduction to option-like payoffs that dynamic hedging is based on.

10.3.1 Fundamental

Fundamental managers believe that currency markets are not semi-strong efficient. That is, they believe there is non-currency-price public information that they can (regularly) obtain that will give them greater than 50% success rate in their exchange rate positions at some horizon in the future – i.e. make their clients a profit.

Fundamental forecasters are deluged with possible contenders for explanatory data – *infla-tion, interest rates, money supply, GDP growth, consumer spending, central bank reserves, bond yields, cross-border asset flows, balance of payments, foreign direct investment, central bank intervention policy, government borrowing, finances and debt*, etc. The list goes on and on. I could list virtually every category in each government's statistical output of economic data, and hardly any would be completely irrelevant. How do managers sift this data for relevance, and how do they build effective models?

The sifting of data is generally determined by the hypotheses that a manager wants to test. If a manager does not have a clear *ex ante* hypothesis, then that is a reliable signal that the model is going to end up with a strong 'data-mining' element.[8] Let me give an example of how the testing process might work. (I have kept it simple to illustrate the process, not to build a credible model.)

10.3.1.1 Hypothesis

Let us suppose that the hypothesis is that exchange rates that are higher than purchasing power parity levels have a tendency to go down (increasing with the distance from parity levels), and that rates that are lower than purchasing power parity levels have a tendency to go up (increasing with the distance from parity levels). It is intuitively appealing and the inputs are relatively simple.

However, it is not quite as simple as it may seem. This hypothesis may be true, but still not be a way for the manager to make money. This is because the manager can only deal in interest-rate-adjusted spot rates – i.e. currency surprise. So for the model to be any use, the hypothesis must be changed to: 'spot exchange rates that are higher than purchasing power parity levels

---

[8] Data mining is the (dismissive) name given to models which are built by choosing as explanatory variables those series that fit the data, rather than those which reflect a well-defined theory. It is pretty much the same thing as 'curve fitting'.

Box 10.5   Capital account

National accounts' economists separate balance of payments data into current and capital account. The way the national accounts process works is that physical imports and exports are recorded in detail, while imports and exports of services (including interest and dividends in both directions) are much more roughly estimated (since there is no port documentation) as 'invisibles'. If these two do not add up to zero, then the balancing item is called 'capital account'. Interestingly, countries with exchange control regulations may have much better invisibles data than those that don't, although exchange controls will almost certainly also spawn a black market, where there is by definition no data.

Capital account transactions, being a residual, are enormously varied. Taking, say, the US perspective, the most obvious ones are cross-border lending and investment in securities – e.g. Japanese public and private sector purchase of US Treasury and other securities 'financing the US deficit'. Other less obvious forms of capital account transactions are, for example, US investment institutions hedging their foreign exchange exposure or a quoted US company building new US plant with the proceeds of a share placing. All these are examples of capital inflows into the US. The last case (where I am assuming some foreign ownership of the quoted company) is that foreign owners subscribe to the share placing.

The current/capital split is defended on the grounds that current account performance is a great deal more predictable than capital account. But it is worth remembering that the sum of the current and capital account is always zero; which implies to the logical non-economist that the capital account is just as predictable as the current account. The only question is the exchange rate that is necessary to achieve that.

---

have a tendency to generate negative currency surprises (increasing with the distance from parity levels), and spot rates that are lower than purchasing power parity levels have a tendency to generate positive currency surprises (increasing with the distance from parity levels)'. If this hypothesis proves to be supported by the evidence, and is stable over time, then in theory it could be the basis for a fundamental model.

10.3.1.2   Inputs

1. We can proxy the changes in purchasing power with the relative change in consumer price indices in the relevant countries (we will need the date that the later of the two inflation levels is announced to avoid the anachronistic mistake).
2. We need a level for purchasing power parity. This could perhaps be the inflation-adjusted average spot rate over a long data period (say 20 or 30 years). But see below the discussion of purchasing power parity.
3. We will have to have a series of spot rates to calculate where current rates are in relation to purchasing power – and forward rates have no role in this calculation.
4. We will need a series of currency surprise – or more particularly an interest-rate-adjusted index of the exchange rates. We need the latter because we might want to vary the horizon over which this hypothesised effect applies. It might not work in a month, but might work over two years.

We also need to pick a currency pair to start with. We will use USD/GBP as an example, but in a live modelling environment, this would be many pairs. We need to choose a modelling frequency: most econometric models are no more frequent than monthly, whereas trading models are almost always daily frequency.

10.3.1.3   Regression

Most econometric models use a technique called 'regression', whose basic principles are as follows. A hypothesis is established, say that future changes in log currency surprise are determined in part by the distance that the spot rate is from purchasing power parity. If interest-rate-adjusted log currency index $= c_t$, then future changes at horizon n months $= c_{t+n} - c_t$. Suppose that $x_t = \%$ over/undervaluation of sterling using PPP values as the benchmark. The regression equation

$$y_t = a + bx_t + e$$

where $y_t = c_{t+n} - c_t$ is a standard linear regression equation, testing whether y is explained by x; a and b are constants (which will be calculated in the regression), and e is the error term (i.e. the unexplained variations in y).

10.3.1.4   Correlation

Because we are only testing the relationship between one external factor (PPP) and changes in future exchange rates, we can run correlations between these two series. We will have about 20 years of monthly data, so about 240 points in the series. For this number of observations, correlation coefficients above about 0.13 (or -0.13) are statistically significant (i.e. we can reject the hypothesis that the two series are unrelated).

10.3.1.5   Trading model

As well as testing the statistical relationship between series, we can also test whether trading rules set up to attempt to exploit the relationship can make money. Any trading will be conducted in the currency surprise series (since this is exploitable), not the spot return series (since this is not investible). The rules can be infinitely varied. I have shown three. The first two take positions for certain predetermined horizons (say 24 months): they are a variable position (i.e. proportionately shorter of sterling as it gets increasingly overvalued) and a 'long/short' switch as the spot rate crosses PPP. The third model does not have a horizon, instead it takes proportionate positions each month dependent on sterling over/undervaluation vs. PPP. These are adjusted end-month on the basis of new PPP levels.

10.3.1.6   PPP

All three modelling approaches require additional inputs from the modellers to get results. The horizon (the time over which PPP is presumed to work) is one variable; perhaps more critical is the PPP reference levels. Calculating definitive PPP is not a science. While it is possible to analyse the price of traded goods, and determine exchange rates that equalise those prices, there are a wide variety of imponderables that make the calculation not definitive. Taxation differences, product specification differences, differences in financial structure of the respective economies, transport and distribution hurdles, and so on.[9] One way out of this uncertainty is perhaps to use the long-term inflation-adjusted historical average of exchange rates, on the basis that these will have oscillated round a long-term equilibrium (presumably something near to PPP). The problem with this is: what historical period do you use? If the period is contemporary with the testing period (in this case 1980–2002), then there is anachronistic data in the model. If it is earlier, it may be less relevant, and pre-1971, there were fixed exchange rates in which market clearing could not operate effectively.

Box 10.6   Purchasing power parity

PPP is an important theory for the determination of exchange rates. It is important because it is the bedrock of the argument as to whether exchange rates are over- or undervalued. The core theory runs as follows. A large part of industrialised economies' GDP is tradeable goods (cars, food, drink, clothes, consumer durables). We can take a basket of these goods, and convert their domestic prices in different countries into a common currency (say the USD) at current exchange rates. This will show a dispersion of countries' price levels – e.g. that a hamburger in Japan is twice as expensive as a hamburger is the US, implying that the yen is overvalued against the dollar.

The PPP argument is that relative price levels will tend towards parity as arbitrage takes over. If an identical CD player can be sold for twice as much in Sweden as in Singapore, then traders will export more CD players to Sweden, and less to Singapore. If repeated across the economy, this will increase the balance of deficit in Sweden, and increase the balance of payment surplus in Singapore, depressing the Swedish exchange rate and raising the Singaporean, tending to equalise the prices.

While superficially attractive, there are a number of major flaws in this theory. The key flaws from the economic perspectives are: non-tradeable country-specific factors like labour costs, taxes, property prices and infrastructure affect domestic prices, but are not arbitrageable. There are also the effects of tariffs, transport costs, differential product specification costs and differential indirect taxes on damping arbitrage for the elements which are tradeable. Finally, and perhaps most important, is the dominance of capital flows in the short-term determination of exchange rates. This can allow PPP overvaluation, together with large balance of payments deficits, to persist for many years without exchange rate movements to compensate (or even with perverse exchange rate movements).

For a quantitative 100-year study, see Alan M. Taylor, *A Century of Purchasing-Power Parity*, National Bureau of Economic Research Working Paper No. w8012, November 2000. It also has a very good bibliography.

I have chosen to test the following models on data 1980–2002, with PPP equilibrium levels calculated from 1971–1990 average actual price and exchange rate levels. This assumes that the secular differences in economic structure will be reflected in the 30-year averages. Hence if an exchange rate appears constantly overvalued in the OECD statistics (like, say, JPY), this systematic bias is eliminated by adjusting for the 30-year averages. In other words, the 30-year

---

[9] The OECD (Organisation for Economic Co-operation & Development) publishes monthly PPP values for OECD member states. They publish, *inter alia*, the ratio of actual exchange rates to those that would give common price levels across member countries. Such published statistics, however, do not solve any of the problems listed above.

average PPP level for each currency is defined as 100. A currency is therefore overvalued if it is trading at an adjusted PPP level of >100, and undervalued if it is trading at a level of <100. In this example, I have already mentioned that I use only one pair (USD/GBP), although of course in the live modelling environment I would look at all major pairs (and probably some minor).

With all these caveats, and remembering that this is an artificial exercise, let's look at the results on actual data.

10.3.1.7 Model results

Each of these models gives different results (Table 10.1). Model 1 gives very high correlations, rising continuously with horizons to about 80 months, falling thereafter. At these horizons it is possible to get 0.8 correlation. Prima facie evidence, perhaps, that future currency surprise is explained by deviations from PPP? Model 2 strongly supports this contention, showing incontrovertible t-stats for the explanatory variable of >10. Likewise, the trading models are all profitable, but with different horizons showing peak performance. It all looks good, but is it the makings of a successful fundamental model? Not necessarily.

There are a number of points to make. The most obvious is that when the PPP equilibrium level is varied, to test the sensitivity of the model to this value (which should be important if the theory is right), two of the three trading models are insensitive to the changes. Both models still make money when every trade is 'short' of sterling, or alternatively every trade is 'long' of sterling. For this to be the case, the market must have exhibited a mean-reverting element over this period (at least at the horizons tested). This means that the model 'looks' like a fundamental model, but is in fact a technical model, making money out of mean reversion.

Table 10.1 Fundamental model results

Type of model	Target to be modelled	External variables	Results
1 Correlation	Change in future currency surprise	% spot over/undervalued vs. PPP	>0.8 – peak horizon 85 months
2 Regression	Change in future currency surprise	% spot over/undervalued vs. PPP	t-stat for PPP >10 depending on horizon
3 Trading model – fixed horizon forward position proportionate to ratio	Cumulative profits	% spot over/undervalued vs. PPP	Profits peak at 13 months horizon
4 Trading model – fixed horizon forward position +/− depending on over/undervaluation	Cumulative profits	% spot over/undervalued vs. PPP	Profits plateau between 15–30 months horizon
5 Trading model – variable horizon forward position +/− depending on over/undervaluation	Cumulative profits	% spot over/undervalued vs. PPP	Profitable for all PPP levels

We can cast further doubt on the model by a split test – the model makes five times as much in 1980–91 as it does in 92–02, and in 98–02 makes almost nothing.

Finally, this exercise has looked at one bilateral currency relationship. A fully-formed fundamental model needs to look at many more than one currency pair. It may need to rank the strength of the signals generated to ensure that risk is being most efficiently rewarded, and it will need to fit into the risk/return requirements that the investor demands.

10.3.1.8   Forward rate bias

The foreign exchange market, like the commodities markets, not only has spot prices actively quoted and traded every day, but also a range of forward prices up to one year horizon. As we have seen, the forward discounts and premiums (vs. spot) are themselves a source of information, and since they are additional information outside the univariate price series, they probably have to be put in the 'fundamental' style pot. This is a little tenuous: most currency overlay managers would not call the forward rate bias a 'fundamental' effect, but in the arbitrary styles currently fashionable, FRB probably goes in this pot. I will not spell out here an active process which exploits the forward rate bias, since I covered this quite extensively in Chapter 9.

10.3.1.9   Summary on fundamental modelling

I have not brought the modelling exercise to a conclusion. I have not looked at the volatilities of the value added, and so the quality of the value-added series is as yet untested. But the experience described above is common: powerful relationships at first look, and then with closer and closer attention the reasons for the relationships become less clear, or emerge as counterintuitive, or are 'picking up' the statistical influences of other variables. The evidence, which regrettably is mostly anecdotal, is that fundamental inputs into currency overlay are inadequate, on their own, to provide an effective active overlay process. The key shortcomings are *instability* of explanatory relationships, and the *unresponsive* nature of fundamental models.

Instability is a very serious shortcoming indeed in modelling. It arises from explanatory models that are generally incomplete; that is, they are missing significant explanatory elements which, at least for some periods, are important contributors to overall price moves. Fundamental modelling faces the almost impossible task of including all these variables if a model is to be stationary (the opposite of unstable in this context). But as a modeller increases the number of these variables (e.g. is the Malaysian Central Bank active today Y/N?), the danger increases that the intuitive basis for the model – the core hypotheses – are diluted and lost. This will lead to high R^2s and t-stats in the modelling period, and huge disappointment in the live period.

Even if a robust stationary model can be constructed, there is the problem of 'responsiveness'. The model constructed above had an element of responsiveness built in – the PPP over/undervaluation calculation is dependent on the spot rate, and this introduces an element of 'lagged dependent variable' into the equation. 'Lagged dependent variable' describes the situation where part of an explanatory variable (PPP over/undervaluation) is itself an earlier value (exchange rate) of the value we are trying to predict (also the exchange rate). Lagged dependent variables bring their own statistical problems, and we will look at these in Section 10.4, where lagged dependent variables are the *sine qua non*.

10.3.2   Technical

Managers who use the 'technical' currency overlay style believe that the currency markets are not weak form efficient. In other words, they believe that the markets' own price history has predictive power for future prices. I have already stated earlier at the start of this chapter that I believe the evidence strongly supports this position. The chapters (Chapter 4 and Chapter 9) that describe the structure of the currency market, and its dominance by non-profit sensitive participants, explain why this belief can be well founded, and that this inefficiency can persist.

This forms the background to technical managers. The detail is largely statistical. If there is information in the price available at time t which is predictive (however indirectly) of future prices, then this is the basis for a successful technical model. We can explore a similar process to that undertaken by the fundamental modeller above. Let's set the scene.

10.3.2.1   Hypothesis

Let us suppose that the hypothesis is that exchange rates exhibit *trends*. This sounds like a rather simple statement, but establishing exactly what it means, and testing it, is far from simple. For example, the signals can be based on any price – spot is fine if it works, but the assessment of whether signals can make money must be based on currency surprise. Trends in one direction do not last for ever, and so there will be decisions to make about the horizon of any trend signal, and turning-point processes.

10.3.2.2   Inputs

We need a daily database with spot and forward rates. We may need higher frequency data if intra-day strategies are to be modelled, and even higher frequency if any signal is to be 'instantaneously' actioned. We also need to pick a currency pair to start with. We will use again USD/GBP as an example, and data 1973–2002.

10.3.2.3   Correlation

We can run correlations between the currency returns and prior period currency returns, or in algebraic form:

$$\text{Correlation } (y_t, y_{t-1}), \quad t = 1972\text{--}2002, \quad \text{variable frequency}$$

We can vary the horizons of the returns (i.e. one-day correlated with prior one-day, or five-day correlated with prior five-day) to see whether any autoregressive effect changes with horizon. Positive correlations imply trends (positive serial correlation), negative imply mean reversion (negative serial correlation). We are not constrained to the same horizons for the past returns and the future returns, i.e. we could test the correlation between one-day returns, and the prior three-day returns. We will explore this route of enquiry in more detail in Section 10.3.2.4. For this exercise, we can show the results from varying the horizon of the returns similarly for both series. If we use about 30 years of daily data, we have about 7550 points in the series. As the horizons extend beyond one day, the number of independent observations falls – two-day returns have 3775 independent observations, etc.

Correlation coefficients can be tested for statistical significance. The formula for this is:

$$t = r \left(\frac{\sqrt{n-2}}{\sqrt{1-r^2}} \right)$$

where t is a t-stat measure, r is the observed correlation coefficient and n is the number of pairs of observations. If $t > 1.96$, then the observed correlation is positive and significant at the 95% level (two-sided test). Similarly, if $t < 1.96$, then the correlation is significantly negative. For 7500 observations, the significance level is 0.022 (or −0.022) (i.e. apparently very low). As the horizon period rises, the level required for significance will also rise. We show the results for the 1973–2002 period in Figure 10.1.

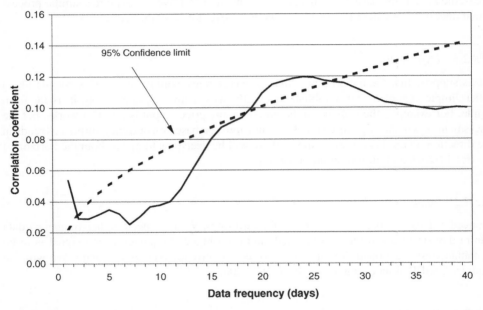

Figure 10.1 Correlation coefficient curve (USD/GBP, 1973–2002, lagged dependent variable, variable data frequency)

Only daily data appears to offer any real significance over this long data period, despite the marginal significance of 25-day data (or roughly monthly). All the horizons show positive correlation, indicating that this relationship has trended over history. However, if we were building a model to use in live trading, we would be building it over the 'testing period', and running it over a 'live' period, outside the testing period. This requires the relationship we establish in the testing period to persist into the live period. This 'stability' is core to the modelling process, and is discussed in Chapter 10 in more detail.

For this example, we can look at the 'split test' of correlation: this is dividing the data into three roughly equal-length periods – 73–82, 83–92, 93–02. Each of these can be tested independently, as the graph in Figure 10.2 shows.

Regrettably, this new information thoroughly undermines our previous hypothesis. It is not so much that the USD/GBP does not trend, because it clearly did in the 20 years 1973–1992, but that it changed its behaviour in the last 10 years, and became a mean-reverting

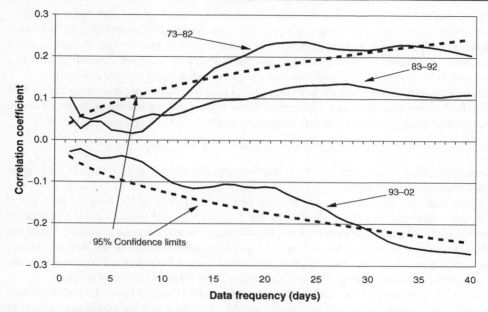

Figure 10.2 Correlation coefficient curves (USD/GBP, 1973–2002, lagged dependent variable, split tests, variable frequency)

currency with negative autoregressive behaviour (although at longer horizons than the trending behaviour).

10.3.2.4 Regression

We can express a basic trends hypothesis in the following format:

$$y_t = f(y_{t-1}, y_{t-2}, y_{t-3}, \ldots, y_{t-n}, e)$$

where $y_t = c_{t+n} - c_t$, where $c_t =$ interest-rate-adjusted log currency index, and e is the error term (i.e. the unexplained variations in y). Expressed in words, this is a rather general model which says that returns in period t are (partially) explained by returns in periods $t - 1$, $t - 2, t - 3, \ldots, t - n$. This type of model is called a *lagged dependent variable* model. The *dependent variable* is y_t, called such because in the model context it is dependent on the explanatory variables. If we can get a dependent variable for a future period to be substantially explained by variables whose values we already know (lagged), then we have the makings of a forecasting model.

We could also re-specify the model slightly into:

$$y_t = f(x_{t-1}, x_{t-2}, x_{t-3}, \ldots, x_{t-n}, e)$$

where $x_t = p_{t+n} - p_t$, and $p_t =$ log spot price. This might reflect more closely what drives the price – and despite appearances, this is still a lagged dependent variable model.

It is usual to model y, the log currency surprise (sometimes called currency *returns*), rather than c, the log interest-rate-adjusted *price*. Returns are the rate of change of prices, and in continuous maths would be called the first differential. Modelling returns (rather than price) is more useful because the random-walk-like nature of prices means that today's price is always 95%+ determined by yesterday's price, so price models give overwhelming (but rather indiscriminate) credence to lagged dependent variables. By contrast, even if there is serial correlation in currency returns, it is weak. So currency returns today are determined only to a small extent by yesterday's returns: this is the value we want to get as high as possible.

I have chosen to model log currency surprise (y_t) with five lagged dependent variables, each one period earlier than the other. I have used linear regression, the statistical details of which are available in any good econometric modelling textbook.[10] The regression model is:

$$y_t = a + b_1 y_{t-1} + b_2 y_{t-2} + b_3 y_{t-3} + b_4 y_{t-4} b_5 y_{t-5} + e$$

where b_1, b_2, b_3, b_4 and b_5 are constants (parameters) and e is the error term (i.e. picking up all the unexplained variations).

Again, like the correlation model, we can vary the frequency of the data – I have tested 1–30-day frequency. Just to be clear, a 30-day frequency model would have the dependent variable as the 30-day currency return (i.e. log currency surprise), let us say starting today and ending 30 days in the future. The first lagged dependent variable would be the 30-day currency return ending today, starting 30 days prior; the second lagged dependent variable would be the 30-day currency return ending 30 days prior, and starting 60 days prior, and so on.

To complete the testing, I examined the regression results using only one lagged dependent variable – the lagged-one-period dependent variable. I then ranked the explanatory power of all the alternative regressions by an F-ratio – essentially a statistical test of how confident we can be that the amount of variation explained by the model is not zero. A high ratio means we can be very confident; confidence levels are given by the F-distribution. The model with the highest F-ratio, giving us the highest confidence that the model has genuine explanatory power, was the simplest – the single one-day lagged dependent variable on daily data.

Summary results for this example regression model are shown in Table 10.2. To the uninitiated, it may be surprising that a very simple model gives us most confidence. It does not give us the best R^2 – a 5-lagged-dependent-variable 18-day frequency regression explains over five times as much of the variation. But as we add explanatory variables, we add significantly to the chance that their explanations are spurious.

Table 10.2 Regression results (USD/GBP, 1973–2002, autoregressive model)

Criteria for 'best regression'	F-test
F-ratio	21.51
F-test confidence	99.99964%
Best frequency	1 day
b_1 coefficient value	+0.053(+ = trends; − = mean reverting)
t-stat for b_1 coefficient	4.4
Best model specification	Independent variables: single one-period lagged
	Zero intercept

Finally, we need to look at a split test. Having seen the results of the correlation split test, we can already guess the result: 1993–2002 will have a negative b_1 coefficient.

---

[10] For example Johnston and Dinardo, *Econometric Methods*, 4th edn, McGraw-Hill, 1996, ISBN 0-07-913121-2.

The results to prove it are shown in Table 10.3. We see that b_1 is negative, but not significantly so over this period, and the F-ratio is not high enough for us to be at all confident that the model explains anything at all.

Table 10.3 Regression results – split test (USD/GBP, 1993–2002, autoregressive model)

Criteria for 'best regression'	F-test
F-ratio	1.70
F-test confidence	81%
b_1 coefficient value	-0.028 ($+$ = trends; $-$ = mean reverting)
t-stat for b_1 coefficient	-1.42

Regression models are explanatory, not trading processes. To convert significant regression results into a trading model, the modeller is required to develop a process. This might be a 'momentum' model, in which the parameters that are identified in a regression as having significant explanatory power are then pressed into service to take an active currency position (proportionately 'long' for predicted price rises and proportionately 'short' for predicted price falls). I show results of a simple version of such a model below.

10.3.2.5   Trading models

The rules of trading models can be infinitely varied. Their purpose is to codify actions that a currency manager needs to take at time t to 'maximise' the chance that the result, once the position is closed, is a profit.

I have constructed and tested two models. The first is a moving average model, the second is a momentum model.

Moving average model: A moving average model is one where a simple trading rule is established: buy the currency that is rising at the moment a shorter trailing moving average of the spot rate crosses a longer trailing moving average. Such a model will exploit positive serial correlation if it exists; the reverse rule would be applied if it is believed that markets are mean-reverting. Note that it is perfectly possible for markets to be both trending and mean-reverting at the same time. The effects can apply at different horizons – say trending up to 3 months, but mean-reverting at 2 years. I will be testing shorter effects in this modelling. Moving averages are expressed in days, and in modelling this kind of process, one can visualise the shorter trailing moving average (say 2 days) being a damped proxy for the current price, and the longer trailing moving average (say 18 days) being a proxy for a 'trend' line. When the shorter crosses the longer, the model is implicitly saying that the trend has changed, and therefore the position should too.

I have constructed a moving average model which uses the *spot* rate as the trend indicator (i.e. as the constituent parts of the moving averages), and which takes a 1 or -1 position (long and short) depending on the relative values of the moving averages. However, the profits or losses from this position are recorded from the subsequent currency surprise, not the spot rate. It is in theory possible (although only with wide interest rate differentials) that the moving average model could correctly predict the spot rate, but that the position would be loss-making because of the interest rate differential erosion. The model also builds in transaction costs

---

Box 10.7   Mean reversion

This is a common expression used to describe a particular type of market behaviour, but what exactly does it mean? It is a rather loose expression, but in 'non-mathematical' speak it means that (a) market movements are not random and (b) the market is more likely to reverse a previous move than continue it. The horizon over which mean reversion applies is very important in determining its effect on market prices, and the kind of active process to exploit it.

Very short horizon mean reversion
This is where the mean reversion applies over the shortest of horizons – say one day. This means that if the market goes up one day, it is more likely to reverse that move tomorrow rather than continue it. This behaviour is characteristic of illiquid markets, and the 'choppy' market prices this brings about are often the result of the absorption process of large orders in the market.

Mid-horizon (moving average) reversion
Under this model, the market has a 'memory' of a moving average of past prices, and there is an 'elastic band' which is trying to move the market level back towards these historical levels. The moving average can be of a wide range of maturities. It is supportable as a proposition that exchange rates are mean-reverting over 5-year horizons.

Fixed mean
Under this model, the mean is not a moving average of historic prices, but a broadly fixed value. The most obvious potential example of this is real (inflation-adjusted) interest rates; they vary day-by-day and year-by-year, but they tend to revert to a value centred around (say) 3%. This is perhaps the purest example of mean reversion.

Mean reversion and trending can co-exist. Indeed there is strong evidence that exchange rates are trending over 'market memory' horizons – say 0–1 years, but mean-reverting over 5-year horizons. This is not particularly surprising: market movements are the result of the collective behaviour of the market's participants, and the complex interactions of sentiment and underlying economic variables may perfectly well have different horizons.

---

for changes in the position. This kind of detail is important in modelling, since one key and necessary condition of a model that proves successful in practice is one that fully represents all the factors encountered in the live trading process.

The results for this model are shown in Table 10.4. I have used 'information ratios' (broadly speaking, annualised return divided by annualised standard deviation of returns – see Box 10.8) as the 'performance' result, and this is calculated from the daily value-added calculated from this model. From the table, the reader can see that the best result was from the 2- and 18-day combination.

The table also neatly illustrates the effect of transaction costs. The values for 10- and 12-day moving averages are repeated in both row and column. The difference of 0.2 (i.e. 0.52 − 0.72) information ratio is twice the effect of the transaction costs, which is therefore 0.1 information

Table 10.4   Information ratios of moving average model, daily data (1973–2002)

Shorter moving average (days)	Longer moving average (days)						
	10	12	14	16	18	20	22
1	0.58	0.54	0.64	0.73	0.71	0.67	0.66
2	0.56	0.60	0.63	0.75	0.76	0.61	0.52
4	0.61	0.65	0.58	0.60	0.43	0.41	0.39
6	0.48	0.60	0.52	0.42	0.29	0.36	0.34
8	0.45	0.59	0.42	0.35	0.27	0.31	0.30
10		0.52	0.44	0.38	0.32	0.40	0.33
12	−0.72		0.23	0.33	0.37	0.28	0.18

Box 10.8   Information ratio

The expression 'information ratio' was first coined by Nobel Laureate William Sharpe as a useful way of measuring the 'skill' of active managers. The principle on which it rests, 'risk-adjusted excess return', is the same as his parallel measure for securities – the Sharpe ratio.

The information ratio is the average added value of a portfolio (portfolio return less benchmark return) divided by the tracking error (see Box 6.1). This value (generally lying in the −1 to +1 area) records how much risk a manager is taking to achieve the recorded value added.

Information ratios are calculated on an annual basis, so if quarterly, monthly or higher frequency data is used, it must be annualised first. Information ratios greater than 0 indicate that a manager might have demonstrated skill. But active managers have to deviate from benchmark returns to add any value at all, and so there is, on the face of it, a roughly 50% chance that a manager with an information ratio greater than 0 will have achieved it by chance. We can test this by using the property of the very useful Central Limit Theorem. In summary, if we multiply the information ratio by the square root of the number of years for which the averages are calculated, we will get a 't-stat'. Roughly speaking, if this number is greater than 1.7, it tells us that there is a 95% chance that the manager has demonstrated skill not luck.

There is a 'rule of thumb' in evaluating managers that an information ratio of 0.5 is good, and 0.75 is excellent. It is highly unlikely that any active manager can demonstrate a prolonged information ratio of 1. An active manager with a (more typical) 0.4 information ratio would have to show a 16-year track record for this to prove skill, whereas a 0.75 information ratio manager could prove this in 5 years.

---

ratio. The effect of transaction costs is less with wider differences of moving average horizon – at 2 and 18 it is about 0.06 information ratio.

This apparently stable state of affairs is, unfortunately, upset when we apply the same split test as in the case of correlation above. If we take the best moving averages (2 and 18), we can calculate the information ratios for each of the split periods (Table 10.5). So the last 10 years has shown negative returns for this strategy, while the previous 20 years gave a staggering

Table 10.5   Moving average model – USD/GBP, 2- and 18-day, information ratios for different periods

Period	Information ratio
Whole period (1973–2002)	0.76
1973–82	1.52
1983–92	1.22
1993–2002	−0.54

average of an information ratio of 1.37. This 'change of market nature' fits in with the negative serial correlation we detected.

The temptation is to attempt to develop the next level of refinement to provide a filter to give 'early warning' of the change from positive to negative serial correlation. This kind of thinking is appealing, but has to be treated with caution. This is for the reasons set out earlier in the chapter. It encourages the idea that with enough explanatory variables, all the 'moving parts' of this series' generator will be captured. A better response, in my opinion, is for the modeller to take the trouble to try to understand, if such a thing is possible, the reason(s) for positive serial correlation appearing in the data in the first place. If these are accurately identified, then if these factors change or disappear, independently of the data, the modeller can progress to predicting such market behaviour changes with a well-founded likelihood of success.

Momentum model: A momentum model can take many forms. The moving average model is a particular type of momentum model. In this section, we will look at another type of model, which in this example is our regression model above.

I will illustrate one class of models in the large universe of possible autoregressive models. Interested readers can find a great deal on univariate[11] time series analysis, as it is called, in econometric and statistics textbooks. It is worth noting that this universe also covers autoregressive second and higher moments – like autoregressive volatility[12] and so on. Finally, staying with univariate modelling, we could (although not here) move away from the strictly statistical into pattern recognition and pattern matching. This moves us into the world of charts and chartists, and more esoteric processes like fractals.[13]

In an effort to keep the example manageably simple, for these illustrative purposes I have built a momentum trading model that applies the 'best model' from the regression analysis above, and turns it into a signal-generation process for position-taking. This is not the principal technique applied to building momentum models, which will be simulation techniques (see Box 10.9). However, in this example, I have chosen to set the size of the position (long or short of GBP) to the size of the predicted move from the autoregressive model. Since the 'best' model is so simple, this is actually proportionate to the size of the move the previous day. The model is reset daily, and gives daily returns, which makes it easy to calculate information ratios. I have chosen to show the results with and without transaction costs. This is because a very 'hair trigger' model like this, which changes the position every day, and which tries to exploit a very

---

[11] Univariate means that there is one time series (the price), and all modelling is conducted on the basis of this information alone.

[12] For example GARCH (Generalised Auto-Regressive Conditional Heteroscedasticity), a univariate modelling process for non-stationary volatility.

[13] Fractals are self-similar geometric shapes. 'Self-similar' means that they look the same however much you enlarge or reduce them. There is a lot on fractals in maths and art textbooks, and on the web.

Box 10.9 Simulations

A significant part of the research and development process of active currency overlay managers is spent building and testing trading models. These are routinely tested in historical *simulations*. In a simulation, a model which has been developed using a range of historical data (usually up to the present time) is 'run' over history to simulate the trades it would have generated had it been live at the time. These simulations can be used to refine models to produce very high value added and low tracking errors (leading to high information ratios) for the whole period tested.

Well-designed simulations are a very valuable tool for managers in their active process development efforts. However, good simulation design requires:

• Full accounting for transactions costs;
• Care over the exact historical timing of information arrival (to avoid trades being 'executed' prior to the arrival of the relevant information);
• High-quality price information;
• Care taken to ensure that the simulated trading process is replicable in live trading (i.e. frequency of price monitoring, lags in executing real transactions).

However, the most important aspect of simulations is that they will generally produce historical results that are consistently better than those achievable in live trading. Why is this?

In the currency markets, it is not primarily due to lack of liquidity or optimistic pricing in the model. Rather, it is the conceptual problem of model selection. Models which survive the 'cuts' imposed by the testing and simulation process will be 'better' (i.e. have better historical returns) than those that do not. Surviving models may have a proportion of their good performance explained by real and stable inefficiencies, but also a proportion explained by chance. The random element is likely to revert to the mean (i.e. zero performance) for the future (live) period; only the 'real' element will contribute any value added.

The disappointment engendered by underperformance of live models has tarnished simulations as a tool. This is shooting the messenger – the problem is not the simulations but the modelling process. The most effective modellers are those that understand the survival problem, and build models which may on the face of it produce inferior historical returns, but which continue to produce similar returns in live trading.

weak effect over very short intervals of time (one day), has a very high cost/benefit ratio. This is clearly shown in the results (Table 10.6).

The results are not particularly appealing – transactions costs (even at the low level achievable in the currency markets, I have assumed 3 bp round-turn on outright forwards) have a very debilitating effect on results. The 93–02 period stands out as being pretty disastrous. Clearly there is some work to do on this model to make it remotely usable.

10.3.2.6 Summary technical modelling results

Summary results are provided in Table 10.7. As we have seen, behind these superficially attractive results is a great deal of non-stationarity. 30 years of daily data is a huge amount

Table 10.6　Momentum model – USD/GBP, 'best fit' regression, information ratios for different periods

Period	Information ratio (without transactions costs)	Information ratio (with transactions costs)
Whole period (1973–2002)	0.67	0.36
1973–82	0.50	0.21
1983–92	1.37	1.08
1993–2002	−0.36	−0.76

Table 10.7　Technical model results

Type of model	Target to be modelled	External variables	Results
1 Correlation	Change in future currency surprise	Lagged dependent variable	t-stat = 4.65 at 1-day autoregressive
2 Regression	Change in future currency surprise	Lagged dependent variable(s)	Best F-ratio = 21.5 at 1-day lag
3 Trading model – moving averages	Cumulative profits	Lagged dependent variable	IR peaks at 0.76 at 2- & 18-day MAs
4 Trading model – momentum	Cumulative profits	Lagged dependent variable	IR peaks at 0.36 at 1-day frequency

(c. 7550 days), and the models have no difficulty whatever in finding highly significant explanatory models in all of the techniques. However, none of these techniques, as they stand, would have allowed their users to make money in the last 10 years – in fact they would have lost money.

In this exercise, I have looked at one exchange rate series over a particular period of time. Of the major currency pairs, USD/GBP happens to exhibit the most extreme changes to the nature of its distribution. Other pairs have changed less, or not at all, or have become more trending with the passage of time. What this exercise will have illustrated, I hope, is that technical modelling can demonstrate persistent inefficiencies, but that exploiting these inefficiencies requires a well-founded belief in the underlying causes of the inefficiency as well as technical modelling expertise. So successful modellers under this reasoning should be experts in the foreign exchange markets first, and mathematicians second, not the other way round.

I have concentrated on one currency pair, but of course there are many. One of the advantages of technical modelling is that it can choose, on the basis of recent currency behaviour, which pairs are conforming to the core model. This is a further powerful tool, which, in the right hands, can make the technical style one of the most powerful.

Finally, technical model building requires an understanding of the needs and constraints of the client. Unconstrained technical models can undoubtedly make money over time, but if they require a US-based client to take positions, long or short, in, say, JPY/GBP, is this acceptable? Certainly a conventional overlay mandate, as we have seen above, imposes certain constraints on the manager: 0–100% hedge ratios, all positions being part of a pair with the base currency, and the size of the position being determined by the underlying asset holdings in those currencies.

10.3.3   Option-based

The currency option market developed in the mid-1980s, and is now large and very liquid. It certainly qualifies on these grounds for inclusion as a suitable instrument for the currency overlay manager. Options are instruments which, as we have seen in Chapter 3, give the option holder rights but no obligations in return for the up-front payment of a fee (the premium). Conversely, options confer on the writer (seller) obligations but no rights in return for receipt of the fee. Given the complexity of the concepts, and the maths surrounding options, the reader should have familiarised himself with the contents of Chapter 3 before embarking on this section.

This section looks at the additional dimensions of decision-making that options give the overlay manager, and the routes that might allow systematic exploitation for value added. Underlying these descriptions is the presumption, given very strong credence in the earlier sections of this chapter and in Chapter 9, that currency markets are not efficient, and therefore that results from analysis and active management can be positive on average over time.

10.3.3.1   Passive option buying in serially correlated markets

Passive option buying is not a popular currency management style. It looks too 'passive' for most active currency managers, and perhaps, more pertinently, their clients. However, there is a perfectly respectable and mathematically sound case to be made that passive option buying has positive expected value added.

We have established from a variety of evidence offered in previous chapters that many currency pairs exhibit trends. I have argued that this trending behaviour has its foundations in the structure of the foreign exchange market. It has shown persistence, and the structure of the foreign exchange market has not materially changed over the period – it is still dominated by profit-insensitive players. Let us take an example of how such an option-buying process might work.

We will make the working assumption that implied option volatilities are equal historical volatilities calculated from the daily vols, and we will test this assumption later. We will look at 12-month options, since the evidence of trending indicates that we should extend the option maturities as far as possible. What are we trying to exploit? Figure 10.3, reproduced from Figure 9.1, shows the volatility differentials for the major currency pairs.

We will be trying to establish whether we can buy options at the daily volatility generated Black–Scholes model premium, and hold them to receive an average payoff that reflects the annual volatility. Let's start with the theory, which I will summarise in a mathematically simplified way.

The Black–Scholes model formula for an at-the-money forward option (put or call) boils down to:

$$\text{FV 1-year option premiums} = (0.796/2) \times \text{volatility} \qquad (10.1)$$

Taking each of the terms in turn:

FV (future value) option premium means the amount payable contemporarily with the payoff value, i.e. at maturity and not up front. The up-front premium payable would be the FV divided by the 1-year interest rate, but then to compare with the payoff value we would have to multiply by the interest rate (because the option writer holds the money for one year before it is needed).

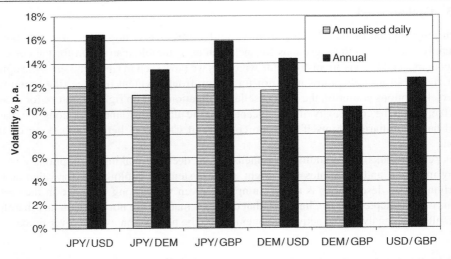

Figure 10.3   Volatility measured at different horizons – volatility of currency surprise (1981–2002), daily volatility annualised and annual volatility

0.796 is the multiple applied to volatility (standard deviation) to calculate the absolute average outcome of a normal distribution (see footnote 2 in Chapter 6); /2 because half the time a call/put expires out-of-the-money and gives zero payoff value.

Volatility is calculated from the log of currency returns (i.e. currency surprise), annualised by calculating daily volatility and multiplying by $\sqrt{262}$. I will convert log values back to percentages after all the algebraic manipulation required.

Using exactly the same logic, and formula, we can also calculate the average expected payoff value. This will have all the same elements of the previous formula, except that the volatility is the average 1-year volatility.

Average historical outcome: If we take the history of DEM/EUR against the USD (I will call it DEM/USD here) as an example, Figure 10.3 tells us the *daily annualised* percentage volatility calculated from the logs is 11.69%. The average option premium under our assumptions is therefore:

$$\exp[(0.796/2) \times \log(1 + 11.69\%)] - 1 = 4.50\%$$

The average *annual* volatility for DEM/USD (also from Figure 10.3) is 14.38%. It follows that the calculated average payoff value is:

$$\exp[(0.796/2) \times \log(1 + 14.38\%)] - 1 = 5.49\%$$

So on the face of it, the trending behaviour observed may be a cause of 'undervaluation' of option premiums, and therefore render passive option buying a profitable strategy.

Implied volatilities – the real test: I have collected a nearly 6-year series of daily implied volatility quotes from a major currency option provider bank for DEM/USD. An example of these quotes is shown in Figure 3.5. However, we need to test 12m option quotes (not 3m option quotes as shown in the graph). I will use the 12m *offer* quotes, the implied volatility the bank is using to price its options offered to customers. Its bid volatilities average 0.25% lower than the offer volatilities over this period. Its volatilities are expressed as percentages, although as explained in Appendix 2, these are really logs (i.e. percentages in continuous time). Banks do not exponentiate their option calculations based on logs back into proper percentages. However, since they charge clients option premiums based on the quoted percentage multiplied by the option principal, I will treat the quotes as percentages.

Applying the test: We are going to calculate option premiums, and the actual payoff values experienced, for DEM/USD 1997–2002 daily:

1. We can calculate the FVs of at-the-money option premiums from the implied vols without interest rates using equation (10.1). Puts and calls will be the same price because of arbitrage (put + forward purchase = call, although this arbitrage only works at-the-money forward). This will give us a series of option premiums.
2. We can double this cost, because in the 'value for money' test we are going to buy doubles (i.e. buying both a put and a call). This will take away any dependency on arbitrary direction of exchange rate moves from the assessment.
3. Then we need to calculate the payoff values for one-year DEM/USD puts and calls. Note that I have not distinguished the numerator and the denominator, and as long as we work in 'log space', we do not have to – the results are the same.
4. Payoff values are not guesswork or averages. They are fact. Here is an example. One-year DEM/USD LHS forward rate on 2 Jan 1997 was 1.5009. This was the price to buy DEM, sell USD. One year later, on 2 Jan 1998, the LHS spot was 1.8042. The payoff in log terms was log(1.8042/1.5009) = 0.1841 for the profitable option (in this case the DEM put/dollar call), and zero for the DEM call/Dollar put. I take 4 bp off the profitable log value to account for the fact that the put and call strikes will be marginally different, reflecting a 4 bp one-year outright bid/offer spread, and the cost of closing the profitable option at spot. This leaves us 0.1837 in log terms as the double profit.
5. Converted back to percentages, the payoff was exp(0.1841) − 1 = 20.16%.
6. The premium for a single option from the volatility quote in this case was 3.52%, or 7.04% for the double. The profit on this observation (i.e. a double bought on 2 Jan 1997) was 20.16% − 7.04% = 13.12%, or 6.56% for the single equivalent.

Figure 10.4 shows the net value of the single option equivalent payoff values minus option premiums for the purchase periods Jan 97–Nov 2001 (maturing Nov 2002). We can clearly see that this net payoff is quite volatile, but that it delivers +44 bp of value added over the period. This is not a spurious finding – it fits in with the trending nature of data we have studied, and what we know about how banks price option premiums. Table 10.8 gives summary information.

Table 10.8 One-year DEM/USD options, averages 1997–2001 (purchase dates)

Average option premium (FV)	4.38%
Average (put + call)/2 payoff value	4.82%
Average gain per option %	0.44%
Max gain %	11.93%
Max loss %	−5.61%

This result arises from one definitive value (payoff) and one less transparent value (option premium). How can we be more confident about how option premiums are quoted? I have compared the option premiums (from implied vols quoted by a major bank) with historical volatilities calculated from spot rates on a rolling backward-looking 6-month period. So for

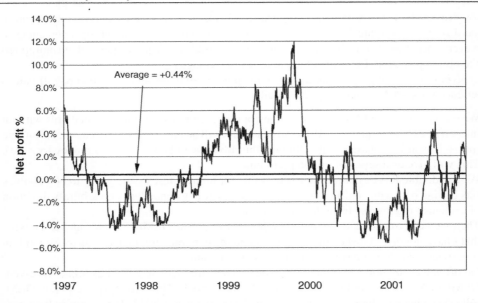

Figure 10.4   One-year DEM/USD put + call options – payoffs less premiums ($/DEM (latterly EUR) options, 97–02, 12m maturity)

2 Jan 1997, the log of the spot changes 2 Jul 1996–2 Jan 1997 would be the source data, and this sample's standard deviation would be annualised, and used as the source to calculate the 'historical' option premium using equation (10.1). The graph of the implied (quoted) and the historical rates is shown in Figure 10.5. Quoted premiums are clearly closely based on historical volatilities, over this period they have averaged 4.38% vs. 4.21% for the historically calculated – a difference of 17 bp.

All of the above is an example; it covers one particular period, for one currency pair, neither the most trending nor the least on the basis of Figure 10.3. It does illustrate, however, that there is a potentially interesting opportunity for overlay managers in this area of 'passive' option buying.

10.3.3.2   'Active' option trading

The Black–Scholes formulation assumes constant volatility. If this assumption is relaxed, as it plainly is in real markets, then there is a premium placed on successful prediction of volatility.

10.3.3.3   Volatility forecasting

Volatility, more specifically implied volatility, has become a recognised market in the world of option trading. Option traders, when asked what they do, will often reply that they 'trade volatility'. Indeed several banks offer OTC products which allow their customers to buy and sell 'volatility' directly. There are several issues that surround volatility trading. The first is that what is traded is implied volatility, not historical volatility. In a sense this makes the market peculiarly circular. Implied volatility is, in effect, a forecast of future volatility. Any manager wishing to successfully 'trade' volatility is being required to forecast future changes in the forecasts of

Figure 10.5 Quoted and historical volatility option premiums (DEM (EUR)/USD, 1997–2002, 1-year options, ATMF, FV premiums)

volatility. Actual volatility may not come into the equation at all! The second point is that volatility is an artificial construct, predicated on (almost certainly violated) assumptions. 'Volatility' is traded because the Black–Scholes formulation assumes a lognormal random walk for the underlying markets, and volatility is the annualised standard deviation of these changes. However, as we have seen above, violation of the Black–Scholes assumptions (in particular uncorrelated random changes) can radically affect even the straightforward calculation of volatility.

Turning to implied volatility forecasting, there is very little academic literature on this area, particularly in foreign exchange. There have been no systematic studies of implied volatility forecasting reliability or success, and the vast majority of the (mainly bank-sponsored) research in this area has concentrated on the relationship between historic volatility and implied volatility. But for forecasting purposes, this is of marginal use, since even a reliable implied volatility model based on historic volatility simply shifts the burden of forecasting to another variable – historic volatility.

Historic volatility (a misnomer since the history may be only a few seconds old) is an average of indeterminate length of the magnitude of changes in the underlying market. Historic volatility can be calculated as the observed standard deviation of a sample of changes in recent history, and this is in practice applied with the assumption that the true (underlying) standard deviation has been constant throughout the sampling period. With increasing length of history, this would be fine if volatility were indeed constant (in line with Black–Scholes assumptions), but it is not fine if population volatility is either non-normal, randomly variable over time, or predictably variable based on other inputs.

Over the past few years modellers have recognised that the underlying variance/volatility is not constant and have contrived to use more sophisticated models to deal with this. GARCH models forecast underlying variance as a (complex) function of past values. This is a more realistic standpoint but unfortunately leads to an exponential growth in the number of parameters which need to be estimated (are they variable too?, when do we stop?), with all the attendant drawbacks.

10.3.3.4   Other active option strategies

Putting aside volatility forecasting, what else can an active manager do with options to enhance returns? Banks will trade options profitably by making prices, not taking them. A currency manager, without a customer-orientated dealing room, client base, brand and market position and capital, cannot do this.

A manager may use options as a downside-controlled way to take currency market bets in either direction, but this is not using option expertise so much as general currency market expertise to add value.

10.3.4   Dynamic

10.3.4.1   Option replication

Very early in the history of currency risk management, in the early 1980s, before currency options became available, currency managers recognised that option-like payoffs were an attractive goal. We have seen in the earlier sections on option models that Black–Scholes' 1973 paper asserted that it was possible to exactly replicate an option position with a dynamically adjusted portfolio of the underlying securities (or forward contracts in this case). Various assumptions violations mean that this assertion is not, in practice, true. Nevertheless, some sort of approximation is possible, and this section explores the various approaches managers have taken to this approximation.

10.3.4.2   Dynamic hedging overlay style

As the OTC option market in currency options started in the second half of 1984, so the money-centre banks who were offering them began to more or less crudely hedge the resulting exposure using dynamic, or 'delta', hedging techniques. The concept of delta hedging is broadly speaking to hold a position in the underlying market whose change in marked-to-market valuation per small (1 bp) movement in the underlying market is equal and opposite to the change in marked-to-market valuation of the option sold. A bank that sells a large portfolio of options in one currency pair can combine these to create a portfolio delta, which is the elasticity of the whole portfolio of options with respect to a 1 bp movement in the underlying market. As an example, an outstanding option sold to a third party, say a $1m call against a third currency, could have a marked-to-market valuation which varies by $350 for a 1 bp movement in the exchange rate. Since a $1m position in the underlying market would have a $100 change in marked-to-market valuation per 1 bp move, this would be called a delta of 0.35 or 35%. Deltas will range between zero and one for 'vanilla' options, but can vary widely and wildly for exotic options. There is a common further measure of the shape of the delta curve with respect to the exchange rate which measures its instantaneous 'curvature', and this is called the gamma. There are a whole lot more Greek letters denoting the elasticities of the option valuation with respect to time, volatility, etc., but they are of interest more to bank risk managers than to the general currency overlay reader.

The argument for currency overlay managers offering a dynamic hedging style of currency risk management runs like this. Buying currency options to protect against adverse currency movements in the fund context is attractive for two reasons: it reduces volatility if correctly targeted and benchmarked, and it satisfies the asymmetric risk-aversion utility curve that mean-variance analysis is poor at coping with. From the evidence presented above, it can also exploit trending markets to add value.

But a manager has to buy currency options from banks. This is true whether or not they are OTC or exchange-traded, since the market-makers on the major exchanges are the major money-centre banks. Banks sell currency options with the prospect of securing a profit on the combination of the premium received for the sale and their cost of covering their risk. They can cover their risk in one of two ways: buying options from third parties or running a delta hedge in the underlying market. Since there are no natural writers of currency options who write them without a delta hedge (in contrast to equity options where institutional holders may well write 'covered' options), banks generally are the ultimate writers of currency options. One way or another, therefore, options written to customers will be matched by a delta hedge run by a bank with the prospect of profit to the bank. Delta-hedging currency managers (or *dynamic hedgers*) offer, at the least, a delta hedge run on behalf of the investor to reduce the cost of the option premium by the amount of the prospective bank profit. They may also offer other advantages: flexibility in tailoring specific option specifications; high liquidity of the forward market compared to the option market; cash flow improvement (no up-front option premiums); and less sensitivity to market volatility in marked-to-market valuation.

In a perfect Black–Scholes world these advantages would be unsullied by any disadvantages. The Black–Scholes model tells us that any option can be exactly and risklessly replicated by a portfolio of the underlying security (foreign currency or forward contracts in this case). As we have seen earlier in this chapter, however, Black–Scholes markets do not exist, and one of the effects of this is that option replication is not a riskless exercise.

What is the effect of this in practice? To simplify the discussion, I propose to discuss the replication of one vanilla option with the following specification:

Put currency	Japanese yen
Call currency	US dollar
Put amount	1bn yen
Strike rate	100 yen/$
Initiation date	1 Jan 1996
Expiry date	1 Jul 1996 (date for exercise)
Maturity date	3 Jul 1996 (date for payoff cash flows)
European style	
(i.e. exercisable only at expiry)	
Premium (% dollar amount)	3.02% (=$302 000)
Premium payment date	3 Jan 1996

Suppose that an investment fund wishes to 'buy' this option on 1 Jan 1996. If it wishes to buy it by replication and not in the OTC market, what will a typical dynamic hedging currency overlay manager do? At the moment when the 'option' is established, the overlay manager will use a Black–Scholes model variant (a variant to cope with forward contracts with no yield and no cash requirement), input the option specification and current market data, particularly the 6-months forward yen/$ rate and a volatility value. The volatility value may be current implied volatilities, historical volatilities or some model value from the manager's volatility forecasting model. The model will provide a series of outputs, the most important of which is the sensitivity of the marked-to-market valuation (in effect the option premium) to changes in the yen/$ exchange rate – the hedge ratio or delta. If this comes out at, say, 45.6% on the first data entry, then the overlay manager will sell 45.6% × yen 1bn = yen 456m against dollars in the forward market. The manager may choose to sell at any forward date, but the obvious 'default' value would be to sell for a maturity of 3 Jul 1996.

What happens next is very much manager-specific, but Black–Scholes theory requires that the manager then conducts *continuous* monitoring of the exchange rate, and continually adjusts the hedge ratio to stay in line with model output, which will vary as the exchange rate and volatility changes and time passes. Black–Scholes require that this process is literally continuous, so that thousands of deals could in theory be conducted in the space of a second, or indeed in a nano-second. This requirement is clearly impractical, so the manager must embark on a series of approximations to get as close to this as possible. Firstly, a manager must decide on monitoring frequency and procedures. Does monitoring take place at fixed frequency: once a second, once a minute, once an hour, once a day, once a week? If monitoring is fixed frequency, what about 24-hour dealing? What about illiquid times of day, when perhaps only a thin Middle Eastern market is available? What about weekends, what about Bank Holidays? If monitoring is not planned to be fixed frequency, how is it conducted? If it is triggered by a certain level of exchange rate movement, how is this movement monitored, continuously? If monitoring is high frequency, does this always trigger adjustments in the hedge position, even if these are small? Are there buffer exchange rate zones or buffer dealing sizes that keep dealing frequency under control? How is volatility monitored? Do market implied volatilities drive the hedge ratio, or historical or model output volatilities?

The variety of answers to these and more questions provide ample material for manager differentiation – and many of the issues here have been dealt with in other contexts earlier in the book. But there is a straightforward test that a customer can apply. Has the option replicator succeeded in replicating the payoff value of the option being replicated, and at what cost? The arithmetic of this is simple. Take the two possible states that an option can expire in: in-the-money and out-of-the-money. If the option expires out-of-the-money, then the payoff value is zero. In this case the cost of the dynamic hedge is the closed sum of the dollar values of all the forward contracts relating to the option. If the option expires in-the-money, then the payoff value will be positive. If the close-out spot rate on 1 Jul 1996 is 108, then the payoff is $740 740.74 [=(1bn/100) − (1bn/108)]. The cost of the dynamic hedge is then the difference between the closed sum of all the associated forward deals, and $740 740.74. As an example, if the delta hedge yields $550 000, then the cost of replication was $190 740.74 (=$740 740.74 − $550 000) or 1.91% of the dollar principal.

The key question that arises from the process described is whether it consistently reduces that cost below buying the equivalent options in the market, and how wide is the variability of the cost. The evidence is difficult to find, in particular since option replication either by banks or by overlay managers is a commercial undertaking not open to public scrutiny. Under some fairly rigid assumptions about the monitoring process, however, it is possible to simulate the results of delta hedging using actual option premiums and underlying market rate histories. It appears from this slim evidence that delta hedging under these rigid assumptions is not materially lower cost than typical option premium offer prices, but nor does it have materially higher cost variance. Any cost savings experienced by dynamic overlay customers are likely to be the result of the managers' proprietary refinements.

Dynamic hedging can also be operated entirely outside the Black–Scholes model environment, and a subclass of dynamic overlay managers do this. Under their processes there is no assumption of lognormality, of continuous markets, or even of volatility levels. Their payoff outcomes are identical to delta hedgers, but the composition of their costs is different. Their costs will be higher or lower than delta hedgers, dependent on whether their models more or less effectively exploit market non-randomness. (Note that with pure lognormal random walk markets, all strategies are ultimately identical at zero net return less transaction costs.)

Dynamic currency overlay managers (or option replicators) represent one of the largest style classes of currency overlay managers. Many overlay managers will not use this style exclusively, but many rely on it as the core of their active process.

11
Active Currency Overlay – Evidence of Performance

This is a short chapter. There is now some evidence of the performance of currency managers, but much of it is proprietary, and it ages quickly. In summary, however, there is good evidence that the universe of currency managers have on average delivered outperformance against passive benchmarks over the 14-year period 1989–2002. There seems to be some 'reversion towards the mean', in that earlier studies showed higher outperformance than later studies, and as the universe has expanded.

11.1 SURVEYS

11.1.1 Currency overlay performance surveys

Currency overlay as a recognised activity in the institutional investment market started in 1985, when this firm (Record Currency Management) secured a mandate to actively hedge the US dollar exposure of the Water Authorities Superannuation Fund – then a public UK fund. Several more mandates followed in the UK in that and subsequent years. The earliest US mandates were 1988/9. The sector grew quite rapidly, largely on mandates from the larger US public and private sector funds. It began to spread to continental Europe, Australia and the Far East in the mid-1990s. The UK is still relatively undeveloped in currency overlay, despite having the second largest pool of defined benefit pension assets after the US. Performance measurement of currency overlay managers is a relatively recent phenomenon, but there are now at least three sources from which we can draw data.

11.1.1.1 The 'Strange Report'

In 1997, an ex-currency overlay manager, Brian Strange, then working in his own small consultancy, Currency Performance Analytics, persuaded 11 currency overlay firms to submit detailed client-by-client data on their performance (vs. benchmark) for all their currency overlay accounts, live and terminated. A further three submitted composite data. The subsequent report, published May 1998, showed that, on average, currency overlay managers had added about 1.9% p.a. in the period since 1989, the earliest data submitted. The average tracking error in this study was 3.5%, giving an average information ratio of 0.54. The total number of currency overlay accounts was 152, and from this client base 1783 client-quarters were analysed. A number of different ways of segmenting the data were illustrated, and in each a story of consistent manager behaviour and consistent value-added emerged.

There was little in-depth analysis of why a universe of specialist managers could perform so well *en masse*, but it was noted that a significant proportion of the client-quarters covered the 3-year 1995–97 period, when the dollar was broadly strong, the most popular benchmark was unhedged, and the dollar was the most common base currency. Currency overlay mandates of this specification would be expected to add value!

11.1.1.2   Watson Wyatt

The actuarial and investment consulting firm Watson Wyatt have picked up the mantle left by Brian Strange (Brian left the consulting business, and now works for an overlay manager). The US arm have continued collecting data on currency overlay performance, and have recently released[1] their latest findings. Up to the end of 2000, the 5-year median value added of currency overlay managers in their universe who are operating to a USD base and an unhedged benchmark has been 1.32% p.a. The equivalent figure for a 50% hedged benchmark is 0.84%.

11.1.1.3   Frank Russell

Frank Russell is an investment consulting firm who have tracked and researched currency overlay managers for longer than any other consultant, and have built a database from contemporary data (rather than *ex post*) supplied by the managers. They published a report in September 2001 in which they analysed the performance data from 24 currency overlay managers. Their data ran from July 1995 to June 2001, and they found an average outperformance of 1.47% p.a. They analysed the data in somewhat more detail than the Strange Report, and reported value added of 0.94% p.a. for 50% hedged benchmark accounts. Unhedged benchmark accounts showed 2.45% p.a. outperformance, and fully hedged benchmark accounts 0.20% underperformance. This data tends to confirm the suspicion voiced in the Strange Report that time- and mandate-specific factors were distorting the figures in a favourable way.

These reports are now uploaded quarterly.

11.1.2   Performance summary

The three surveys discussed above, and some other unpublished performance surveys, all point to there being identifiable value added in currency overlay when measured at the level of universe of overlay managers. That this unusual finding is possible is explained by the nature of the FX market – that currency overlay managers have identified and are exploiting one or more persistent market inefficiencies at the expense of the vast majority of the FX market who are constrained in their behaviour and/or are not profit- or price-sensitive.

11.2   WHO LOSES?

Elsewhere in the book (Chapter 4, Chapter 9) I have described the mechanics and structure of the foreign exchange market in some detail. If the (small) universe of currency managers has made money on average over nearly 15 years, then the remainder of the FX market, not measured by investment consultants, loses. This is definitional.

I have commented elsewhere that the possibility of consistent average outperformance by the universe of overlay managers is a highly unusual position for a group of managers to be in, particularly where there is no real debate about the nature of the benchmark against which they are measured (this is not the 'outperformance' of bond managers holding credit measured against government bonds). To be fully intellectually rigorous, however, I should emphasise

---

[1] Brian Hersey and Kurtay Ogunc, Watson Wyatt Presentation, 25 June 2001.

again that there cannot be overall outperformance generated by the currency market in total. Taking all of the participants, including the market-making community, global outperformance is zero. The observation we have made from the surveys, and from the evidence presented in earlier chapters, is that an identifiable class (overlay managers) has made money. This is an observation about style, since the general style that overlay managers adopt (discounting the differences within the overlay universe) is more successful as a trading strategy than at least one other of the groups that make up the total FX market.

12

Implementing Currency Overlay

In this chapter I set out a 'check-list' for investors considering currency overlay – whether designed to reduce risk, or add value, or both. I also cover some of the practical questions that clients have asked when they establish currency overlay programmes. The answers I give reflect the *realpolitik* of getting mandates started as well as the theoretical considerations covered in the remainder of the book.

Let's start with the 'check-list'.

12.1 SUMMARY CHECK-LIST

I will raise and answer a number of practical points, which I will summarise in table form in Section 12.1.14.

12.1.1 What mandate type?

Currency overlay investors generally come in two categories:

1. Those who wish primarily to reduce their existing international portfolio's exposure to currency risk.
2. Those who wish to tap a source of excess return from active management of currencies.

These two aims may also co-exist, in which case answers to both halves of the question are relevant.

(1) *Risk reduction*: To reach the decision to implement a risk-reduction currency overlay programme, an investor would normally have conducted an asset allocation study, in which 'hedged equities' was one of the categories included in the range of assets studied. As a result of the study, the investor would generally be asked to choose (often with the help of an investment consultant) a benchmark hedge ratio for international equities. This is a fundamental asset allocation decision, similar in strategic importance to the domestic:international equities split, and second only to the equity:bond split decision. Many investors do not have a strong instinct for currency and its implications, and therefore they often find this decision difficult to make. The author's experience is that as a result this decision can be delayed for years, or indeed never properly addressed. It is a minority of investors who systematically analyse the strategic role of currency exposure within their portfolio, and determine a policy, based on these studies, that matches their goals. It is not uncommon for investors to choose an arbitrary benchmark hedge ratio (say 50%) without a full assessment of the implications on the portfolio. While this may appear a little crude, nevertheless it can result in beneficial action where a fuller analysis and more study would result in paralysis and inaction.

Active or passive? Once an investor has chosen a strategic position which requires overlay, then he has to decide whether to implement it with an active overlay or a passive overlay. The decision will be determined by two factors. The *first* (and overriding) is whether the investor believes that active currency management can add value. He clearly also needs to believe that he (together with his consultant if he uses one) is capable of choosing an active manager that will add value in the future. In currency overlay this may in practice be much easier than in other active manager searches: as one consultant put it, 'it is quite hard to find an established currency manager who does not add value over time'.

The *second* factor is whether the investor has a desire for an asymmetrical overlay return pattern. Irrespective of their beliefs about long-term value added, many investors are attracted to the idea of limited negative performance (and unlimited positive performance) of any overlay. Asymmetrical return is also associated with asymmetrical cash flows, so the amount of cash outflow in periods of domestic currency weakness is limited to a predetermined amount rather than dependent on currency movements alone. These asymmetric active mandates are a characteristic of dynamic and option-based styles in particular.

Finally, investors may choose to implement a risk-reducing overlay without adopting a hedged benchmark. While this creates a wide tracking error, it does have the merit of an understandable benchmark in which 'cash-in' from the overlay means positive performance versus the benchmark, and the positive performance is associated with negative performance of the unhedged international assets. It would be highly unusual, and hard to justify, the adoption of a passive overlay programme with an unhedged benchmark.

(2) *Value-added*: With the increasing length of track records possessed by the main currency overlay firms, most investment consultants and many investors now accept that active currency overlay is capable of generating positive excess returns over long periods of time. As discussed elsewhere in the book (Chapter 4, Chapter 9) this is not the result of chance, nor an unfathomable 'mystery'. The structural conditions that allow currency market inefficiencies to persist also allow the median currency overlay manager to make money.

The design of a pure 'value-added' (or 'alpha') active currency portfolio is different from a risk-reducing currency overlay, although strictly speaking it is still an overlay since it does not require a capital allocation. The key criteria for a successful 'alpha' mandate are: (a) wide latitude given to the manager for cross-hedging and 'net-short' positions (i.e. able to exploit any directional movement in any major currency pair); (b) a clear and unambiguous benchmark (zero return is as good as any); (c) a clear expression of the nominal amount of the mandate; and (d) a tracking-error target or limit built into the investment guidelines (see below and Appendix 4).

Where the investor has both strategic risk reduction and active value added as goals, then these two, sometimes conflicting designs, have to be knitted together.

12.1.2   For risk-reducing overlay – benchmark hedge ratio

The benchmark hedge ratio is, as already discussed (and illustrated) elsewhere in the book (particularly Chapter 6 and Chapter 8), a technically complex area, with some differing academic views, although the views amongst most expert practitioners and consultants are broadly similar, and expressed in this book.

A *purist approach* is to first choose passive or active overlay based on the investor's beliefs about the continuing ability of currency managers to add value. Then, with that choice in hand, to optimise the allocation of international assets (usually equities in this context) with an additional overlay asset class, as described on p. 134. The optimised portfolio then becomes the strategic asset allocation, and the scale of the active overlay as a percentage of international assets becomes the strategic (benchmark) hedge ratio. Using the values from Table 5.6 (which allows active currency overlay), this would mean a 100% benchmark hedge ratio for all portfolios apart from the most risk-loving – the 15% whole-portfolio volatility target – which would have an 82% benchmark hedge ratio. If passive overlay is the chosen route, then similarly all portfolios apart from the most risk-loving would have a 100% hedged benchmark. However, without active overlay's value added to maintain its appeal to the optimiser, the removal of the risk constraint sends the benchmark hedge ratio near to zero. However, this purist approach is just that, and I have yet to come across such thorough-going purism in any strategic asset allocation decision.

An *analytical but realistic* approach is to conduct this and other analyses, and then reach a common-sense compromise asset allocation. Most large investors (pension funds, endowments) still favour home bias even though there is no theoretical support for it. They will often measure nominal volatility rather than volatility relative to long-bond returns (reflecting their liabilities), and they will often declare support for one particular asset class over another without a clear description of why they hold that belief. Under these circumstances, a recognition that unmanaged currency exposure gives risk without return will lead such an investor to choose a fully or partially hedged benchmark. This is likely to lead to a benchmark hedge ratio between 50% and 100%, and the final part of the decision will probably depend on the materiality of the international exposure, the maturity of the fund and (for a pension fund) the strength of the sponsoring parent relative to the fund's liabilities.

An *intuitive* approach would be to accept that currency hedging reduces risk, and therefore that any hedging has merit. Without any further analysis the intuitive investor may wish to minimise the regret from hedging,[1] and this will lead to a 50% hedged benchmark. It also provides a symmetrical platform for any active currency overlay that does not allow cross-hedging or net-short positions.

Finally, many investors are sensitive to the cash flows that arise from currency overlay. The detailed analysis of the costs of managing cash flows in Chapter 6 shows that this sensitivity may not be justified, but nevertheless it exists. High benchmark hedge ratios naturally lead to high potential cash flows from overlay. This may lead some investors to choose lower benchmark hedge ratios than pure risk-reduction considerations would imply, and sometimes unhedged benchmarks (although only for active overlay).

12.1.3   Investment guidelines – active

I have included sample investment guidelines in Appendix 4. The key considerations for an active mandate are the *scale*, the *benchmark* (discussed above), the *restrictions* and the *targets*.

The *scale* is largely self-explanatory, for risk-reducing currency overlay it is normally the marked-to-market valuation of the international assets to be overlaid. It may exclude unhedgeable currencies, although this is usually marginal.

Under *restrictions* come the permitted hedge ratio range (0–100%, 25–75%, 50-150%, etc.), whether cross hedging is permitted (i.e. active positions in currency pairs which exclude the investor's base currency, and possibly the target currencies), and if cross hedging is permitted, the range, and scale, of currencies that can be traded. Some mandates may have a restriction (i.e. an absolute limit) on downside performance, or on negative cash flows, although this can have the effect of limiting the expected value added of the mandate. Well-designed investment

---

[1] See Gardner, G.W. and Wuilloud, T., *The Regret Syndrome in Currency Risk Management: A Closer Look*, Russell Research Commentaries, August 1994.

guidelines give clear instructions in the event of breaches of restrictions, with timetables and consequences.

Finally, *targets* are the key measures on which the success or otherwise of the mandate will be judged. These are typically the tracking error of the actual performance versus the benchmark performance (see Section 7.6), and the average annual excess return (or value added) versus the benchmark. Some investment guidelines can have more complicated targets ('capture 75% of the increase in value of currencies and limit the losses to 50% of their fall in value'), and the test of these guidelines is how easy they are to monitor and give an unambiguous 'yes' or 'no' to the question of whether they have been hit or not. In my experience, typical targets for active mandates with a 50% hedged benchmark might be 'tracking error of 2.5% p.a. with a 1% p.a. excess return'.

12.1.4   Investment guidelines – passive

Similar considerations apply to passive mandate investment guidelines as to active ones, but with all the measures writ smaller. The restrictions are likely to be dominant in the operation of the mandate, and the targets should be set on the basis of the manager's assessment of the impact of the restrictions. Typical targets for a passive mandate with a 100% benchmark hedge ratio might be 'tracking error of 25 bp p.a. with a –5 bp excess return' if the benchmark is costless (i.e. based on mid-prices), or 'tracking error of 25 bp p.a. with a 5 bp excess return' if the benchmark is based on WM/Reuters left- and right-hand side prices.

12.1.5   Investment guidelines – alpha

Investment guidelines for an 'alpha' mandate should be much simpler than for a risk-reducing mandate. Guidelines should still have the *scale, benchmark, restrictions* and *targets* mentioned above, but they can all be virtually one-liners.

Scale can be a nominal amount (preferably in the investor's base currency) to represent the denominator against which percentages are calculated. Because a currency alpha programme does not require an initial investment, a clear expression of the scale is important. The investment guidelines should make clear how the scale changes over time. Under conventional geometric linking of returns, the scale would reflect the cumulative returns since inception. As an example, if the initial scale of an alpha mandate is $100m, then the scale of the mandate under the given assumed monthly returns would be as in Table 12.1.

Note that on p. 84 I explicitly state that monthly returns of overlay alone cannot properly be geometrically linked without including the returns of a 'carrier asset'. However, alpha is different. The exercise we are conducting here is to express the returns of active currency management with a consistent denominator so the returns can be represented as percentages. If the overlay manager is given these guidelines, then the manager can quite properly rebalance the size of currency positions based on the returns of the currency alpha programme, rather than, in the case of currency overlay, based on the returns of unhedged international assets. Under these circumstances, geometrically linking alpha returns is legitimate.

There is another perfectly acceptable approach to take on changes to the scale of the alpha mandate, and that is to have no changes that are not explicit. This would mean that returns from currency alpha would be 'washed away', and in the example above, the scale would remain constant at $100m. This approach would mean that the overlay manager would not have to routinely rebalance his alpha process. It would remain legitimate in principle to geometrically

Table 12.1 Example of mandate size changes – initial
mandate size ($m) = $100m

Month	Assumed monthly returns	Mandate value ($m)
0		100.00
1	0.21%	100.21
2	0.36%	100.58
3	0.24%	100.81
4	−1.72%	99.08
5	1.17%	100.25
6	1.23%	101.47
7	0.49%	101.97
8	−0.24%	101.72
9	0.72%	102.46
10	0.08%	102.54
11	0.77%	103.33
12	−0.26%	103.06

link the returns (for example for the purposes of analysis and comparison), but the resulting compound returns would not reflect the live portfolio, which in effect would exhibit simple returns.

The most appropriate *benchmark* for mandates under guidelines similar to these shown above is almost certainly zero. It has the powerful twin benefits of simplicity and transparency.

Restrictions on an alpha mandate may be necessary for legal or regulatory reasons (say no net short positions versus the home currency, or limitations on the range of currencies traded). The guidelines will also have to express an annual tracking error, and this could be either framed under this section (implying an absolute tracking error limit), or under the 'targets' section, implying no absolute limit. For maximum efficiency, the overlay manager would be given no additional restrictions over those strictly necessary to fulfil legal and regulatory obligations.

The most obvious *target* for the alpha mandate is the annual return target. This has to be expressed in the direct context of the tracking error – they are directly proportional.

12.1.6   Bank FX lines

Whatever the type of overlay, an overlay mandate will require the overlay client to have FX lines at a panel of banks. The client may have minimum requirements for credit ratings for the banks, but subject to that restriction, the overlay manager would be expected to suggest the panel based on the particular needs of the client, to negotiate lines between the client and each bank, and to advise the client on the most effective documentation to secure their contractual rights. Where possible, a client's security is usually best served by entering into IFEMA[2] agreements with their counterparties. IFEMA provides a framework for netting (i.e. legally offsetting) matching pairs of forward contracts where one deal reverses the other, and all the other terms, except the contract rate, are the same. This is intended to avoid possible

---

[2] IFEMA (International Foreign Exchange Master Agreement) is a standard set of terms agreed by the British Bankers Association and the US-based Financial Markets Lawyers Group. It was first issued in 1993, and substantially amended and extended in 1997. It is widely accepted in the main foreign exchange centres as 'standard terms' governing foreign exchange contracts. A wider version (Foreign Exchange and Options Master Agreement (FEOMA)) covers OTC options as well as forwards.

'cherry picking' of profitable forward contracts by the receiver of one bankrupt contract party, and the repudiation of the loss-making ones.

Except under unusual circumstances, a client can expect to be granted FX lines by banks without any requirement for an initial deposit or margin, and without any 'variation margin' (see p. 49 for more on margins). This means that the client retains control over the timing of cash payments and receipts from the settlement of forward FX contracts.

12.1.7   Bank contract confirmation

The manager and the chosen bank counterparties need to establish a fail-safe mechanism for the confirmation of verbal forward contracts. There are now well-established electronic platforms (for example CMS (formerly FX Match)) which allow both parties to upload deal details into an independent system, and which then provide exception reports where details do not match. The client does not have to be involved in this process, but they need the confidence that it is effective – forward contracts differ from conventional asset purchases in that they are not settled immediately – and of course the delay is the length of the forward contract. Since this is routinely several months, and can be up to 12 months, early and reliable confirmation is at a much greater premium than for conventional cash-settled assets. Where a client's custodian is asked to record and value outstanding forward contracts, the information that the custodian gets should be after successful confirmation.

12.1.8   Investment management agreement

Currency overlay is an investment management assignment, and it should be contractually treated just like a more conventional assignment in equities or bonds. While the investment guidelines for currency overlay are overlay-specific, the investment management agreement can be largely a standard form.

12.1.9   Reporting requirements

How currency overlay is reported is critical to the client's perception of its value, and indeed its performance. The important point here is that the chosen benchmark genuinely reflects the perception of the client (i.e. in answering the question 'how did the currency overlay manager do?'), and that reporting accurately follows the benchmark decision. As an example: suppose the client chooses a fully hedged benchmark, has given the manager 0–100% hedge ratio leeway (with cross hedging bound by these restrictions too), and the overlay manager is reporting on a period when the domestic currency is weak. The currency overlay will be 'losing money', and there will be cash outflows. However, it is likely that the active currency overlay will be adding value versus the benchmark, since only by getting the direction 100% wrong for all currencies could the manager perform as badly as the benchmark. Hence the excess return versus benchmark will be positive, and may be very positive, even while cash haemorrhages. If the currency overlay reports to the client highlight the positive performance, and the client is content with the performance of the manager, then the reporting and the benchmark are congruent. If, on the other hand, the client is uneasy about the cash outflow, or is concerned about the impact of the currency overlay's performance on the whole portfolio, then the benchmark should probably be reviewed, since it clearly does not represent the 'neutral' position of the client. The reporting should then follow the revised benchmark.

Two features of currency overlay mean additional reports over and above conventional mandates. The first is cash flow. Cash flow is a (delayed) reflection of the gross performance of the overlay, although not, as we have seen above, of performance versus the benchmark. However, efficient management of the whole portfolio requires that cash flow is forecast as far ahead as possible (although that may not be very far, depending on the overlay manager's choice of forward contract maturities). These forecasts need to be communicated to the client in cash flow forecast reports. The second is the credit exposure that the client runs when there is strong positive gross performance from the overlay. Under these circumstances, and again depending on the maturity of the forward contracts, the client may wish to know the bank counterparties who owe him substantial amounts of money. This is not academic – where there are concerns with the credit of a large indebted counterparty, it is possible to close out forward contracts and accelerate the settlement of the cash by negotiation with the bank in question.

12.1.10   Periodic cash and contract reconciliation

The client will usually choose to use his custodian to record forward contracts undertaken by his overlay manager, and to reconcile these, and the resulting cash flows, with the manager on a regular basis. However, the role of the custodian is a little different in currency overlay from conventional asset management. Forward currency contracts (which are the dominant instrument used by overlay managers) are not initially 'valuable' in the way that equities or bonds are. So the conventional role of the custodian to 'look after' the securities in a portfolio does not apply in the case of currency overlay. It is perfectly possible, therefore, to not involve the custodian in the overlay record-keeping process, and still retain the security of a third-party check on the accuracy (and existence) of the forward contracts from the bank confirmation process.

12.1.11   Bank contract settlement procedures

Except in special circumstances (like manager transition), forward currency contracts will be closed out by the overlay manager prior to maturity. In many cases, the closing-out contract will not be executed until the spot date, which is two days prior to the maturity date (see p. 37 for details). This means that the manager and bank counterparty must then agree the amounts of cash settlement, and the manager is responsible for informing the custodian of the amounts to be paid and received for each relevant value date. The client must be satisfied that the checking, reconciliation and authorisation processes are reliable and secure, although generally speaking the client will not be required to play an active part in this process.

12.1.12   Benchmark calculation

Aside from the strategic decision of what the benchmark hedge ratio is to be (for risk-reducing mandates) or what the return benchmark is to be (for alpha mandates), it is clearly important that the client is satisfied that the calculation of the benchmark is accurate and transparent, and ideally independent of the manager. As discussed previously (Table 7.1), there are a number of index providers that produce hedged benchmarks. If one of these fits the mandate for the underlay, then the hedged (or a mix of hedged and unhedged) version provides a ready-made currency overlay benchmark. However, mostly the actual weights of the international assets to be hedged will not exactly match the weights of proprietary indices, and many clients will therefore want to develop a bespoke benchmark. There are only three candidates who are generally in a position to design and calculate a bespoke benchmark: the custodian; the client's investment consultant, and the currency overlay manager.

In the author's experience, custodians have little expertise in currency hedging and currency benchmarks, and their strength lies only in the routine calculations required once the formulae and data sources are established. There is considerable expertise in some of the larger investment consultants, although it tends to reside in specialist currency research units or in particular individuals. Most investment consultants are not geared up to provide regular, systematised monthly reports – so while they may be able to design a benchmark, they probably cannot deliver it in real time.

The most detailed expertise, together with systems and processes, to deliver real-time benchmarks lies with currency overlay managers. For many clients, the disadvantage of the loss of independence brought about by using their manager to also calculate the benchmark is overcome by the convenience and accuracy that a knowledgeable and informed manager can bring to the calculation. If the calculation methodology is transparent, and the data source is published and independent, then the loss of independence may be more imaginary than real.

12.1.13 Performance measurement

Performance measurement flows naturally out of the benchmark calculation and the reporting of the gross overlay performance. The excess return of the gross overlay performance over the benchmark performance is the bedrock of the performance measurement, and the volatility of that value – tracking error – is the other key measure. With these two values, the progress of the overlay mandate can be monitored, and compared to the targets in the investment guidelines.

The principal responsibility for reporting lies with the overlay manager. A well-designed performance report will give the client clear and unambiguous performance reporting. The client, however, may also want the custodian to replicate the key elements of the performance report, both as confirmation of the source numbers (marked-to-market valuation of outstanding forward contracts and cumulative cash flow) and as an independent calculative check. The consultant is likely to be involved in the design-only phase.

12.1.14 Summary check-list

Check-list item	Considerations	Decision/action made by
Mandate type	(a) Risk reducing (active or passive); (b) alpha only	Investor/consultant
For risk-reducing overlay – benchmark hedge ratio	International exposure and risk aversion	Investor/consultant
Investment guidelines – active	Active risk/return positioning	Investor/manager
Investment guidelines – passive	Tracking error/cash flow considerations	Investor/manager
Investment guidelines – alpha	Size of mandate/active risk/return positioning	Investor/manager
Bank FX lines	Spread of counterparties and credit ratings	Manager
Bank contract confirmation	Fail-safe	Manager/bank/proprietary electronic confirmation system

(*cont.*)

Check-list item	Considerations	Decision/action made by
Investment management agreement	Commercial, prudential and regulatory considerations	Investor/manager
Reporting requirements	To match investor's needs	Investor/manager
Periodic cash and contract reconciliation	Fail-safe third-party process	Manager/custodian
Bank contract settlement procedures	Secure/accurate/daylight risk-minimising	Manager/custodian
Benchmark calculation	Transparent and independent	Consultant/index provider
Performance measurement	Independent and accurate	Manager/consultant/custodian

12.2 PRACTICAL QUESTIONS AND ANSWERS

Question: I believe that active currency management is no more likely to make money than active equity management. Does this mean I can forget about overlay?

Answer: If an investor is not convinced that they can identify an active currency manager, this rules out active overlay and currency alpha. However, whether or not currency can add value, there is a significant reduction in risk available (by adopting a fully or partially hedged benchmark) at almost zero cost for most investors. This would be the adoption of passive overlay.

Question: I believe in active currency management. Do I need to have a complete review of my strategic hedge ratio before looking for active currency managers?

Answer: No. An investor can exploit currency inefficiencies using currency alpha without changing any strategic benchmarks.

Question: How do I manage cash flows from overlay?

Answer: For active overlay, limits can be built in to cash outflow. For many investors, this cash requirement will be less than their normal cash allocation, and therefore no special arrangements need to be made. For larger overlay programmes, or for passive programmes, the investor may need to ask the overlay manager and custodian to arrange a process for cash to be realised from (or invested in) low-trading-cost securities (large cap equities, bonds). Alternatively, the investor can hold higher cash allocations with a futures overlay that 'equitises' or 'bondises' the cash.

Question: Can I have overlay without cash flows?

Answer: Not for equities. However, it is possible to extend the cash horizon by the use of longer-dated forward contracts. For bonds, however, cash flows can be matched to the interest and bond payments, and in effect become invisible – and this is effected by a currency swap.

Question: What fees should I expect to pay for overlay?

Answer: Management fees are highly dependent on scale, complexity and other client-specific factors. However, as a guideline, average fees for active overlay tend to be in the 10–15 bp p.a. region (assuming a $500m mandate), and average fees for passive overlay are 3–5 bp p.a. Fees for currency alpha depend on the target level of return, but will generally have a management (asset-based) fee component (perhaps 20–25 bp p.a. depending on target return) and a performance-based component (say 20% of new high-water-mark).

Question: What exactly does 'cross hedging' involve?
Answer: Cross hedging is where the manager will undertake forward currency contracts between two currencies, neither of which is the investor's base currency. This will generally, although not always, mean that the investor increases exposure to one currency (the bought currency) beyond the exposure in the underlying assets. If that is the case, then the hedge ratio for at least one currency will lie outside the 0–100% range. If, despite cross-hedging contracts, hedge ratios of all currencies continue to lie in the 0–100% range, then it could be argued that cross hedging is not really taking place, since that effect could be replicated by doing all deals via the base currency.

Question: I have a very low international asset allocation. Can I use overlay?
Answer: You can use currency alpha to exploit currency inefficiencies. If your total international exposure is very low (say less than 10% in each asset class), then there is unlikely to be a good case for active or passive risk-reducing currency overlay.

13

Looking Ahead

This is a speculative chapter, and since it will reflect my unsubstantiated opinions, it is likely to be of less interest than the earlier chapters with evidence and analysis. It will also be short.

13.1 DEVELOPMENT OF ACTIVE MANAGEMENT STYLES

The process by which management styles in any asset discipline become established is a study in itself. A keen observer of investment managers may observe a number of characteristics which seem to be enduring:

- Styles go in fashion – and like fashion, are to some extent 'returning'.
- There is a process of 'style natural selection'.
- Styles become established in any asset class quite early in an asset class's life; despite small changes at the margins, and the vagaries of fashion, they persist.
- Advances in information processing technology have allowed some quantitative styles to develop, but have not dominated style changes.

Currency management styles have conformed to these guidelines quite well. Within a very few years of the advent of currency overlay, three core styles emerged – fundamental, technical and option-based/dynamic hedging. Most managers still recognise these descriptions, and they still give clients and consultants a reasonable guide as to the way a manager constructs a process. Some managers have argued that they no longer fit well into these categories, although my instinct tells me that existing style categories will continue to be pressed into service, even if the fit is not perfect.

What about completely new ways of identifying and exploiting currency movements? We could perhaps look at other asset classes to prompt our thoughts. Equity managers use the top-down/bottom-up distinction, and growth/value distinction, to cut styles along two planes. There are also ethical, contrarian/momentum, quantitative and style rotators. They also deal with different classes – large cap, small cap. Hedge funds also have a wide variety of styles unique to them: event-driven (takeovers, distressed situations); global macro (anything and everything), market neutral, convertible arbitrage, and so on. Bond managers, dealing with a very specific asset class, probably have no styles which could transfer to currency. Any opportunism they have displayed in the past in their own currency management of international bond portfolios can be wrapped up in the opportunistic hedge fund style description below.

Can any of these concepts apply to currency managers?

13.1.1 Top-down/bottom-up

This distinction perhaps resonates with the following in currency: a top-down manager is one who starts the hunt for inefficiencies in the structure of the currency market. The structure applies to all currency pairs, so general statements can be made about all currencies, not just specific pairs. 'Top-down' currency managers would be students of the market place; they would gather and analyse the nature and motivations of the currency market players, pore over BIS reports when they are issued, lobby for more frequent data about participants and their behaviour, try to assess the effect of changes in the banking industry on the market, and study the changing behaviour of other, identifiable, classes of player such as corporate treasurers, central banks and various investor groups. By contrast, bottom-up managers might be thought of as pure fundamental managers, concerned with the full range of specific factors which impinge on each currency pair. They try to become more knowledgeable about each pair than everyone else in the market (a task so difficult it borders on the impossible).

13.1.2   Growth/value

It is a struggle to shoe-horn this distinction into the currency context. Its closest parallel is perhaps the 'search' for value in currencies by analysing and exploiting the forward rate bias, since a currency's interest rate is the closest thing we can get to a value measure. However, the lack of the concept of price/earnings ratio (p/e) in currency, and the role of expectations in the movements of p/e values, means that the analogy largely fails.

13.1.3   Contrarian/momentum

I have put contrarian with momentum as two ends of a similar spectrum. They do have a parallel in currencies, which is technical analysis. While contrarians are not formally quantitatively or technically driven, in practice they are mean-reversion supporters. The intellectual argument is a little more sophisticated. A contrarian argues that if 'everyone' thinks that stock X or index Y is going up, then that means that all the investors who have the ability to buy it, already have. This means that the only flexibility left to the major participants (who are long) is to sell. This forms the basis for the argument to do the opposite to the 'herd'. There are very few situations in the currency market when the 'herd' is clearly identifiable, and even then usually with the benefit of hindsight. Herds require an element of community and common values/language and culture. These do not exist to any extent in the FX markets. There are many herds, and they all see the world differently. Momentum managers are more overtly technical, but underpinning their approach is to go with the prevailing price trend, and therefore implicitly with the herd. This makes their behaviour mirror the technical trend-follower.

Both of these styles resonate to 'what everyone else is doing', and so concern themselves with game theory as well as just price movements. The game theory element is less evident in the currency markets than in smaller markets because of the diversity of players, their varied motivations and the opacity of their activities.

13.1.4   Ethical

Ethical managers probably do not have a counterpart in currency management. The only parallel that could be drawn is the possible future emergence of a repugnant regime in the current members of the global FX market – currently less than 20 countries. However, one of the characteristics of repugnant regimes is that they tend to deprive their population of freedoms. The continuance of a freely tradeable exchange rate in dictatorial conditions is therefore unlikely, and similarly the emergence of the currency of a repugnant regime into the global market is equally unlikely.

13.1.5   Hedge fund styles

Most of the style categories are inappropriate for currency overlay managers. The only substantive style which has incorporated active currency management is the global macro style. Two events stand out in which hedge funds of this style entered the currency market in a substantial (and price-changing) way.

The first is the celebrated case of George Soros and the pound sterling in September 1992. This was, in effect, an event-driven opportunity in which George Soros used the assets of his main hedge fund vehicle, the Quantum Fund, to speculate against the self-imposed lower limit of the pound versus the DEM in the (now defunct) European Exchange Rate Mechanism (ERM). It appears that Soros took a leveraged position of about £10bn against the pound, and this was one of the straws that broke the camel's back – the UK government capitulating to the market pressure, and (permanent) withdrawal from the ERM. This was a highly publicised win for George Soros, who was rumoured to have made £1–2bn in the Quantum Fund.

The second entry of hedge funds into the currency market was less happy. This is the period in 1998 when a group of hedge funds 'spotted' what they regarded as an opportunity to take a short position against an already weak yen, and be 'paid' for it – the yen 'carry' trade. They were 'paid' to do this by the interest rate differential between the yen and the USD – yen could be 'borrowed' much cheaper than USD could be deposited. The 'opportunity' turned out to be a chimera – in two days on 7/8 October 1998 the yen appreciated by about 12%, and the currency market showed real disarray (it was almost a one-way market) – a truly rare event. The trigger for this startling movement was the risk-control processes of the hedge funds trying to close out their rapidly worsening positions all at the same time and in the same direction. Hedge funds collectively lost a great deal of money, and perhaps even more confidence in this debacle. Currency overlay managers were not totally unscathed, but the diversified nature of their portfolios and their diversified styles saved them any serious embarrassment.

There are other examples of event-driven 'opportunities' being spotted by hedge funds, but many of the lesser known were thoroughly unsuccessful. One of the most important is a series of unsuccessful attacks on the 7.80 HK dollar parity with USD – and the adverse interest rate differential was serious punishment for the lack of success.

Will this style enter the currency overlay style universe? I believe that the answer is probably not. Currency overlay's attraction is its ability to provide more predictable and stable results, from established processes, rather than speculative opportunities with undiversified risks.

13.1.6   Summary on styles

None of the existing style descriptors of equity or hedge fund managers fit the needs of currency overlay clients particularly well. Nor do they play to currency overlay managers' strengths. My own instinct is that technical, fundamental and dynamic hedging styles will (continue to) lose their very distinct characters, and that managers with become less differentiated by these criteria. I believe that all these managers are already exploiting the same inefficiencies, and indeed many of the processes of an overtly fundamental manager may match those of an overtly technical manager.

The distinction that I think will become increasingly drawn is, on the one hand, managers who rely on the full rigour of models and processes; and on the other hand, discretionary 'expert' managers who are guided by models and indicators, but who take individual decisions on the basis of their judgement. We could call these *systematic* and *discretionary*. As with all styles, there will be gradations in between the poles, but the meaning is quite clear. Some commentators, and managers, already use one or both of these descriptions to categorise managers. I think this trend will continue.

13.2   NATURAL SELECTION OF OVERLAY MANAGERS

According to Mercer, the investment consultant, the first stand-alone currency overlay mandate was signed in April 1985. Prior to this, several (probably around three or four) of the current universe of managers (or their principals) had activities in active currency management. However, none of the contracts under which these activities were undertaken were identifiably currency overlay. By the late 1980s, there were still comparatively few managers offering currency overlay (perhaps six or seven), and there were very few currency overlay mandates. The early 1990s saw rapid growth in the number and scale of overlay mandates, particularly from US pension funds (and some endowments). This encouraged the formation of new overlay managers to service (and stimulate) this demand, and the manager universe grew substantially. A number of the new managers were formed as independent firms by principals who mainly came from investment banks rather than investment managers. Some developed out of a 'currency desk' in existing (larger) investment managers. By the late 1990s, the number of managers with $1bn or more under management was probably in the teens.

There was a slow-down in the growth of overlay from US institutions after the mid-1990s, but other investing countries, notably Australia, the Netherlands, Switzerland and latterly the UK have continued to create new overlay mandates as their international allocations have risen, and the currency risk has been recognised and dealt with. The currency overlay universe now (in early 2003) probably numbers 40 managers. Many are quite small, and many are also new to overlay. As with all active management populations, there has already been a certain amount of culling of managers, and this will continue. The managers who have been proven most able to survive so far have been those with a well-differentiated style and strong 'brand', and those with backing from a large international asset manager, investment bank or custodian. The most vulnerable are the newest, who lack a stand-alone track record, and those with a scale too limited to weather difficult trading conditions.

Fees in active currency management are low by the standards of other active management classes. Active currency overlay fees are likely to be in the range 5–50 bp p.a., depending on the scale and complexity of the account. Most active overlay managers will average around 10–15 bp. If we round this to 12 bp, then this is $1.2m in annual fees per $1bn of overlay. Passive mandates would attract fees of 1–10 bp, with most managers averaging passive fees of 2–3 bp for large mandates, although significantly higher for small mandates.

There is no evidence that there is any serious upward pressure on fees, particularly in depressed asset return environments. Likewise, the fee levels are probably sufficiently low that there is unlikely to be downward pressure from aggressive pricing from new or growth-orientated participants.

Table 13.1 gives some very rough guesstimates of the currency overlay market at end-2002 (it is based on international assets shown in Table 2.2). The penetration percentages are my (rounded) estimates; this produces spuriously accurate estimates of overlay mandates in $bn. The accuracy is spurious, and should therefore not be relied on. Most of these mandates will be active overlay, the mix is probably 80:20 active:passive at the time of writing.

Table 13.1   Overlay geographical penetration analysis

Country	International assets (US$bn)	% Penetration	Overlay mandates (US$bn)
US	569	9%	51.2
UK	291	3%	8.7
Switzerland	119	5%	6.0
Netherlands	100	10%	10.0
Japan	64	3%	1.9
Canada	33	3%	1.0
Sweden	29	2%	0.6
Australia	23	55%	12.4
Hong Kong	8	6%	0.5
Germany	9	6%	0.5
Belgium/France	8	13%	1.0
Total	**1251**	**7%**	**93.7**

Source: Record Currency Management Estimates, December 2002.

From this information, we can calculate a very rough approximation of the fee revenues available to the currency overlay manager universe:

$$\text{Assets} \times \text{Average fee rate} = \text{Annual income}$$
$$= \$94\text{bn} \times [(0.8 \times 12\,\text{bp}) + (0.2 \times 3\,\text{bp})]$$
$$= \$96\text{m}$$

This means that 40 firms are sharing revenues of $96m, or around $2.5m each if it was equally spread (which it is not). $2.5m is probably below the critical fee income level required to support the research, product development, systems and compliance costs at the minimum level necessary to be a viable manager. This implies that one or more of three things are likely to happen: consolidation of the smaller players into the larger; closure or withdrawal of the smaller players; or significant growth in the overlay market.

There is no immediate evidence from the stated intentions of investors that overlay will experience rapid growth over the next few years. Overlay is likely to continue to increase penetration in existing international allocations, and these may well grow with the continuing trend of internationalisation. Countering this, there is some evidence that international allocations in the US have peaked, and that the disappointing return experience of many US investors will cap their desire for more international diversification.

13.2.1   Conflict of interest

There is a final point to be made on overlay managers' income. There are some overlay managers that are part of large investment banks. To the extent that mandates permit them to deal with their own dealing desks, this is a source of customer FX turnover, and therefore profit, to the dealing room. One or two FX dealing rooms have established 'overlay' teams based in the dealing rooms, and they are quite explicit about their desire to increase customer turnover. These are not serious overlay managers, and they will always be hugely compromised by the conflict of interest and the dealing culture of their employers.

More difficult to dismiss are bank subsidiary overlay managers who are set up, and operate out of, an investment management arm of the bank. Many of these are serious and successful overlay managers; it rests with the client to specify the overlay contract in such a way that they can be certain that conflicts of interest do not arise. My recommendation to any client would be to forbid such a manager from dealing with their associated bank. This (harsh) prescription is the only one that can guarantee no conflict.

13.3   EXTENDING THE RANGE OF HEDGING INSTRUMENTS

The current range of hedging instruments available to an overlay manager is so liquid, low-cost and flexible that it seems churlish to want more or different. From my experience, the only serious drawback from the customer's perception of the current range is the regularity, and size, of the cash flows associated with the maturity, and rolling, of forward contracts.

Innovation in this area may reduce the hurdles for some investors embarking on overlay, and it is possible that currency swap technology holds the key. The scope of this book does not allow me the space to explore such designs in any more detail.

13.4   WILL INEFFICIENCIES GROW OR SHRINK?

Markets are never static creatures, and the FX market is no exception. For most asset markets, the answer to this question is that current inefficiencies will shrink and disappear, and new inefficiencies, currently absent or undreamt of, will appear. The active manager in these markets is therefore like the hunter – equipped to spot, chase and kill the prey wherever it appears.

For the FX market, I think the answer is different. The FX market, as I have laboured in this book, is a leviathan that is the clearing-house for a very large volume of trading that is not directly profit-oriented. The secret of how current inefficiencies will develop therefore lies in accurate prediction of how the structure and make-up of the market will change. I see little short-term structural change in the market's customers. The market's suppliers, the banks, have undergone radical consolidation over the past 10 years, but this has not markedly changed the clearing or price-setting mechanisms. In the more distant horizon, I see a continuing rise in capital account FX trading (which includes hedge funds and currency overlay managers, and also conventional asset managers, as well as investment banks on behalf of, for example, M&A clients). However, the rate of growth is not likely to be high as long as asset markets remain depressed, and since these sources are a relatively small proportion of the current price-taking customer community at the moment, they will remain so in the mid-term.

This leaves the door open for existing inefficiencies to continue to exist, despite their being openly recognised and discussed among the active currency management community. The style of active manager that will thrive in this environment is less like the hunter (responsive, restless, instinctive, action above care) and more like the farmer (planner, order, knowledge, process, care above action). The best farmers are those who possess the properties above, plus an entrepreneurial and intellectually curious streak that leads them to investigate new methods of production, new processes and new machinery. The best overlay managers will possess these qualities too.

13.4.1 Can outperformance by currency overlay managers continue?

The short answer is 'yes'. The inefficiencies that currency overlay managers exploit are related to the unique structure of the FX market, not to any particular style or 'view' held by current participants. However, most textbooks on financial economics will tell you that price inefficiencies are unlikely to be anything more than temporary, since arbitrage will ensure that any 'free lunch' is fully exploited until it goes away. Why is this not true in the FX market?

It is not true for all the reasons discussed in previous sections: the arbitrage is risky, its existence is not self-evident, it is heavily dependent on specialist FX market expertise, it competes with other opportunities for risk capital, and there is a limited amount of long-horizon risk capital in comparison with the huge volume of capital that flows through the market daily.

My prediction is that over, say, the next decade, the apparent value added of the median currency overlay manager may decline, but still remain above zero after costs. This may come about more as a result of the size of the currency overlay manager universe increasing, than by any diminution of the inefficiencies in the FX market. The best, and most consistent, firms will continue to add significant value, but entry of less sophisticated players may dilute the value added of the universe. In my view it is unlikely that any increase in the assets under management in the active overlay universe will by itself be sufficient to significantly reduce or eliminate the persistent inefficiencies in the FX market.

References/Useful Reading

AIMR Benchmarks and Performance Attribution Subcommittee Report, John C. Stannard *et al.*, August 1998.

AIMR Conference Proceedings, Currency Risk in Investment Portfolios, 1998.

Aitchison, J. and Brown, J.A.C., *The Log-normal Distribution*, Cambridge University Press, 1963.

Bernstein, W.J. and Wilkinson, D., 'Diversification, rebalancing, and the geometric mean frontier', *Efficient Frontier* (www.effisols.com), January 1998.

Black, F. and Scholes, M., 'The pricing of options and other corporate liabilities', *Journal of Political Economy* **81** (May/June 1973) 637–659.

Black, F., 'Living up to the model', *Risk Magazine*, March 1990.

Black, F., 'Universal hedging', *Financial Analysts Journal*, July–August 1989.

Brigham, E.F. and Houston, J.F., *Fundamentals of Financial Management*, The Dryden Press, 8th edn, 1998.

Clowes, M.J., *The Money Flood*, John Wiley & Sons, 2000.

Econometric Methods, Johnston and Dinardo, McGraw-Hill, 4th edn, 1996.

Fama, E.F., 'Market efficiency, long-term returns and behavioural finance', *Journal of Financial Economics* **49** (1998) 283–306.

Fama, E.F., 'Efficient capital markets', *Journal of Finance* **46** (Dec 1991) 1575–1617.

Fama, E.F., 'Random walks in stock market prices', *Financial Analysts Journal*, September–October 1965.

Fitzgerald, M., *Financial Options*, Euromoney Publications, 1987.

Gardner, G.W. and Wuilloud, T., 'The Regret Syndrome in Currency Risk Management: A Closer Look', Russell Research Commentaries, August 1994.

Gartland, W.J. and Letica, N.C., 'The basics of interest-rate options', chapter 59 in Fabozzi, F.J. (ed.), *The Handbook of Fixed Income Securities*, McGraw-Hill, 5th edn, 1997.

Haugen, R.A., *Modern Investment Theory*, Prentice Hall, 1993.

Jorion, P., 'Mean/variance analysis of currency overlays', *Financial Analysts Journal*, May–June 1994.

JP Morgan/Reuters, 'RiskMetricsTM – Technical Document', 4th edn, 1996.

Karnosky and Singer, 'Global Asset Management and Performance Attribution', Research Foundation of The Institute of Chartered Financial Analysts, February 1994.

MacDonald and Stein (eds), *Equilibrium Exchange Rates*, Kluwer Academic, 1999.

Markowitz, H.M., 'Portfolio selection', *Journal of Finance* **7** (1952) 77–91.

McCutcheon, J.J. and Scott, W.F., *An Introduction to the Mathematics of Finance*, Butterworth-Heinemann, 1986.

Nesbitt, S.L., 'Currency hedging rules for plan sponsors', *Financial Analysts Journal*, March–April 1991.

Perold, A.F. and Schulman, E.C., 'The free lunch in currency hedging: implications for investment policy and performance standards', *Financial Analysts Journal*, May–June 1988.

Rogoff, K., 'The purchasing power parity puzzle', *Journal of Economic Literature* **34**(2) (1996).

Rosenberg, M., *Currency Forecasting: A Guide to Fundamental and Technical Models of Exchange Rate Forecasting*, Richard D. Irwin & Co, 1996.

Rosenberg, M., The Deutsche Bank Guide to Exchange Rate Determination, May 2002.

Sarno, L. and Taylor, M., 'Official intervention in the foreign exchange market: is it effective, and if so, how does it work?', *Journal of Economic Literature* **34**(3) (2001).

Sharpe, W., 'Asset allocation: management style and performance measurement', *Journal of Portfolio Management*, Winter 1992.

Siegel, J.J., 'Risk interest rates and the forward exchange', *Quarterly Journal of Economics* **89** (1972) 173–175.

Taylor, A.M., 'A Century of Purchasing-Power Parity', NBER Working Paper No. w8012, November 2000.

Tobin, J., 'A proposal for international monetary reform', *Eastern Economic Journal* **4** (1978) 153–159.

Appendices

APPENDIX 1 – BOUNDARY CONDITIONS FOR FORWARD ARBITRAGE

The following sets out the maths that applies in each case:

Case 1 The 'no spread' world – sterling investor replacing a sterling deposit with a hedged dollar deposit.

Case 2 Real markets – sterling investor replacing a sterling deposit with a hedged dollar deposit.

Case 3 Real markets – dollar investor replacing a dollar deposit with a hedged sterling deposit.

Case 4 Real markets – borrowing one currency to lend the other, the outer bounds of the arbitrage.

Case 1 – No spreads

Invest in sterling direct:

(1)	Invest an amount of sterling	£DEP
(2)	Interest =	£DEP × £LIMID/12
(3)	Total £ value 1 month	£DEP[1 + (£LIMID/12)] = £RET

Invest via the dollar:

(4)	Invest	£DEP
(5)	Convert to $ =	£DEP × $£MIDSPOT = $DEP

where $£MIDSPOT is expressed as dollars/sterling:

(6)	Interest =	$DEP × $LIMID/12
(7)	Total $ value 1 month	$DEP[1 + ($LIMID/12)] = $RET
(8)	Total £ value 1 month	$RET/$£MIDFWD

The arbitrage is perfect where the total £ value 1 month is equal from both investing routes, i.e. (3) = (8), or:

(9)   £DEP[1 + (£LIMID/12)] = $RET/$£MIDFWD

Substituting from (7):

(10)   £DEP[1 + (£LIMID/12)] = {$DEP[1 + ($LIMID/12)]}/$£MIDFWD

and rearranging to find the forward rate ($£MIDFWD):

(11) $£MIDFWD = {$DEP[1 + ($LIMID/12)]} / {£DEP[1 + (£LIMID/12)]}

Substituting from (5):

(12) $\pounds MIDFWD = \{(\pounds DEP \times \$\pounds MIDSPOT) \times [1 + (\$LIMID/12)]\}/$
            $\{\pounds DEP[1 + (\pounds LIMID/12)]\}$

and simplifying:

(13) $\$\pounds MIDFWD = \$\pounds MIDSPOT \times [1 + (\$LIMID/12)] / [1 + (\pounds LIMID/12)]$

Or in words, *the forward rate is equal to the spot times the ratio of 1 + interest rates* (the ratio has the numerator interest rate on top).

We can substitute example values as follows:

$$\$\pounds MIDSPOT = 1.5346 \qquad \$LIMID = 2.0938\%$$
$$\pounds LIMID = 4.9688\%$$

which gives the forward rate as follows:

(14) $\$\pounds MIDFWD = 1.5346 \times [1+ (2.0938\%/12)]/[1 + (4.9688\%/12)]$
            $= 1.5346 \times (1.001745/1.004141)$
            $= 1.53094$

and therefore the 'FX swap' expressed in 'FX points' (1 point = 1/10 000th of $1) at mid-prices is:

(15) $1.53094 - 1.5346 = -36.6$ points

Case 2 – Sterling investor with spreads

Invest in sterling direct:

(1)   Invest an amount of sterling   £DEP
(2)   Interest = $\pounds DEP \times \pounds LIBID/12$
(3)   Total £ value 1 month $\pounds DEP[1 + (\pounds LIBID/12)] = \pounds RET$

Invest via the dollar:

(4)   Invest   £DEP
(5)   Convert to $ = $\pounds DEP \times \$\pounds RHSSPOT^* = \$DEP$

where $\$\pounds RHSSPOT$ is expressed as dollars/sterling:

(6)   Interest = $\$DEP \times \$LIBID/12$
(7)   Total $ value 1 month $\$DEP[1 + (\$LIBID/12)] = \$RET$
(8)   Total £ value 1 month $\$RET/\$\pounds RHSFWD^*$

One further piece of information is needed, and it refers to $\$\pounds RHSSPOT$ and $\$\pounds RHSFWD$. The way in which the forward market is priced is by forward FX points, so, for example, the forward discount of the pound in the previous example might be quoted as $-37/-36$ (i.e. a 'one point' spread). This means that for the deal contemplated above, the bank will sell the customer dollars at the spot rate, and simultaneously buy it back from them for 1-month maturity at 36 points better (better to the investor) rate (i.e. lower number). The bank will not charge a spot spread, because no spot risk is being taken by them. But in this example, the amount that this investor wants to sell forward is larger (by the interest received) than the amount they are buying, so there will be a very small outright forward deal, which will not only attract a full spot and forward spread, but will be used by the bank as the spot rate off which they will price the whole deal (and this will be the right-hand side (RHS)). In a pure FX swap (i.e. the two amounts of dollar being identical), the bank is indifferent to the spot rate used, and might accept LHS, mid or RHS without preference.

This is why I have used $\$\pounds RHSSPOT$ as the spot conversion rate, whereas normally the investor would *buy* dollars at $\$\pounds LHSSPOT$. From the foregoing, we can define the forward rate in this case as follows:

(9)   Outright forward rate: $£RHSFWD = $£RHSSPOT + ($£RHSSWAP
             /10 000)
where $£RHSSWAP is the RHS swap points expressed in FX points.

   Using exactly the same algebra as in the previous case, we can derive the forward price
which is just 'no arbitrage'. So mirroring the previous equation (13):
   (10) $£RHSFWD = $£RHSSPOT × [1 + ($LIBID/12)]/[1 + (£LIBID/12)]
We can substitute example values drawn from market data as follows:

$$\$£LHSSPOT = 1.5345 \qquad \$LIBOR = 2.1250\%$$
$$\$£MIDSPOT = 1.5346 \qquad \$LIMID = 2.0938\%$$
$$\$£RHSSPOT = 1.5347 \qquad \$LIBID = 2.0625\%$$
$$£LIBOR = 5.0000\%$$
$$£LIMID = 4.9688\%$$
$$£LIBID = 4.9375\%$$

   (11) $£RHSFWD = 1.5347 × [1+ (2.0625%/12)] / [1 + (4.9375%/12)]
                        = 1.5347 × (1.001719/1.004115)
                        = 1.53104
and therefore swap points:
   (12)   1.53104 − 1.5347 = −36.6 points
which is the same value as the mid-price calculation.

   So, perhaps a little surprisingly, the arbitrage kicks in instantly – if the UK investor is ever
offered better than −36.6 points (i.e. a larger number), the US investment route will risklessly
make him more money than an investment in sterling. It is worth noting that the spot bid/offer
spread is irrelevant for this arbitrage – even if interest rates are very high, and, say, the amount
of the sale of dollars was 10% more than the amount of the purchase.

Case 3 – Dollar investor with spreads

Invest in the dollar direct:
   (1)   Invest an amount of dollars $DEP
   (2)   Interest = $DEP × $LIBID/12
   (3)   Total £ value 1 month $DEP[1 + ($LIBID/12)] = $RET
Invest via sterling:
   (4)   Invest $DEP
   (5)   Convert to £ = $DEP/$£LHSSPOT = £DEP
where $£LHSSPOT is expressed as dollars/sterling:
   (6)   Interest =   £DEP × £LIBID/12
   (7)   Total £ value 1 month   £DEP[1 + (£LIBID/12)] = £RET
   (8)   Total $ value 1 month   £RET × $£LHSFWD
The algebra from here is similar to the previous cases, but we have reversed the direction of
the foreign exchange transaction, so we divide where previously we multiplied and vice versa:
   (9) $DEP[1 + ($LIBID/12)] = £RET × $£LHSFWD
Substituting from (7):
   (10) $DEP[1 + ($LIBID/12)] = £DEP[1 + (£LIBID/12)] × $£LHSFWD
and rearranging to find the forward rate ($£LHSFWD):
   (11) $£LHSFWD = {$DEP[1 + ($LIBID/12)]}/{£DEP[1 + (£LIBID/12)]}

Substituting from (5):

(12) $£LHSFWD = {$DEP[1 + ($LIBID/12)]}/ {($DEP / $£LHSSPOT)
× [1 + (£LIBID/12)]}

Simplifying and rearranging:

(13) $£LHSFWD = [1 + ($LIBID/12)] / {(1/ $£LHSSPOT)
× [1 + (£LIBID/12)]}

(14) $£LHSFWD = $£LHSSPOT × [1 + ($LIBID/12)]/[1 + (£LIBID/12)]

Or in words, *the forward rate is equal to the spot times the ratio of 1+interest rates* (the ratio has the numerator interest rate on top). This is the same algebra as Cases 1 and 2 – just the LHS and RHS are different. So it does not matter whether the investor who exploits these arbitrage opportunities is dollar-based or sterling-based.

Substituting with values above:

(15) $£LHSFWD = 1.5345 × [1+ (2.0625%/12)] / [1 + (4.9375%/12)]
= 1.5345 × (1.001719 / 1.004115)
= 1.53084

and therefore swap points:

(16)   1.53084 − 1.5345 = −36.6 points

which is again the same value as the mid-price calculation. This means that the dollar-based arbitrageur will make riskless gains if the swap points are numerically less than this −36.6 (i.e. if they were 36). So there are zero bounds for this arbitrage, even in the real world (since the sterling investor will make money if the swap points are numerically higher than −36.6, (i.e. 37). This is surprising – normally the transactions costs of the real world mean that arbitrage has a 'neutral' area where it is profitable for no-one.

Case 4 – Borrowing one currency to lend the other

The final case we will examine is where an arbitrageur is not a natural lender or borrower. Here, he will have to borrow one currency and lend another, which will mean that he will have to overcome the interest rate bid/offer spreads to be able to exploit the arbitrage. The base currency of the investor is irrelevant (and even could easily be a third currency) – the key is the boundary forward points beyond which the arbitrage is profitable.

The principle of this arbitrage is simple: let's start with an investor borrowing sterling to invest in dollars. The maths is identical to Case 2, except that equation (3) in case 2 will have a £LIBOR term in, not a £LIBID. This works through to the following equation (matching (10) in Case 2):

(1) $£RHSFWD = $£RHSSPOT × [1 + ($LIBID/12)] / [1 + (£LIBOR/12)]

Substituting values:

(2) $£RHSFWD = 1.5347 × [1+ (2.0625%/12)] / [1 + (5.0000%/12)]
= 1.5347 × (1.001719 / 1.004167)
= 1.53096

and therefore swap points:

(3)   1.53096 − 1.5347 = −37.4 points

So if the RHS of the swap points rises higher than −37.4 (e.g. 38), then the borrowing sterling/ lending dollars arbitrage is profitable.

A similar boundary can be established for the LHS of the swap. The maths is identical to Case 3, except that equation (3) in Case 3 will have a $LIBOR term in, not a $LIBID. This works through to the following equation (matching (14) in Case 3):

(4) $£LHSFWD = $£LHSSPOT \times [1 + ($LIBOR/12)] / [1 + (£LIBID/12)]$

Substituting values:

(5) $£LHSFWD = 1.5345 \times [1+ (2.1250\%/12)] / [1 + (4.9375\%/12)]$
                    $= 1.5345 \times (1.001771 / 1.004115)$
                    $= 1.53092$

and therefore swap points:

(6) $1.53092 - 1.5345 = -35.8$ points

So if the LHS of the swap points falls below -35.8 (e.g. 35), then the borrowing dollars/lending sterling arbitrage is profitable.

These arbitrage possibilities make currency forward rates virtually always a pure mathematical result of relative interest rates. The question of whether this always means that interest rates determine forward rates is a sophisticated question, the answer to which involves the relative weights of money following domestic interest rates or forward rates. Most of the time domestic rates dominate, but sometimes it is clear that forward rate expectations dominate.

This has been most visible recently in the attacks against the French franc peg versus DEM (1982 and 1983), sterling peg versus DEM (1992), French franc versus DEM (1993) and Hong Kong dollar versus US dollar (1998), when domestic interest rates became distorted by views of the future exchange rate. At its most extreme, French franc 'Euro' (i.e. offshore) overnight rates went to 3000% p.a., equivalent to an 8% devaluation the next day. This was only possible because of exchange control, which kept domestic French rates to about 20% p.a.

APPENDIX 2 – LOGNORMAL RETURNS

Setting out the problem

In practical fund management, we are often faced with time series of returns (or asset values), and need to summarise the characteristics of these series with *annualised returns* and *volatility*. Let's take a 1-year period of total monthly returns from some conventional asset (say an equity; Table A2.1) and ask the simplest questions: what are the observed annualised return and SD?[1]

Table A2.1

Period	Returns
1	2.4142%
2	4.9287%
3	1.3992%
4	2.5029%
5	−1.4179%
6	6.6249%
7	5.5299%
8	4.4657%
9	2.9206%
10	0.1610%
11	−3.5356%
12	−3.6404%

---

[1] I use *volatility* and *SD* interchangeably.

Return

The compound return is the product (less 1) of (1 + period return) for the 12 periods. The reader might like to ascertain himself that this is 24.02%. We do not need to do any explicit annualising because the 12 periods are one year's worth. There are two other obvious arithmetic or hybrid methods, which I mention to dismiss:

$$\text{Arithmetic average} = \text{Average of monthly returns} \times 12 = 22.35\%$$
$$\text{Hybrid} = \{[(\text{Average of monthly returns}) + 1]^{\wedge}12\} - 1 = 24.79\%^2$$

I dismiss these measures because they fail our basic definition; the asset value after one year of the asset above is $124.02 for a starting value of $100.

Note that in this example the arithmetic average return is lower than the compound; this is commonly (but not universally) the case for positive return series when annualising monthly data over only one year. However, when we annualise longer series of data, the effect is reversed, and compound returns are typically lower than arithmetic. This effect is emphasised by high volatility series, a phenomenon often referred to as 'volatility drag'.[3]

Volatility

This is a much less straightforward problem. Firstly, we should note that the answers in the returns section above were all given without mentioning logs.[4] In volatility calculations, however, we will find that logs are essential. Let's go back to first principles.

The series in Table A2.1 was generated by a lognormal random generator model. For each month, the model selected a random point on a normal distribution[5] with mean R and volatility V. In this model, $R = 0.007943$ and $V = 0.040346$. We will come back to why these values were chosen later. The randomly generated values for the 12 months were as given in Table A2.2. Note that while I have labelled these values 'log values' there is nothing

Table A2.2

Period	Log values
1	0.023855
2	0.048110
3	0.013895
4	0.024721
5	−0.014281
6	0.064147
7	0.053824
8	0.043688
9	0.028788
10	0.001609
11	−0.035997
12	−0.037083
Sum of logs	0.215276

---

[2] I use '^' to mean 'raise to the power of'. This means $\sqrt{x}$ and $x \,\hat{}\, 0.5$ are identical.
[3] McCutcheon and Scott (1986) show the mathematics of volatility drag on p. 293.
[4] Throughout this appendix 'log x' or 'ln x' means log base e of x, and 'exponential of x' or 'exp(x)' means e^x. $e = 2.7182818\ldots$.
[5] In Microsoft Excel this can be calculated by using =NORMINV(RAND(),R,V), where R = mean return and V = volatility.

particularly 'log' about them at this stage; they are normally distributed, for example. However, to create a lognormal distribution of returns, we take these numbers and treat them as if they were logs. This means that to 'apply' them to asset values over time we take the exponential of each of these values, and multiply the end-month asset values by these exponential values.

Table A2.3 shows this mathematical process clearly in each of its stages. We can recognise column (e) as our series of returns.[6] We also note that returns = exp(logs) − 1. At this juncture we can also succinctly show that compounding returns using geometric linking exactly matches the lognormal model. The annualised return using compounding is 24.02%. The sum of the logs in column (b) is 0.21527. Exp(0.21527) − 1 = 24.02%. For longer periods than a year (say from Table A2.4 later) the reader might like to take the average monthly log return and multiply by 12. The exp()−1 result will be identical to the annualised compound return produced by geometric linking $[=\{(\text{asset value at end/asset value at start})^{f/n}\}-1$, where f = data frequency per year and n = no of periods].

Table A2.3

(a) Period	(b) Random log value	(c) Exponential value [=exp(b)]	(d) Asset value ($) [=c(t)d(t−1)]	(e) Returns [={d(t)/d(t−1)}−1] or [c−1]%
			100	
1	0.023855	1.024142	102.41	2.41%
2	0.048110	1.049287	107.46	4.93%
3	0.013895	1.013992	108.97	1.40%
4	0.024721	1.025029	111.69	2.50%
5	−0.014281	0.985821	110.11	−1.42%
6	0.064147	1.066249	117.40	6.62%
7	0.053824	1.055299	123.90	5.53%
8	0.043688	1.044657	129.43	4.47%
9	0.028788	1.029206	133.21	2.92%
10	0.001609	1.001610	133.42	0.16%
11	−0.035997	0.964644	128.71	−3.54%
12	−0.037083	0.963596	124.02	−3.64%
Sum of logs	0.215276			

Turning again to volatility, we know that the SD of the population from which these returns were drawn was 0.040346. However, we also know that they were transformed by the exponential function to reach percentage returns. So to get to the volatility of this return series, we could go through the same transformation process. Firstly, we take the SD of column (b).[7] The reader might like to ascertain for himself that it is 0.033646. But this is the volatility of the 1-month log values, whereas we want the annualised volatility. The Central Limit Theorem

---

[6] We could have done it a different way: we could have taken the log of the initial asset value of $100 [ln($100) = ln$4.60517] and added the numbers in column (b) in sequential order to give us a ln(asset value) each month. Log asset values are not particularly intuitive, but once exponentiated they come out fine. Using this method, asset value at the end of the year is: exp(4.60517+0.215276) = exp(4.820446) = 124.02.

[7] $\text{SD} = \sqrt{\dfrac{\sum\limits_{i=1}^{n}(l_i-\bar{l})^2}{n-1}}$ where l_i = ith period log value, $\bar{l}$ = average value of l in the sample, and n = number of observations in the sample. There is some debate about the denominator being n or $n-1$. Using $n-1$ gives an unbiased estimate of variance (but not SD = $\sqrt{}$ variance). However, I will use it as most investment management users do. See however the AIMR section.

tells us that the SD of the mean of a sample size of n independent observations from a normal population with SD= V is $V/\sqrt{n}$. However, we are not averaging here, we are summing – we want the sum of the 12 observations to make up the year's return. We therefore get $nV/\sqrt{n}$, or rearranging, $V\sqrt{n}$. So the annualised SD of this series is $0.033646 \times (12 \textasciicircum 0.5) = 0.116553$. Note that we can only *sum* returns if they are log returns; if we try to sum percentage returns to annualise, we are being inconsistent with geometric linking. So $nV/\sqrt{n}$ is only valid for log returns, not percentage returns. The users of the conventional percentage SD calculation have probably not realised this.

But this value is in logs. To convert to percentages as defined, we have to transform using the exponential function: $SD = \exp(0.116553) - 1 = 12.36\%$. So you would think that, following this logic, the volatility of this series was 12.36%. I should just say that the population SD of 0.040346 is derived from wanting to generate a 15% annualised volatility series. If $V = 0.040346$, then $\exp(\sqrt{12}V) - 1 = 15\%$.

Industry Practice

Faced with the return series in Table A2.1, I suspect when asked to calculate the sample SD, most industry participants would take a straight SD of the percentages, and multiply by $\sqrt{12}$. This comes to 11.79%.[8] There are a number of points to make here.

The first is that if returns are lognormal, then an SD cannot be calculated as if the returns are additive (i.e. as the SD of the % period returns). Just imagine a very high volatility investment of $SD = 50\%$. What happens if the returns are negative 3 SDs? Does the value of the investment go to less than zero? Figure A2.1 shows the range of percentage changes for a series with a mean annual return of 10% and SD of 15% for (a) lognormally calculated percentage changes for -4 to $+4$ SDs (the SD applied to the log of the % returns and converted back to %) and (b) additive percentages for the same range (the SD applied directly to the % returns). It shows quite clearly that additive percentages underestimate the risk of high returns, and overestimate the risk of low returns. In short, additive percentages show no convexity.[9]

We should note that the 1 SD positive value for the log series is $26.5\% = \exp[\ln(1.1) + \ln(1.15)] - 1$, whereas for the additive series it is 25% (10% + 15%). This is my guess as to industry practice: what evidence do we have for this?

MSCI

MSCI, the index provider, has published very comprehensive index methodology[10] and, in summary, it uses additive returns to calculate the annualised return of the SD. Their formula is:

$$\text{Annualised volatility} = \sqrt{\frac{\sum_{j=1}^{n} (TR_j - \overline{TR})^2}{n-1}} \times \sqrt{12} \qquad (A2.1)$$

---

[8] In Microsoft Excel terms =STDEV(Series)*(12\textasciicircum 0.5).
[9] Convexity in returns (and asset values) is characteristic of lognormal processes, and for the mathematically-minded the second differential of the curve in Figure A2.1 is positive for the convex process, zero for the additive process.
[10] www.msci.com/risk/index.html

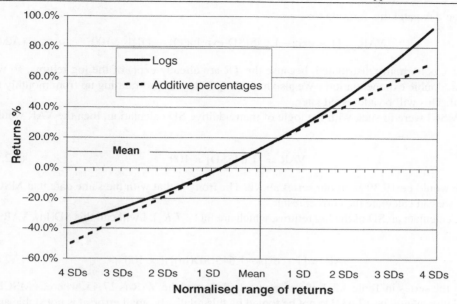

Figure A2.1   Lognormal return distribution for a series with mean 10% and SD 15%

where TR_j symbolises the monthly total return, $\overline{TR}$ is the average total return and n is the number of data points used in the calculation.

MSCI's TR value is a percentage monthly return; they spell out in great detail their methodology for annualising TR, and they do so correctly using geometric linking and annualising by raising the product of $(1 + TR)$ to the power of $12/m$, where m is the number of months to be annualised. All of which is fine, and fits exactly with log methodology as described above. It is all the more worrying then that they abandon their log methodology when it comes to the calculation formula above for the SD of the series, and calculate the SD of the % TR_j, rather than via $\ln(1 + TR_j)$. Their formula therefore treats returns as if they were additive, and incorporates no convexity.

Interestingly, MSCI go on in their methodology document to show a Value at Risk (VAR) calculation as follows:

$$VAR = (1 - e^{[-1.645\sigma]}) \times 100 \qquad (A2.2)$$

where 1.645 implies a 95% confidence level, σ is the monthly standard deviation (volatility) of the monthly total returns and e is a constant term having an approximate value of 2.718.

Assume Poland has a VAR of $15. This implies that for every $100 invested in Poland, there is a 5% chance of losing $15 or more in a given month. This is particularly odd, because the introduction of the e-power function (or exp()) would be absolutely correct if the SD was an SD of log returns, but is absolutely mathematically wrong for an SD of total return %.

Rewriting the formula (A2.2) using the exp function:

$$VAR = [1 - \exp(-1.645SD)] \times 100 \qquad (A2.3)$$

We could expand this formula to:

$$\text{VAR} = [1 - \exp(-1.645\{SD(\exp(\ln(x)) - 1)\})] \times 100 \qquad (A2.4)$$

where x is normally distributed, because the TR are already exp() of the log returns, so we have a 'double exponentiation'. We also have the problem of pro-rata-ing up from monthly to annual. This will be addressed later.

If MSCI were to stick with the logic of their additive SD calculation, then the VAR would be:

$$\text{VAR} = [1.645SD] \times 100 \qquad (A2.5)$$

which would be 19.39 from our series above. The irony is that with the same data that MSCI have, we can calculate the correct result.

We calculate an SD of the log returns, which are $\ln(1+TR_j)$. I will call this SD(ln). VAR is then:

$$\text{VAR} = [1 - \exp(-1.645\{SD(\ln)\})] \times 100 \qquad (A2.6)$$

Using the series in Table A2.3, the correct calculation of the VAR is 17.45, whereas MSCI's calculation would be 17.63. Do not be fooled by this relatively small error; it is not stable and it could be much larger depending on the data set and the annualisation process. More of this later.

AIMR

What about the Association for Investment Management and Research (AIMR)? AIMR is the US performance reporting standards setter, and is the leading partner in the new global performance standard – GIPS. AIMR has published its preferred methodology for the calculation of SD in Appendix B of the 1993 Performance Presentation Standards. It describes SD formulae in two places (external and internal risk). The basic formulae are the same, and are as follows.

'Standard deviation of portfolio performance over time (S_p) is a measure of volatility... calculated as follows:

$$S_p = \sqrt{\dfrac{\displaystyle\sum_{i=1}^{n}(C_{ASSETi} - MEAN(C_{ASSET}))^2}{n}} \qquad (A2.7)$$

where C_{ASSETi} is the asset weighted composite return in the ith time period, and n is the number of periods in the study.'

AIMR do not mention the lognormality issue at all, although like MSCI they imply that returns are lognormal by their insistence on geometric linking for returns over time. Like MSCI, they too see the SD of percentage returns as the appropriate measure. By way of an aside, AIMR take some time to justify the use of n rather than $n - 1$ as the denominator. It is a statistical debate at a tangent to the present issue – so I will ignore it.

Textbooks and academic literature

There is a huge volume of textbook and academic literature from which to draw samples of common usage. I have picked two textbooks at random: Haugen (1993) and Brigham and Houston (1998). The latter is particularly relevant because it is a recommended text for the CFA – the US (and now worldwide) industry standard investment management qualification. Both of these books unequivocally calculate SDs of investment returns using the (incorrect) methodology shown earlier, or generically:

$$SD = \sqrt{\frac{\sum_{i=1}^{n} (r_i - \bar{r})^2}{n - 1}} \tag{A2.8}$$

where $r_i = i$th period return in %, $\bar{r}$ = average value of r, and n = number of observations in the sample.

However, a number of commentators remark (in passing) that log returns are the 'correct' measure, but then go on to say that 'percentages are good enough'. An example of this comes from Gartland and Letica (1997) in the bond market literature: 'The intuitive approach to calculating a percentage volatility is to find the standard deviation of daily *returns*, assuming a normal distribution. This approach is equivalent to the lognormal assumption as long as the distribution can be characterized as being equally normal and lognormal and the changes in prices are taken on a small interval, such as daily.'

These comments seem to abound – that percentages are fine as long as the volatilities and/or time period are small. Of course this is wrong. A daily SD of 1% (and most commentators would say that 1% is 'reasonably small') annualises to 17.48% if correctly calculated via logs, and to 16.19% if incorrectly calculated direct. A 2 SD movement upwards is 38.01% (if calculated correctly via logs), and only 32.37% if calculated incorrectly with direct percentages. These are not second-order errors.

What about the founders of modern portfolio theory? Markowitz (1952), a model of clarity of thought struggling against computational odds, does discuss logs in relation to compound returns and their geometric mean. However, he is principally concerned with his emerging theory of efficiency, and the mathematics of combining stocks to form efficient portfolios. Because period returns are easy to observe and intuitively appealing, he chooses to stick to returns as his core 'random variable'. While recognising the inadequacy of adding returns over time rather than compounding, he seeks to provide a quadratic formula for approximating the compound return from return data rather than effecting a fundamental transformation of his return data into logs. It is quite possible that this approximation (adopted, I suspect, largely because of the computational difficulties of wholesale transformations into and out of logs) has carried on down the years just because no one has thought hard about an alternative. So in the end, Markowitz calculates the SD of returns directly, not via logs.

Investment banks and option traders

One final industry sector has not yet been considered. This is one where the exact calculation of volatilities for the pricing of options and other exotic derivatives is critical, since large volumes of trades are transacted on the basis of these calculations every day. It consists of the options desks of the major investment banks.

From a brief survey of custom, practice and use in this sector,[11] it is clear that logs are universally used for SD calculations, but that, bizarrely, the logs are not converted back to percentages, but left as logs with a '%' sign on the end. This is extremely confusing, but as long as this is consistently and universally applied, no errors will arise. In particular, annualising will be intuitive, and the errors described in the section below will not arise. However, if this convention is universally applied to returns and SDs, then a return of 10% under this convention would turn $100 into $110.52 at the end of one year. This is because the 10% here is a log, and the asset value will be multiplied by exp(0.1) to get the next value. Exp(0.1) is 1.1052. This is equivalent to continuously compounding 10% over infinitesimal time. While mathematical models find this easy to do, investors find continuously compounding hard to handle and even harder to re-create with data!

This treatment is confirmed in the textbooks written for the investment banking community. Fitzgerald (1987), writing about option pricing, describes a fully consistent log calculation of SD, but right at the end he says:

$$\text{'Annual volatility} = 0.003625 \times \sqrt{365}$$
$$= 0.069 \text{ or } 6.9\%\text{'}$$

His use of % is confusing, as it implies that it refers to returns, when in fact it refers to $\ln(1 + r)$ where $r = $ returns. It is also interesting that he uses 365 as the annualising factor.

So the investment banking conventions violate our investment management convention of 10% return meaning you have $110 at the year-end from your $100. I see nothing wrong in the investment banking community continuing to use logs as the basis of everything they do, but I do not believe their usage would translate well to the investment management community.

Finally, as an aside, I am not sure that many participants in the investment banking community really understand that they are dealing with logs, particularly since everything they do is expressed as $x\%$. I see logs as a particular language (call it Latin), and percentages as another language (call it English). There is an exact translation process to convert one to the other. But for option traders to describe an implied volatility as '12%', when this is in fact a log value of 0.12 (which would translate to a return volatility of $\exp(0.12)-1 = 12.75\%$) in my view runs the risk of using Latin words that look like English words but have a different meaning. I will always use the convention of $x\%$ when referring to percentages, and $y.yyy$ when referring to logs.

It is possible that the reader is already convinced by the theoretical arguments presented above. However, there may be a strong element of 'so what?' from readers who see the errors I have demonstrated to be rather esoteric, and the SD of % returns to be a reasonable approximation of the more precise log-based SD. I hope that the following example will convince waverers. Let us suppose we are dealing with a very volatile stock – say an Internet stock – whose volatility we wish to measure. The monthly returns for 2 years are given in Table A2.4. This stock has observed annualised volatilities as follows:

1. Correct (ln) calculation   SD= 109.03%
2. SD on return percentages   SD = 78.60%
3. SD of log   SD = 0.7373

---

[11] See, for example, JP Morgan (1996). There is a very good analysis of the relative merits of percentage and log returns in section 4.1. They choose log returns for all their calculations, but they do note that this is not as convenient as percentages for portfolio cross-sectional analysis. They do not 're-translate' log returns back into percentages, but nevertheless they use '$x.xx\%$' notation.

I suspect that the differences between values 1 and 2 is large enough to worry the most hardened 'approximator', and it of course brings into question the whole concept of percentage changes that can in theory be larger than 100%. Raw percentages cannot cope with this level of volatility; by contrast, log returns can cope with any level of volatility. The first thing that any modeller will notice when faced with annualised volatility of 109% (or indeed 78%) is that there seems to be a high chance each year that the value of the stock will go negative. Since this is impossible in a limited liability company's equity, he is forced to override at zero value, or put in some other 'fudge factor' to prevent this possibility.

Table A2.4

Period	Returns	Period	Returns
1	29.12%	13	−18.05%
2	−23.96%	14	19.67%
3	27.42%	15	14.34%
4	−10.09%	16	−15.19%
5	62.09%	17	6.21%
6	−19.81%	18	2.71%
7	−25.54%	19	4.10%
8	−16.53%	20	22.76%
9	−22.20%	21	39.29%
10	−6.82%	22	9.34%
11	2.04%	23	−20.34%
12	3.60%	24	18.67%

The third value quoted is the un-exponentiated SD of the logs. This is 'Latin', and what option traders would quote. The uninitiated might note that the second and third values are quite close, and so perhaps all this is a fuss about nothing (mirroring the close VAR values in the MSCI methodology). But let's subtly change the specification of the series above, and we shall see how wrong this complacency is.

Let us suppose instead that the series in Table A2.4 is annual data rather than monthly. This is clearly a less volatile series, and obligingly we have 24 years' worth of data. What are the three volatilities now?

1. Correct (ln) calculation   SD=23.72%
2. SD on return percentages   SD =22.69%
3. SD of log   SD =0.2128

Here the relative relationships have changed, with the third value now the most distant from either of the other two. This changed relationship is caused by the annualising process; it is a symptom of convexity, and is considered in the next section in more detail.

Annualising

When we annualise independent returns for periods less than a year, the industry universally uses the rules of the Central Limit Theorem, which, as mentioned previously, boils down to multiplying monthly SD by $\sqrt{12}$ and daily SD by $\sqrt{262}$ to get annual SD.[12]

---

[12] In some markets the convention is to use 250, approximately the number of working days (weekdays excluding Bank Holidays) in a year, rather than 262, approximately the number of weekdays in a year.

If we take our lognormal model, which is additive, then we can use the Central Limit Theorem and achieve accurate results. However, in the process of converting the log returns into percentages that we can use and which we understand, we have to exp() those log returns. In fact, 'lognormal returns' is a slight misnomer – so called because if you transform the return series using logs you get a normal distribution. But if you start the other way, with the normal distribution, returns are the exponential of this normal series. You could call this 'exponentiated normal returns'. This fits the skew of returns, which is upwards.

Returning to the annualising question, we have to exp() the log series after annualising. This means that by multiplying a log (by, say, $\sqrt{12}$), we are raising the exponentiated value to a power. This is convexity in action.

If all of this is confusing, a practical example might help. Suppose we have monthly data, the SD of which we wish to annualise. Table A2.5 shows the error generated by the conventional annualising process versus the log methodology. To read the table, take a value of column (a),

Table A2.5

Volatility of monthly series	Volatility of the logs	Annualised vols	Annualising ratio	% Error vs. $\sqrt{12}$	'Months'
(a)	(b) = ln(1 + a)	(c) = exp(b$\sqrt{12}$) − 1	(d) = c/a	(e) = (d/$\sqrt{12}$) − 1	(f) = d^2
			$\sqrt{12}$ = 3.4641		12.00
1.0%	0.00995	3.51%	3.5070	1.24%	12.30
2.0%	0.019803	7.10%	3.5503	2.49%	12.60
3.0%	0.029559	10.78%	3.5940	3.75%	12.92
4.0%	0.039221	14.55%	3.6382	5.02%	13.24
5.0%	0.04879	18.41%	3.6827	6.31%	13.56
6.0%	0.058269	22.37%	3.7277	7.61%	13.90
7.0%	0.067659	26.41%	3.7731	8.92%	14.24
8.0%	0.076961	30.55%	3.8190	10.24%	14.58

say 4%. This is the observed monthly SD, calculated by the correct log method, converted into percentages by the exp function. Column (b) shows the related monthly log SD, and column (c) the correctly calculated annualised SD. The remainder of the columns show the annualising ratios and the error versus $\sqrt{12}$, with column (f) showing the ratio converted into months. So for an asset with a monthly SD of 4%, this translates to an annual SD of 14.55%, 5% [column (e)] higher than would be calculated by a straight factor of $\sqrt{12}$ or 3.4641. This equates to $\sqrt{13.24}$ months rather than $\sqrt{12}$ months.

This is a very radical finding, the importance of which cannot be underestimated for investment analysts, managers and consultants. As mentioned earlier, the one area where the problem does not arise is in option-pricing models – since no exponentiation ever appears to take place, and the traders just talk in 'logs', i.e. 'Latin'.

The solution

Unlike many problems in investment, however, there is a simple solution. The correct methodology is available (and shown above), it is not computationally complex, and modern spreadsheets like Excel can easily compute it. The correct methodology will completely solve all the approximation problems and errors encountered in relation to SDs. Incidentally, it also resolves Siegel's paradox (1972), which apparently gives positive combined returns for two currency market participants with opposing base currencies irrespective of the currency movement (see Box 5.3).

To recap the solution, we take the observed return series, and instead of calculating a direct annualised SD by taking the SD % and multiplying by $\sqrt{12}$, we take the log(1+returns) and take the SD of this [I'll call it SD(ln)]. We then multiply SD(ln) by $\sqrt{12}$, and calculate the exponential $[\exp(SD(\ln)^* \sqrt{12})-1]$. This is the 'correct' SD, expressed in % not in logs. Table A2.6 is a simplified version of Table A2.3, with the order of SD calculation clearly shown.

Table A2.6

(a) Period	(b) Returns	(c) Logs [=ln(1+b)]	
1	2.41%	0.023855	
2	4.93%	0.048110	
3	1.40%	0.013895	
4	2.50%	0.024721	
5	−1.42%	−0.014281	
6	6.62%	0.064147	Setp 1 – Calculate monthly SD of log returns
7	5.53%	0.053824	
8	4.47%	0.043688	
9	2.92%	0.028788	
10	0.16%	0.001609	Step 2 – annualise monthly SD (monthly *$\sqrt{12}$)
11	−3.54%	−0.035997	
12	−3.64%	−0.037083	
SD monthly		0.033646	
SD annualised		0.116553	Step 3 – Convert to percentages (= exp(SD)−1)
SD log expressed as %		**12.36%**	

APPENDIX 3 – AIMR® REPORT

AIMR Benchmarks and Performance Attribution Subcommittee Report
August 1998

The AIMR Performance Presentation Standards Implementation Committee, which sponsored the formation of this subcommittee, encourages the public to comment in writing on these standards. This report outlines guidelines concerning benchmark reporting. The subcommittee will develop a report on performance attribution at a later date.

AIMR Performance Presentation Standards
Benchmarks and Performance Attribution Subcommittee

John C. Stannard, CFA, Chair
Frank Russell Company

Mary C. Cottrill, CFA
California Public Employees'
Retirement System

Jeffrey P. Davis, CFA
State Street Global Advisors

James E. Hollis, III, CFA
Standish, Ayer & Wood, Inc.
Robert E. Pruyne
Scudder, Stevens & Clark, Inc.

Brian D. Singer, CFA
Brinson Partners, Inc.

James L. Kermes
Glenmede Trust Company
Neil E. Riddles, CFA
Templeton Global Investors, Inc.

Peter T. Willett, CFA
State Street Global Advisors

Summary recommendations

The committee's report below examines some of the major factors involved in the choice of a benchmark for an investment portfolio or composite. As a result of its deliberations, the committee recommends the following changes to the AIMR standards:[13]

The AIMR standards should require that, where a benchmark exists, it must be included in the performance presentation. The name of the benchmark plus any other significant information (such as tax basis, etc.) must be disclosed. Where no benchmark exists, an explanation must be provided.

This requirement will take effect from an effective date (e.g. 1/1/99 – to be determined by the AIMR PPS committee). Use of benchmarks for periods prior to that effective date will be recommended but not required.

According to prevailing conditions (e.g. portfolio or composite strategy, index availability) a benchmark may consist of two or more indexes chain-linked together over time.

If a firm introduces a new benchmark to replace one used earlier for a certain composite, it must disclose fully the reason for doing so (such as the recent availability of a better benchmark).

Introduction

Benchmarks are important tools to aid in the planning, implementation and review of investment policy. They clarify communication between the investment fiduciary and the investment manager and provide a point of departure for assessing return and risk.

The terms 'benchmark' and 'index' are often used interchangeably. But while indexes are most often used as benchmarks, a benchmark is essentially the starting point for evaluating success. So we might define a benchmark more generally as follows:

An independent rate of return (or hurdle rate) forming an objective test of the effective implementation of an investment strategy.
A benchmark may take any of the following forms:

1. A well recognised published index
2. A tailored composite of assets (or indexes)
3. A peer group (or '*universe*') of similar funds or portfolios

---

[13] This subcommittee has stated its recommendations in general terms rather than by specifying specific changes to specific items in the AIMR PPS Handbook. In this regard, our goal is to state recommendations clearly enough that the implementation committee has an unambiguous basis for making changes in the Handbook.

What makes a good benchmark?

Properly used, a benchmark should be a focal point in the relationship between the manager and the fiduciary body overseeing the prudent management of the assets. Thoughtful choice of a benchmark will make the relationship between these parties more effective and enhance the value of the investment strategy. The most effective benchmarks are:

1. Representative of the asset class or mandate
2. Investable (e.g. a viable investment alternative)
3. Constructed in a disciplined and objective manner
4. Formulated from publicly available information
5. Acceptable by the manager as the neutral position
6. Consistent with underlying investor status (e.g. regarding tax, time horizon, etc.)

Benchmarks can be misused. Indeed choosing a bad or inappropriate benchmark can undermine the effectiveness of an investment strategy and lead to dissatisfaction between client and manager. Most problems associated with benchmarks arise from not observing the basic rules set out above (e.g. the manager doesn't understand benchmark construction or the benchmark doesn't match the mandate). But problems can also arise from setting multiple benchmarks which conflict with each other (e.g. outperform cash in the short term and equity in the long term). The remainder of this appendix reviews the uses of benchmarks in certain special situations and provides guidelines for investors when using and applying the AIMR Performance Presentation Standards.

Use of peer groups (*'universes'*) as benchmarks

The process of selecting an appropriate benchmark often involves a choice between an index (or composite index) or a peer group universe of managers. Each has advantages and disadvantages. Published indexes of 'unmanaged' assets are the most commonly preferred and frequently used form of benchmark, but a universe of managers may be a suitable alternative in some cases.

The major advantage of using a universe as a benchmark is in situations where no widely recognised index of unmanaged assets exists to reflect the asset class or investment strategy. Examples of such situations would be real estate, private equity and venture capital. In these situations a collection of managed products rather than unmanaged assets often best represents the asset class. What is often thought of as an index for real estate, private equity or venture capital, for example, is in most cases actually a universe of managed assets or products.

Universes do offer certain benefits in performance comparisons. Universes represent achieved results of manager portfolios which are effectively available as investment alternatives for investment fiduciaries (fund sponsors, etc.); they take full account of transactions and other trading costs and they reflect decisions taken by investors across the board (e.g. to underweight Japan relative to the index). But as the sole benchmark for comparing performance, universes are subject to certain drawbacks. These include:

1. They are not available real time, resulting in a time lag for comparison.
2. There is no established oversight process for determining universe participants and whether the universe accurately represents the entire asset class or style of management.

3. Survivor bias[14] will develop over time as some managers are deleted from the universe.
4. They are not replicable or investable.
5. They do not permit the manager to move to a known neutral position.

Style analysis

Style analysis is an increasingly popular technique used to determine portfolio exposures to various investment 'styles', e.g. large-capitalisation growth. The styles themselves are generally described as passive indexes and in its broadest sense, style analysis includes the techniques used to calculate these indexes. Typically, style indexes will break a broad market index down into four (or more) mutually exclusive components usually defined as large and small (or small/medium), growth and value segments. A style analysis model will then aim to quantify the exposures of a portfolio to these four style components as expressed by the indexes (and the underlying exposures to securities within the index universes). The basic tenet of style analysis is that a passive portfolio can be constructed by combining the four indexes. Therefore, a manager can be considered to add value only when performance exceeds the passively constructed portfolio. Added value can be achieved by varying the index exposures over time or by security selection within the index universes.

Application of style analysis is beneficial, but results of style analysers must be carefully interpreted. The most popular approach, developed by Sharpe,[15] is a statistical technique, which assesses the styles embedded in a portfolio based on correlation with the relevant underlying index. Due to the similar performance of certain indexes, style analysers can identify index exposures where none actually exist. This is especially perplexing for global portfolios where exposures to regional indexes show up even though no assets are actually held in the region. Also, this approach is based on data measured over a fixed time horizon (say five years) and may not be sensitive to sudden changes in style. Another method assesses the style of a portfolio based on its underlying characteristics (e.g. P/E, yield, etc.). This approach is more sensitive to style changes although the model techniques must be adjusted market by market for underlying conditions and accounting measures. Style analysis results must be analysed with due regard for these factors.

When using style indexes in performance presentations, investors should be careful to ensure that the style index, or blend of indexes, is representative of portfolio objectives and risk constraints. Failure to do so will lead to misleading impressions of outperformance. In this regard, the results of style models must be carefully interpreted in the light of the strengths and weaknesses of the analytical approach involved.

Benchmarks for multi-currency portfolios

Most investors recognise that currencies have a large impact on the returns of international and global portfolios. There is less appreciation however for the role that currencies play in the choice of an international or global benchmark. When selecting a multi-currency benchmark, the investor (implicitly or explicitly) makes both a decision on a set of underlying assets

---

[14] Survivor bias occurs where terminated accounts drop out of the sample – hence the average or median return is biased based on the surviving (and usually better-performing) portfolios.

[15] William Sharpe's article 'Asset allocation: management style and performance measurement' published in the *Journal of Portfolio Management* (Winter 1992) presents the method now generally known as *returns-based style analysis*.

and a decision on the desired level of embedded currency exposure. While AIMR here does not make a recommendation in favour of the unhedged or the hedged benchmark, we do regard the determination of currency exposure in the benchmark as an important fiduciary responsibility.

Investors should, in addition, aim to analyse the effects of currency movements and currency decisions separately from the underlying assets. There are three basic reasons for doing so. First, currency is a large source of return and risk, both in terms of benchmark selection and active management. Second, modern performance attribution methods allow asset selection skill to be differentiated from currency selection skill. Third, currency performance and attribution results highlight the significance of the choice between an unhedged, a partially hedged, or a fully hedged benchmark. This section sets out some of the factors to consider when making the benchmark decision in the context of currency management. Note that the guidelines below are not intended to explicitly define a calculation methodology but simply highlight the factors which managers must be aware of when managing portfolios. Specific methodologies for analysing currency return must be developed in the light of underlying portfolio structure and analytical needs.

Relative interest rates and the forward premium

Investors often use the change in spot exchange rate (over a holding period) as a measure of the influence of currency on their portfolios (i.e. of the 'unhedged' currency return). However, this approach is misleading since it fails to reflect the actual returns that can be obtained by currency instruments and ignores the effect of the forward currency premium[16] (referred to hereafter simply as the forward premium). In fact we get better information about the true effect of currency if we split the return derived from the change in spot rates into two separable components:

1. The forward premium which is known in advance and is driven by short-term interest rate differentials.[17]
2. The component of the change in spot rate *not* accounted for by the forward premium and which is commonly called the *currency surprise*.[18]

The reason we identify these two components separately is that they help explain an important fact. Investors cannot eliminate currency effects entirely and earn the *local return*.[19] They can only eliminate the currency surprise component while retaining the forward premium component. Thus, the hedged return is different from the local return and is the return that the foreign investor will earn that is free of currency risk.

---

[16] The forward premium can be positive (if interest rates in the foreign currency are lower than the home market) or negative, i.e. giving a forward discount (if rates abroad are higher).

[17] The interest rate differentials are 'short-term' because liquidity in the forward currency market only extends to short-term contracts, i.e. up to one year.

[18] The notion of 'currency surprise' (calculated as exchange rate movement less forward premium) is one useful basis for evaluating currency effects and currency decisions. Karnosky and Singer set out an alternative methodology in the ICFA Research Foundation publication 'Global Asset Management and Performance Attribution'. This approach also recognises the impact of relative interest rates by adjusting nominal market returns by the risk-free rate. The Karnosky and Singer methodology is consistent with the currency surprise and forward premium framework.

[19] The *local return* is the foreign asset return expressed in terms of the foreign currency. For example, a German equity portfolio owned by a US investor with a value of DEM100m at end-period 1 and DEM103.2m at end-period 2 has a local return of 3.2% for period 2. This return is irrespective of the spot currency movement of the Deutschmark.

Relative interest rates have a significant effect on currency returns, the pricing of hedging instruments such as forward foreign exchange contracts and currency analysis. While forward premiums might be thought of as a 'cost' of hedging, it is perhaps more accurate to consider them a 'hedging return component'. They exist because currency-hedged returns for cash (riskless assets) are forced (by arbitrage) to be equal irrespective of the market or currency in which the investor holds the cash. So if you invest in a high interest rate, foreign cash market and attempt to lock in that higher yield by hedging the currency, the forward premium will force you to realise a loss in the currency market which is equal and opposite to the interest rate market gain.

An excellent example of the currency surprise phenomenon is provided if you imagine that you are a British pound investor reviewing the performance of the pound (£) against the Deutschmark (DM) from 1972 to 1997. Commentators often claim that the pound was weak over this period since £100 converted into DM in 1972 would have been worth £253 at the end of 1997 purely through the pound's spot depreciation. But in fact if the investor had sold DM forward for pounds, the total investment would be worth £340. This is because the cumulative forward premium (based on the relative interest rates between the UK and Germany) was greater than the pound's actual depreciation. In fact, the currency surprise of the Deutschmark was negative by £87, and the hedged return outperformed the unhedged return.[20]

Accordingly, in choosing a benchmark, investors should recognise the shortcomings of using the spot-to-spot exchange rate difference. In particular, they should note the existence of the forward premium and, where appropriate, separate the spot movement into its two components – the forward premium and the currency surprise. In practical terms, this means don't use spot-to-spot exchange rates as the basis for evaluating the success or impact of currency decisions.

Unhedged benchmarks versus hedged benchmarks

Unhedged benchmarks, such as the MSCI EAFE Index, are those where no adjustments are made for hedging positions. The unhedged return for each country in the benchmark consists of the combined effect of the local asset market return and the spot currency return. The benchmark therefore contains a currency component comprising both currency surprise and forward premium. Unhedged benchmarks are used when the investment mandate does not include a consistent hedged position although currency activity may be allowed as a means of adding to return and/or reducing risk. They might be used for example by investors with relatively low allocations to foreign assets and/or investors who actively desire currency exposure.

---

[20] This example can be expressed algebraically as follows:

$$\text{Change in spot rate return } (c) = \text{Forward premium } (f) + \text{Currency surprise } (s)$$

$$\text{Hedged return } (h) = \text{Unhedged return } (r) - \text{Currency surprise } (s)$$

In this example, $c = 153\%$, $f = 240\%$ and $s = -87\%$ (i.e. $c = f + s$). Since the Deutschmark value of the converted £100 doesn't change (i.e. local return = 0), we have:

$$\text{Unhedged return } (r) = \text{Change in spot rate return } (c)$$

$$h = r - s = 153\% - (-87\%) = 240\%$$

That is, the hedged return effectively outperforms the unhedged return.

When the neutral position for an investment strategy involves the strategic hedging of some or all of the currency exposure, then a hedged benchmark (or index) is used. Such benchmarks may eliminate all currency exposure (a *fully hedged benchmark*) or they may eliminate a fixed proportion (between 0% and 100%) of the currency exposure. The proportion chosen is often called the *benchmark hedge ratio*. The return for each country in the fully hedged benchmark consists of the sum of the local asset market return and the currency premium. The currency surprise component of the spot currency return is eliminated.

Once again a manager can use active currency strategies to seek additional return but the neutral position is to hold hedges equal to the benchmark hedge ratio. Hedged benchmarks might be used for example by investors with material allocations to foreign assets who wish to eliminate the volatility of foreign currencies.

Benchmarking currency overlay

Broadly speaking a currency overlay strategy is one in which the management of currency is carried out separately from the remainder of the portfolio – even though it may be carried out by a single manager or within a single organisation. Currency overlay is generally linked to the management of currency exposure within the portfolio – if a fund employs a currency manager but has no foreign currency assets this is not thought of as currency overlay.

Currency overlay assignments can either be active or passive. Passive currency overlay versus an unhedged benchmark means neutralising the currency effect (or more specifically currency surprise) implicit in the active country position while (fully) hedged passive overlay means eliminating (all) currency surprise. Active currency overlay strategies seek to participate in upside currency gain while protecting against downside currency losses.

Note in particular that, because the forward premium cannot be hedged away, hedging an asset will give you the hedged return (local plus premium) not the local return. This relationship is fundamental to the understanding of such strategies. Accordingly, the possible components of currency overlay assignment might be broken down into:

(A) Hedged asset return[21]   the hedged return on the assets comprising the underlying portfolio
(B) Currency surprise[22]   the asset-weighted currency surprise component by market
(C) Overlay return[23]   the effect of the overlay strategy (i.e. active and/or passive positions) arising from the negative of the currency surprise

Such strategies can also either be fully or partially hedged (i.e. the benchmark hedge ratio can vary between 0% and 100%). These breakdowns are not significant in themselves other than that they enable us to distinguish between different components of the strategy and define benchmarks accordingly.

The aim in selecting an appropriate currency overlay benchmark is that it must reflect the nature of the assignment. Since currency overlay is typically managed separately from the

---

[21] The sum of the local market forward premium and the local asset return.
[22] Commonly referred to as the *implicit* currency component.
[23] Commonly referred to as the *explicit* currency component.

Table A3.1

| Benchmark definition | Description of benchmark return* | |
	Unhedged benchmark	Fully hedged benchmark
Asset + currency + overlay (A + B + C)	Hedged asset return + currency surprise (=local asset return + spot return)	Hedged asset return (=local asset return + forward premium)
Currency + overlay (B + C)	Currency surprise	Nil
Overlay only (C)	Nil	Negative currency surprise

* Partially hedged benchmark structures can be constructed as the weighted sum of unhedged and fully hedged benchmarks shown above (e.g. 50% hedged currency + overlay is 50% of currency surprise).

underlying foreign assets, performance should be correctly attributed by portfolio or manager and it is important to identify which components of the assignments are the direct responsibility of the currency overlay manager. The benchmark can be legitimately expressed either as the asset + currency + overlay return [(A) + (B) + (C)], as the currency + overlay return [(B) + (C)], or as the overlay return [(C)] only.

Some examples of possible benchmark specifications are shown in Table A3.1. An investor should define a consistent currency overlay benchmark based on the strategic considerations of the fund. These considerations will include: the maturity of the fund, the size of its international asset allocation and the fund's risk/return trade-off. The structure of the benchmark will depend on the nature of the assignment and the component of the overall strategy to be measured.

Other practical considerations

The following further factors must also be considered when designing currency overlay benchmarks:

1. The portion of the underlying assets that will form the basis for calculating the currency overlay return – all foreign assets, or just those for which currency hedging is practicable at reasonable cost.
2. The treatment of deviations from benchmark currency weights in the underlying portfolio.
3. Treatment of issues such as mid versus bid/offer pricing of contracts and treatment of illiquid currencies should be considered and where necessary treatment should be consistent between the portfolio and the benchmark.
4. The flow of information on the allocation of the assets being overlaid and the practical frequency for rebalancing back to benchmark – in practice, weekly or monthly rebalancing is probably more practical than daily.

One-way ticket effect

The *one-way ticket effect* describes the fact that a currency overlay manager with an unhedged benchmark can only benefit from hedging a currency when that currency is weak. Conversely, a currency overlay manager with a fully hedged benchmark can only benefit from 'lifting' hedges when the currency is strong. This leads to an asymmetrical, 'one-way ticket' influence on returns for currency portfolios. Investors should recognise that periods of continuous 'one-way' currency movement can last for very long periods, so performance targets for shorter periods should take this into account.

Partially hedged benchmarks reduce this problem, and a benchmark hedge ratio of 50% eliminates it. However, where strategic considerations make setting a partially hedged benchmark undesirable, alternatives include setting differential currency performance targets in periods of base currency weakness or strength or, probably a better course of action, allowing the currency cycle to run its course. Alternatively, an investor might set a band for currency allocation around the benchmark position, e.g. plus or minus 20% of the benchmark weight. Since, for a non-domestic currency assignment, this may give rise to a foreign currency exposure of more than 100% of the portfolio,[24] this decision must be taken with due consideration for the risk parameters of the portfolio, and any legal or other limitations.

APPENDIX 4 – SAMPLE INVESTMENT GUIDELINES

General remarks

[CURRENCY MANAGER] will be responsible for the execution of a currency overlay programme for [INVESTOR] 'the Client' as follows:

[CURRENCY MANAGER] will actively manage the currency overlay on the Client's international investment portfolio comprised of [equities] [bonds] [property] [cash].

Benchmark

[CURRENCY MANAGER]'s performance will be measured against an [unhedged] [50% hedged] [fully hedged] currency benchmark. See [Annex] for a description of the performance benchmark calculation. The overlay programme benchmark is determined by the Client and can be modified or adjusted by the Client upon written notice to [CURRENCY MANAGER].

Mandate size

The initial mandate size is equal to the whole of the Client's international equity portfolio as reported to [CURRENCY MANAGER] by the Custodian (see below). The Client may vary this mandate size at any time by giving written notice to [CURRENCY MANAGER].

Return and risk objectives

[CURRENCY MANAGER] should achieve an outperformance on the currency overlay programme against the benchmark's performance of [1%] p.a. net of all costs and fees over a market cycle of 3 to 5 years. A detailed description of the performance calculation is provided in the [Annex – Calculation Methodology].

[CURRENCY MANAGER] should achieve the return objective with a target tracking error of [2.5%]. The tracking error is the annualised standard deviation of the monthly outperformance of the overlay programme versus the benchmark.

---

[24] Or less than zero for a fully hedged benchmark.

Eligible currencies

[CURRENCY MANAGER] may only undertake spot and forward currency exchange contracts in currencies that are part of the currency overlay programme as specified below.

The actively managed overlay programme will only be implemented in the following currencies: [US dollar, Japanese yen, euro, Swiss franc, Swedish krona, Australian dollar, Canadian dollar, Hong Kong dollar, Singapore dollar]. [CURRENCY MANAGER] may, at its discretion, decline to enter into hedges in any of the above currencies if either the portfolio exposure in that currency falls below a tradeable market amount, or if lack of liquidity in the market for forward currency contracts adversely affects the performance of the overlay.

[CURRENCY MANAGER] may elect to hedge a less liquid currency exposure (whether or not included in the above list) by entering into forward contracts in a proxy currency (which will be in the list above). Any proxy hedging will be approved in writing by the Client prior to trading, and the list of proxies may be changed only with the written approval of the Client. An example of a proxy might be to undertake US dollar contracts to hedge a Hong Kong exposure. Proxy hedging will not be undertaken tactically – only as a strategic decision to minimise the costs of transactions.

The currency composition of the active overlay programme will be designed by [CURRENCY MANAGER] and must be communicated to and agreed in advance with Client. Without the consent of the Client, [CURRENCY MANAGER] may not make any changes to the currencies that are part of the overlay programme.

Investment restrictions

[CURRENCY MANAGER] may only enter into forward contracts such that the hedge ratio (the foreign currency amount of the net outstanding sales of the forward currency divided by the portfolio asset value denominated in that currency) does not lie outside the range [−3%] and [103%].

Counterparties

[CURRENCY MANAGER] may only enter into transactions with counterparties that have long-term senior debt or unsecured claims paying ability rated at least [Aa3 by Moody's] and have ratings for short-term instruments of [P1] (or the equivalent ratings from other rating sources), and with the prior written approval of the Client.

The creditworthiness of all counterparties must be monitored by [CURRENCY MANAGER] on an ongoing basis. [CURRENCY MANAGER] should take all reasonable steps to protect the Client's assets in the event of adverse changes to a counterparty's creditworthiness. It is acknowledged that it is [CURRENCY MANAGER]'s practice to remove a downgraded Bank (which falls below the permitted minimum) from the active dealing list, but to allow forward contracts to run off without premature close-out or accelerated settlement.

Rebalancing

The rebalancing of the overlay programme will take place on a monthly basis, on the [5th] working day of the month, except where specifically instructed by the Client, or where the Custodian has failed to provide updated portfolio data. [CURRENCY MANAGER] will normally receive portfolio information from the custodian by the [4th] working day. In case further re-balancing is to take place it is the Client's responsibility to inform [CURRENCY MANAGER] timely about expected changes to the investment portfolio to allow [CURRENCY MANAGER] to adjust the overlay programme accordingly. Adjustments to the overlay programme will be made when the unhedged value of the underlying stock in the market relating to one currency differs from the size of the overlay in that currency by more than [3%] of the [sterling] [dollar] [euro] amount of exposure. [CURRENCY MANAGER] will set all hedges to expire on the [5th] working day of the month.

Cash flows

The overlay programme will periodically realise positive and negative cash flows upon settle-ment of the foreign exchange contracts. These settlements will be effected once a month and reduced in size if possible by using 'settlement netting' arrangements with the counterparties. Any cash positions may only be held in cash accounts that belong to and are controlled by the Client. [CURRENCY MANAGER] must notify and reconcile the settlement amounts with the Custodian Bank at least two business days prior to the settlement date.

Any positive cash flows will be 'swept' from the currency overlay portfolio based upon written instructions from the Client. Cash requirements to settle foreign exchange contracts will be funded from cash sources at the discretion of the Client.

Custodian

The actual underlying investment portfolio will be made available electronically from the Cus-todian Bank. Further necessary information will be provided by the Client. It is [CURRENCY MANAGER]'s responsibility to monitor the portfolio monthly and to collect the necessary data from the Custodian and the Client.

Further restrictions

At no time should the net value of all outstanding contracts sold exceed 103% of the underlying value of the assets being overlaid. Forward currency contracts are limited to 13-month forward settlement dates or less.

[CURRENCY MANAGER] may not deal with any affiliated firms of [CURRENCY MAN-AGER] as counterparty to any currency contracts.

Communications

[CURRENCY MANAGER] is responsible for ongoing communication with the Client. [CUR-RENCY MANAGER] must promptly notify the Client of any significant changes to [CUR-RENCY MANAGER]'s investment or portfolio strategy, organisational structure, financial condition or the personnel managing the portfolio.

Reporting

Monthly [CURRENCY MANAGER] will issue reports by the 12th working day of the fol-lowing month as follows:

(a) Monthly overlay valuation report
(b) Monthly overlay performance report
(c) Bank credit exposure report
(d) Monthly transaction and cash flow report
(e) Monthly market summary
(f) Trailing 12-month and prospective 12-month cash flow report
(g) Cash flow at risk report
(h) Quarterly Executive Summary

The report formats will be designed by [CURRENCY MANAGER] based on the Client's requirements. Semi-annually [CURRENCY MANAGER] will present the performance of the programme to the investment committee, and annually to the full Board of Trustees.

Investment guideline compliance

[CURRENCY MANAGER] will certify in writing, each quarter, that they remain in compliance with the investment guidelines, and that they have reconciled their transactions that quarter, and the outstanding contract inventory, with the Bank counterparties.

If, at any time, [CURRENCY MANAGER] feels that the investment guidelines present an impediment to the investment strategy, [CURRENCY MANAGER] should discuss the matter with the Client as soon as practical.

If, at any time, a specific guideline is not being adhered to, the Client should be notified as soon as possible but always within five business days after the discovery of a breach of a guideline.

Addresses and contact persons

Client
    [CURRENCY MANAGER]

Index

Index compiled by Annette Musker

Printed and bound in the UK by
CPI Antony Rowe, Eastbourne

Printed and bound by CPI Group (UK) Ltd, Croydon, CR0 4YY

05/04/2023

03208763-0001